The Community Forests of Mexico

The Community Forests of Mexico

Managing for Sustainable Landscapes

EDITED BY DAVID BARTON BRAY,
LETICIA MERINO-PÉREZ, AND DEBORAH BARRY

University of Texas Press ⌁ *Austin*

Support for this book comes from an endowment for environmental studies made possible by generous contributions from Richard C. Bartlett, Susan Aspinall Block, and the National Endowment for the Humanities.

Library of Congress Cataloging-in-Publication Data
    The community forests of Mexico : managing for sustainable landscapes / edited by David Barton Bray, Leticia Merino-Pérez, and Deborah Barry. — 1st ed.
      p.   cm.
    Includes bibliographical references and index.
    ISBN 0-292-70637-5 (cl. : alk. paper)
    1. Community forests—Mexico. I. Bray, David B. II. Merino-Pérez, Leticia. III. Barry, Deborah.
SD569.C66   2005
333.75′0972—dc22
                         2004022777

To the ejidatario *and* comunero *families of the forest communities of Mexico, in the hopes that this book will be one more* granito de arena *toward all of us learning how to become better forest stewards.*

Contents

Acknowledgments **xv**

PART I. **Introduction, History, and Policy**

Chapter 1: Community Managed in the Strong Sense of the Phrase:
The Community Forest Enterprises of Mexico **3**
DAVID BARTON BRAY, LETICIA MERINO-PÉREZ, AND
DEBORAH BARRY

Chapter 2: Contested Terrain: Forestry Regimes and Community
Responses in Northeastern Michoacán, 1940–2000 **27**
CHRISTOPHER R. BOYER

Chapter 3: Forest and Conservation Policies and Their Impact on
Forest Communities in Mexico **49**
LETICIA MERINO-PÉREZ AND GERARDO SEGURA-WARNHOLTZ

Chapter 4: Challenges for Forest Certification and Community
Forestry in Mexico **71**
PATRICIA GEREZ-FERNÁNDEZ AND ENRIQUE ALATORRE-GUZMÁN

PART II. **Social Processes and Community Forestry**

Chapter 5: Indigenous Community Forest Management in the
Sierra Juárez, Oaxaca **91**
FRANCISCO CHAPELA

Chapter 6: Empowering Community-Based Forestry in Oaxaca:
The Union of Forest Communities and *Ejidos* of Oaxaca,
1985–1996 **111**
RODOLFO LÓPEZ-ARZOLA

Chapter 7: New Organizational Strategies in Community Forestry in Durango, Mexico   **125**
PETER LEIGH TAYLOR

Chapter 8: Community Adaptation or Collective Breakdown? The Emergence of "Work Groups" in Two Forestry *Ejidos* in Quintana Roo, Mexico   **151**
PETER R. WILSHUSEN

PART III. **Ecology and Land Use Change in Community Forestry**

Chapter 9: Ecological Issues in Community Tropical Forest Management in Quintana Roo, Mexico   **183**
HENRICUS F. M. VESTER AND MARÍA ANGÉLICA NAVARRO-MARTÍNEZ

Chapter 10: Land Use/Cover Change in Community-Based Forest Management Regions and Protected Areas in Mexico   **215**
ELVIRA DURÁN, JEAN-FRANÇOIS MAS, AND ALEJANDRO VELÁZQUEZ

PART IV. **The Economics of Community Forestry**

Chapter 11: Vertical Integration in the Community Forestry Enterprises of Oaxaca   **241**
CAMILLE ANTINORI

Chapter 12: The Managerial Economics of Sustainable Community Forestry in Mexico: A Case Study of El Balcón, Técpan, Guerrero   **273**
JUAN MANUEL TORRES-ROJO, ALEJANDRO GUEVARA-SANGINÉS, AND DAVID BARTON BRAY

PART V. **Global Comparisons and Conclusions**

Chapter 13: The Global Significance of Mexican Community Forestry   **305**
DAN KLOOSTER AND SHRINIDHI AMBINAKUDIGE

Chapter 14: Community Forestry in Mexico: Twenty Lessons Learned and Four Future Pathways   **335**
DAVID BARTON BRAY

Appendix: Acronyms Used   **351**

About the Contributors   **357**

Index   **363**

List of Figures and Tables

Figures

Figure 4.1. A decade of forest certification in Mexico: Field-assessed and certified sites annually, 1994–2003   **78**

Figure 5.1. Organization levels and interdependence   **100**

Figure 5.2. Organization of a community member of UZACHI   **101**

Figure 5.3. UZACHI organization   **105**

Figure 6.1. Structure of an indigenous community with CFE   **116**

Figure 6.2. Structure of UCEFO   **119**

Figure 8.1. *Ejido* members of the Sociedad Sur (SPFEQR)   **155**

Figure 9.1. Total harvested volume of mahogany and Spanish cedar in Quintana Roo, 1938–2001   **184**

Figure 9.2. The Quintana Roo study areas   **186**

Figure 9.3. Population structure of *Swietenia macrophylla* in part of the permanent forest area in X-Hazil   **197**

Figure 9.4. Map of transect 1 in X-Hazil, showing eco-units   **202**

Figure 9.5. Transect of forest in aggradation phase   **204**

Figure 10.1. The LUCC study sites   **218**

Figure 10.2. Flowchart illustrating the methodological steps followed to produce LUCC Analysis, derived statistics, and maps   **222**

Figure 10.3. Flows depicting processes of land cover conversion and permanence analyzed   **223**

Figure 10.4. Rates of change calculated according to Puyravaud (2002)   **224**

Figure 10.5. Trends of change between anthropogenic and natural cover for the *ejidos* of OEFHG-Guerrero (a); the *ejidos* of OEPFZM-Quintana Roo (b); the protected areas (c); and both groups of *ejidos* (Guerrero-Quintana Roo) (d)   **226**

Figure 10.6. Spatially explicit distribution of the conversion processes, 1979–2000, in the 10 *ejidos* of OEFHG-Guerrero [online]   **225**

Figure 10.7. Spatially explicit distribution of the conversion processes, 1980–2000, in 12 *ejidos* of OEPFZM-Quintana Roo [online]   **225**

Figure 10.8. Annual rate of change (a) for the *ejidos* analyzed in each region independently and the PAs; and (b) for the *ejidos* joined and the PAs   **228**

Figure 11.1. Historical comparison of timber processing capability in sample communities, Oaxaca 1986–1997   **247**

Figure 11.2. Marginal effects of key variables on the level of vertical integration   **262**

Figure 12.1. Porter's Diamond   **277**

Figure 12.2. Trend of the distribution of profits in El Balcón   **289**

Figure 12.3. Balcón timber harvest by species, 1987–2000; projected harvest, 2001–2010   **292**

Figure 12.4. Trends in percent of cost by production activity in El Balcón, 1989–2000   **294**

Figure 13.1. Tenure in some forest-rich countries   **308**

Figure 13.2. A comparison of community forestry according to characteristics of local management power and local benefit   **324**

Figure 14.1. Four future paths for Mexican CFEs   **340**

Tables

Table 1.1. Three estimates of number of forest communities in Mexico   **9**

Table 1.2. Estimates of number of forest production communities in Mexico, and 1992 forest permits   **10**

Table 1.3. PROCYMAF classification of Mexican forest communities   **11**

Table 1.4. Proposed new classification of Mexican forest communities and CFEs **12**

Table 4.1. Principles of good forest management (FSC) **73**

Table 4.2. Forest sites and area certified by region by FSC **74**

Table 4.3. Community forest operations certified by FSC **77**

Table 5.1. Area of the UZACHI **102**

Table 5.2. Carbon capture area and sequestration costs **104**

Table 5.3. State of marginalization: Rankings of UZACHI communities **107**

Table 7.1. Timber and wood industry in Durango's urban areas, 1993–1998 **131**

Table 7.2. Forest industry production in Durango, 2000 **132**

Table 8.1. Work group timber volumes and income in Caoba, 2000 **159**

Table 8.2. Work group timber volumes and income in Petcacab, 2000 **162**

Table 8.3. Mahogany buyers in Petcacab, 2001 **167**

Table 8.4. Comparison of work group dynamics in Caoba and Petcacab **171**

Table 8.5. Comparison of community forest enterprises (CFEs) and work groups **175**

Table 9.1. Richness of trees and epiphytes in the vegetation study **194**

Table 9.2. Abundance of tree species in four forest *ejidos* in Quintana Roo **195**

Table 9.3. Annual diameter growth per diameter class for forest species in sampling plots totaling 1.5 ha in the *ejido* Naranjal Poniente, Quintana Roo **199**

Table 9.4. Surface areas (m^2) of different development phases in eco-units **206**

Table 10.1. Summary outline of the organizations of *ejidos* where the LUCC study was conducted **220**

Table 11.1. Summary statistics and predicted sign of key variables **256**

Table 11.2. Average revenue, cost, and profit by level of integration (new pesos) **265**

Table 12.1. El Balcón products and sale (real) prices (domestic market) **285**

Table 12.2. SWOT analysis, El Balcón **296**

Acknowledgments

This book would not have been possible without the vision and the generous support of the Ford Foundation and the William and Flora Hewlett Foundation. This book is part of a larger project, funded by both of these foundations, to carry out new research on the impacts of Mexican community forestry on the communities and their forests, and the extent to which it can be considered a global model. We would like to thank Dr. Gerardo Segura-Warnholtz, director of the Proyecto de Conservación y Manejo Forestal de la Comisión Nacional Forestal (PROCYMAF), who has been a major source of insight and inspiration for his leadership in strengthening community forestry in Mexico. Countless others who supported this book—and more importantly, community forestry in Mexico—will go unnamed here, but you know who you are.

We would also like to thank Skya Murphy, whose unwavering editorial eye and conscientious attention to detail have made the manuscript far better than it otherwise would have been. Thanks are also due to the Department of Environmental Studies at Florida International University, and the Instituto de Investigaciones Sociales at the Universidad Autónoma de México for crucial institutional support. Finally, the authors would like to take this rare opportunity to publicly thank their families for support in this and just a few other things in life: thanks to Victoria Floor, Erik Bray, and Abigail Bray, and to Baltazar Lopez and Gabriela Lopez-Barry. Leticia Merino-Pérez thanks Daniel, Ayari, and John for all the joy and support they give.

The Community Forests of Mexico

PART I

INTRODUCTION, HISTORY, AND POLICY

CHAPTER 1

Community Managed in the Strong Sense of the Phrase: The Community Forest Enterprises of Mexico

DAVID BARTON BRAY, LETICIA MERINO-PÉREZ,
AND DEBORAH BARRY

This book examines the historical and contemporary experience of community forest management in Mexico from a variety of perspectives.[1] As this volume makes clear, the community forest sector in Mexico is large, diverse, and has achieved unusual maturity doing what communities in the rest of the world are only beginning to explore: the commercial production of timber. In most of the world, *community forest management* refers to the management of recovering forestlands or non-timber forest products on government lands. The achievement of Mexican communities in the commercial production of timber from common property forests was largely accomplished over the last 30 years, but has roots deep in Mexico's twentieth-century history.

Despite these achievements, the community forest sector in Mexico is still little known outside of Mexico, and insufficiently recognized even within Mexico. It also has many challenges and deficiencies. This volume joins other recent research efforts to begin to address this lack of recognition for an important global model (Bray et al. 2003) and to document and analyze both its achievements and shortcomings. We have here collected a series of articles by established researchers in the field, some presenting new data from research commissioned especially for this book, that examines the phenomenon from historical, policy, economic, ecological, sociological, and political perspectives, frequently in ways that integrate these disciplines. The book also contains accounts by some of the important practitioners from the Mexican nongovernmental organization (NGO) sector, which has been involved in promoting community forestry for over two decades.

A few terminological notes are in order. Throughout this book we will refer to *community forest management* (CFM) as the general phenomenon and to *community forest enterprises* (CFEs) in specific reference to communities that are commercially producing timber with varying levels of integration.[2] The Mexican Revolution in the second decade of the twentieth century left a strong mark on land tenure, creating or reinforcing community properties known as *ejidos* and indigenous or agrarian communities. While there are some differences in origins and governance, both forms establish collective governance of a common territory or property. While these community lands were long defined as held in usufruct from the state, reforms to the Mexican Constitution in 1992 strengthened community ownership of these lands. Unless it is important to distinguish them, the generic term *communities* will be used to refer to both of the common property community land tenure systems that exist in Mexico, *ejidos* and *agrarian communities*, as defined in Mexican agrarian law.[3] Individual forest smallholder private properties exist in Mexico, and are probably more important than realized in the forest sector, but are not covered in this book.

The Forests of Mexico: Extent, Ecology, and Deforestation

According to the 2000–2001 National Forest Inventory, 32.75% of the national territory of Mexico is covered by "forests and rainforests," corresponding to 63.6 million hectares. Of this, 32.9 million hectares (52% of total forests and rainforests) are temperate zone forests and 30.7 million (48% of the total) are tropical forests, both tropical dry forests and rainforests (INEGI 1997).

The temperate pine-oak forests of Mexico cover the Sierra Madre Occidental and the Sierra Madre Oriental, the mountain ranges in western and eastern Mexico, the Volcanic Axis, which joins the two ranges in central Mexico, and the Sierra Madre del Sur along the Pacific coast of Guerrero and Oaxaca. In the south, after breaking at the Isthmus of Tehuantepec, the mountains rise again in the Sierra Madre de Chiapas and the Mesa de Chiapas in southeastern Mexico. It is on the slopes of the Sierras that Mexico's pine and oak forests are found, with the greatest number of pine species of any country in the world, some 72 in two major groups (Perry 1991). There are also some 130 species of oak, with both pine and oak having rates of endemism of over 70% (Castilleja 1996).

Castilleja (1996) has divided the two principal forest vegetation classifications for Mexico—Miranda/Hernández and Rzedowski—into the following classification scheme: Tropical Rainforests (*selva alta perrenifolia*, *selva alta subperrenifolia*, and *selva mediana subperrenifolia*), Tropical Seasonal Forests (including Tropical Dry Forests), Tropical Montane Forests, and Coniferous and Oak Forests. It is the Tropical Rainforests and Tropical Seasonal Forests that have been most heavily impacted by deforestation. Today, Tall Tropical Rainforest (*selva alta perrenifolia*), with canopy heights of over 30 meters and annual rainfall over 3 meters, are estimated to be at about 10% of their original extension, and the largest remaining masses are confined to the Lacandon region of Chiapas and the northern Chiapas-southern Oaxaca region, known as the Chimalapas. Medium-high deciduous Tropical Rainforest extends from northern Veracruz through most of the southern and central Yucatán Peninsula.

Most of the tropical community forest projects in Mexico have developed in *selva mediana subperrenifolia* (medium semideciduous forests) in southern Campeche and southern and central Quintana Roo. Tropical Seasonal Forests (*selvas subcaducifolias* and *selvas caducifolias*) lose up to 50% of their leaves in prolonged dry seasons, and may be less than 10 meters in height. Few if any forest management projects for timber have been developed in these forests. Tropical Montane Forests can be found in an altitudinal belt from 1,000 and 1,500 meters on the western slopes of the Sierra Madre Oriental, parts of the Sierra Madre del Sur, and north and central Chiapas. Because of the relative lack of commercial species in these forests, few community forest projects are found in these forests, either. The Conifer and Oak Forests extend throughout the Sierra Regions, with pines dominating in the higher, colder altitudes and oaks being more common at lower and drier altitudes (Castilleja 1996). The majority of all forest management communities in Mexico are found in the Conifer and Oak Forests, particularly in the states of Chihuahua, Durango, Michoacán, Guerrero, Puebla, and Oaxaca.

These forests contain much of Mexico's vaunted biodiversity. "Although Mexico covers only one percent of the earth's land area, it contains about one tenth of all terrestrial vertebrates and plants known to science. The meeting of the nearctic and neotropical biotic regions, the abundance of topographic islands and the wide climatic variation across its territory are significant factors in Mexico's biodiversity" (Castilleja 1996). Of some 25,000 vascular plant species and 1,352 vertebrate species found in Mexico, 81% of the plant species and 75% of the vertebrates are found in the four types of forest mentioned.

However, as in the rest of the tropics, Mexico's forests have been under assault in recent decades, although studies of deforestation suggest that deforestation rates have varied between tropical and temperate zone areas.

As elsewhere in the tropics, deforestation in southeastern Mexico, where the tropical forests are concentrated, has occurred at alarming rates. In the mid-1980s deforestation rates in Mexico's tropical forests was estimated at around 2% a year, but regional studies showed local rates that range from 4.3 to 12.4% annually (World Bank 1995). De Jong et al. (2000) found that from the mid-1970s to the mid-1990s, a block of the Lacandon rainforest had lost nearly one-third of its mature forest, although there had been very little decline within protected areas. It has been estimated that 40% of the historic Lacandon was lost by 1995 (O'Brien 1998). Trejo and Dirzo (2000) have demonstrated that only 27% of the original cover of seasonally dry tropical forest remains in Mexico.

The rates of deforestation mentioned above include estimates of annual losses of forest cover that range from 365,000 annually to 1.5 million hectares annually. However, a comprehensive recent study of land use/land cover change (LUCC) in Mexico has produced the most authoritative figures to date. The National Land Use Inventory of 2001, carried out by the Instituto de Geografía of the Universidad Nacional Autónoma de México (UNAM) and commissioned by INEGI and SEMARNAT, indicates that the rate of annual forest loss in the 1976–2000 period was .25% for forests, .76% for tropical forests, and .33% for semi-arid scrub forests (*matorral*). This implies an average annual loss of 86,718 hectares for temperate forests, 263,570 hectares for tropical forests, and 194,502 hectares for *matorral*, for a total average annual loss of 545,000, with a 50,000-hectare margin of error. This is based on the most rigorous and comprehensive study to date and incorporates the most trustworthy satellite images from earlier periods (Velázquez et al. 2002).

The principal proximate drivers of this deforestation are thought to be agricultural and livestock expansion (Barbier and Burgess 1996), which are linked to colonization processes. The factors that drive these proximate causes, such as population density, population growth, increased food production, high agricultural export prices, exchange rate devaluation, increased debt-servicing ratios, and roundwood production, can be considered underlying causes, but "exact magnitudes of relationships cannot be reliably estimated" (Barbier and Burgess 1996). Attributing deforestation to particular policies can be challenging since "In practice . . . it is very difficult to determine the overall effects of policy changes on deforestation, as it is likely that a given policy change will have both positive and negative impacts on forest conversion and degradation" (Barbier and Burgess 1996).

Until recently, little effort has been made to link deforestation or stability in forest cover with community forest management (however, see Durán-Medina et al., this volume). The vast majority of community-managed forests are in the mountainous, coniferous zones that in recent decades have shown lower rates of deforestation, although no cause-and-effect relationship has been argued. In addition, tropical land use change has been well below national rates in two areas where community forestry has been prominent, southern Campeche and central Quintana Roo (Palacio-Prieto et al. 2000). It is also noteworthy that, as historical processes, the rise of community forestry in Mexico in the 1970s occurred precisely during the period when tropical deforestation was at its most intensive, and its proponents at the time and since have promoted it as an alternative to deforestation.

Economic Dimensions of Mexican Forests and the Role of CFM in the Forest Sector

Forest production plays only a very minor role in the overall Mexican economy. In the early 1990s the commercial production of timber was slightly less than 1% of the GDP of Mexico, with its share declining nearly 25% since 1987. Historically, very little investment has been made by the government in forestry, and as little as 4% of the total budget for agriculture has been allocated to the forestry agency (World Bank 1995). The forest industry is heavily concentrated in the three states of Durango, Chihuahua, and Michoacán, which have 63% of all industrial installations. Mexican timber production and the forest industry are not considered to be internationally competitive because, according to the World Bank, "production costs (including transport) are high, community-managed forests are inefficient, few forests are actively managed, and lack of infrastructure makes most of the timber inaccessible" (World Bank 1995). Although the World Bank lays part of the responsibility for underperformance of the Mexican forest sector on community forests, this volume will explore some of the factors that mitigate this presumed underperformance and how some aspects of it could become a source of competitive strength in the marketplace.

The exact contribution of community-managed forests to the overall forest sector is not clear. This is not surprising, since there is much confusion even about such basic facts as the total roundwood and sawnwood production in the overall forest sector. FAO and Mexican government figures show dramatically different production levels for both roundwood and sawnwood. One observer of the Mexican forest sector has noted that "the SEMARNAP numbers are probably understated and the FAO numbers overstated. I doubt we could sort this out with a month of hard study" (H. L. Arnold, email, 22 August 2002). Arnold has suggested that a figure of around 25 million cubic meters of roundwood production and 8 million cubic meters of sawnwood production may be close for the 1990s, but despite scattered guesses no one knows the magnitude of production from the community forests.

The Magnitude and Characteristics of Mexican Community Forests and Community Forest Enterprises (CFEs)

It is commonly noted that as much as 80% of Mexico's forests are in the hands of *ejidos* and indigenous communities. This figure reportedly was first used in a 1980 publication by the National Institute of Statistics and Geography (Instituto Nacional de Estadística, Geografía e Informática; INEGI), with no reference to the empirical foundation of the number, but it has become the single most commonly cited figure on the forest sector in Mexico (J. M. Torres-Rojo, personal communication, 2003). It is not known how *forest* might have been defined and thus neither the absolute numbers of communities with forests on their lands nor the total number of hectares of that forest are known with any degree of precision. Table 1.1 shows three different estimates of how many "forest communities" exist in Mexico, ranging from 7,000 to 9,047. Presumably many of these forest communities have only small and degraded patches of forest, and they cannot be regarded as communities where the forest is an appreciable economic resource. The National Ecology Institute (INE) is currently developing a more precise estimate of how many communities have forests in their community lands.

A 1991 INEGI *ejido* census with information on 30,000 *ejidos* indicates the persistent problems with estimating forests on community lands, since it shows that all *ejidos* in Mexico have less than 15 million hectares of forests, an impossibly low figure (Torres-Rojo, personal communication, 2003).

But if we take the 7–9,000 range of forest communities, how many of these can be said to operate CFEs or engage in the legal commercial production of timber? Table 1.2 shows the range of existing published estimates for forest production *ejidos* and includes one data point on the number of logging permits issued, another elusive statistic.

Table 1.1. Three estimates of number of forest communities in Mexico

Source (cited by)	No. "forest communities'
Alatorre Frenk 2000	9,047 "have forests or rainforests"
DGF 1995 (Alatorre Frenk 2000)	7,000 "have forest timber resources"
INEGI 1995 (Merino-Pérez et al. 2000)	8,400 "forest communities"

The table shows a range of figures from a low of 288 to a high of 740. Since most of these figures come from the late 1980s to mid-1990s, it may be useful to compare these numbers to the logging permit data point from 1992. If we assume that the 1992 figure for number of logging permits is typical, this would suggest that the number of CFEs constitute from 16 to 42% of the total logging permits. The remainder would presumably be mostly private property owners. A new national study is currently under way to determine at a greater level of precision how many communities are producing timber in Mexico, their relative degree of control over the process, and their degree of vertical integration. Early incomplete results from this study suggest that the total number may be over 2,400 communities producing timber legally, well above existing estimates (Octavio Magaña, personal communication, 2004).

The significance of community forestry for overall forest management also varies from state to state, and in some states it may not currently be an important part of overall forest management. For example, in Michoacán, only 10% of the forest area is thought to be under management, and only 3% of the forest *ejidos* carry out authorized extraction, two-thirds of them as stumpage communities, the lowest level of vertical integration (see below) (Merino-Pérez et al. 2000).

Typologies of Mexican CFEs

For many years, there was little concern about creating classifications or typologies for Mexican CFEs, since it was a relatively undifferentiated phenomenon. This is no longer the case. The size and complexity of the sector demands a typology of CFEs, but this turns out to be a challenging task. The underlying criteria for classifying the type of communities has been the degree of processing of the tree when sold—from standing to sawnwood—and/or the proximity to the final sale to the buyer. Until

Table 1.2. Estimates of number of forest production communities in Mexico, and 1992 forest permits

Source (cited by)	No. forest production communities
Alatorre Frenk 2000	584
Alatorre Frenk 2000	288
SARH 1992 (Alatorre Frenk 2000)	740
Adapted from Alatorre Frenk 2000; Madrid, 1993	425
Adapted from World Bank 1995	290–380
DGDF 1992 (Alatorre Frenk 2000)	No. *permisos forestales* in 1992 (% CFEs) 1,750 (16–42%)

the 1970s, almost all Mexican forest communities that produced timber were considered either *rentistas*, a term that refers to the fact that communities "rented" their forests to outside loggers, whether contractors or concessionaires, or *empresas ejidales forestales* (forest *ejido* enterprises). As early as the 1940s and continuing into the early 1970s, various government agencies promoted community sawmills under the term "forest *ejido* enterprises." These sawmills were not independent businesses, since they were almost always forced to sell to only one buyer, the concessionaire, at the price it set, and the government agrarian reform agency had a strong hand in administering the mill.

Beginning in the 1970s, as more CFEs began to emerge, and the era of the concessions came to a close (see Merino-Pérez and Segura-Warnholtz, this volume), almost all forest communities were allowed to sell their timber and receive the full market price, not a government-set stumpage fee. Beginning in the 1970s a large number of CFEs emerged, with varying degrees of vertical integration that needed classification. Informal classifications came into popular usage as to whether a community sold timber "on the stump" or "standing timber" (*al tocón*); "at the head of the road" (*a pie de brecha*—they logged and took it to a forest logyard, but a buyer came to take it to the sawmill); "delivered to the patio" (*al patio*) (those that delivered roundwood to the sawmill, implying they had their own logging trucks); and "sawmill" communities, which had their own sawmills.

The first formal effort at classification was carried out by the World Bank (1995), which proposed a very complicated classification scheme with multiple criteria in each category. Although the numbers of CFEs in each category came to be widely quoted, the categorization appears to have been based on questionable assumptions. A much simpler scheme was proposed and developed by the Programa para la Conservación y Manejo Forestal (PROCYMAF), a World Bank/government of Mexico project to finance projects in community forest management. The PROCYMAF classification, developed in 1997–1998, is shown in Table 1.3.

As Table 1.3 indicates, Type I communities have forest resources but are not legally exploiting them for timber; Type II communities have their forests logged by outside contractors, with varying levels of direct participation in the process; Type III communities have some form of CFE where they control the logging process; and Type IV communities have sawmills and do their own marketing. Most of the focus has been on Types II–IV, since Type I communities by definition are not exploiting their forest and do not have any kind of CFE. For ease of reference, and after Antinori (2000), we shall refer to Type II communities as *stumpage communities* (they only sell timber on the stump and may have little involvement with the extraction process, Type III communities as *roundwood communities* ("roundwood" being an industry term for sawn tree trunks), and Type IV communities as *sawmill communities* (they have their own sawmills). Antinori (2000) has also proposed a Type V, which she calls *finished products communities*, communities that produce products

Table 1.3. PROCYMAF classification of Mexican forest communities

Type I	Potential producers: Owners and/or possessors of forestlands with capacity for sustainable commercial production that currently do not carry out logging because they lack an authorized forest management plan or sufficient means to pay for its elaboration.
Type II	Producers who sell timber on the stump (*rentistas*). Owners and/or possessors of parcels subject to timber exploitation where the activity is carried out by third parties through commercial contracts, without the owner or possessor participating in any phase of the extraction process.
Type III	Producers of forest raw materials: owners and/or possessors of forest parcels that have authorized logging and that participate directly in some phase of the production chain.
Type IV	Producers with capacity for transformation and marketing: producers of raw forest materials that have infrastructure for its primary transformation and directly carry out the marketing of their products.

Source: PROCYMAF 2000.

Table 1.4. Proposed new classification of Mexican forest communities and CFEs

Type I	Potential producers: owners and/or possessors of forestlands with capacity for sustainable commercial production that currently do not carry out logging because they lack an authorized forest management plan or sufficient means to pay for its elaboration.
Type II (stumpage communities)	Producers who sell timber on the stump. Owners and/or possessors of parcels subject to timber exploitation where the activity is carried out by third parties through commercial contracts, without the owner or possessor participating in any phase of the extraction process, although owners/possessors may participate as laborers.
Type III (roundwood communities); Phase I: logging team; Phase II: extraction equipment	Producers of forest raw materials: owners and/or holders of forest properties that have authorized logging and that participate directly in some phase of the productive chain. This category contains two phases, Phase I, where the community has its own logging team (logging foreman, scaler, documenter) and Phase II, where it acquires extraction equipment such as skidders, winches, and trucks.
Type IV (sawmill communities)	Producers with capacity for transformation and marketing: producers of raw forest materials that have infrastructure for primary transformation and directly carry out the marketing of their products.
Type V (finished products communities)	Producers of roundwood that have a sawmill as well as other diversified processing infrastructure to give value-added to the sawnwood. These may include driers, furniture and moldings factories, chip mills, etc.

elaborated from sawnwood, which may include dried sawnwood, furniture, and plywood.

Drawing on Antinori's modifications, we propose a modification of the PROCYMAF classification, which appears in Table 1.4.

In this proposed modification, Type I remains the same and Type II remains essentially the same, with the additional criterion that the community may be employed as laborers by the contractors and still be regarded as a Type II community. Type III is modified to include two phases. In Phase I the communities assume direct control of the extraction process by having their own logging team that works with the contractor, under the direction of the *ejido* president. This logging team is normally directed by a person known as *jefe de monte* (logging foreman), who also has other specialized functions.

In Phase II, the community may begin to capitalize itself further by acquiring extraction machinery such as skidders, tractors, winches, and trucks, and may also begin to acquire more specialized administrative functions, especially in accounting. Type IV, sawmill community, remains the same, and a fifth type, "finished products community," is added, with the criteria noted above. A final issue that should be mentioned is, "When do we consider a community to have a CFE?" It has been suggested, for example, that Type II stumpage communities are not operating CFEs, since they do nothing but take the money for selling the timber off their land. It has even been suggested that many Type III communities don't really have CFEs since they keep no books and have no capitalization. In this interpretation, a CFE emerges only when the business is formally incorporated, when a manager or managerial council is established, and when other aspects of a formal business operation are achieved.

It is here argued that all logging communities are CFEs. At the lower levels of integration, they may be enterprises in which no operating capital is maintained, in which all profits are immediately distributed, and which shut down entirely between logging seasons, but these are nonetheless income-generating operations based on common property that make production decisions, even if the decision is to contract out all activities. Thus, you may have poorly capitalized and structured or highly capitalized and structured CFEs, with most in-between, but they all are CFEs.

Mexican CFEs: The Common Property Basis

Common property has been defined as one among three major forms of property: private, government, and common properties. The discussion of historical cases of common property have tended to focus on traditional, local, and indigenous forms of governing natural resource extraction from territories held in common or, in a modern context, natural resources which by their nature do not lend themselves to either private or government tenure forms, such as groundwater or the atmosphere (Ostrom 1990). An important distinction has been made between *open-access* and *closed-access* common property.

Open-access refers to situations where a resource is genuinely without owners, and where no one feels responsible for the maintenance of the resource. It has been suggested that this is not even really a form of common property, but rather of "propertylessness." By contrast, a *closed-access common property* has a clear set of owners. Thus, it has been argued that closed-access common property should more properly be regarded as a form of jointly held private property, like a corporation (McKean 2000). Here the importance of common property terms such as *excludability* (the right and capacity of owners to exclude others from the resource) and *subtractability* (access must be controlled because use by one reduces the capacity of others to use it) are particularly relevant in defining the characteristics of closed-access common property.

The term *common pool resources* refers to the physical dimensions of a resource while *common property regime* (both referred to as CPR) refers to the property rights arrangements or the rules which have been developed to govern access to this physical resource (McKean and Ostrom 1995). Another important distinction in common property theory is that between the management of the *stock* and the *flow* of a common pool resource. In the case of forests, the *stock* is the standing forest while the *flow* is the outputs that come from it. The management issues around the stock and the flow may be quite different (Arnold 1998).

Most of the common property literature focuses on traditional forms of CPR management. These are most commonly characterized as being in a process of dissolution or disappearance, with governments now trying to recover modernized versions of them in the growing perception that they may confer some management advantages at the community level (Arnold 1998). However, Mexico presents a most unusual and little noted case in the common property literature. Some analysts have rather mechanically applied Ostrom's (1990) "design principles" to the Mexican case (Vargas-Prieto 1998), but Mexico actually represents what may be a unique case in the common property literature. While Mexico is rich in indigenous forms of common property management, these indigenous forms were both imitated and overlaid by the massive agrarian reforms that came out of the Mexican Revolution in the second decade of the twentieth century.

This agrarian reform had as its principal land tenure expression the implementation of the two previously mentioned common property forms, *ejidos* and *comunidades indígenas* or *agrarias* (indigenous or agrarian communities), which came to cover about half of the national territory. These land tenure reforms were enshrined in Article 27 of the Constitution of 1917, and remained unchanged until 1992 (Ibarra Mendivel 1996). These agrarian reforms produced a situation where the state created both a common property regime and a common pool resource. The reform of Article 27 in 1992 presented sweeping changes in the *ejido* system, while still retaining state control in reduced ways. The reforms ended the distribution of rural lands; allowed private enterprises, through a mechanism of stocks and bonds, to become owners of rural lands; established the foundation that allowed *ejidos* and communities to exercise greater autonomy in their affairs; established new regulations governing use of property within the *ejidos;* and established new processes for resolving problems (Ibarra Mendivel 1996). This greater autonomy sanctioned a variety of forms of communal management, which were both already present and emergent (see Wilshusen, this volume). Thus, the reform to Article 27 of the Mexican Constitution may be thought of as a form of devolution or decentralization of control over natural resources as it is occurring elsewhere, but marked by the very particular agrarian history of Mexico, where significant state control is still exerted over the use of natural resources, now less out of concern for political control than for environmental protection. Thus, Mexican common property in general, and common property forests in particular, are unique in that in an era with many governments trying to institute new forms of common property, Mexico embarked on a reform, but not dissolution, of a massive state-directed effort to create common property that goes back to the third decade of the twentieth century.

This legal background, and the specific development of community forest management in Mexico, thus distinguishes it from other cases in the common property literature. For example, (McKean and Ostrom 1995) argue that "in most instances common property regimes seem to have been legislated out of existence," yet in Mexico a massive common property regime was legislated *into* existence. McKean and Ostrom (1995) title their article "Common Property Regimes in the Forest: Just a Relic from the Past?" but in Mexico common property regimes in the forest are the widespread legal present, not at all a relic from the past, and have in fact been reinforced by the reforms. In the same vein, contemporary common property regimes have also been characterized as those that have "endured" and those that have "emerged" (Arnold 1998), but Mexico is neither. It represents an ongoing, solid, widespread institutional reality and what has "emerged" over the last two decades may be thought of, in global development terms, as the "second stage" of what common property arrangements may lead to in terms of the erection of community enterprises on a common property base. It is in this sense that Mexico may be said to be "in the vanguard" or "the face of the future" in community forest management globally (Stone and D'Andrea 2001).

In Mexico, we are confronted with a massive, state-structured form of common property management where change in rules over management of forest resources has been driven either by government policy or by changes emanating from formally constituted organizations. Therefore, the more informal institutions-as-rules approach common in the CPR literature has relatively little applicability to the Mexican case. Some of the "rules" of resource use for Mexican *ejidos* are found in the agrarian laws of Mexico, while changes or additions to these rules are driven by training and technical assistance coming through government programs or second-level community organizations. Formal organizations do not play a prominent role in most of the CPR literature, but in Mexico they have been key, including both government organizations and formal civil society small farmer organizations. As Antinori (2000) has noted, "The Mexican agrarian communities are formal institutions that are adapting to a new role in resource production, whereas much of the common property literature assesses informal institutions not recognized by the state apparatus."

There are few examples in the world of formal, market-oriented community enterprises established on the basis of a common property resource, yet Mexico's forest communities have thousands of examples of this phenomenon. Common property administration by local communities is almost always seen in the context of subsistence economies. Almost entirely missing from the common property literature is a "systematic focus on stakeholders in a common property resource responding to larger market opportunities as an alternative source of benefits provided by the common property asset" (Antinori 2000). Yet this is a common occurrence in Mexican CFM.

As governments throughout the world have attempted to decentralize the administration of forest resources, various practices known as "co-management" and "joint management" have emerged (McCay and Acheson 1987). However, the term has usually referred to a mixture of local and state governance over a *publicly owned* resource. In Mexico, we have a case where community autonomy over lands has been strengthened in some aspects, while a strong government presence has been maintained in other aspects, particularly in the regulation of forest extraction. As will be explored further in the conclusions, the Mexican case may be thought of as a form of "joint management" or "co-management," but on the basis of *privately held communal property*. That is, Mexican communities manage their forests for timber with many decisions being made autonomously, but also under a strong regulatory framework provided by Mexican forestry law and the Mexican environmental agency, the Secretaría de Medio Ambiente y Recursos Naturales (SEMARNAT).

Arnold (1998) has conducted one of the most recent and comprehensive reviews of managing forests as common property. The only references to Mexico in the study are in a description of the Plan Piloto Forestal (PPF) in Quintana Roo, and some of its most salient aspects within the common property are not fully delineated. In a later section, the author concludes that the Quintana Roo case, "in which local communities are engaged in commercial logging and processing, shows that complex processes and sophisticated technologies can be handled at this level, given an appropriate institutional framework" (Arnold 1998:54). This is one of the lessons of the Mexican experience, but the fact that the common property system was created by the state early in the twentieth century with, as we shall see, massive transfers of natural forest assets taking place in later periods, and that these are community *enterprises* based on a common property resource, is not emphasized for the unique case that it is.

Thus, the articles in this volume are part of new, more systematic, efforts to understand the dimensions, unique characteristics, achievements, and challenges of Mexican community forest management. As the attentive reader will note, there is uneven coverage of some of the important community forestry regions of Mexico, with a bias toward studies of Oaxaca, and a relative paucity of studies from northern Mexico. There is an easy explanation for this. Oaxaca, with its rich social and ecological matrix of indigenous groups and biodiverse forests, has long been a magnet for student activists, NGOs, and academics. There are probably more NGOs in some neighborhoods of the city of Oaxaca than in all of Chihuahua.

The book is divided into five sections: Introduction, History, and Policy; Social Processes and Community Forestry; Ecology and Land Use Change in Community Forestry; The Economics of Community Forestry; and Global Comparisons and Conclusions. The Introduction, History, and Policy section lays important groundwork for the other articles. The emergence of such a large and relatively consolidated community forestry sector has deep historical roots in twentieth-century Mexico, and these articles outline some of the agrarian and forest policies which created the sector.

Following the present chapter, Christopher R. Boyer takes a detailed look at the local-level historical roots of community forestry, in this case in Michoacán. This is an important first step toward filling in the details on the little known but rich regional histories of community forestry in Mexico. Boyer's article is also a reminder that not all the regional paths of forest communities have led to successful outcomes, making the need to explain how so many have had relative "success" even more compelling. Boyer examines the community of El Rosario, Michoacán, and its neighbors, which today are best known as being a troubled locus of mass tourism that has grown up around visitations to one of the overwintering sites of the Monarch butterfly (*Danaus plexippus*). Boyer demonstrates that El Rosario's current state of diminishing forests and clandestine logging, which threatens the Monarch Butterfly Reserve, is a result of a series of failures to consolidate community forest management in the region. While much of this book is aimed at understanding why and how CFM has been successful in Mexico, Boyer's article joins the crucial literature that helps us understand why so many other efforts at CFM have become beset by disorganization, violence, and corruption, despite the expressed interest of many community members in the sustainable management of their forests (Klooster 2000; Vázquez León 1992).

In the next chapter in this section, Leticia Merino-Pérez and Gerardo Segura-Warnholtz analyze the evolution of Mexican forest policy and the emergence of CFEs. They show how policies of forest concessions and bans slowly began to give way in the 1970s to complex strands of supportive state policy, intertwined with more hostile state policies emanating from different points in the bureaucracy, intensified grassroots mobilizations against forest concessions, and the emergence of urban activists who took to the forests to help communities learn how to manage their own forests. Mexican forest policy has always been beset with tensions between forces that want to realize the ideals of the Mexican Revolution in terms of peasant empowerment and those that regard peasants as incapable of managing their forests for the good of the nation. In the 1930s, there was an ineffectual turn toward empowerment, followed by the long 1940–1970 period, when forest community empowerment was most clearly not on the agenda. Beginning in the 1970s however, forces within and outside the government began to come together to propel a substantial community forest management sector into existence.

In the late 1980s and the first half of the 1990s, the policy pendulum once again swung against community forestry, although by that time the sector had become relatively consolidated and could survive, albeit with difficulties, without consistent government support. However, as the authors detail, beginning with new pro-community forestry programs in the Zedillo administration (1994–2000) and continuing with major new levels of support from the Fox administration (2000–present), we are currently in a period of highly significant state support for community forestry.

In the final article in the History and Policy section, Patricia Gerez-Fernández and Enrique Alatorre-Guzmán analyze the difficult history of forest certification in Mexico. Certification represents an unusual effort to implement forest management policies through the marketplace by encouraging consumers to choose timber products from well-managed forests. Mexico's achievements in forest certification clearly show the strength of the sector in global terms. Only 3% of the 29.63 million hectares which have been certified worldwide are considered "communal," but within this category, Mexico clearly dominates, with nearly half of the communities and half of the certified community forests worldwide. Durango has taken the lead here, with a sectorwide stakeholders effort resulting in 19 certified communities (see Taylor, this volume). Despite this notable achievement, Mexico's communities have little to show for their efforts in terms of increased markets. There have been only a few sporadic sales of certified timber, with most certified communities having sold no certified timber at all. Further, as the big northern timber companies and retailers move toward embracing certification, this will once again leave small producers and communities with no particular competitive edge in the marketplace. As the authors note, new efforts by the Forest Stewardship Council (FSC) to adjust their criteria for small and community producers are under way, and will be crucial if community forestry and other small producers are to gain anything from the certification process.

In the Social Processes and Community Forestry section, the authors review the recent history of the emergence of some of the best-known community forestry organizations in Mexico, with a focus on institutional processes. Francisco Chapela, who first arrived in the Sierra Juárez of Oaxaca in the early 1980s as a student activist and stayed to found with others the NGO of which he writes, Rural Studies and Advising (Estudios Rurales y Asesoría Campesina; ERA), gives a detailed account of some of the institutional factors that led to emergence of the Union of Zapotec-Chinantec Communities (Unión de Comunidades Zapoteco-Chinanteca; UZACHI). Chapela shows how an organizing and training strategy that built human and social capital, and recognized the integration of household, community, and organizational needs was able to support one of the best-known experiences in forest management in southern Mexico.

Rodolfo López-Arzola was also an important community forestry organizer, working as the leader of a government team that also landed in Oaxaca in the early 1980s. López-Arzola gives a personal view of the rise and fall of one of the first autonomous (i.e., not directly sponsored by the government) second-level organizations in Mexico, the Union of Forest Communities and *Ejidos* of Oaxaca (Unión de Comunidades y Ejidos

Forestales de Oaxaca; UCEFO). He details UCEFO's difficult emergence as an organization, its major accomplishments in organization and improved forest management (it introduced the more silviculturally sophisticated Method of Silvicultural Development to Oaxaca), as well as the internal and external tensions that led to its effective dissolution after 10 years. Like Boyer's piece, this is a cautionary tale, warning that apparent consolidation can become dissolution if appropriate support is not provided.

Peter Taylor takes us to Durango in northern Mexico to look at how community forestry is evolving there, and shows how CFEs are evolving into new organizational forms. Most community forest advocates, whether government or nongovernment, have usually promoted the model whereby a CFE administers a common property forest where the community as a whole holds both the stock and the flow of the forest. But Taylor, like Peter Wilshusen in Quintana Roo (see below), shows how communities are now taking institutional issues into their own hands, dividing up the stocks and the flows of the forest and structuring their CFEs in the most diverse ways. The emergence of the so-called work groups throughout Mexico represents a genuine grassroots innovation in CFE organization, and shows that there is no one right way to organize a CFE. Although some community forestry advocates find the emergence of work groups to be troubling, few can be troubled by what Taylor also shows is emerging in Durango, probably the first genuine stakeholder community in Mexican forestry. The private timber industry and CFEs in Durango have understood that they have a common stake in improving production and quality of timber, and are banding together in innovative ways with, for example, timber buyers providing subsidies to communities so that they can become certified.

Peter Wilshusen gives a richly detailed ethnographic analysis of how work groups have evolved in two contrasting communities in the tropical forests of southern Quintana Roo. He shows how in the community of Caoba, despite having low volumes of timber, the work groups have become motors of local economic diversification, while in the much higher volume community of Petcacab, work groups have become a source of great community conflict with little of the proceeds being harnessed to foster genuine community development. He also uncovers the emergence of a fascinating timber futures market in Petcacab as an unexpected by-product of the work groups.

In the Ecology and Land Use Change in Community Forestry section, we enter into one of the most important new areas for research on community forestry. Frequent claims have been made that communities will manage their forests more sustainably than private enterprises, but until now there has been little hard evidence to back up that assertion. In this vein, Henricus F. M. Vester and María Angélica Navarro-Martínez take on one of the most contentious issues in tropical silviculture: What are the factors that encourage the regeneration of mahogany and what is the impact of logging on the population of mahogany in the forest? As they note, most silvicultural prescriptions have argued that mahogany needs to have relatively large clearings in order to be able to successfully grow to canopy-dominating size (although not necessarily to germinate in the first place), and that current silvicultural practices do not permit a sustainable harvest of mahogany over the long run. However, on the basis of new research in the forests of Quintana Roo, they argue that current silvicultural practice will allow continual harvests at current levels—they are more or less "sustainable," an assertion that is certain to spark more debate and research on the subject.

Elvira Durán-Medina, Jean-François Mas, and Alejandro Velázquez present one of the first systematic efforts to examine the impact of community forestry on land use change and to compare it to land use change in another major tenure regime more associated with conservation, formal protected areas, or parks. In a conclusion that will surprise some, they find that the differences between rates of land use change in protected areas and community-managed forests, especially in the tropical area of central Quintana Roo, are not statistically significant, and that there are stronger tendencies for recovery of deforested lands in community forests than in protected areas. Although this does not necessarily say anything about what is going on beneath the forest canopy, it is an important argument for the role of community-managed forests in landscape-level management.

In The Economics of Community Forestry section, the authors began to look at another kind of sustainability, the sustainability of the CFEs as financial and economic entities. Camille Antinori undertakes a brief historical review of the institutional underpinnings of the evolution of CFEs and their roots in the *ejido* and agrarian community governance forms. She analyzes the issue of what she has elsewhere called the "community as entrepreneurial firm," asking how community enterprises operating with a common property resource compete in the marketplace. Antinori's article is based on the first large-scale comparative and quantitative survey-based study undertaken specifically of the CFM sector, in this case 42 CFEs in Oaxaca. Her examination of transaction costs, contractual hazards, and vertical integration demonstrates that CFEs appear to be profitable at all levels of integration and that "communities prefer to integrate forward to avoid contractual hazards with outside entities like private logging firms." She also concludes on the basis of quantitative evidence that the common pool resources contribute to community welfare and that community ownership and control over production assures access to these benefits.

Torres-Rojo, Guevara-Sanginés, and Bray examine the economic underpinnings of one of Mexico's most successful CFEs, that of the community of El Balcón in the state of Guerrero. El Balcón, after a difficult beginning, has stabilized and grown into a CFE with one of the best sawmills in Mexico, a stable and productive relationship with a U.S. timber company, growing export markets, and clear community leadership of the enterprise, while also leaving many decisions to professional management. However, the authors argue that there are weaknesses to the business model that must be addressed if El Balcón is to continue delivering benefits to community members and maintaining their forest as a productive ecosystem. It is suggested that greater investments must be made in the forest, that the forest is currently subsidizing the industry to an unsustainable degree, and that there must be a "reengineering" of the processes of production, investment, and distribution of profits.

Finally, in the Global Comparisons and Conclusions section, Dan Klooster and Shrinidhi Ambinakudige situate Mexican community forestry within a sweeping global review. As the authors make clear, most local communities worldwide are still struggling to organize themselves to co-manage state forest lands as woodlots for firewood, forage, and non-timber forest products, even if they are lands that they have used for hundreds of years. And although important advances are being made in these areas, they conclude that Mexico "confirms the expectations of community forestry proponents: Greater community participation in forest benefits and greater community power over forest management results in better forest use and protection and improved livelihoods for local people." David Bray then summarizes some of the lessons learned from some 30 years of community forestry in Mexico, and where it might be going from here.

Camille Antinori, in her article, comes to the following conclusion: "Therefore, Oaxaca's forests are community-managed in a strong sense of the phrase. The community governance and territorial land claims have national recognition, and a governance structure is in place where (mainly male) community members can determine the distribution of forest benefits while the elected authority on common property matters, the CBC, normally has the power to administer decisions on common property forestry matters." As Antinori is also well aware, many CFEs stumble from crisis to crisis, have serious problems in stable governance, fiscal administration, and forest management, and do indeed, as she notes, continue traditional patterns of suppression of women's rights. However, this does not take away from the fact that an impressive number of CFEs in Mexico, most likely in the hundreds, have achieved the constitution of enterprises that deliver benefits to the community, maintain the ecosystem functions of the forests, and that are, indeed, community managed in the strong sense of the phrase.

Finally, given the magnitude of Mexican community forests, both in number and in territory, they also have very significant implications for Mexican landscapes. To the extent that community-managed forests contribute to the maintenance of forest cover and other ecosystem processes, they may be said to contribute to "sustainable landscapes." The idea of landscape management is one that is frequently found in Europe but less so in Latin America. However, Mexico has many areas where there is still a significant forest matrix and which have been comparatively stable in terms of forest cover, but these regions have been little recognized. These "sustainable landscapes" may be operatively defined as those where deforestation rates are low, in equilibrium, or with net expansion of forest cover, and where multiple institutional processes are present that encourage the preservation of ecosystem structure, composition, and process (Haines-Young 2000; Shepherd and Harshaw 2001). Working landscapes can still retain many crucial ecosystem processes and biodiversity. As Chazdon (1998:1295) has argued, "A tropical landscape containing a matrix of old-growth forest fragments, second-growth forest, logged forest, and agricultural fields could conceivably protect most of the species present in the regional biota." Conservation organizations speak of "designing" sustainable landscapes by rebuilding fragmented forests in biodiversity conservation corridors (CABS et al. 2000; Sanderson et al. 2003). However, we argue in this book that many Mexican forest communities are already managing for sustainable landscapes that have been designed by both grassroots action and government policy over many decades.

As mentioned earlier, this volume attempts to pull together the existing work and reflection by its most important researchers and practitioners on Mexican community-based forestry. The breadth of the topics reflects the focus of existing work, but also reveals areas where there is a lack of systematic inquiry, despite its importance. For example, conspicuously absent is research incorporating a gender perspective in the analysis of Mexican CFM. In general within CFM communities, gender rigidity encapsulates a severe limitation of women's participation in the power structures and decision making of forestry activity. The strong traditional governance systems in the rural communities and the male dominance of the forestry sector, as a whole, often combine to suppress women's rights with little understood implications and consequences.

Deeper inquiry into understanding the benefits of CFM at the household level is also an understudied topic, as is the impact of migration and remittances and their impact on family and community survival strategies, changes in their governance systems, and influence in their economic well-being. Lastly, the role of the generational dynamics of these communities is of crucial importance. Social sustainability must go hand in hand with the analysis of environmental sustainability, which leads us to the need for understanding how CFM is affecting the youth in forestry communities: their access to resources and expertise, and their participation in leadership.

Notes

1. This book is one product of a series of research projects on Mexican community forestry that have been conducted under a Ford Foundation grant with important additional support from the William and Flora Hewlett Foundation.

2. The term *silvicultura comunitaria* (community silviculture) has also been widely used in the Spanish-language literature to refer to all aspects of community forest management. We have not adopted this term here because the use of the term *silviculture* suggests a narrow focus on forest cultivation issues, while CFE is intended to include all aspects of the community enterprise, from forest cultivation and management to industrialization.

3. According to Mexican agrarian law (Ley Agraria 2002), *comunidades* consist of (usually indigenous) people that have been dispossessed of their lands and then been restored these same lands. *Comunidades* were formerly known as *comunidades indígenas* to differentiate them from both from *ejidos* and from communities in the generic, pre-1992, sense, and are now often called *comunidades agrarias* for this same reason.

References

Alatorre Frenk, G. 2000. *La construcción de una cultura gerencial democrática en las empresas forestales comunitarias.* Mexico City: Casa Juan Pablos, Procuraduría Agraria.

Antinori, C. M. 2000. Vertical integration in Mexican common property forests. PhD diss., University of California, Berkeley.

Arnold, J. E. M. 1998. *Managing Forests as Common Property.* Rome: FAO.

Barbier, E. B., and J. C. Burgess. 1996. Economic analysis of deforestation in Mexico. *Environment and Development Economics* 1:203–239.

Bray, D. B., L. Merino-Pérez, P. Negreros-Castillo, G. Segura-Warnholtz, J. M. Torres-Rojo, and H. F. M. Vester. 2003. Mexico's community-managed forests as a global model for sustainable landscapes. *Conservation Biology* 17:672–677.

CABS, CI, and IESB. 2000. Designing sustainable landscapes/planejando paisagens sustentáveis: The Brazilian Atlantic forest. Conservation International Center for Applied Biodiversity Science, Washington, DC.

Castilleja, G. 1996. Mexico. In *The Conservation Atlas of Tropical Forests: The Americas,* ed. C. S. Harcourt and J. A. Sayer, 193–205. New York: Simon and Schuster.

Chazdon, R. L. 1998. Tropical forests—Log 'em or leave 'em? *Science* 281:1295–1296.

de Jong, B. H. J., R. Tipper, and G. Montoya-Gómez. 2000. An economic analysis of the potential for carbon sequestration by forests: Evidence from southern Mexico. *Ecological Economics* 33:313–327.

Haines-Young, R. 2000. Sustainable development and sustainable landscapes: Defining a new paradigm for landscape ecology. *Fennia* 178: 7–14.

Ibarra Mendivel, J. L. 1996. Cambios recientes en la constitución mexicana y su impacto sobre la reforma agraria. In *Reformando la reforma agraria mexicana,* ed. L. Randall, 65–80. Mexico City: UAM Unidad Xochimilco.

INEGI 1997. *Estadísticas del medio ambiente.* Mexico City: INEGI.

Klooster, D. 2000. Institutional choice, community, and struggle: A case study of forest co-management in Mexico. *World Development* 28:1–20.

Ley Agraria. 2002. Mexico City: Anaya Editores.

McCay, B. J., and J. M. Acheson. 1987. *The Question of the Commons: The Culture and Ecology of Communal Resources.* Tucson: University of Arizona Press.

McKean, M. A. 2000. Common property: What is it, what is it good for, and what makes it work? In *People and Forests: Communities, Institutions, and Governance,* ed. C. C. Gibson, M. A. McKean, and E. Ostrom, 27–55. Cambridge, MA: MIT Press.

McKean, M. A., and E. Ostrom. 1995. Common property regimes in the forest: Just a relic from the past? *Unasylva* 46:2–14.

Merino-Pérez, L., P. Gerez-Fernández, and S. Madrid-Zubirán. 2000. Políticas, instituciones comunitarias y uso de los recursos comunes en México. In *Sociedad, derecho y medio ambiente: Primer informe del programa de investigación sobre aplicación y cumplimiento de la legislación ambiental en México,* ed. M. Bañuelos, 57–143. Mexico City: CONACYT, SEP; Casa Abierta al Tiempo, UNAM, SEMARNAP, PROFEPA.

O'Brien, K. L. 1998. *Sacrificing the Forest: Environmental and Social Struggles in Chiapas.* Boulder, CO: Westview Press.

Ostrom, E. 1990. *Governing the Commons: The Evolution of Institutions for Collective Action.* Cambridge: Cambridge University Press.

Palacio-Prieto, J. L., G. Bocco, A. Velázquez, et al. 2000. La condición actual de los recursos forestales en México: Resultados del inventario forestal nacional 2000. *Investigaciones Geográficas* 43:183–203.

Perry, J. P. 1991. *The Pines of Mexico and Central America.* Portland, OR: Timber Press.

PROCYMAF. 2000. *Proyecto de conservación y manejo sustentable de recursos forestales en México: Balance de tres años de ejecución.* Mexico City: SEMARNAP.

Sanderson, J., K. Alger, G. A. B. d. Fonseca, V. H. Inchausty, and K. Morrison. 2003. Biodiversity conservation corridors: Planning, implementing, and monitoring sustainable landscapes. Conservation International Center for Applied Biodiversity Science, Washington, DC.

Sheppard, S. R. J., and H. W. Harshaw. 2001. *Forest and Landscapes: Linking Ecology, Sustainability and Aesthetics.* New York: CABI.

Stone, R., and C. D'Andrea. 2001. *Tropical Forests and the Human Spirit: Journeys to the Brink of Hope.* Berkeley and Los Angeles: University of California Press.

Trejo, I., and R. Dirzo. 2000. Deforestation of seasonally dry tropical forest: A national and local analysis in Mexico. *Biological Conservation* 94:133–142.

Vargas-Prieto, A. M. 1998. Effective intervention: External and internal elements of institutional structure for forest management in Quintana Roo, Mexico. PhD diss., University of Wisconsin, Madison.

Vázquez León, L. 1992. *Ser indio otra vez: La purepechización de los tarascos serranos.* Mexico City: Consejo Nacional para la Cultura y las Artes.

Velázquez, A., J. F. Mas, J. R. Díaz, et al. 2002. Patrones de cambio de uso del suelo y tasas de deforestación en México. *Gaceta Ecológica de la Instituto Nacional de Ecología* 62:17–25.

World Bank. 1995. *Mexico: Resource Conservation and Forest Sector Review.* Washington, DC: World Bank, SARH. 161.

CHAPTER 2

Contested Terrain: Forestry Regimes and Community Responses in Northeastern Michoacán, 1940–2000

CHRISTOPHER R. BOYER

In the early days of the rainy season of 1941, leaders of the *ejido* of El Rosario, Michoacán, wrote to President Manuel Ávila Camacho to tell him about a problem that they had encountered with the neighboring village. The leaders explained that over the past several years they had taken care of the forests on their land reform parcel and done all their logging in strict accordance with federal regulations. But now the neighboring community had requested a grant of some woodlands that the villagers of El Rosario had hoped would be added to their existing land reform parcel. This sort of intercommunity conflict over land and resources was commonplace in postrevolutionary Mexico, but the tone of the villagers' letter was not. Rather than basing their claim to the disputed lands on typical grounds of prior ownership or of their primordial rights to the land they work, community leaders argued that their village deserved the land because they were good conservationists. As the community leaders put it, El Rosario had always sought to use the existing pastures and "keep the woodlands untouched" whereas their neighbors "only want[ed] the forestland in order to log it off" (García and Domínguez 1941).

This letter and others like it from the 1940s were written nearly four decades before terms like "stewardship" and "sustainability" had become the catchwords of national and international development efforts. It would be fully 30 years before El Rosario and its sister communities in the eastern highlands of Michoacán would gain international attention as one of a handful of peasant villages whose collectively held but dwindling forestlands served as the winter breeding ground for Monarch butterflies. Nevertheless, it is clear that the community leaders already found it useful to argue that their good land management was the basis of the community's well-being and that the forest should belong to those who intended to use it in an equitable and environmentally responsible manner. It is true that the leaders may simply have made these arguments because they thought it was what the president wanted to hear—a not unreasonable expectation in an age when some of the nation's most prominent leaders were insisting that the protection of the nation's patrimony could only be achieved through the "rational" use of forests (e.g., de Quevedo 1938). Nevertheless, their words and the actions behind them announced the beginning of El Rosario's long engagement with state-imposed forest management regimes.

Mexico's forestry policies were marked by both continuities and change during the twentieth century. On the one hand, the law varied widely over time. Forestry codes of the 1920s allowed for community-based forestry carried out by state-regulated village producers' cooperatives. In the 1940s, 1950s, and 1960s, the codes were rewritten to favor commercial and parastatal timber producers charged with making "rational" use of resources over wide territories, including those held by peasant communities as land reform *ejidos*. A new regime appeared in the 1970s and 1980s that attempted to use market demand to drive production while simultaneously promoting community production (for a periodization, see Merino-Pérez 2001). On the other hand, two key policy areas have remained constant over time. First, political leaders and forestry experts have repeatedly insisted that Mexico's forests constitute an underutilized but potentially vast source of wealth. They have sometimes gone as far as to claim that "rationally" organized wood products industries could one day be as lucrative as the petroleum sector. Second, these experts and policy makers have consistently argued that rural communities should earn the greatest share of the profits and receive the first jobs when their forests are exploited for timber or resin; yet, for years they argued that their scientific knowledge gave them the right to make most major decisions about how the forests should be used without consulting with the communities themselves (see, e.g., "Exposición" 1923:14; Rodríguez Adame 1963).

The repeated policy shifts in the overall context of scientific paternalism and nationalist developmentalism created a political environment that was at once unstable and yet consistently unfavorable for the highlands of Michoacán. Forestry policies toward the communities were based on a model of village producers' cooperatives in the 1930s, on large-scale regional producers' organizations in the 1950s and 1960s, and ultimately on community forestry and ecotourism associated with the Monarch Butterfly Reserve from the mid-1970s to the 1990s (Chapela and Barkin 1995).

Villagers responded to each new initiative with a combination of enthusiasm, compliance, and resistance, but in the end none of these models proved sustainable. Most initiatives were imposed on the communities with little or no consultation beforehand and thus tended to undermine local autonomy. The communities' economies and ecosystems declined as a result, and villagers' support for locally controlled, sustainable forestry eroded over the course of the twentieth century.

This chapter focuses on the experiences of El Rosario and the neighboring village of El Asoleadero in the eastern highlands of Michoacán, two communities that were among the first in the state to receive grants of *ejido* land reform parcels in the 1920s and that hence have had unusually long experience in negotiating with federal authorities at all levels. They also formed part one of the state's most long-lived producers' organizations (known initially as the Melchor Ocampo Forest Exploitation Unit and later as the Melchor Ocampo Union of *Ejidos*[1]). These organizations promised to achieve the rational use of forest products, yet they failed to deliver the communities from their grinding poverty. Unlike other communities that were also subject to producers' organizations but which eventually succeeded in managing their community resources—communities such as San Juan Parangaricutiro in the more temperate foothills of central Michoacán—the two highlands villages ultimately failed to negotiate the labyrinth of federal forest policies while sustainably logging their forests. The combination of uneven enforcement of laws and regulations, intracommunity tensions, and, eventually, out-migration, overwhelmed community leaders' efforts to moderate and oversee village forestry.

Ecological Paternalism, 1920s–1940s

Postrevolutionary presidents such as Álvaro Obregón (1920–24), Plutarco Elías Calles (1924–28), and Lázaro Cárdenas (1934–40) undertook a massive campaign to transform popular political culture and mobilize the rural people around what they regarded as the collective interests of peasants. They hoped to politically mobilize rural people by assembling them in mass institutions intended to empower them, discipline them, and channel their support behind the postrevolutionary state (Boyer 2003; Knight 1994). These presidents, and Cárdenas in particular, sought to rebuild the fractured national economy and reorganize the government they inherited after a decade of warfare, all while redistributing land—including woodlands—to peasant communities. It was in this context of populism and economic crisis that scientific forestry emerged (or rather, reemerged from a hiatus after its initial appearance the late nineteenth century) as an element of the wider cultural project of state formation. As elaborated by intellectuals such as Miguel Angel de Quevedo, scientific forestry promoted the twin goals of conservation and efficiency, both of which were needed if Mexico was to maximize resource use and harness forest ecosystems to national capitalist development (Simonian 1995:85–97; for a comparison with the United States, see Hays 1959). Yet scientists did not trust peasants to achieve these goals alone and repeatedly charged that peasant communities and, to a lesser extent, commercial logging operations, were inefficient and wasteful. Their solution in the postrevolutionary years was to advocate for legislation that restricted access to the commercial market to only those communities and enterprises that met scientific standards of rational exploitation.

De Quevedo and the experts in the Mexican Forestry Society helped draft the 1926 forestry code, whose lyrical goal was to "regularize the conservation, restoration, propagation, and utilization of forests." The code, which signaled the definitive emergence of scientific models of forest conservation in Mexico, established the legislative basis for declaring protected forest reserves, creating a forest service, and regulating nearly every aspect of logging on public, private, and collectively held lands. The twin goals of allowing for community participation in forestry while safeguarding ecosystems was accomplished through the establishment of an extensive and sometimes labyrinthine set of laws meant to control forest use and foster conservation. For example, watersheds were declared off-limits for logging, and authorization from the Department of Forestry and Game was required for commercial logging on any land regardless of its ownership. The law required private landholders to file a complete forestry plan with the federal government and directed the largest operations to hire a full-time forester. Transportation of timber also came under tight regulation; indeed, it soon became the chief mechanism for enforcement of forestry regulations. The law required every mule team, truck, and railroad car hauling a consignment of commercial forest products to have a complete set of licenses and transshipment orders on hand, and forestry officials could check them at any point along the route (Secretaría de Agricultura y Fomento 1930:47–58).

Although the enabling legislation for the 1926 code placed substantial restrictions on commercial firms, it sought above all to reorient peasant behaviors and attitudes toward the forest. Like the code authorizing the land reform itself, the forestry code obliged land reform beneficiaries to form producers' cooperatives if they intended to sell their timber to outsiders (Secretaría de Agricultura y Fomento 1930:48). In theory, this provision would allow villagers to work their own lands and sell their timber directly to the highest bidder. This in turn would create jobs and remove intermediaries such as sawmill contractors and timber brokers from the production process. The code was meant to confer the greatest benefits of timber production upon the land reform beneficiaries that possessed the forests as they organized themselves into collectivist and easily monitored village associations. But rural people almost universally ignored the law. A full eight years after the law went into effect, only six communities in all of Mexico had formed producers' cooperatives (de Quevedo 1938).

That changed once Cárdenas invited de Quevedo to head up the National Forestry Service and charged him with integrating the peasant timber sector into the government's greatly expanded land reform program. De Quevedo responded by ordering foresters to establish cooperatives throughout the countryside. Within two years, more than 300 community producers' organizations had been established. De Quevedo expected that the co-ops would both develop the peasant economy and provide forestry officials with a mechanism through which they could regulate and oversee peasant logging practices (de Quevedo 1938), and his peremptory attitude toward peasant production eventually brought him into conflict with the president. Nonetheless, his placement of institutional checks on peasant production and behavior fit comfortably within the overall framework of Cardenismo. Indeed, it became the baseline for Mexico's subsequent and largely paternalist forestry policy (on the conflicts between Cárdenas and de Quevedo, see Simonian 1995:107–108; for an example of de Quevedo's pro-cooperative attitude, however, see, e.g., de Quevedo 1937).

A central problem with the cooperative program was that the goal of disciplining and regulating peasants' use of the forests conflicted with the goal of empowering peasants to participate in community-based production. For example, a forest warden reported in 1929 that members of rural communities in the Uruapan area did a brisk timber business on the open market but reacted to his suggestion to form a producers' cooperative with suspicion and enough antagonism that he no longer felt safe in the woodlands without a picket of soldiers to accompany him.[2] More prosaic problems arose as well. Some cooperatives functioned poorly because small-time political bosses (*caciques*) tried to use them as vehicles to enrich themselves and their cronies. And, rural people sometimes resented the overbearing attitudes of the forestry officials who arrived to establish the co-ops. In still other instances, rural people seem to have regarded the cooperatives as unwanted intrusions into community life, particularly within indigenous communities such as those around Uruapan that already had their own local governance systems and forest use practices.

For communities such as El Rosario, the 1926 forestry code and its requirements for the establishment of cooperatives brought new possibilities for local control over timber production, as well as new forms of dependency on the state. The cooperative became an important part of local politics in El Rosario, as its leaders emerged as mediators with major political leaders. After all, the director of the cooperative had enough stature within the community that he felt he was in a position to write to the president of the republic on behalf of his community—a role usually reserved for a village's top religious and administrative leaders. The cooperative also provided tangible benefits for its members and served as a conduit through which conservationist ideals entered village leaders' political discourse. In short, it functioned as a conduit between the postrevolutionary state and the community hierarchy. But how, precisely, did this relationship play out in practice?

The forests of the northeastern Michoacán highlands had been contested terrain for nearly a hundred years by the time that the Mexican Revolution opened the way to land reform. The high alpine forests were comprised of pine, oak, and oyamel trees, and they had been home to a substantial population of Otomí indigenous people who had arrived there in the early days of the colonial period. By the late nineteenth century, the United States–owned American Smelting and Refining Company (ASARCO) had acquired most of the timberland surrounding the El Oro/Angangueo mining complex, and the predominantly indigenous families who lived in the region regularly complemented subsistence agriculture by sending their men to work for the company. Most local men worked at least on a casual basis as woodcutters, harvesting timber and hauling it to company-owned sawmills where it was cut for use as mineshaft stays, railroad ties, and fuel for the locomotives. A handful of villagers worked as miners as well.[3]

The land reform had made its debut in the highlands in 1921, when a self-styled indigenous leader by the name of Jesús Aguilar arrived in the community of El Asoleadero (El Rosario's neighbor) and convinced villagers to present a formal request for an *ejido* land grant. The mining company almost immediately began a campaign of threats and intimidation, the first step of which was to cancel all labor contracts with men from the community. Nevertheless, the villagers persisted, and the people of El Asoleadero occupied their new *ejido* the following year. Unfortunately, the new grant was not good land for agriculture. As early as 1921 a government agronomist had judged its high altitude and red clay soils as unsuited for growing corn or wheat. Virtually the only way for villagers to make a living—both then and now—was through logging and cattle ranching.[4]

The villagers of El Asoleadero found themselves in difficult economic straits once the company fired them, so it hardly seems surprising that they began to log the woodlands even before the president of the republic had given his final approval to the establishment of their *ejido*. Nor did villagers heed the local agent of the Land Reform Commission, who insisted that they could not begin their operation until they had formally established a producers' cooperative.[5] A mere two years after the community occupied its tract of woodland, its dependence on the local timber industry was clear for all to see. Indeed, a forest warden determined that a timber broker had become the dominant voice within village politics by the late 1920s.[6] Yet, it also appears that the village logging operation functioned relatively smoothly in the 1930s thanks to the participation of at least some key members of the community. The village headmen who had helped to set up the cooperative emerged by the decade's end as dedicated partisans of revolutionary ideologies, and its leaders began to discuss issues of regional politics with the leaders of other Otomí communities in the area. Perhaps most importantly, the village logging cooperative was formally if belatedly established in 1937, allowing villagers to sell timber on the open market.[7]

Problems did break out in the mid-1940s, however, when El Rosario requested its own land reform parcel. The plot that the community solicited encompassed a stand of timber that the members of El Asoleadero regarded as their own. As we have seen, the leaders of El Rosario were quite comfortable writing to the president and employing the discourse of conservation to explain why they deserved the land more than their neighbors. They depicted themselves as ecologically minded peasants who intended to act as faithful stewards of the forests. How far these villagers might have gone to make their behavior conform to their rhetoric is an open question, but the discourses that people use to explain—or even to misrepresent—their behavior to outsiders are at least potentially able to structure their identities and attitudes in the long run. If the rhetoric of conservation had become an ingrained element of community life in El Rosario, it may well have underwritten conservationist practices in the long run (Matthews 2003; and see Boyer 2000). Encouraging signs were visible elsewhere in the state as well. For example, Michoacán was the nation's largest producer of pine resin, and four community-based resin-tapping cooperatives had been formed in the Uruapan area during the late 1930s and were still functioning and deriving value from the forest in the face of a 1937 ban on logging.[8] Yet neither these cooperatives nor the nascent producers' organization survived for long. By the 1940s, Mexican presidents were already turning away from the earnest, albeit paternalist, drive to develop peasant-based models of forestry. Enticed by the prospect of rapid industrialization, Mexican leaders of the 1940s and 1950s promoted large, often state-owned forest products enterprises that received exclusive rights to exploit timberlands covering vast regions, including stands that were located inside land reform communities. The government's emphasis on the community as a possible locus, not merely of forest production but of forest *preservation*, had come to an end and did not reappear for another four decades.

Central Planning, 1940s–1980s

Mexico's political economy underwent a major transformation as World War II dawned. U.S. demand for Mexican primary-sector products soared, leading to a revival of the Mexican economy and simultaneously to government efforts to curb social demands that could threaten continued economic development. The populism of the Cárdenas years began to give way as the Mexican state turned toward industrialization—a policy that favored urban workers over peasants. The change was felt almost immediately in forestry legislation. The 1926 code derived from the paternalism and positivistic disregard for peasant productive practices that characterized the postrevolutionary years, but it nonetheless departed from the assumption that community-based timber production could meet at least part of the nation's demand for timber products. By the 1940s, however, the pro-industry and pro-development strategy that gripped national leaders demanded a different legal structure.

In 1940, the same year Cárdenas left office, a new forestry code was passed that matched the spirit of the times. It encouraged the establishment of semi-public corporations known as Industrial Forest Production Units (Unidades Industriales de Explotación Forestal, or UIEFs), which were envisioned as a mechanism for "rationally" managing the extraction of timber on a regional level. The new productive units would necessarily supplant existing community-based producers' cooperatives, which as discrete, local entities had neither the geographic scope nor the working capital to exploit the nation's forests on the scale that the nation's modernizing leaders envisioned. The conservationist paternalism of the 1926 law was replaced by a sort of economic paternalism, in which the stumpage fees generated from logging—the so-called *derechos de monte*—were held in an escrow that communities could only access if they petitioned the Department of Agrarian Reform (Secretaría de la Reforma Agraria) (Merino-Pérez 2001:80). In case there was any lingering confusion about the direction that the federal government envisioned for forestry policy, a further elaboration of the law was published in 1952 that gave UIEFs jurisdiction over all forests that were located within their boundaries, regardless of whether the acreage was held as common land by indigenous communities, ejidal land in land reform communities, or fee simple private property (*Diario Oficial de la Federación*, 11 January 1952).

The new code's authors regarded the UIEFs as a mechanism that would simultaneously limit community access to the market (thus assuaging foresters' concerns that peasant production was incompatible with conservation) and meet the political imperative of creating jobs and economic infrastructure in rural areas. All this could be accomplished, it was believed, by subjecting local needs to the allegedly more rational oversight of regional forest managers.

Policy makers intended the UIEFs to produce most of the raw material needed for the broader project of rapid industrialization, and indeed many UIEFs became the primary suppliers of forest products to private or parastatal enterprises such as paper companies. In other words, the UIEFs functioned as concessions of raw materials to select businesses, and it didn't take long for entrepreneurs to seize upon the opportunity to solicit these concessions and thus create monopsony conditions for themselves. The government had formed approximately 30 UIEFs by 1960, most of which had 25-year concessions to the land under their respective jurisdictions, though some concessions were slated for as many as 60. Together, the UIEFs controlled over 5.8 million hectares, or over a sixth of all forests in the nation.[9]

Yet even in the early 1950s, some observers already recognized that the UIEFs were not living up to their promise of rationalizing resource use on a regional scale or providing a satisfactory defense for the integrity of forest ecosystems. Writing in what was then the nation's premier daily newspaper, Filberto Gómez González observed that many of the UIEFs had not provided an economic boost to most rural communities under their authority, nor had they improved the efficiency of timbering operations, all because they had "fallen into the hands of bunglers and politicians." He noted that stricter measures such as the formation of forest reserves and national parks had not produced any better results since the people who had been charged with administering them had often elected to log them off (*El Universal*, 19 October 1951). The UIEFs clearly suffered from the seemingly limitless cupidity of their administrators, but also problematic was their use of the so-called Mexican Method of Forest Management, which if properly applied would encourage a natural succession from pine to oak and thus reduce the commercial value of the forest (Snook and Negreros 1986). On the other hand, it is far from clear that the UIEFs employed any selection technique at all, electing instead to simply clear all the trees from the areas they worked. Moreover, they failed to inject much new capital into their territories because the UIEF concessionaires typically set an artificially low price for timber, effectively compelling land reform beneficiaries and other nominal owners of forests to subsidize their production (Barrena 1961:12).

The potential advantages of UIEFs were not lost on the elite families that dominated the timber industry in Michoacán, nor on the pro-development and pro-government members of the State Forestry Commission. Both of these groups began to argue in the early 1950s that community cooperatives, at least the few that continued to function in the Uruapan area in the 1940s, had failed to protect forests or to develop the regional environment and should be subsumed within UIEFs.[10] In 1950, the largest and most successful of these new parastatal enterprises was established in another part of Michoacán with a total of 5 million pesos capitalization (3.1 million from 23 Mexican investors and 1.9 from 7 Spanish ones): the Michoacana de Occidente received the right to log over 113,000 hectares of the relatively sparsely inhabited Michoacán hotlands and coastal region.[11]

According to its promoters, the Michoacana de Occidente had acquired the "most modern" machinery available from the United States and Europe even before receiving final permission to begin operations. Writing to ex–President Cárdenas, who had become the unofficial overseer of Michoacán's forest development while serving as the executive director of the Comisión de Tepalcatepec in the 1950s, the Michoacana's administrators also promised to follow an "economic-social program of action that will ensure the scientific utilization of the forests [as well as] good salaries, houses, schools, and hospitals for our workers and their families."[12] The Michoacana made its first cuts in 1952 and soon emerged as the most highly organized such venture in Michoacán, although it came at the cost of closing down four small-scale logging operations that functioned in the region at the time. Nevertheless, it did set many residents to work in its tapping and logging operations, and even had some success at reforesting the land it had exploited. In its first few years of full operation, its annual production reached approximately 320,000 cubic meters of pine, about a tenth that much of oak, and over 1.5 million gallons of resins.[13]

Most UIEFs did not enjoy anything near that degree of success, however, even if "success" is judged only on the basis of reported production. By contrast, the northeastern highlands of Michoacán was home to what by nearly any standard was one of the nation's least successful UIEFs. The El Oro, Angangueo y Tlalpujahua UIEF was a concession given to a parastatal corporation dubbed Montes-Industriales-Minas, and it received control of the struggling mining operation and timberlands throughout the area, including the ejidal lands of El Rosario, El Asoleadero, and others. It was a substantial mandate. The mine's previous owner, ASARCO, had found it difficult to turn a profit ever since the 1910s, and since that time has elected instead to lease its holdings to small-scale operators. As far as the federal government was concerned, the importance of the mining complex by the 1940s lay less with its ability to produce ore than with its potential to provide employment to skilled workers in the region. The mines continued to be the largest single employer in the area and the major consumer of forest products from nearby communities, meaning that the newly formed parastatal company received very favorable terms for the purchase of timber. The UIEF's timber concession, combined with a statewide ban (*veda*) on all other logging activity established in 1950, guaranteed it a monopoly on legally harvested timber in the area. (The Michoacana del Occidente, formed four years later, received a similar exemption from competition.[14]) By the middle of the decade, then, community leaders in the eastern highlands found that they needed permission from Montes-Industrias-Minas to cut wood from their own *ejido*, even for such seemingly trivial operations such as the felling of 1,500 board feet of wood to be used for house repair and the construction of a community meeting house.[15]

The villagers of El Rosario had no trouble recognizing that change was in the air. The community forestry cooperative had ceased to exist sometime in the late 1940s, and members of the community began to search for more land to sustain themselves. Yet, the creation of the UIEF blocked the community from direct access to the timber market, forcing the villagers to seek new land that could be cleared and converted into pasturage for cattle. It appeared at one point as if that strategy would pay off. In 1950, it seemed possible that the community would receive some lands carved out of a nearby hacienda, and dozens of villagers invaded the hacienda with rifle in hand and began to harvest as much timber as they possibly could, casting away the professed conservationism of the previous decade.[16] The villagers presumably used the wood the same way most other people who illegally harvested timber in that area did, employing it for their domestic needs, converting it into charcoal for sale as cooking fuel in the town of Zitácuaro, or delivering it directly to sawmills and furniture shops in one of the nearby cities (Gutiérrez Jarquín 1969:329).

The villagers had every reason to work quickly. According to the owners of the hacienda that had been invaded, the villagers knew that they would probably never be given permanent possession of the land and decided instead to take it by force. Then they would attempt to sell as many logs as they could before they were ordered to leave. Even if the villagers did receive permanent possession, they would be able to argue that the land should be classified as pasture for their cattle, not as forestland subject to the UIEF's control. It eventually turned out that the community was ineligible to receive the disputed property because it lay inside Mexico state, not Michoacán. By the time the villagers finally abandoned the land in 1956, the hacienda owner claimed that they had just about eliminated the forests altogether.[17]

In 1964, Montes-Industriales-Minas lost its concession after the forestry department determined that it had failed to abide by the terms of its charter. The mining operation still had the option of buying timber from villagers, but it now had to pay prevailing market price. It was not long before the company collapsed altogether. As the communities began to reorganize for limited entry into the market, officials in the Michoacán State Forestry Commission convinced them to form a regional co-operative—technically, a Forest Planning Unit or Unidad de Ordenación Forestal—that comprised roughly the same area and the same 37 *ejido* land reform communities and 9 indigenous villages with communal lands that had previously been subject to the UIEF. Like their immediate predecessors, the foresters who helped to organize the "Melchor Ocampo" Association of *Ejidos*, as the new institution was known,[18] intended to promote rapid development in the countryside while still conserving the forest for future generations (Gutiérrez Jarquín 1969:294). Also like the UIEF, the Association of *Ejidos* was essentially hierarchical in structure, having been established by the federal Subsecretariat of Forests and Game for reasons that responded to administrative and economic imperatives, rather than responding to demands articulated by the communities themselves. And, of course, foresters with technical expertise retained the authority to determine the extent and location of (legal) logging operations throughout the area.

Unlike the UIEF, however, the Association of *Ejidos* sought to generate community participation in both production and long-term conservation. The authors of the planning unit's forest inventory emphasized that they rejected the notion that "the campesino is incapable of acting as an entrepreneur" and condemned previous institutional arrangements that had kept rural people "marginalized from the production regimes in their own forests." Therefore, the Association of *Ejidos* was organized so that the member communities directly received contractors' licenses to log their land (gaining the status of so-called *permisionarios*) as well as the right to seek their own credit to get local production under way. The foresters recognized that most peasants lacked the scientific training or the economic means to establish a regime of sustainable forestry on their own, but the foresters were nevertheless quite sanguine about villagers' ability to harvest and market their own timber without resorting to middlemen or contractors, at least as long as they did so under the foresters' guidance (Gutiérrez Jarquín 1969:332, 340–342). Foresters hoped the Association of *Ejidos* would both stimulate community-based production and "create norms related to all aspects of the silvicultural use of the woods, in order to conserve, develop, and increase these resources in order to achieve the maximum sustainable yield" (Gutiérrez Jarquín 1969:2).

Yet, the about-face in institutional context ended up generating resentments within the highlands communities. Villagers suspected forestry officials and some community members of enriching themselves, and poor communication between the forestry department and the communities, combined with intervillage rivalries, created an atmosphere of confusion and resentment. In 1976, for example, El Rosario community leaders complained that not once in the 12 years that the Association of *Ejidos* had operated had they been notified of their community's share of the profits from the association's furniture workshop and sawmill. They also wondered why the producer association was able to provide trucks and other vehicles for foresters but not for members of the *ejido* communities.[19] The persistence of such questions apparently undermined many people's confidence in the organization and drove a wedge between community members and leaders, as well as between communities and the forestry department.

Something of the scale of these problems can be gleaned from a 1986 postmortem written by experts from the Michoacán State Forestry Commission. Among other problems, the commission noted that the Association of *Ejidos* never received the amount of credit originally envisioned, making it impossible for it to achieve production goals. As a consequence, member communities ceased to receive their annual revenues after the organization's first six years of operation. The experts also cited other factors that impeded the organization's success, including the ill-will and obstructionism of local timber companies as well as community members' own lack of education and understanding of the nature of the Association of *Ejidos*–what the foresters called peasants' "total ignorance of [the Association's] administrative and accounting practices." Perhaps most importantly, the Association of *Ejidos* (which, like the UIEF before it had received a legal monopsony on its member communities' wood products) paid less than prevailing market values for wood and resin, which led to 10 communities resigning from the organization in the early 1980s. By 1985, it was clear that the Association of *Ejidos* was mired in debt and deeply unpopular with highlands communities (Comisión Forestal 1986:8).

In 1986, the Association of *Ejidos* collapsed altogether and was replaced by new union of *ejidos*, the Unión de Ejidos para el Desarrollo Rural Integral "Melchor Ocampo," which was authorized to promote community production in a gamut of enterprises beyond forestry alone (Sánchez 1994:73–76). But the move came at a bad time for such producers' organizations because government was in the midst of yet another structural shift.

Neoliberals and the Turn to Community Forestry, 1980s–2000s

The economic crisis of the early 1980s set off a seismic shift in Mexico's political economy, as presidents moved to replace state intervention in the economy with neoliberal structural adjustment policies that emphasized privatization, international trade, and the withdrawal of funding for a gamut of social services. One of the most noteworthy of these neoliberal reforms came in 1992, when President Carlos Salinas de Gortari put an end to the continued redistribution of land and modified Article 27 of the Constitution to allow for the privatization of most forms of collective landholding, though forestland was excluded (Bray and Wexler 1996). The neoliberal turn of the 1980s and 1990s placed increasingly heavy strains on the countryside and soon produced a massive out-migration, yet it also put an end to highly centralized rural development schemes such as the defunct UIEF and the "Melchor Ocampo" Association of *Ejidos*.

In El Rosario and El Asoleadero, some market pressures became apparent even before the much-vaunted neoliberal initiatives of the 1980s. Already in the mid-1970s, the government began to withdraw support for the mining concern, which by then had been transformed into a government-funded workers' cooperative called the Compañía Impulsora Minera de Angangueo. But the forests that the miners' cooperative had received (along with the nearly played-out mining veins) were not sufficient to meet its needs. Decades of land reform and intensive exploitation by the UIEF had whittled the old woodlots down to a few hundred mostly deforested hectares, leaving the mining operation in the unaccustomed position of having to purchase wood from local producers at prevailing market prices. Worse still, these prices began to rise rapidly thanks to the 1986 formation of the Melchor Ocampo Union of *Ejidos*, which had allowed highlands communities to find alternative markets for their timber. The increasing resentment between the miners' cooperative and the highlands communities provoked a series of confrontations that began in 1974 and finally came to a head in 1980, when community members from El Rosario, "with the use of violence," blocked the transport of timber that the mining company had cut on land that the community claimed to control. After that, the company quit pressing for the disputed land, and within another six years, it had failed altogether.[20]

As the decades-long conflict with the mining company slowly ground to a halt, the villagers of El Asoleadero and El Rosario soon confronted another major institution that made claims on their woodlands, now for purposes of conservation. In the early 1970s foreign researchers discovered what community members had always known: their forests served as breeding grounds for the Monarch butterfly. As interest in this discovery expanded, in 1980, the federal government established a modest refuge for the Monarch butterflies that flock by the millions to the region's oyamel trees every winter. Six years later, it expanded the reserve and gave it its current name, the Reserva Especial de la Biosfera Mariposa Monarca, expanding its area to 16,100 hectares in several different parcels, some of which included acreage from both communities' land. The villagers were not consulted about whether a reserve should be created or how it should function; indeed, the community members of El Rosario felt sufficiently alarmed when they heard rumors that the reserve would be expanded in 1984 that they wrote President Miguel de la Madrid asking for an audience to discuss it with him, apparently to no avail.[21]

The federal authorities' peremptory actions and overall lack of communication with villagers did not improve much with time. In 1991, the community leaders of El Rosario complained that no federal official had ever visited the community to explain what had become of the cash that the *ejidos* of the region were supposed to receive from a one-time cut that they had been authorized to make within the Monarch reserve. The community desperately needed the money, because it had no way to capitalize on the increasing tourist traffic into their *ejido* to see the butterflies. The authorities had refused to pave the road that tourists used; as a result, the visitors' cars kicked up dust as they traveled up to the parking area and spoiled the homemade food that the *ejidatarios* had laid out for sale on the sides of the access road. Many residents turned in desperation to clandestine logging within the reserve.[22] Indeed, the rate of deforestation in El Asoleadero seems to have accelerated about the time that the Monarch reserve was formed in 1986 (Merino-Pérez 1999). One probable cause for the increased pressure on the land was that alternative sources of employment began to dry up at about the same time. Not long after the creation of the butterfly reserve, the mining cooperative collapsed and closed its doors for good. The union's three sawmills ceased operations soon afterward. Even a local cut-flower growers' association failed. These stoppages took a heavy toll. Observers from the State Forestry Commission were distressed to find in 1986 that poor sanitation, a lack of potable water, and insufficient protein in villagers' diets had created endemic malnutrition and gastric illness (Comisión Forestal 1986:69).

These economic imperatives, combined with the lack of a strong local tradition of community-based forestry, led a substantial number of highlands communities to engage in clandestine logging, disregarding both the guidelines set by the federal and state forestry departments and the boundaries of the Monarch reserve. Clandestine logging provided a marginal salve at best for impoverished villagers, yet it harmed the interests of those communities that obtained the proper permits. Local sawmills paid only a fraction of the market value for illegally harvested timber, often taking discounts of 50 or 70% on "pirated" sawlogs, and yet the high volume of the clandestine business kept the regional price for even legally harvested timber products at an artificially low level (Merino-Pérez 1999). As the economic situation grew more and more bleak, some villagers apparently gave up on life within the communities and decided to migrate to the United States. Sometimes they pirated a few logs and sold them to local sawmill owners to pay for their passage.[23]

The new Union of *Ejidos* formed in 1986 in the wake of the association's collapse could do little to improve the situation. The union never lived up to its original promise of giving villagers direct access to the market, and within a decade or so of its founding, it was all but defunct (INI 2002). By the late 1980s, the accumulated stresses within the communities had begun to undermine the viability of even the most established subsistence strategies. The authority of respected community leaders had declined to such a point that they could no longer prevent their comrades from engaging in clandestine logging on a fairly routine basis. A remarkable letter written in 1988 illustrates the difficulties that even well-meaning members of these communities faced at this time. According to Gustavo Guzmán, the leader of a community volunteer group that patrolled communal forests in El Asoleadero:

> The forest commons of this *ejido* are being exploited in an indiscriminant and clandestine way, both by the members of this community as well as by outsiders who don't have the proper authorization. In my rounds, I have found that clandestine loggers are leaving the hills without a single tree left standing . . . I tell you all this because I consider it my obligation, but I also think that the authorities are obliged to give us the means [we need to confront this situation]. It is simply impossible for a mere community watch to confront the immeasurable ambition of rapacious woodcutters. I therefore find it necessary to tender my irrevocable resignation from my post, so that I may avoid these burdens in the future.[24]

Guzmán's letter announced not only his intention to give up his position with the community watch, but in a sense his abandonment of the notion of community-managed forestry itself. In an anguished acknowledgment of the multiform stresses on his homeland, he seems to imply that the community had lost the internal coherence to manage its woodlands on its own.

Conclusions

Over the course of the twentieth century, the residents of El Rosario and El Asoleadero found ways of accommodating to those policies and the institutions they considered advantageous, but they were always prepared to evade laws and regulations that did not suit them. They invaded lands, occupied sawmills, and of course clandestinely harvested timber. Yet these commonplace transgressions do not mean that villagers were unwilling to participate in the various forestry regimes put into place over the years.

On the contrary, community members often engaged with the successive management regimens, including the community producers' cooperative of the 1930s, the UIEF of the 1950s, the Production Unit/Association of *Ejidos* of the 1970s, the Union of *Ejidos* of the 1980s, and most recently the butterfly reserve of 1990s. Yet with the possible exception of the producers' cooperative, none of these organizational schemes harnessed villagers' productive capacities to a viable plan of forest exploitation.

There were a number of barriers to community forestry in the highlands, including intervillage rivalries, antagonisms with timber consumers such as the mining operation and local sawmills, local traditions of resource use, inconsistent forestry policies, and the effects of villagers' poverty in an environment in which logging is often the best available means of generating income. Perhaps the most fundamental problem was the lack of communication and consultation between government officials and forest communities, on the one hand, and within communities themselves, on the other. Top-down implementation of forestry policies and a concomitant lack of transparency seems to have undermined many of the community members' support for the consecutive frameworks governing forest exploitation. Broken or incomplete lines of communication on the regional level made it nearly impossible for local leaders to understand and respond to the constantly changing laws, decrees, and institutional requirements laid down by state and federal bureaucracies. This misapprehension often seems to have made it impossible for community leaders to keep their fellow villagers informed about developments involving regulations or disbursements of money; no doubt it made it possible for them to misappropriate community funds as well. In a sense, however, it hardly matters whether village leaders were corrupt or not, since the lack of transparency produced the appearance of malfeasance and aroused villagers' suspicion.

Even if the lines of communication had been perfect, members of highlands communities such as El Rosario and El Asoleadero would still have had ample cause to resist most forms of forest legislation during the postrevolutionary period. Between the 1920s and the 1970s, most forestry policy measures explicitly sought to achieve conservation by limiting peasant access to the market for forest products. Initially, policy makers in the mold of de Quevedo sought to place organizational hurdles such as the producers' cooperatives in the way of communities that sought to sell their timber. By the 1940s, new policies placed even more substantial restrictions on villagers' ability to use their own resources. Instead, they often subjected communities to powerful organizations such as the UIEFs. The local impacts of these policies were far from negligible and often exacerbated tensions both within rural communities and among them as well. Such tensions have increased pressures on the very forest ecosystems that federal law was supposed to protect. Resolutions to these problems were late in arriving to the Michoacán highlands: whereas state and national governments began to promote community forestry and direct access to the market in many parts of Mexico as early as the 1970s (Bray and Merino-Pérez 2002:34–41), communities in the northeastern highlands faced substantial impediments to marketing their timber until the formation of the Union of *Ejidos* in 1986. Even then, they never received the scale of support that community forestry projects did elsewhere in Mexico.

Finally, the failure of community forestry in the northeastern highlands stems in no small degree from the poverty of the soils and household economies of Michoacán's northeastern highlands. The area's high altitude lowers the yield of corn *milpa* agriculture, and the soils, once they are deforested, can support little more than cattle ranching on a modest scale. As a result, the maintenance of forest cover is even more critical in the highlands than in most other parts of western Mexico. In El Asoleadero, El Rosario, and the neighboring communities, however, forest resource use is necessarily a primary source of income rather than a supplemental one, and cash-strapped villagers often have no alternative but to over-exploit their forests to survive. This, perhaps, is the saddest irony of the failures to establish a robust tradition of community forestry in the highlands. Community members have at least nominally recognized the value of managing their forests ever since 1941, when its leaders wrote to President Ávila Camacho to describe themselves as ecological peasants. Yet the imperious needs of the moment combined with a legacy of failed management plans have led them to exhaust the forestlands on which their subsistence depends. In light of community members' relative openness to the various development initiatives, the failure of successive producers' organizations to achieve a viable regime of sustainable community-based production in the northeastern highlands can only be interpreted as a history of missed opportunities.

Notes

AUTHOR'S NOTE: I would like to acknowledge the helpful commentary and editorial assistance of Deborah Barry and David Bray, both of whom labored mightily to help me refine this chapter. Funding for this research was provided by the Academy for International and Area Studies of Harvard University and by an Arts,

Architecture, and Humanities award from the Office of the Vice-Chancellor for Research at the University of Illinois at Chicago.

1. Respectively, the Unidad de Ordenación Forestal "Melchor Ocampo" and Unión de Ejidos para el Desarrollo Rural Integral "Melchor Ocampo."

2. Report of forest warden Andrés Orozco, Uruapan, 26 December 1929, AGN-PF, caja 719, exp. 8600.

3. Also, Angel Granados, interview with the author, Tlalpujahua, 24 February 1995.

4. Boyer 2003: Chapter 2; Report of Pedro Pineda, 13 October 1921, RAN-M, "El Asoleadero."

5. Report of engineer Augusto Hinojosa, 15 May 1925, RAN-M, "El Asoleadero."

6. Transcription of letter from Adolfo González to Procurador de Pueblos (Morelia), 10 January 1928, RAN-M, "El Asoleadero."

7. Comisión Nacional Agraria delegation office chief in Morelia to Departamento Forestal, 13 July 1937, RAN-M, "El Asoleadero."

8. Banco Nacional de Crédito Agrícola to Lázaro Cárdenas, 12 December 1938, Archivo Histórico del Centro de Estudios de la Revolución "Lázaro Cárdenas," Jiquilpan, Mich., Fondo Cárdenas, caja 32.

9. *Mexico Forestal* 34(2), 1960:1–7; Merino-Pérez 2001.

10. For an example of a 1930s-era forestry cooperative in the village of Aranza (Paracho) that continued to function until the 1950s, see AHPEM-B, caja 722, exp. 18483.

11. José Antonio Arias and Alberto Pichardo Juárez to Dámaso Cárdenas, 14 October 1950, AHPEM-B 6/3; Unidad Industrial de Explotación Forestal Michoacana del Occidente, S. de R. L., "Proyecto General de Ordenación Forestal" Uruapan, December 1959 (unpublished mss.), p. 4.

12. José Antonio Arias, general director of Michoacana de Occidente, to Lázaro Cárdenas, Uruapan, 30 April 1951, AHPEM-B, caja 6, exp. 3.

13. Untitled document apparently written by Enrique Beltrán labeled "La Comisión Forestal de Michoacán," ca. 1961, Archivo Particular de Enrique Beltrán (Mexico City), caja 22, exp. 28; Unidad Industrial de Explotación Forestal Michoacana del Occidente, S. de R. L., "Proyecto General de Ordenación Forestal," Uruapan, December 1959 (unpublished mss.), pp. O-R.

14. See Unidad Industrial de Explotación Forestal Michoacana del Occidente, S. de R. L., "Proyecto General de Ordenación Forestal" Uruapan, December 1959 (unpublished typescript), pp. 6–7.

15. Roberto Bastida S. to Presidente del Comisariado Ejidal San Francisco de los Reyes, 10 January 1956, AHPEM-B, caja 8, exp. 3, doc. 261.

16. Jesús M. Téllez to Delegado del Departamento Agrario en Morelia, 8 January 1954, RAN-M, "El Rosario."

17. Dolores Carmona de García to Delegado del Departamento Agrario en Morelia, 27 August 1956, RAN-M, "El Rosario."

18. Technically, the land was managed by the Unidad Ejidal de Ordenación Forestal "Melchor Ocampo," which in turn gave all net profits from timbering operations to the Asociación de Sociedades Locales de Crédito Ejidal Forestal

"Melchor Ocampo," comprised of the *ejidos*, communities with common lands (*tierras comunales*), and 279 private property owners.

19. Transcribed in report of Jerónimo Morales Pallares, 19 October 1976, RAN-M, "El Rosario," exp. "Organización."

20. Julio Larios López to Departamento de Quejas, 9 June 1982, RAN-M, "El Asoleadero," exp. "Dotación de Tierras."

21. Rosario Jerónimo González Paredes et al. to Miguel de la Madrid, 14 February 1984, RAN-M "El Asoleadero," exp. "Dotación de Tierras."

22. Leobardo González Cruz to Carlos Salinas de Gortari, 15 February 1991, RAN-M, "El Rosario," exp. "Organización." As the letter makes clear, the onetime cut was the result of a negotiation between the federal government and the community: The Secretariat of Agrarian Reform had earlier embargoed some of the community's funds as punishment for clandestine logging in the area. When community members protested, however, the authorities relented and allowed one legal cut within the reserve.

23. Author's confidential interview with a Michoacán forestry official, Morelia, 8 August 2001.

24. Gustavo Guzmán Guzmán to Delegado del Departamento Agrario en Morelia, 9 May 1988. RAN-M, "El Asoleadero."

References

Barrena, R. 1961. Unidades de ordenación forestal. *México Forestal* 35(4):11–15.

Boyer, C. R. 2000. The threads of class at la virgen: Misrepresentation and identity at a Mexican textile mill, 1918–1935. *The American Historical Review* 105(5):1576–1598.

———. 2003. *Becoming Campesinos: Politics, Identity, and Agrarian Militancy in Postrevolutionary Michoacán, 1920–1935*. Stanford, CA: Stanford University Press.

Bray, D. B., and L. Merino-Pérez. 2002. The rise of community forestry in Mexico: History, concepts, and lessons learned from twenty-five years of community timber production. Ford Foundation Report.

Bray, D. B., and M. B. Wexler. 1996. Forest policies in Mexico. In *Reforming Mexico's Agrarian Reform*, ed. L. Randall, 217–228. Armonk, NY, and London: M. E. Sharpe.

Chapela, G., and D. Barkin. 1995. *Monarcas y campesinos. Estrategia de desarrollo sustentable en el oriente de Michoacán*. Mexico City: Centro de Ecología y Desarrollo.

Comisión Forestal del Estado de Michoacán, Area de Servicios Técnicos. 1986. Estudio dasonómico general de la Unión de *Ejidos* para el Desarrollo Rural Integral "Melchor Ocampo" S. de R.I. de los municipios de Angangueo, Aporo, Ocampo, Senguio, Tlalpujahua y parte de los municipios de Tuxpan y Zitácuaro del Estado de Michoacán: Memoria. Unpublished typescript.

De Quevedo, M. A. 1937. Informe sobre los principales trabajos desarrollados por el Departamento Forestal y de Caza y Pesca durante el año de 1936. *México Forestal* 15(1–2):3–9.

———. 1938. Resumen de los principales trabajos desarrollados por el Departamento Forestal y de Caza y Pesca, durante el año de 1937, *México Forestal* 16(1–3): 17–21.

Exposición de motivos que funda el Proyecto de la Ley Forestal de Arboleadas. 1923. *México Forestal* 1(1).

García, C., and F. Domínguez. 1941. Letter to the Presidente de la República. Archivo Histórico del Registro Agrario Nacional, Morelia (RAN-M), El Asoleadero.

Gutiérrez Jarquín, J. T. 1969. Proyecto General de Ordenación Forestal, Unidad Ejidal de Ordenación Forestal "Melchor Ocampo," Ocampo, Michoacán. (Unpublished typescript).

Hays, S. P. 1959. *Conservation and the Gospel of Efficiency: The Progressive Conservation Movement, 1890–1920.* Cambridge, MA: Harvard University Press.

INI. 2002. Diagnóstico de los pueblos indígenas de Michoacán. http://207.248 .180.194/bibdf/ini/estatal/michoacan%20DX%20web/10_Organizaciones% 20sociales%20en%20las%20regiones%20indigenas.htm. Accessed 3 October 2002.

Knight, A. 1994. Popular culture and the revolutionary state in Mexico, 1910–1940. *Hispanic American Historical Review* 74(3):393–444.

Merino-Pérez, L. 1999. *Reserva especial de la biosfera mariposa monarca: Problemática general de la región.* Mexico City: Departamento de Comunicación y Difusión Pública del Secretariado de la Comisión para la Cooperación Ambiental.

———. 2001. Las políticas forestales y de conservación y sus impactos sobre las comunidades forestales. *Estudios Rurales* 18 (September–December 2001):74–115.

Matthews, A. S. 2003. Suppressing fire and memory: Environmental degradation and political restoration in the Sierra Juárez of Oaxaca, 1887–2001. *Environmental History* 8(1):77–108.

Rodríguez Adame, J. 1963. La industria forestal será como la petrolera, *Excelsior* 20 Feb. 1963.

Sánchez, X. M. 1994. *Características ecológicas generales de la región forestal oriental del estado de Michoacán, México.* Morelia: Universidad Michoacana de San Nicolás de Hidalgo, Secretaría de Difusión Cultural.

Secretaría de Agricultura y Fomento, Dirección Forestal y de Caza y Pesca. 1930. *Ley forestal y su reglamento.* Mexico City: Talleres Gráficos de la Secretaría de Agricultura y Fomento.

Simonian, L. 1995. *Defending the Land of the Jaguar: A History of Conservation in Mexico.* Austin: University of Texas Press.

Snook, L. K., and P. Negreros. 1986. *Effects of Mexico's Selective Cutting System on Pine Regeneration and Growth in a Mixed Pine-Oak Forest.* Washington, DC: USDA Forest Service, 1986.

CHAPTER 3

Forest and Conservation Policies and Their Impact on Forest Communities in Mexico

LETICIA MERINO-PÉREZ AND GERARDO
SEGURA-WARNHOLTZ

Over the past century, forest use in Mexico has been subject to almost continual debate. Both state and federal governments have frequently intervened in the sector, to a much greater degree than in other areas of rural life. These interventions have included direct government participation in logging, the control and concession of resource user rights, regulatory action, and conservation strategies, among others. This paper's main objective is to analyze the forest policies implemented by various Mexican governments over the second half of the twentieth century and to comment on their impact. The general areas tackled by this research are as follows:

- The debate regarding forest resources and the main issues that have informed political action and policy making
- The ways in which government institutions have intervened in the forestry sector, including industry, silvicultural practices, and forest communities
- The form and levels of control that the state has placed on forests and, in contrast, the margin of control that communities have maintained over their forests
- The impact of public policies and the responses developed by communities

Even though specific analysis of the different forest laws that existed during the twentieth century does not form part of this research, reference will be made to these laws for each of the periods examined. We will examine state policy using the four analytical themes mentioned above, and place it in the context of the political and economic conditions of the different historical periods.

After discussing the pre-1940 historical background, we will focus on the following periods. The proposed time periods are only suggestive; the processes overlap in time in complex ways and in different regions of the country.

- Concessions to private companies and forest bans (1940–1972)
- Concessions to state-owned companies (1972–1982)
- The rise of community forest enterprises (CFEs) (1982–1992)
- Economic globalization and policy uncertainty (1992–2002)
- Development of innovative forest policies in the context of political transition (2003–present)

Historical Background

The 1857 implementation of the Leyes de Reforma de la Constitución Federal radically modified access to land and natural resources of the indigenous communities that made up the majority of the country's rural population. With the intention of attracting investment and modernizing the country, the government opted to privatize communal and church lands. Temperate and tropical forests occupied great expanses of indigenous territory, both because ethnic groups historically occupied them and because they served as "refuge areas" where indigenous peoples escaped the rigors of European colonialization (Aguirre Beltrán 1991).

In the second half of the nineteenth century, under the protection of the Leyes de Reforma and as the country underwent "modernization," English and North American companies and investors received massive land concessions to cut down timber, build roads, construct railways, and open mines. Neither logging nor land use in general was subject to any kind of regulation, and this open-door policy had a great impact on the forests of central and northern Mexico (Gonzáles 1992). This policy, which was thought to promote the country's development, resulted in wholesale dispossession for the majority of campesino and indigenous communities—to such a degree that the Mexican Revolution of 1910–17 was largely driven by a desire on the part of campesinos to reclaim control over their land and natural resources.

Campesino and indigenous demand for land rights attracted little attention for the first 10 years after the end of the revolution. At the same time, forest policy took a conservationist turn, focusing on the reduction of deforestation. Miguel Angel de Quevedo, Mexico's leading forest conservationist in the first decades of the twentieth century, thought that forests should be maintained as, or converted into, public property. He sought to strengthen the government control over forests in a highly centralized manner reminiscent of the conservation policies popular in North America at the time. In this context, he encouraged the drafting of the first forest law of the twentieth century, which increased regulations on forest extraction and severely restricted campesinos' use of the forest. Under the Forest Department, the government created a conservationist and repressive forest bureaucracy (Klooster 1996, 1997).

The agrarian reform implemented by the government of President Lázaro Cárdenas (1934–40) was designed to respond to campesinos' land rights claims. The majority of these claims were for agricultural land. By the end of his presidency, however, more forestlands were handed out to communities, representing approximately 18% of the country's forest area. The remaining forests were located mainly on state-owned lands or on private property. During the period, agrarian policy focused primarily on agricultural development and paid little attention to forest development, though the government did support community resin extraction in central Mexico's temperate forests and chicle extraction in the southeast (Klooster 1997; Bray and Merino-Pérez 2002).

Rentismo is a Mexican forestry term that refers to logging carried out by contractors under short-term contracts. Under this system, which prevailed from the 1920s to the 1970s, communities had little knowledge of authorized extraction volumes and prices, and no incentives were given to local forest owners. *Rentismo* logging operations were largely inefficient and damaged the forest. Contracts between the contractors and forest communities were inequitable and abusive, and corruption of community leaders was often a problem. It was estimated in the 1950s that "of the different types of forest in the country, 34% had been exhausted, 44% had been subject to logging but were still exploitable, and only 22% were still considered virgin forest" (Villaseñor 1956, cited by Klooster 1997:134). The problems associated with logging under *rentismo* were a perverse result of the 1926 Forest Law, which, in its eagerness to limit extractions, restricted contracts to one year, thereby encouraging contractors to extract the maximum amount of resources in the limited time they had.

Concessions to Private Companies and the
Establishment of Forest Bans (1940–72)

Governments after Cárdenas focused on the development of a national industry and internal markets. Within the context of import substitution, the country's dependence on forest products imports and the underutilization of forests were both problems that, in the mind of government officials, called for a radical change in policies and laws.

The Forest Law of 1940 considered that domestic forest use, subsistence agriculture, and *rentismo* were the central causes of forest deterioration. Under this law, forests would be placed at the service of industrial development in order to guarantee a constant supply of raw materials at low prices. The most significant change in the 1940 Forest Law was the reestablishment of forest concessions in order to encourage long-term investments. The government initially granted 30 logging concessions in many of the country's richest forest regions, as in the states of Chihuahua, Durango, Oaxaca, Chiapas, and Quintana Roo. The concessions were usually for 25 years, although some were for up to 60 years (Klooster 1997). The concessionaire companies established heavy restrictions on traditional forest user groups, with public force being used to impose and enforce these measures. The communities that had been given back property rights in previous years were only given the options of selling timber to the concessionaires or not using forest resources. In exchange they received a fixed stumpage fee from the agrarian agency. Payments, however, were not handed over directly to the communities but were deposited in a fund managed by the agrarian agency. Communities could only access this fund by presenting and having approved specific investment projects. Many communities were unaware of the existence of this fund (Bray and Merino-Pérez 2002; Merino-Pérez 2002).

Over the next few years, concessionaires constructed a network of forest roads and strengthened local logging and extraction capabilities. As a result, the local owners of the forests acquired a growing understanding of the commercial value of their resources and of the importance of regaining control over their use and management. Although the concession period may have provided a base for the creation of a community-based forest economy, local forest owners were also beginning to witness the high economic and environmental costs that logging entailed. Although forest cover was maintained, after decades of logging a great swath of forest had lost much of its commercial tree species (Snook and Negreros 1986). For many years, these companies realized a huge income from logging activities, none of which was reinvested in improved forest management, or in the communities. As Zabin (1992 : 406) notes, many timber industries during the import substitution era were inefficient and depended too heavily on protected markets, the equipment was rarely upgraded, and production costs were always high.

Despite the "productivist" nature of that period, conservationist thinking was still prevalent and had some degree of influence. Thus at the beginning of the 1950s, forestry bans in a number of different regions were established. By 1958 forest bans affected some 58% of the country's forest territory (Hinojosa-Ortiz 1958). Despite the supposed contradiction between forest bans and forest concessions, both policies shared common features: the centralization of control over forest resources and the loss of rights for campesinos living in forest regions.

State Intervention in the Forestry Sector:
Concessions for State-Owned Companies (1972–82)

The beginning of Luis Echeverría's presidency (1970–76) marked a new direction for rural policy making. From the end of the 1960s onward, expressions of campesino discontent increased as a result of decades of campesino productive decapitalization. Responding to these protests, the government restarted the agrarian reform process, expropriating some large agricultural properties in Sinaloa and Sonora and redistributing large chunks of national territory, especially tropical forests and arid lands. This new form of land distribution modified Mexico's forest regions to such a degree that by the middle of the 1970s, some 65% of the country's forests were the property of campesino communities (Gonzáles Pacheco 1981, cited by Klooster 1997).

However, there were relatively few investments that would allow communities to manage their forests, with priority given to agriculture and livestock. The National Livestock Program and the National Land-Clearing Commission (Comisión Nacional de Desmontes) provided subsidies to farmers to clear forests. Colonization policies that encouraged farmers to move from crowded areas in central Mexico to tropical areas led to the clearing of 80% of the country's humid rainforest. Further losses were particularly acute during the 1970s, when annual rates of deforestation rose to 1.5 million hectares, according to one analyst (Toledo 1992).

During this same period, the state promoted an ambitious policy of authoritarian rural modernization (Bartra 1997). There was large-scale public investment in dams, highways, and rural road construction, and the development of "green revolution" agricultural research. Subsidized access to fertilizers, herbicides, and improved seeds allowed many communities to cultivate marginal land, such as forested mountainsides, for both commercial and subsistence agriculture, which served to increase deforestation rates in central and southern Mexico. Government policies also sought to develop campesino forestry capacity through the creation of community forest enterprises (CFEs) (Bray et al. 2003; Barkin and Chapela 1994). The management and administration of CFEs, however, still involved the established rural bureaucracy, through the Secretariat of Agrarian Reform (Secretaría de Reforma Agraria; SRA) and the Rural Credit Bank.

The forest sector also attracted much criticism. While the series of forest bans had failed to protect forests, they had seriously affected the welfare of campesinos and small-scale timber producers, as well as increasing the rate of illegal logging. Marginalizing the traditional owners from the benefits of forest use and blocking their regulatory capacity, the forest bans actually created a scenario of "open access forest resources" and illegal logging, leading to corruption among forestry workers, *ejidos*, and communal authorities. The concessions had not even fulfilled the objective of overcoming the trade deficit in forest products. The official response to this problem was to increasingly centralize the management of the forestry sector, supported by the state's direct control over forestry activities (Bartra.1997).

In 1960, a new forest law was passed that sanctioned the creation of state-owned forestry companies. The concessionaire companies became public property, and new forest concessions were handed out to these new parastatals. By 1976, at the end of Echeverría's government, 26 such publicly owned forestry enterprises existed, operating in the forests of Durango, Guerrero, Chihuahua, Nayarit, Jalisco, Quintana Roo, Chiapas, and Oaxaca. By the end of the 1970s, these enterprises played a major role in the country's timber production.

During the 1970s, campesino discontent with the forest concessions policy had spread to various regions of the country. Responding to this, and acting as a parallel forest policy, the SRA encouraged the participation of *ejidos* and local communities in the forestry sector. A fund was created for the acquisition of equipment and training, and the development of regional community organizations was promoted. By the middle of the 1970s, approximately 257 agrarian groups had received financial support to develop forestry activities, and 1,046 agrarian communities had been integrated into regional forestry unions promoted by the SRA (Klooster 1997). Despite all this investment, the results from these initiatives were mostly disappointing. On the one hand, the resources made available to community-based forestry activities were, in the majority of cases, quite poor, and on the other, it was agrarian bureaucrats and not the forest communities themselves that were the driving force behind the creation of these CFEs. These bureaucrats tended to exercise strong organizational, technical, and administrative control.

Through the SRA the state exercised another type of control. It was directly involved in handing out concessions, it defined the stumpage fee, and it controlled the trust fund into which the stumpage fee was deposited. All important decisions regarding community management of forest resources, such as sales or equipment purchases, had to be sanctioned by SRA staff, whose participation was a necessary part of the application for logging permits and the election of *ejido* authorities. Communities' property rights over forest resources were highly ambiguous. Although the communities were recognized by the state as the true forest owners, at the same time government institutions exercised direct control over these resources and, in some cases, they appropriated most of the benefits. Lack of effective property rights[1] over forest resources led some communities to perceive their local forests as marginal resources, and some even viewed them as an obstacle in the way of full land ownership.

The state-owned forestry enterprises failed to meet expectations, and there appeared to be little difference between them and those private companies that had operated during the earlier period of forest concessions. Their relationship with local forest communities had also become conflictive. Despite the expansion of these state-owned companies, *rentismo* remained an important part of forestry activities. The communities resented the appropriation of resources by concessionaires and many resorted to illegal logging. Under these conditions, the majority of the state-owned enterprises suffered from severe undersupply (Victor Suárez, personal communication, 2002).

Insufficient financing, a lack of personnel, and the centralization of management decisions have all been constants in the application of forest policies. Despite a reduction in supervisory capacity, the different forest laws maintained high levels of bureaucracy and layers of administrative red tape. All of these laws required annual permits for the felling and transporting of timber and all trees logged had to be marked. To comply fully with these demands required the hiring of forestry professionals, a position that fell outside the reach of the vast majority of campesino communities (Klooster 1997). The law did not differentiate between campesino and industrial uses of forest resources, even when it was obvious that only private enterprises had the capacity to comply with the numerous, complex requirements that legislation imposed.

Campesinos Regain Control of the Forests and CFEs Are Established (1982–92)

During the second half of the 1970s, problems with raw material supplies were common for many of the state forest enterprises. Consequently, some forestry officials felt that increasing campesino control over forestry activities could be a viable strategy to increase the supply of timber. In addition, the political costs of forest concessions were beginning to be felt. In the states of Oaxaca, Guerrero, and Durango, regional alliances of communities were created to combat the renewal of concessions (Alatorre Frenk 2000; Bray and Merino-Pérez 2002; Chapela 1999; Gonzáles 1992; see also Chapela, this volume, and López-Arzola, this volume).

Within the Forestry Subsecretariat of the Secretariat of Agriculture and Hydraulic Resources (Secretaría de Agricultura y Recursos Hidráulicos; SARH), a group of progressive officials created the General Office of Forest Development (Dirección General de Desarrollo Forestal; DGDF), which sought to promote the establishment of CFEs. This proposal for community-based forestry faced opposition from timber merchants, forest engineers, and state governors, all of whom had links with the state-owned forestry enterprises. Initial attempts at establishing autonomous CFEs by the DGDF took place in regions that had been subject to forest bans, such as Chinahuapan, in the state of Puebla; Zacualtipan, in Hidalgo; Hueyacocotla, Zongolica, and Cofre de Perote, in Veracruz; Tlaxco, in Tlaxcala; and Valle de Bravo, in the state of Mexico (Bray et al. 2003; Gonzáles 1992). The full development of these enterprises was held back by a lack of technical assistance and training, limited access to adequate machinery, forest deterioration, and control of timber markets by contractors. Increasingly, however, the achievements of some communities highlighted the potential of community-based forestry, as occurred with the Puebla Plan, some of whose *ejido* members have been managing their forests since the 1970s.

Soon after Miguel De la Madrid (1982–88) took office as president, the majority of forest concessions came to an end. The new administration initiated the implementation of structural adjustment policies, which sought to pay off external debts and liberalize the economy. Paradoxically, campesino demands to put an end to forest concessions were suddenly being listened to within the context of a new political paradigm that sought to reduce the state's role within the national economy. The state-owned forestry enterprises began to be dismantled.

Many of the communities that had been affected most by the concessions decided to start their own operations and regain control over their forest resources. The DGDF supported many of these, providing technical assistance and training to help in the creation of CFEs. For campesino communities, the appropriation of forestry activities implied running an enterprise far more complex than traditional forest management. With assistance from the DGDF, several hundred agrarian communities and *ejidos* established their own CFEs. In some cases they also managed to strengthen their organizational structures, incorporating into their traditional management schemes new elements in order to improve planning, financing, accountability, and the payment of taxes.

Many of these new enterprises could take advantage of existing timber markets, an established road network, and the presence of *comuneros* and *ejidatarios* whose members had already been trained in logging operations during the concessions period. In the short periods of time that these enterprises were operating, the income from forestry activities increased considerably, many local jobs were created, and some have managed to raise enough capital to acquire machinery for logging and timber processing. In many cases communities developed mechanisms to effectively protect their forestland, something that is conspicuously absent when community-based forestry is not present. These mechanisms include surveillance against illegal logging, forest fires, and plagues (Alatorre Frenk 2000; Bray 1991; Bray and Merino-Pérez 2002; Merino-Pérez 1997, 2002; PROCYMAF-SEMARNAP 2000).

Although forest communities regained a degree of control over their forests, the federal government, through the SRA and SARH, maintained a strong influence over the internal management of CFEs. SARH directly provided technical forestry services to the majority of communities and controlled the services of those community-based forestry unions that had obtained a technical service concession. The SRA imposed a series of conditions on community forestry, including the need for obligatory savings funds, the adoption of specific organizational forms, and administrative supervision of CFEs. Despite the paternalistic nature of this intervention, for many communities SRA and SARH represented the only form of external assistance available.

Community forestry in Mexico has been possible thanks to the coming together of several factors. It is in part the fruit of agrarian reform policy, part a product of the struggle by forest communities for control over their resources, and part the result of the political will of a group of reformist government workers and independent advisors who became convinced of the viability of community forest management. As a result of communities regaining control over forest management, participation in community forestry has increased noticeably. In 1992, some 10 years after their beginnings, 40% of national wood production and 15% of processed timber was being generated by community-based forestry enterprises (Bray and Merino-Pérez 2002).

Pressure from regional forestry organizations and the DGDF staff were reflected in the Forest Law of 1986, which abolished forestry concessions and recognized the rights of local communities to manage their forest resources. This law also established the requirement to develop an integrated forest management plan and gave communities their first opportunity to hold the title of technical forestry services provider. For the first time in the history of Mexican forest legislation, communities were considered central actors within the sector.

The policy of promoting CFEs was most evident in those older concession regions where there still existed commercially valuable timber resources. Areas of poorer forest or those that lacked established commercial species were not affected by this policy. Also of relevance during this period was the strengthening of the urban-based conservationist movement, which, in alliance with international ecological groups, instilled new blood into the country's conservation policy. This movement supported the establishment of new or enlarged protected areas, mostly as Biosphere Reserves (BRs). The BR scheme sought to overcome the limitations of national parks, which had been based on the public appropriation of communal land and now suffered from serious environmental problems. In contrast, the BRs formally allowed the traditional forest owners to maintain property and offered them incentives to promote conservation measures and encourage sustainable resource use. In reality, however, this new scheme still deprived forest owners of their property rights by imposing total and indefinite bans on forest use in the core zones of the reserve and by imposing very strong restrictions in the buffer zones.

Economic Globalization and the Introduction of Diverse Forest and Conservation Policies (1992–2002)

In 1986, while the DGDF was promoting community-based forestry, Mexico joined the GATT (General Agreement on Tariffs and Trade) and began to gradually increase imports of forest products. While private forest companies (during the forest concessions period) operated within the context of a closed national market, the new community-based enterprises were being faced with growing competition from low-cost imported timber. Natural resource policies during this period were increasingly geared toward the private sector.

But by the early 1990s, community-based forestry was not seen as an important aspect of forestry policy. Investment in community forestry was limited both financially and spatially, and communities were not supported by government programs targeted to helping them develop their capacity to compete within a globalizing economy. During the government of Salinas de Gortari (1988–94), structural adjustment policies were strengthened, and major reforms to the agrarian legislation occurred in 1991 and 1992. These reforms attempted to create a market for agricultural land and encourage greater investment in the countryside. Although this move increased the fragility of the *ejido* system, it also implied the end of the SRA's control over campesino communities (Gordillo et al. 1999). The changes to agrarian law ended "strong state intervention in the internal business of the *ejidos*, particularly with regard to their decision-making processes and access to their goods and public services" (De Janvry 1996:71). Under the new agrarian policy, communities had greater autonomy, although financial and training support from the government was withdrawn. During the 1990s, reduced public investment in the countryside favored consumption subsidies and poverty relief programs over productive investment. In the forestry sector, the reduction in public spending translated into the suspension of the technical assistance programs and training and consultancy given to forest communities that the DGDF had provided for more than a decade.

Although modifications to agrarian legislation created the possibility of privatizing the *ejidos'* agricultural lands, common property forest resources could not be divided and would revert to the state if the *ejido* were privatized. This restriction ran the risk of generating incentives to decrease forest cover. With the aim of encouraging greater investment in forestry, the new agrarian law allowed *ejidos* to enter into associations for up to 30 years with private operators, allowing forest plantation owners to control (albeit temporarily) areas of up to 20,000 hectares (Téllez Kuenzler 1994).

Also in 1992 a new forest law was enacted. One of its most significant features was its promotion of the role of the private sector. Another change was allowing communities to freely access the market for technical forestry services, something that had previously been controlled by SARH. In the short time since forest industry and transport regulations have been abolished, illegal logging rates have increased dramatically (Cuauhtémoc Gonzáles Pacheco,[2] personal communication, 1998 and 1999). The liberalization of the market for technical forestry services led to the deterioration of the forest and its resources. Since the law did not stipulate minimum quality criteria to guide forest management, price became the critical factor in the selection of technical assistance. Like its predecessors, the 1992 Forest Law failed to acknowledge or address a key issue, the lack of incentives to encourage forest owners to conserve and/or sustainably manage their forest resources.

Since the signing of the North American Free Trade Agreement (NAFTA) in 1994, the country's economy has opened up. Since that time, and as a consequence of the temporary overvaluation of the peso at the end of Salinas's presidential term, Mexico's timber market saw an inundation of cheap wood from the United States, Canada, and Chile. Since then, the production costs of timber products in Mexico have often been higher than the cost of imported products, generating great difficulties for small timber producers competing with subsidized foreign plantation production (Merino-Pérez 1992).[3] The economic viability of some producers was based more on macroeconomic policy than on investments and real productive capacities.

During the presidency of Ernesto Zedillo (1994–2000) campesino development continued to lose importance. Resources destined for the agricultural, livestock, and forestry sectors fell from 6.6% to 3.8% of total public spending and income of rural producers fell 70% (*La Jornada*, 2 September 2000). The Secretariat of the Environment, Natural Resources, and Fisheries (Secretaría del Medio Ambiente, Recursos Naturales, y Pesca; SEMARNAP) was created by the Zedillo administration, integrating various environmental policy areas into one cabinet-level agency. SEMARNAP assumed responsibility for the forest sector, which had always been subsumed under the ministry of agriculture, and sought to increase the environmental sensitivity of forestry. SEMARNAP had as its objectives resource use guaranteeing the conservation of the country's forests, an increased role of forestry in economic development, the sustainable use of forest resources, the valuation of forest environmental services, and the improvement of the quality of life of the campesino communities living in forest areas (PROCYMAF-SEMARNAP 2000).

SEMARNAP, created at a time of structural adjustment policies and cuts in rural investment, operated with a very tight budget. Such limitations affected the agency's ability to meet its basic responsibilities, such as the surveillance and sanctioning of illegal environmental breaches and the regulation of forest activities. For example, in 1998, the Federal Attorney General for Environmental Protection (Procuraduría Federal de Protección Ambiental; see PROFEPA 1998) had just 150 inspectors, based in state capitals, to carry out forest monitoring in all of the country's forest areas. Their job was made all the more difficult because of overall institutional weakness and the fact that deregulation of forestry activities had led to an increase in illegal logging. There were also problems with the process for granting logging permits. Each application for permits had to be repeated annually and could take up to three to four months. This increased considerably the costs of logging and generated tension between forest communities and SEMARNAP.[4]

In 1997 the forest law was modified again. This time the focus was on regulating large-scale forest plantations producing wood destined for pulp and paper production. It was reasoned that these plantations would allow Mexico to capitalize on the high biological productivity of its forests. It was also argued that the environmental benefits that these plantations would produce made them worthy of government subsidies. In 1996, President Zedillo announced that the government would provide fiscal support and would absorb 65% of the production costs (over a seven-year period) of plantation projects approved by SEMARNAP (Paré and Madrid 1997).

Campesino and civil opposition to the project was initially able to influence some areas of the new law and criteria were established to guide plantation management and mitigate possible environmental impacts. The 1997 Forest Law (see PROFEPA 1997) again tried to introduce some controls over the forestry industry and timber transport, although industry regulation continued to be weak, with timber storage and processing capacities constantly surpassing authorized levels (C. G. Pacheco and R. Caro, personal communication, 2002).

Repeated questioning from forestry organizations regarding the level of financial support given to forestry plantations led SEMARNAP to design a forest development strategy that provided new support programs specifically for local forest communities: the Programa de Desarrollo Forestal (PRODEFOR) and the Programa para Conservación y Manejo Forestal (PROCYMAF). Despite the significance of this move, the limited resources these programs received lessened their impact. In 2000, the combined budgets of PRODEFOR and PROCYMAF was under 300 million pesos and during its first year PRODEFOR received only 7 million pesos. The budget of the Programa para el Desarollo de Plantaciones

Forestales (PRODEPLAN), which provided subsidies to plantations providing raw cellulose material for the paper industry, was considerably higher (F. Chapela, personal communication, 2003).

The innovative character of PROCYMAF should be mentioned. This program began in 1996 as a pilot project operating in the state of Oaxaca. The program recognized that "patterns of forest deterioration were a result of inadequate policies" and also that "the situation regarding forest resources is associated with the social and economic problems being experienced in rural areas . . . and in order to . . . promote sustainable development, one must consider raising the quality of life among local rural communities" (PROCYMAF-SEMARNAP 2000:101–102). The state of Oaxaca was of special interest because some 90% of its forest area was under communal control, and there were a number of cases of successful community-based forest management, favored by the strong organization of many of its communities and the validity of traditional governance structures (PROCYMAF-SEMARNAP 2000:101–102).

PROCYMAF is involved in a wide range of activities, including the provision of technical assistance and training, Participatory Rural Appraisals (PRAs), and community land use planning, much of it aimed at explicitly strengthening community social capital for the collective management of community forests. Other areas of support seek to help communities improve market access through market studies, ecotourism projects, forest certification, and the establishment of water-bottling plants, among others. PROCYMAF has also been involved in the creation of Regional Natural Resource Committees, which have become important sources of information for forest communities, as well as helping with discussions and conflict resolution (PROCYMAF-SEMARNAP 2000).

In Oaxaca, PROCYMAF's and PRODEFOR's work in 2000 resulted in a 62% increase in timber production, an 89% increase in the production of non-timber products, a 78% increase in communities with forest management programs, 30% of the state's forest area under management plans, a 33% rise in the number of forest-sector jobs created, a 283% increase in community forestry–related incomes,[5] and the existence of 12 communities under certified forest management schemes (SEMARNAT 2001).

One of the SEMARNAP's management priorities was promoting conservation policy. During its existence, SEMARNAP increased the overall area and number of protected areas by creating 30 new Biosphere Reserves (SEMARNAP 2000). SEMARNAP's emphasis on restricting natural resource use as the backbone of conservation policy paradoxically resulted in changing land use practices and the illegal logging that for much of the twentieth century had been associated more with forest bans. The weight of this policy contrasts starkly with the weak capacity of the agencies actually working in the country's protected areas on fundamental issues such as forest monitoring and the regulation of sustainable resource use. Until 2000, the expansion of the National System of Natural Protected Areas was in itself being used as an indicator of the progress of conservation policy, without the aid of any proper evaluation or information about the loss of vegetation and resources in zones under official protection (Garibay and Bocco 2000).

This paper does not question the importance of conserving areas of natural vegetation; rather, it advocates for a truly decentralized conservation policy, understood not only to mean the devolution of governmental functions but also the recognition of rights for local communities (Agrawal and Ostrom 2001). To consider campesino communities as central players in conservation and strengthen their roles within this field will allow policy makers to face up to the rights and needs of communities as traditional forest owners with an interest in preserving regions, resources, and environmental services.

Communities continued to manage their forests through the 1990s, despite facing multiple pressures, including competition from international timber producers, droughts, forest fires, illegal logging, lack of financing, government inefficiencies, and short-sighted government policies.

Innovative Forest Policy within the Context of Political Change (2003–present)

President Vicente Fox (2000–present) took over governing the country in the middle of a severe economic recession that was particularly serious for campesino producers, whose profits were falling within the context of a liberalizing national marketplace. Even the most developed and efficient community timber producers in the country, such as the community of San Juan Nuevo Parangaricutiro in Michoacán, had production costs that on average were much higher than those of Chilean producers supplying the Mexican timber market.[6]

The Fox government's Plan Nacional Forestal, or PNF (National Forest Program; 2001–6), changed the bureaucratic structure and program focus for the sector, giving it a level of attention and resources that it had not experienced during the previous three presidential administrations. The PNF highlights the rich biodiversity of Mexican forests and the tenure conditions of the country's forestlands, and it is particularly innovative because it recognizes the existence of "successful sustainable forestry management experiences, which include more than one million certified hectares of good forest management" (CONAFOR 2002), and because it proposes that these be supported and developed as part of the overall strategy to fight forest degradation. This was the first time that an official forest planning instrument referred to the contribution of community-based forestry. The PNF also stated that there is a "lot of potential in the development of markets for environmental services" and proposes its active promotion (CONAFOR 2002).

The new government also created the National Forest Commission (Comisión Nacional Forestal; CONAFOR). This is a high-level commission directly under the Secretaría de Medio Ambiente y Recursos Naturales (Secretariat of the Environment and Natural Resources; SEMARNAT),[7] but with additional links to ministries of the interior, agriculture, and defense. CONAFOR is responsible for the promotion and preservation of the country's forests, which basically includes all activities except for forest regulation, which remains in the hands of SEMARNAT. In administrative terms, thanks to the creation of CONAFOR the forest sector gained a level of importance and recognition that it had not had during the previous decade. CONAFOR has also taken on the goal of promoting the decentralization of policy decisions, allowing state governments a greater role in promoting and regulating forestry activities (CONAFOR 2003).

CONAFOR continued with the forest programs that had been created during the final years of SEMARNAP: PRODEFOR, PROCYMAF, and PRODEPLAN, all of which experienced meaningful changes. PROCYMAF's budget increased tenfold, enabling it to expand its work into the states of Guerrero, Michoacán, Durango, Jalisco, and Quintana Roo. It also provided PROCYMAF with sufficient funds to create a new program entitled Campesino Biodiversity Conservation (Proyecto de Conservación de la Biodiversidad por Comunidades Indígenas de los Estados de Oaxaca, Michoacán, y Guerrero, México; COINBIO), the goals of which include the promotion of conservation areas and practices within forest communities, decreed by the communities themselves, and the creation of markets for environmental services.

PRODEPLAN's framework was also modified. By the end of President Zedillo's term, resources assigned to PRODEPLAN could not be spent on plantations because of bureaucratic requirements.[8] The new version of PRODEPLAN benefited smaller landholdings that had not been considered by the previous administration. Emphasis also switched from pulp production to a broader spectrum of options, including tropical trees, Christmas trees, non-timber forest products, and even firewood, all of which were aligned somewhat more closely with local community conditions and had a stronger focus on environmental restoration. Consequently, from 2001 to 2002 the number of projects financed by PRODEPLAN increased from 58 to 758, while the area of forest financed increased from 59,000 to 197,000 hectares. The participation of forest communities also increased dramatically, from 15% of PRODEPLAN beneficiaries in 2000 to 85% by the end of 2002. Another important difference from the previous scheme regarded the species composition of these plantations. Moving from a program that concentrated on plantations for pulp production, in 2002 the area occupied by such monoculture plantations was only 30% of the total area being financed. The participation of communities in PRODEPLAN is important when one considers that on the whole, global demand for forest products tends to be increasingly met by plantations (CONAFOR 2003).

PRODEFOR has undergone a transformation similar to that of PRODEPLAN. Its operational rules have been developed in discussion with various social actors, and they have incorporated new technical assistance and investment components that are more sensitive to local needs. These presently include carrying out specific silvicultural practices (such as forest thinning), administering small-scale fires to induce forest openings, and providing CFEs with financing to acquire sawmills and machinery needed for logging and drying. In addition, PRODEFOR is trying to incorporate some of the experiences of PROCYMAF into its programs, such as the promotion of productive diversification.[9] They have also taken steps to improve the quality of technical forest service providers, planning to widen the register of service providers in order to include professionals other than forest engineers and to begin training activities to help communities establish their own service providers. Another important development for PRODEFOR is that they have strengthened their links with various state governments, thanks to the establishment of agreements that clearly set out the financial commitments of all parties involved. Finally, it is important to note that, despite increases at the beginning of the current presidential term, PRODEFOR's budget has virtually remained the same over the past two years (CONAFOR 2003).

CONAFOR has the following goals: the standardization and integration of the country's forest information systems, the development of productive chains, support for the creation and development of CFEs, the promotion of forest certification, and the creation of national and international financing mechanisms to support forest activities in different regions of the country.

Two years after its creation, the performance of CONAFOR has in many ways been encouraging, although it is still too early to carry out a proper evaluation. Many of the commission's focal areas are an expression of the demands of various campesino organizations that they have been involved with over the years, demands that CONAFOR is now in a position to take on board and promote. Despite the advances made with regard to the sustainable management of Mexican forests (many of which represent the consolidation of many of CONAFOR's proposals), it is important to mention some of the tough challenges that are still to be faced by policy makers, communities, and forestry enterprises. Needed are the development of

- support and promotion schemes for communities that participate in the government's forest management and forest use programs;
- ways to combat the growing competition faced by Mexican forest producers from imported timber products, which are often heavily subsidized;
- adequate financing in support of forestry activities;
- environmental services marketing that will generate direct benefits for the traditional owners of forestlands while also respecting their rights over the management of such resources;
- ways to discourage out-migration from forest regions, which tends to deprive communities of their young people and to weaken both community social capital and the community institutions for collective resource management;
- effective coordination between forestry and conservation policy; and
- better relationships between privately owned enterprises and the local forest communities.

To face these challenges head on will require effective civil and governmental action, which will have at its core the transformation of rural-urban relations, the generation of significant benefits for forest owners, respect for, and the development of, communities' ability to self-manage forestry activities, and the overall reevaluation of rural spaces and local community life.

Notes

1. Agrawal and Ostrom (2001) define property rights as exclusion, access, extraction, management (or regulation), and lineation (purchasing, sales, and mortgage).

2. At the time these communications took place, Cuauhtémoc Gonzáles Pacheco was the Director of Forest Surveillance of the Procuraduría Federal de Protección Ambiental.

3. In 2000 the Chilean company Terranova sold timber in Mexico at prices 35% lower than the equivalent national product.

4. Authorization applications often dragged on into the rainy season.

5. The increases mentioned refer to the values/indicators presented in 1995, when timber production was equivalent to 408,000 cubic meters, and non-timber production equivalent to 318 tonnes. Seventy-seven communities were under a management plan and the area under forest management was 500,000 hectares. Thirty thousand jobs were created through forestry activities and income generated was approximately 1.1 million pesos (SEMARNAT 2001).

6. Personal communication from the manager of Nuevo San Juan Parangaricutiro's CFE.

7. The Fox government reorganized the environmental ministry, changing the name from SEMARNAP to SEMARNAT.

8. One of the causes of this was the 50% fall in international paper and pulp prices during 1998.

9. A PRODEFOR official noted that the program had previously been too timber centered, or *maderocéntrico.*

References

Agrawal, A., and E. Ostrom. 2001. Collective action, property rights and decentralization in resource use in India and Nepal. *Politics and Society* 29:294–316.

Aguirre Beltrán, G. 1991. *Regiones de refugio, obra antropológica* IX. Mexico City: Fondo de Cultura Económica.

Alatorre Frenk, G. 2000. *La construcción de una cultura gerencial democrática en las empresas forestales comunitarias.* Mexico City: Procuraduría Agraria/Casa Juan Pablos.

Barkin, D., and G. Chapela. 1994. *Monarcas y campesinos.* Mexico City: Centro de Ecodesarrollo.

Bartra, A. 1997. *Guerrero bronco. Campesinos, ciudadanos y guerrilleros en la Costa Grande.* Mexico City: Sinfiltro e Instituto para el Desarrollo Rural Maya.

Bray, D. B. 1991. La lucha por el bosque: Conservación y desarrollo en la Sierra Juárez. *Desarrollo de Base* 3(15):13–25.

Bray, D. B., and L. Merino-Pérez. 2002. The rise of community forestry in Mexico: History, concepts and lessons learned from twenty-five years of community timber production. A report in partial fulfillment of a grant from the Ford Foundation.

Bray, D. B., L. Merino-Pérez, P. Negreros-Castillo, et al. 2003. Mexico's community-managed forests as a global model for sustainable landscapes. *Conservation Biology* 17:672–677.

Chapela, F. 1999. La Gestión comunitaria de los bosques en el sur de México. Paper presented at the Taller de Análisis sobre el Deterioro de los Recursos Forestales y el Cambio Institucional en el Campo en México. Mexico City: UNAM and SEMARNAP.

CONAFOR. 2002. *Programa Nacional Forestal 2001–2006.* Mexico City: SEMARNAT-CONAFOR.

———. 2003. CONAFOR presentation at the second forest forum of the UN. www.conafor.gob.mx. Accessed May 2003.

De Janvry, A. 1996. *NAFTA and Agriculture: An Early Assessment.* Berkeley: University of California Press.

Garibay, C., and G. Bocco. 2000. Legislación ambiental, arias protegidas y manejo de tecursos en zonas indígenas forestales: El caso de la región del Pico del Tancítaro, Michoacán. In *Sociedad, Derecho y Medio Ambiente*, ed. Martha Bolaños, 10–45. Mexico City: Procuraduría Federal de Protección Ambiental and Universidad Autónoma Metropolitana.

Gonzáles A. M. 1992. Los bosques de las tierras mexicanas: La gran tendencia. *El Cotidiano* 48:3–6.

Gordillo de Anda, G., A. de Janvry, and E. Sadoulet. 1999. *La segunda reforma agraria de México: Respuestas de familias y comunidades, 1990–1994.* Mexico City: Fondo de cultura Económica y El Colegio de México.

Hinojosa-Ortiz, M. 1958. *Los bosques de México: Relato de un despilfarro y una injusticia.* Mexico City: Instituto de Investigaciones Económicas de la UNAM, Mexico City.

Klooster, D. 1996. Como no conservar el bosque: La marginalización del campesino en la historia forestal mexicana. *Cuadernos Agrarios* 14(6):144–156.

———. 1997. Conflict in the commons: Rules and conflicts around a common pool resource management in San Miguel Peral, Oaxaca, México. PhD diss., University of California, Los Angeles.

Merino-Pérez, L. 1992. Contrastes en el sector forestal: Canadá, Estados Unidos y México. *El Cotidiano: Revista de la Realidad Mexicana Actual* 8:67–73.

———. 1997. *El manejo forestal comunitario en México y sus perspectivas de sustenabilidad.* Mexico: CRIM-UNAM, WRI, SEMARNAP and CCMSS.

———. 2002. Las políticas forestales y de conservación y sus impactos sobre las comunidades forestales. *Estudios Agrarios, Revista de la Procuraduría Agraria* 18:45–65.

Paré, L., and S. Madrid. 1997. Ley forestal y subsidios a plantaciones forestales privadas. *La Jornada del Campo* (56):4.

PROFEPA. 1997. Ley Forestal. Mexico City: Procuraduría Federal de Protección al Medio Ambiente.

———. 1998. Informe tribunal 1995–1997, Mexico City.

PROCYMAF-SEMARNAP. 2000. Voces del monte: Experiencias comunitarias para el manejo sustentable de los bosques de Oaxaca. Mexico City: SEMARNAP.

SEMARNAP. 2000. Textoguía forestal. Mexico City: SEMARNAP.

SEMARNAT, Delegación en Oaxaca. 2001. Perspectivas para la conservación y manejo de ecosistemas forestales. Mexico City: SEMARNAT.

Snook, L. K., and P. Negreros, 1986. Effects of Mexico's selective cutting system on pine regeneration and growth in a mixed pine-oak (pinus-quercus) forest. In *Current Topics in Forest Research: Emphasis on Contribution by Women Scientists*, ed. S. V. Kossuth and N. A. Pywell, 108–114. Asheville, NC: Southeastern Forest Experiment Station.

Téllez Kuenzler, L. 1994. *La modernización del sector agropecuario y forestal.* Mexico City: Fondo de Cultura Económica.

Toledo, V. M. 1992. La crisis ecológica a escala planetaria y el nuevo rol del campesinado. In *Las organizaciones campesinas e indígenas ante la problemática ambiental del desarrollo,* comp. G. Alatorre et al., 17–27. Mexico City: Memoria.

Zabin, C. 1992. El mercado de la madera en Oaxaca. *Cuadernos de trabajo: Empresas y desarrollo.* Mexico City: Inter-American Foundation.

CHAPTER 4

Challenges for Forest Certification and Community Forestry in Mexico

PATRICIA GEREZ-FERNÁNDEZ AND
ENRIQUE ALATORRE-GUZMÁN[1]

In this chapter we evaluate the development and current status of forest certification in Mexico at the closure of its first decade, from the beginning in 1994 through the end of 2003. It is particularly crucial to analyze the Mexican case since, as we shall see below, Mexico has the largest number of both community forest enterprises (CFEs) and certified community forests in the world (Bray et al. 2003). The first section of this chapter discusses briefly the concept of forest certification and the various schemes that exist at the global level, with a particular focus on the Forest Stewardship Council (FSC), an international program developed to create a global system of operational forest certification. The second section focuses on the importance of community forest certification globally. The third section looks at the progress of forest certification in Mexico, including data on the number of community forests evaluated and certified during the past 10 years. The fourth section looks at the challenges and opportunities that have been identified for these community forests. The fifth section concludes the chapter with a reflection on the current limitations of certification for communities and the need to include other actors and options in this process in order to fulfill the objective of improved forest management.

The Forest Certification Concept

Forest certification is a relatively recent concept that emerged in the 1990s as a response to the limited success of both the embargoes placed on tropical timber by civil groups during the 1970s and 1980s and the forest bans established by various governments trying to reduce rates of illegal logging and deforestation. The FSC was founded in 1993 as an international nongovernmental organization (NGO) with the goal of creating the first worldwide system of operational forest certification. Its overall purpose has been to promote the better management of forests by means of market mechanisms that reward good management practices and provide a guarantee to the end consumer of the forest product that the wood has been harvested using sustainable practices. The standards developed include environmental protection as well as the provision of direct benefits to the forest owners, local community members, and workers (see Table 4.1). Interest in voluntary certification has come as much from private companies as it has from the general public and governments. This is because companies have begun to experience the effect of consumer interest in buying certified products, especially in Europe.

There are many skeptics regarding the future of forest certification, but it seems that the concept is here to stay. The last three years have seen the area of certified forests increase exponentially, while the number of new schemes has proliferated. In addition to the FSC, there is the Pan-European Forest Certification (PEFC) and at a national level, Canada, the United States, Malaysia, Indonesia, and other countries have established their own certification schemes. According to Atyi and Simula (2002), in January 2002 there were a total of approximately 109 million hectares of certified forest worldwide, involving a number of different schemes. Of these, the majority were found in Europe (54%) and North America (38%), followed by a far more limited presence in Latin America (3%), Africa (3%), and Asian-Pacific countries (2%). Atyi and Simula also observed that there had been an important change in the distribution and size of forest area certified by each particular scheme, with the FSC declining in importance. In 2002, the FSC accounted for 23% and the PEFC for 38%, with the remainder (39%) made up of the different national certification schemes.

Despite the strong emergence of other schemes, the FSC is still the only worldwide certification program. Recent statistics indicate that the FSC seal has certified 567 forest management areas in 59 countries, covering a total area of 40 million hectares.[2] As can be seen in Table 4.2, Europe is the region with the greatest area of forest and number of FSC-certified sites, and Latin America is second in number of areas and third in total certified area. For Latin America these figures represent the total amount of certified operations, since FSC is the only seal operating in the region. The certification programs accredited by FSC working in Latin America are Rainforest Alliance's SmartWood Program, with 73% of the total; the Sociéte

Table 4.1. Principles of good forest management (FSC)

Principle 1: Compliance with laws and FSC principles
Forest management shall respect all applicable laws of the country in which they occur, and international treaties and agreements to which the country is a signatory, and comply with all FSC principles and criteria.

Principle 2: Tenure and use rights and responsibilities
Long-term tenure and use rights to the land and forest resources shall be clearly defined, documented, and legally established.

Principle 3: Indigenous peoples' rights
The legal and customary rights of indigenous peoples to own, use, and manage their lands, territories, and resources shall be recognized and respected.

Principle 4: Community relations and workers' rights
Forest management operations shall maintain or enhance the long-term social and economic well-being of forest workers and local communities.

Principle 5: Benefits from the forest
Forest management operations shall encourage the efficient use of the forest's multiple products and services to ensure economic viability and a wide range of environmental and social benefits.

Principle 6: Environmental impact
Forest management shall conserve biological diversity and its associated values, water resources, soils, and unique and fragile ecosystems and landscapes, and, by so doing, maintain the ecological functions and the integrity of the forest.

Principle 7: Management plan
A management plan—appropriate to the scale and intensity of the operations—shall be written, implemented, and kept up to date. The long-term objectives of management, and the means of achieving them, shall be clearly stated.

Principle 8: Monitoring and assessment
Monitoring shall be conducted—appropriate to the scale and intensity of forest management—to assess the condition of the forest, yields of forest products, chain of custody, management activities, and their social and environmental impacts.

Principle 9: Maintenance of high conservation value forests
Management activities in high conservation value forests shall maintain or enhance the attributes which define such forests. Decisions regarding high conservation value forests shall always be considered in the context of a precautionary approach.

Principle 10: Plantations
Plantations shall be planned and managed in accordance with Principles and Criteria 1–9, and Principle 10 and its Criteria. While plantations can provide an array of social and economic benefits, and can contribute to satisfying the world's needs for forest products, they should complement the management of, reduce pressures on, and promote the restoration and conservation of natural forests.

Table 4.2. Forest sites and area certified by region by FSC (as of 5 January 2004)

Region	No. certified forest sites	Area covered (millions of hectares)
Europe	234	25.20
Latin America	149	4.40
North America	117	8.00
Asia-Pacific	41	1.12
Africa	26	1.60
Total	567	40.40

Source: www.fscoax.org.

Générale de Surveillance (SGS), with 16%; and Scientific Certification Systems (SCS), with 11%. In Mexico, SmartWood is the only program to date providing forest management and chain of custody certification.

The role of FSC, in addition to the development of international standards for good forest management practices, is to be the accrediting agency that periodically audits the organizations that provide the FSC seal and certification based on those standards (see Table 4.1). A fundamental aspect of the FSC scheme is that its credibility is ensured by its function as a "third-party evaluation." This means that it is conducted by an independent body with no links to the forest operation to be evaluated, the forest industry, or with the local or state government. In addition, two external and independent experts review the results of every evaluation.

An important element contributing to the FSC's credibility is its board of directors, made up of representatives from all sectors involved in forest management: environmental NGOs, rural development organizations, human rights and labor organizations, the timber industry, wood products retailers, and forest products consumer organizations, all from various countries. These diverse interest groups actively participate in defining the principles and criteria on which the FSC scheme is based (see Table 4.1), and they maintain quality control of the certification of logging operations and the chain of custody for manufacturers and retailers. Integrating an operational standard from this diversity of interests has been a difficult task, and the result is a generic standard that sets broad outlines on how to achieve forest sustainability.

The FSC program certifies logging operations that incorporate and recognize all the components within the established principles and criteria. The program monitors a broad range of practices that operations should comply with, including silviculture, prevention of negative environmental impacts, environmental restoration, conservation of biological diversity, economic profitability, and generation of social benefits (see Table 4.1). Many of these are requirements that go further than those established in the various national forest laws. This framework calls for the quality of forest management to increase gradually over the five-year period of the renewable certification contract.

However, even though FSC forest management standards are generic, they were designed with larger timber operations in mind. For CFEs, as we shall see, full compliance with these standards is expensive. It should be noted that chain-of-custody standards for manufacturers do not include aspects related to the environment or worker rights; the focus is on managerial systems that monitor the flow of the certified wood from the forest to the end consumer, ensuring that it is not combined with timber from noncertified sources. Both forest owners and manufacturers are subject to annual supervision in order to evaluate their compliance with conditions identified during evaluation.

Importance of Community Forest Certification

The main goal of forest certification was to create a market incentive to reward well-managed forest areas through the creation of market niches and improved prices for certified forest products. Unfortunately, market prices respond to multiple situations that mitigate this hypothesis, such as bank interest rates, global and national economic cycles, and oversupplies from global plantation production. In this market turbulence, certified products can only rarely get higher prices than noncertified ones. Any price premium may also accrue to end-product manufacturers, rather than timber producers such as the CFEs.

This situation has created a paradox, since this presumed market incentive for good management practices is not generating the additional income that was supposed to be used to invest in sustainable management practices. For the certified CFEs, who own their forests, this means that even if they make the commitment to care for their forests and improve management quality, the certification does not cover the related costs.

In practical terms, only forests blessed with good resources and managed by entities with some technological and organizational sophistication are able to get the FSC seal. This also explains why internationally private and publicly owned forests, rather than communal ones, dominate certification, as we shall see. The fact that certified products still do not, and may never, attract a higher price in the marketplace highlights the need for some sort of subsidy that will cover the extra costs of raising the quality of forest management in most, but possibly not all, CFEs. This is especially true for communities with low volumes of production or small forests. Currently, FSC is reviewing procedures for so-called Small and Low Intensity Managed Forests (SLIMF) to try and increase their access to certification. However, costs are not the only limiting factor in CFEs getting and maintaining certification.

Data on the distribution of property types under FSC certification shows that 53.6% is private, 43.4% public, and only 3% is communal property. The significance of Mexico within the communal category becomes clear when we look more closely at the global distribution of certified community forests. As Table 4.3 shows, as of January 2004, Mexico has 39% of the communities and 43% of the certified communal forest area worldwide. The fact that 80% of Mexico's forest cover is under community ownership supports these statistics (White and Martin 2002).

Given the global weight of Mexico's certified community forests, a review of the first 10 years of experience with certification is in order; the case of Mexico provides a crucial means of understanding the significance, expectations, and lessons for the growing number of community-managed forests worldwide.

Ten Years of Certification in Mexico

Forest certification in Mexico began basically at the same time as international certification. Although an initial visit was made to Quintana Roo *ejidos* by SCS's Green Cross Programme in 1991, because "no scheme or internationally recognized certification procedure existed, this was later classed as a pre-certification visit for the more regulated assessment of 1994" (Maynard and Robinson 1998:21). In 1993–94 the SmartWood Program of the U.S. NGO Rainforest Alliance evaluated forest management in five *ejidos* in southern Quintana Roo as a pilot for its certification program. Once FSC was founded in 1995, three of these *ejidos* were certified under its seal. However, after this start, the certification process stagnated because the concept was little known and a national market, to which most production in Mexico is sold, did not exist for certified products (see Figure 4.1).

To address this issue, from 1997 to 1998 a national coalition of NGOs,

Table 4.3. Community forest operations certified by FSC (as of January 2004)

Country	Certified community forests	Certified area (ha)	Type of forest	Tenure
Mexico	27	532,740	Natural forests	Communities
Guatemala	12	300,401	Natural forests	Communities
United States	3	219,628	Natural forests	Communal-indigenous
Brazil	4	48,890	Natural forests	Communities
Germany	12	42,324	Semi-natural forests & plantations	Communal cities
Honduras	2	37,277	Natural forests	Communities
Philippines	1	14,800	Semi-natural forests & plantations	Communities
Italy	1	11,000	Natural forests	Communal cities
Switzerland	2	7,078	Semi-natural forests & plantations	Communities
Netherlands	1	3,896	Natural forests	Communal
Japan	1	2,079	Semi-natural forests & plantations	Cooperative
Sweden	1	1,450	Natural forests	Communities
Austria	2	751	Semi-natural forests & plantations	Communal cities
Canada	1	400	Natural forests	Communal-indigenous
Total	**70**	**1,222,714**		

Source: www.fscoax.org.

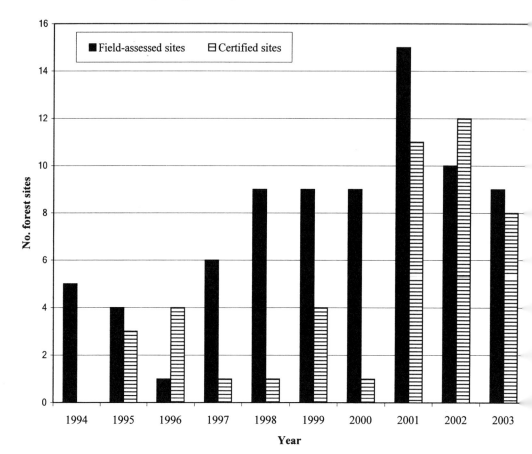

Figure 4.1 A decade of forest certification in Mexico: Field-assessed and certified sites annually, 1994–2003. *Source:* CCMSS-Certification Department database, as of December 2003.

the Consejo Civil Mexicano para la Silvicultura Sostenible (CCMSS; Mexican Civil Council for Sustainable Silviculture) and the national and regional community forestry organizations undertook a campaign to promote certification among the most developed CFEs. From that time, *ejidos* and communities in the states of Quintana Roo, Oaxaca, Hidalgo, Michoacán, Durango, and Chihuahua began to show more interest in getting certified.

During the first years of certification in Mexico, from 1996 to 1999, the communities' main interest in certification was that it provided an external evaluation on the quality of their forest management program, helping them to identify strengths, weaknesses, and needs, as well as offering the hope of a price premium in the marketplace. Certification helped local communities to show the general public and the regional and national media that an external evaluation by a third party proved that they were committed to good forest management practices. They also felt that it would increase the chances of receiving support from the government and foundations to develop and strengthen future management and conservation activities.

By 1998 some companies and exporters of forest products noticed that international markets were demanding certified wood, opening up a new market niche for their products. This fact created interest, even at the local markets, because the high costs of national timber production made it difficult to compete with low-cost imported plantation timber. From 1999 to 2001 the involvement of the private sector provided a new stimulus to forest certification. In 2002 and 2003, government funds from PRODEFOR opened up the opportunity for more communities to get involved. Figure 4.1 shows this 10-year trend of expansion in the number of community forests and area certified in Mexico.

According to the CCMSS database,[3] by December 2003–January 2004 the total number of certified operations in Mexico was 36 community (including 4 communities joined in a regional certified organization) and 5 small private forest enterprises. The total certified area covered 642,128 hectares, producing 1,438,597 cubic meters of certified wood annually, in the states of Durango, Chihuahua, Michoacán, Oaxaca, Quintana Roo, and Guerrero. This volume represents approximately 13% of total timber production annually in the country. There is also one *ejido* that has earned certification for chicle as a non-timber forest product (NTFP).

These figures change every two or three months, since new operations are being field-assessed, certified, or they end their certification period without seeking renewal. The discontinuity shown in Figure 4.1 between the number of assessed and certified sites shows part of the complex process of forest certification: after the field assessment, some operations need to improve certain aspects before they can get the certificate, others are cancelled due to a lack of compliance with commitments made, and some have their assessment report in review or their certificates in process. In addition, the number of exporting manufacturers interested in certifying their chain of custody has increased, with 17 currently certified and some others interested.

Durango has taken the lead in forest certification in Mexico (see Peter Taylor's article, this volume), since half of the chain-of-custody certified exporters operate there and currently 25 CFEs are certified; another 7 are in some stage of the certification process. Some of the exporting companies are so eager to have certified supplies of timber that they are willing to pay the certification costs of some communities. However, as noted, none are yet giving a price premium for certified log and timber products. Furthermore, up to now, no domestic manufacturers of wood products have sought certification.

Given the large number of community forests in Mexico there is a potential for continued dynamic growth over the next few years, if the needed support reaches them. The CCMSS reports that in 2002, the Comisión Nacional Forestal (CONAFOR; National Forest Commission) received 34 requests for government subsidies to support certification costs (Madrid and Chapela 2002), of which only 14 had started the certification process. A recent study carried out by the CCMSS in eight forest states[4] identified 824 community forests with production levels ranging from 1,730 to 23,000 cubic meters annually (Cao Romero and Mondragón 2002), although the levels of production and organization for many of them will probably never justify the costs of certification. Given that there are no updated statistics, nor a comprehensive national database, a realistic estimate of potentially certifiable communities is difficult. Other studies have suggested widely varying numbers of communities producing timber, from 54 to 324 communities, varying by level of organization and resource base (Madrid 1993; SEMARNAP 1995:25).

Several experts believe that in the next decade we will probably see an increase in the number of communities interested in certification, but not in the number of communities actually certified, since most of the long-standing CFEs are already included. This trend is emerging already (Figure 4.1). In all of these communities, incentive programs are needed to improve both the quality of forest management and the levels of community organization. Thus, it is essential to develop parallel projects to identify community forests ready for certification, as well as those who are interested but who require assistance before getting to that stage.

As we have said, sales of certified timber have been scarce and without premium prices, but there are enough straws in the wind to suggest that certification could increase if a market promotion strategy is implemented. NORAM de México, an exporter of oak charcoal, opened up the certification market niche in the state of Durango. This company is the only one paying *ejidos* for a secondary product that would otherwise fall on the forest floor as debris, and occupying this new market niche has generated extra income for the *ejidatarios*. In Guerrero the *ejido* El Balcón is exporting timber through a healthy working relationship with Westwood Forest Products of Washington State in the United States, which encourages them to pursue certification. From 1996 to 2001, El Balcón exported 40–45% of its volume, which represented 65% of total sales. From late 1995 to late 2001, they exported approximately US$19 million worth of timber to Westwood (Bray and Merino-Pérez 2003). In December 2002, El Balcón got its FSC certificate and is now exporting certified timber. San Juan Nuevo Parangaricutiro in Michoacán received certification four years ago and exports certified moldings to Home Depot in the United States (ironically, the furniture they sell to a well-known Mexico City department store does not use the certified seal). Finally, the Society of Forest Production *Ejidos* of Quintana Roo exported $302,016 worth of tropical timber between 1994 and 1997, and they have continued to sporadically export certified timber since then (Maynard and Robinson 1998). In 2002, one of these *ejidos* founded a trading company in an attempt to increase the market of certified tropical wood.

Challenges and Opportunities

The challenges discussed here are in line with the conclusions from a recent study by Forest Trends (Molnar et al. 2003) summarizing the problems that communities have in the certification process. Those most relevant to Mexico include the following:

1. *High international standards.* FSC developed an ambitious standard for forest management, originally tailored for big timber corporations. Results from evaluations of the performance of CFEs on the basis of these standards can generate tensions with local communities. For instance, most community operations in Mexico pay little attention to worker safety, few include formal and periodic training, and almost none have monitoring systems for forest, social, and economic impacts. Recently in Oaxaca an issue arose during a field evaluation when a community expressed objections to some of the FSC criteria, complaining that they went beyond Mexico's environmental laws, which are enforced by the Procuraduría Federal de Protección Ambiental (PROFEPA). In particular, they complained about criteria that challenged their communal organization and traditions by citing a lack of voting rights in the General Assembly for a group of working women. Certifiers argue that the use of international standards that are higher

than local and national laws has been one of the main positive impacts on the forest industry worldwide. But the issue here is that certification goes beyond environmental management into delicate issues of local customs.

2. *Expense and further requirements of certification on the certification contract.* It has been estimated that certification in Mexico costs around US$60,000 over a five-year period (Madrid and Chapela 2002). This is a substantial amount for small CFEs, especially when there have been few sales of certified timber from the majority of these communities. Just over half of this estimate is for the certification process itself, including the initial evaluation, four annual audits, and annual fees, although this varies depending on the size of the operation. The rest of the estimate considers the costs of fulfilling the commitments made to improve forest management practices in the certification contract. However, these latter costs should not be considered as solely another certification cost. In fact, these are the investments needed to improve forest quality and reveal the lack of attention to Mexican rural areas during the last two decades. These costs should be a shared responsibility of Mexican government and society as a whole; the government could help in establishing a strategy for training, infrastructure, and developing markets, and society could pay for these certified products.

3. *The lack of sales and a price premium.* Certification was initially promoted as a means to get a higher price in the market, but as the market begins to move toward certification, a price premium has not emerged. The lack of sales has left some communities who were originally certified uninterested in getting recertified and otherwise understandably confused about how it works. In Oaxaca, the community of La Trinidad did not understand why they had to pay for what was believed to be a prize, nor did they like the clause in the contract saying that any dispute would be adjudicated in New York (Alatorre Frenk 2000). La Trinidad is correct to be concerned about the cost of certification. A recent International Tropical Timber Organization (ITTO) report confirmed the worst fears of communities: "In general certification costs tend to be much heavier for primary producers than processors. On the contrary, the benefits of certification, which relate mainly to market access, tend to be realized by actors down in the supply chain: at present, the main winners from forest certification appear to be far from the forest, particularly in the case of tropical forests" (Atyi and Simula 2002).

4. *Continued dependence on external subsidies to support certification costs.* From 1994 to 2000, many of the subsidies for the certification of forest communities came from international sources, such as the Ford, Inter-American, and MacArthur Foundations, and the North American Environmental Cooperation Fund. Recently, the Mexican government has emerged as an important new actor in support of certification. The current government of President Vicente Fox has made explicit its interest in certification as a mechanism for promoting better forest management. This interest has been manifested through the Forest Development Program (Programa de Desarrollo Forestal; PRODEFOR), a program for forest owner subsidies first launched in 1998 that has expanded its objectives to fund an increased range of forest-related activities. In addition, the Program for Forest Conservation and Management (Programa para la Conservación y Manejo Forestal; PROCYMAF), a project sponsored jointly by the World Bank and the government of Mexico to promote community forestry in Oaxaca and several other states, has also been supporting certification (PROCYMAF 2000). Some of the communities requesting certification have a new strategy in approaching certification, asking for preevaluations that result in a work plan to get ready for certification. This step-by-step process could be a model for future certifications of less developed CFEs.

5. *The feasibility of some recommendations for community forests.* CFEs represent a very special form of forest enterprise, with specific cultural and economic situations. Given that communities sell primarily to a domestic market and have diversified livelihood strategies, the usefulness of FSC certification has been questioned because of its inability to make recommendations that capture the complexity of the integrated management systems of non-timber, timber, and rotational agriculture, and to help communities make optimal choices for landscape management (Madrid and Chapela 2002; see also Molnar et al. 2003). This suggests a significant backing away from the greater expectations created when the forest certification concept was first launched. It is being realized that, even with the adaptations of FSC standards to Mexican realities, the certification process faces very complex local and regional dynamics that cannot be solved by only one instrument.

Despite these problems, it is clear that certification is advancing in Mexico and that widespread interest is present. As we have argued, this interest is due to a variety of factors, including the recognition that certification brings prestige in local, national, and international circles, and that this has both tangible and intangible value. Community leaders seek certification to show their effectiveness and to mobilize community support for forest management. Certification can be used to help resolve community conflicts over forest management, and it also helps maintain a competitive edge in the marketplace (Madrid and Chapela 2002).

Conclusions and Recommendations

Certification is controversial. Nonetheless, it still represents both a viable *strategy* and a necessary *process* to support community forestry and to encourage a new stage in its development. A strategy because this global movement has opened up specific market opportunities that can trigger a flow of resources to Mexican community forestry and allow certified products the chance to compete in new niche markets. A process, because it could trigger a wide range of support mechanisms to improve the overall quality of forest management in Mexico, and to increase, gradually, the direct and indirect benefits for the inhabitants of these forests. The forest certification process is a valuable instrument, but has shown its limits. The response of markets is urgent, as is the intervention of programs and actors working in synergy to reach the same goals.

Through the 87 forest operations evaluated to date,[5] an overview of the current situation of community forestry that pinpoints its strengths and weaknesses is possible. Eight key areas require attention from a wide variety of social sectors in order to reach the goal of making a difference in the forest management of these communities. Despite some obvious differences, community operations share a notable similarity in their social, ecological, and productive conditions. Many show the chronic weaknesses and stagnation in the Mexican forestry sector that are due to decades of underinvestment and lack of technical assistance and training.

The eight key areas requiring attention are (1) improvement of forest and sawmill productivity; (2) updating forest databases, surveys, and the forest management planning process; (3) development of guidelines for good forest management practices; (4) multiple-level training for forest owners and forest and mill workers, as well as technical staff; (5) strengthening of CFEs through managerial and administrative training; (6) monitoring systems in the forest to evaluate the effect of management, as well as the social and economic impacts of forest activities; (7) biological and ecological studies for a better understanding of these managed ecosystems and identification of landscape elements that should be protected; and (8) a marketing strategy for the promotion of the concept at a national level to awaken the domestic demand for certified wood and products.

Some of these actions are the direct responsibility of the forest owners; others are the responsibility of their technical forestry staff; still others require the participation of external institutions and enterprises. There is a clear need to establish links between academic institutions, NGOs, *ejidos*, and forest communities, as well as with financial supporters, to fulfill all these needs. Without improved markets, however, progress will be limited.

As certification becomes a norm in the marketplace, even certified communities will continue to suffer many of the disadvantages they currently face. This raises the question of the need for another specialized label that would recognize timber and NTFPs produced by communities and indigenous peoples. In the United States and Canada, for example, Native American tribes are discussing the possibility of an "indigenous forest products" label that recognizes their unique production conditions (Molnar et al. 2003). As has been noted, "It may be timely to analyze the potential to produce wood and nonwood forest products harvested or processed by communities to acknowledge their commitment to sustainable forest management, their historical practices and accomplishments, and their future aspirations. There may be a role for market labeling based on an ethical or fair trade category of standards, drawing upon existing government and local geo-referenced databases, landscape quality data generated by communities, and documentation of community management" (Molnar 2003:36).

Forest certification is an important process, but it is immersed in a global, national, and local context that calls for other options, or modifications of the existing ones. Certification, as currently constituted, may not be the answer for most communities. A specific market promotion strategy tailored for CFEs, involving information campaigns in Mexican domestic markets for consumers and retailers, is imperative, and currently does not exist.

Regarding the certification process, a step-wise or step-by-step option might be better adapted to CFEs and their economic constraints, and might make certification a more inclusive option. Mexican forest communities and their CFEs, like an increasing number of communities and indigenous forest enterprises in the rest of the world, represent a unique contribution to the forest economy and conservation of these forest ecosystems. It is this uniqueness that should be recognized in the marketplace.

Notes

1. Both authors were in charge of the Consejo Civil Mexicano para la Silvicultura Sostenible, A.C., Certification Office. The opinions expressed in this chapter are their own.

2. FSC updated statistics: Certified Forest List. Doc. 5.3.3; 29 April 2003. Forest Management Report by Continents, 5 January 2004. Search on FSC-Certificates data bank, 14 January 2004 (www.fscoax.org).

3. CCMSS-Certification database figures differ from FSC's figures due to lags in updating the latter. These numbers include those operations that are in the process of obtaining their formal certificate.

4. Campeche, Chihuahua, Chiapas, Durango, Guerrero, Michoacán, Oaxaca, and Quintana Roo.

5. Total number of field assessments performed in Mexico up to December 2003.

References

Alatorre Frenk, G. 2000. *La construcción de una cultura gerencial democrática en las empresas forestales comunitarias*. Mexico City: Casa Juan Pablos, Procuraduría Agraria.

Atyi, R. E., and M. Simula. 2002. Forest certification: Pending challenges for tropical timber. Unpublished paper. ITTO International Workshop on Comparability and Equivalence of Forest Certification Schemes, Kuala Lumpur.

Bray, D. B., and L. Merino-Pérez. 2003. El Balcón, Guerrero: A case study of globalization benefiting a forest community. In *Confronting Globalization: Economic Integration and Popular Resistance in Mexico*, ed. T. A. Wise, H. Salazar, and L. Carlsen, 65–80. Bloomfield, CT: Kumarian Press.

Bray, D. B., L. Merino-Pérez, P. Negreros-Castillo, G. Segura-Warnholz, J. M. Torres-Rojo, and H. F. M. Vester. 2003. Mexico's community-managed forests: A global model for sustainable landscapes. *Conservation Biology* 17(3):672–677.

Cao Romero, M., and V. M. Mondragón. 2002. *Estimación y diagnóstico del mercado potencial para la certificación forestal en México*. Xalapa, Veracruz: CCMSS, A.C.

FSC. 2002/2003. *Forests Certified by FSC-Accredited Certification Bodies*. August 2002 and April 2003. Available from http://www.fscoax.org/html/5-3-3.html. Lista de Bosques Certificados. DOC. 5.3.3, 30 August 2002. FSC. Accessed 6 October 2002 and 29 April 2003. Forest Management Report by Continents up to 5 January 2004 downloaded from FSC website.

Madrid, S. 1993. Análisis social: La participación de grupos indígenas y no indígenas en actividades forestales y de conservación. Obstáculos y oportunidades de los ejidos y comunidades forestales en México. Unpublished study of Mexico's forestry subsector completed for the World Bank.

Madrid, S., and F. Chapela. 2002. La certificación en México: Los casos de Durango y Oaxaca. Report. Washington, DC: Forest Trends.

Maynard, B., and D. Robinson. 1998. *Ethical Trade and Sustainable Rural Liveli-*

hoods—*Quintana Roo Forest Certification Case Study.* Chatham, UK: Natural Resources Institute.

Molnar, A., et al. 2003. *Forest Certification and Communities: Looking Forward to the Next Decade.* Washington, DC: Forest Trends.

PROCYMAF. 2000. *Proyecto de conservación y manejo sustentable de recursos forestales: Balance de tres años de ejecución.* Mexico City: SEMARNAP.

SEMARNAP. 1995. *Programa forestal y de suelo, 1995–2000.* Mexico City: Secretaría de Medio Ambiente, Recursos Naturales y Pesca.

White, A., and A. Martin. 2002. *Who Owns the World's Forests? Forest Tenure and Public Forests in Transition.* Washington, DC: Forest Trends, Center for International Environmental Law.

PART II

SOCIAL PROCESSES AND COMMUNITY FORESTRY

CHAPTER 5

Indigenous Community Forest Management in the Sierra Juárez, Oaxaca

FRANCISCO CHAPELA

In this chapter, the experiences of communities living in the Sierra Juárez, also known as the Sierra Norte of Oaxaca, and in particular communities that organized themselves into the Unión de Comunidades Zapoteco-Chinanteca (UZACHI), will be examined. This organization consists of three Zapotec communities and one Chinantec community. Each one of these is autonomous and has its own internal governance mechanisms. Together, they created UZACHI to be a regional body, a union, to support the management of their forests and to face common problems collectively. This is an opportune time to carry out an evaluation of UZACHI, which was established 10 years ago. Such an evaluation can help identify lessons that can be applied to the design of future institutional arrangements that support sustainable natural resource management and rural development policies. The history of UZACHI will be placed in the context of the larger struggle of Oaxacan indigenous peoples to regain control of their land and their resources after the Spanish Conquest. The concepts of natural and social capital will also be employed to help illuminate some contemporary dimensions of UZACHI's success in community forest management.

The Mexican state of Oaxaca is located in a region with great natural endowments favoring the development of community forestry. It is located in southern Mexico, where mountain chains running from the coast of the Gulf of Mexico converge with those from the Pacific Ocean. The confluence of these two mountain systems resulted in an abrupt topography, producing a range of climatic variations and microclimates. The geology in this part of Mexico is very complex, and consequently is home to a very wide range of soil types. One can find within Oaxaca practically all the main ecosystems and vegetation assemblages found in

Mexico. In fact, the list of plants and animals in Oaxaca is the most extensive in Mexico, famed for its high level of biodiversity.

Cultural Diversity and History

This great variation in natural environments has impeded the use of a single model to manage natural resources. Instead, through cultural evolution dating back 10,000 years, local Oaxacan communities have developed traditional techniques to adapt to the microenvironments typical of the state. In addition, cultural heritage has developed unique aspects in each of the 15 ethnic groups found in Oaxaca, adding an important dimension to the state's diversity. Thus, the traditional natural resource use patterns of the Huaves, Mazatecos, Zapotecos, and Chinantecos, as well as many others, show important differences even though they sometimes share similar environmental conditions.

The enormous variation in geography and cultures has historically limited large-scale exploitation of the state's natural resources. During Spanish colonization, only those valleys that could be irrigated or sustain livestock were occupied by Spanish haciendas, with the indigenous peoples being pushed up into the mountain slopes, where they further adapted traditional technologies, organizational systems, and resource management institutions. The Spaniards demanded payments from these local communities, but the traditional management systems were maintained. Although the indigenous territories were not officially recognized, the size of their territory was used as the base to determine the tribute to be paid to the crown representative.

When the country began fighting for independence in the first two decades of the nineteenth century, indigenous communities were under the control of the central government, while maintaining autonomy in technical and productive areas. In the second half of the nineteenth century, the liberal party promoted the creation of new property rights in Mexico with the objective of "modernizing" the rural sector. These policies failed to recognize the territorial rights of indigenous communities, meaning that the majority of Mexico's indigenous population began the twentieth century without the legal right to use their own territories. Traditional management systems broke down in many parts of the country. In Oaxaca, however, the resilience of many traditional institutions and organizations, along with the physical difficulties of establishing a state-led system of natural resource exploitation, allowed for the persistence of traditional resource management systems. Throughout the twentieth century, Oaxacan communities fought for the reestablishment of their traditional territorial rights. The availability of colonial tax documents, known as *títulos primordiales*, was their strongest argument for the devolution of territorial rights. These struggles by Oaxacan communities and the frictions they caused with neighboring communities due to unclear boundaries generated innumerable conflicts throughout the last century across all the 570 municipalities in Oaxaca.

However, the majority of Oaxacan communities have started the twenty-first century with a reconfirmation of their territorial rights, and the history of their appropriation of forest management and timber production is the best example of how they have regained rights over their natural resources, adapting traditional governance structures and institutions to this new task.

Natural Capital and Social Capital

As forests and clean water become scarcer, the concept of natural capital has emerged to recognize the economic value of biological resources. Environmental economists have observed that conventional economic theory and analysis fail to internalize the environmental impacts of economic production. Realities such as the contamination of the environment or the exhaustion of the natural resource base are rarely incorporated into private-sector accounting systems. To have a more realistic picture of the economic situation, we must add to conventional accounting figures data that reflect more comprehensively the flows of wealth, not just cash and physical capital, but also *natural capital* (such as forest stocks, seeds, or soils). With this, one would have a more realistic picture of the economic situation. The unsustainable exploitation of natural capital makes a country poorer, not richer, in the long run (Daly 1993).

From an environmental economics perspective, a community forest enterprise (CFE) management plan should seek to increase levels of capital through the accumulation of machinery, equipment, and infrastructure, while also increasing the value of the natural resource base. Similarly, Ostrom and Ahn (2001) noted that education and technical training are forms of investment in human and social capital, with the objective of improving long-term productive capacity. Ostrom and Ahn also see the cost of time and effort in creating an organization as an investment in social capital. These organizations can then set objectives and establish rules that can improve the economic competitiveness of the CFE or intercommunity organization, and, therefore, they can be considered social capital.

Within this conceptual frame, the UZACHI struggle can be viewed as a movement that responded to a concern of local indigenous communities to preserve their natural capital and increase their human and social capital, thus increasing their financial capital and cash flows. This does not mean that the people of UZACHI now all have cars and VCRs; rather, as a result of investments in social, human, and natural capital, they are able to provide their families with a decent way of life, demonstrated by life expectancies, literacy rates, and numbers of professionals that are well above the average for Mexico.

The Struggle to Halt the Destruction of Natural Capital: From Concessions to UZACHI

Halfway through the twentieth century, the majority of Oaxaca's local and indigenous communities had yet to secure the full reinstatement of their territorial property rights. Then in 1956, despite many communities being in the middle of the political and legal process of renegotiating these rights, the government decided to administer the communities' forests as if they were public resources. Responding to the dominant institutional schemes of the time, the government awarded concessions to forestry companies in exchange for a stumpage fee (*derecho de monte*), which was administratively fixed far below the market value. Further, the concessionaire then controlled all activities in the forest, totally alienating the communities from their own forests. Thus, there was no incentive for the communities, government, or the concessionaire to make investments in the forest. In the case of Oaxaca, the region of the Sierra Norte was given as a concession to the paper company Fábricas de Papel Tuxtepec (FAPATUX), while the Sierra Sur was given to the company Bosques de Oaxaca, which had a plywood, board, and veneer factory. The responsibility for the elaboration of forest management plans fell to a forestry engineer who was contracted by the companies under authorization from the government. In this way, over 3.4 million hectares of Oaxacan community forestlands were given out in concessions from 1941 to 1978 (SARH-SFF 1980).

The latest struggle for the rights of indigenous people over their land and the disposition of their forest resources began at the end of the 1960s.

This was manifest by the struggle of 15 communities, led by San Pablo Macuiltianguis, which refused to sign the logging contracts and launched a boycott for higher salaries, increases in stumpage fees, investment in roads, and fulfillment of promises like scholarships for children. It is revealing that these communities did not yet envision managing and logging the forests themselves. A *comunero* in Macuiltianguis said of this period: "We seem like workers and not owners of the forest. That's why we have always had a rebellious position with respect to the enterprise since it carries away all our wealth and our sweat and doesn't leave us anything . . . we are the most beaten down, while those that work for the enterprise, the workers as well as those that have their confidence, earn triple what we take out" (Alatorre Frenk 2000:59). The Unión de Pueblos Abastecedores continued its strike for six years before FAPATUX finally ceded to some community demands.

These forest struggles can be linked to other movements of the period and to the confluence of rural and urban struggles in Mexico in the 1970s and 1980s. The 1968 university students' movement in Mexico sparked the reappraisal of many issues, such as the role of peasants in modern Mexico and the relationship between urban and rural areas. León Jorge Castaños, a former undersecretary for forests and wildlife and one of the foremost supporters of community forestry in Mexico, believes the 1968 movement to have been an important event for community forestry in Mexico:

> The 1968 students' movement made many people aware of their social
> commitment. It broke down silences and official monologues, and
> led the 1970–1976 Federal Administration to introduce a number of
> operational initiatives that provided real support for urban and rural
> social causes . . . [At the same time] some other movements and
> independent peasant struggles were developing, typically made up
> of peasant communities upset with the way they had been treated
> in the past and adamant that they would reject the presence of any
> concessionary business that would work against their interests in the
> future—as happened in Northeast Durango and in the South and North
> Oaxacan Sierras. (Castaños 1999)

The "democratic opening" under President Luis Echeverría (1970–76) led to a political divide, where the government shifted from a "Soviet" model, with only one effective state party, a welfare state, and very strong political leaders, to a new competitive and more plural political system.

One of the manifestations of this was the relative empowerment of rural forest communities in the early 1970s. The democratic opening gave renewed hope to rural groups that believed that, if community organization was promoted and given enough support, long-term progress could be achieved in Mexico. In contrast to the nonparticipatory form of national development of the 1950s and 1960s, which led to the 1968 crisis, new approaches saw rural communities as the main actors in a process of sustainable national development.

Forest communities took full advantage of the historical moment. For the first time, they had the chance to talk directly with the government about their property rights, which had been recognized in principle after the revolution, but which were almost forgotten during the post–World War II economic expansion. Now local communities began demanding full recognition of their property rights and the right to control their own forests. Community empowerment, the crisis within state-owned forestry companies, and the increasingly visible technical constraints of the concessions regime, led communities to switch from asking for better work conditions or wages, as in the late 1960s, to demanding that control over the logging business to be handed over so that they could create their own CFEs.

Another important institutional change that contributed to set up the scenario for the development of community forestry was Mexico's decision in 1976 to enter the GATT[1] agreement and pursue a Structural Adjustment Plan (SAP). Under this SAP, state-owned companies were to be sold or closed if possible. Taking advantage of this, Oaxacan communities suggested that—if state-owned companies were being closed down—the communities themselves could take care of forest management in their territories, thereby regaining control over their natural resource base.

In 1981 the concession period for FAPATUX in the Sierra Norte and Bosques de Oaxaca in the Sierra Sur expired. By 1979 the companies had already begun to lobby the government for another 25-year concession period, but there was a growing awareness in the communities of just how much they were losing from the concession scheme. By 1980, the forest communities of Oaxaca formed a mass social movement, with regional communities ready to protest the renewal of the concession and concerned about the preservation of their cultural and natural heritage. In the Sierra Norte, the Organización para la Defensa de los Recursos Naturales y el Desarrollo Social de la Sierra Juárez (ODRENASIJ) coordinated mass protests involving more than 30 communities. Simultaneously, other communities from the Sierra Sur mobilized themselves to successfully deny an extension of Bosques de Oaxaca's concession. In the Mixe zone, the Coordinadora para el Desarrollo de la Región Mixe (CODREMI) was formed, involving the participation of some 60 municipalities from the Mixe indigenous group; in the isthmus region the Unión de Comunidades Indígenas del Istmo (UCIRI) was formed, made up of 30 local communities.

It quickly became evident that the communities would need professional support. They recruited professional sons of community members and a lawyer to help take legal action against the forestry concession decree. They also sent delegations to the National Autonomous University of Mexico (Universidad Nacional Autónoma de México; UNAM), the Autonomous Metropolitan University (Universidad Autónoma Metropolitana; UAM), the Autonomous University of Chapingo (Universidad Autónoma de Chapingo; UACH), and the National School of Anthropology. In this way the communities made contact with a group of graduates from the UAM, who, over the following years, developed the technical aspects of a community-based forest management program. From this initial group, Estudios Rurales y Asesoría Campesina, A.C. (ERA), was formed. ERA identified two possible options for dealing with the needs of the communities. One was to directly resolve, as professionals, the technical problems in forest management. The second option was to form a technical corps within the communities that would be given the support necessary to find the technical solutions themselves. ERA opted for the second approach and developed a range of formal training activities to develop a body of qualified and skilled community members. They did not identify their goal as "developing human and social capital," but this is in fact what they were doing.

Disquiet and unrest with state-owned companies grew steadily; concessionaires were no longer seen as the vanguard of progress but as entities that were destroying the community's natural capital. This increased tensions and led to demonstrations against the state companies in Oaxaca. The Mixe carried out militant demonstrations against FAPATUX, demanding its removal from community territory (Castro 1985). The communities that would later compose UZACHI struggled for the right to use the forests in their territories (Bray 1991).

Unsurprisingly, government officials did not support changes in the institutions of the forestry sector. However, such was the scale of social mobilization that it forced institutional changes within the national forest sector. Thus, a new forestry law was passed on 19 December 1985 (Díaz 1985) and published in early 1986 (see also Merino-Pérez and Segura-

Warnholtz, this volume). This new law accepted that, under regulation by the forest agency, a private, professional team in the employ of the communities could develop the legally required forest management plans, instead of the Forest Service (Ley Forestal 1986). In spite of its limitations, this law helped to dismantle paternalist structures and opened up opportunities for more participatory forest management approaches, particularly the organization of unions of communities that banded together to provide their own forest technical services and management plans, as in the case of UZACHI.

A second big institutional change came on 6 June 1986, when the Forest Commission was created under the leadership of León Jorge Castaños (*El Heraldo*, 6 June 1986:5). The commission was given the goal of coordinating forest initiatives in the public and private sectors, rather than making the decisions by itself, as the Forest Service had done. This new approach contrasted sharply with the ideology of the omnipresent Forest Service, limiting government intervention to the role of referee over nongovernment initiatives. In Castaños's (1999) words, "All this was done to put an end to the damage and problems associated with logging bans, concessions and [state] companies, and to put the focus back on the [natural] resource owner."

The forestry unions that were formed after the 1986 law quickly moved beyond labor demands to demand greater control over forest resources and industries. They developed their own technical staff and their own forest management approaches. In addition to the two objectives of constructing technical capacity and forming a regional forestry management and negotiating body, there was also the question of addressing past mistakes. If UZACHI was to successfully obtain and maintain control over regional forestry production, it would be a mistake to reproduce many of the unsustainable logging practices carried out by the state forestry company. The restoration of communal rights was UZACHI's principal goal; the goal of more sustainable logging practices developed over the next decade, with the explicit aim of increasing natural capital. Thus, UZACHI began to view forestry not from a short-term business perspective but from a communal one, where the well-being of the next generations is seen as being just as important as that of the current one. Community-led foresters developed a new approach in UZACHI's 30,000 hectares, most of which was forested, with some interesting features. For example, land use planning addresses community needs in a comprehensive way. This means that the objectives of crop production for subsistence, availability of pasturelands, and maintenance of wildlife areas are as important as the objective of wood production. The paper mill urgently needed raw materials, so their management objective was to get them at any cost. For communities, timber production is a means to get cash, but is not the only use of the forest. There are areas suitable for timber production, while others are dedicated to water catchments, wildlife refuges, or non-timber products areas. Forest improvement is as important as timber extraction. Because one explicit management objective is to assure that future generations inherit productive forests, extracted volume leads to current well-being, and improvements to remaining stands leads to future well-being. Forest management under community control also eventually led to a transition out of the Método Mexicano de Ordenación de Montes (MMOM; Mexican Method of Forest Management) to a more flexible system called the Método de Desarrollo Silvicultura (MDS; Silvicultural Development Method). Among other things, MMOM did not allow sufficient space for the regeneration of pine, encouraging a transition from pine forests to oak forests, and reducing the commercial value. MDS opens larger spaces, encouraging pine regeneration and preserving the genetic quality of the forest. It is recognized that to manage a forest is to manage a complex ecological system, where no effective control can be achieved by merely controlling for some simple variables such as minimum cutting diameter or maximum allowable volume. An adaptive management approach is used instead, where monitoring and evaluation are important tools to keep the management system directed to the main strategic objectives.

Community Forest Management and Circles of Interdependence

Community management of natural resources takes advantage of family, communal, and regional organization, forming a system in which the three levels of organization mutually depend upon each other in what may be thought of as circles of interdependence, as illustrated in Figure 5.1.

The family remains the basic unit of production in the forest communities of the Sierra Norte. It is at the family level that basic subsistence and income-generating activities such as agricultural production and wooden arts and crafts are carried out. Individual family members may also work as employees in the CFE, and the family member who is a registered *comunero* can help make management decisions about the forests and other community properties through the General Assembly. Beyond the family level are the networks of extended families, or *guelaguetza*, whereby vari-

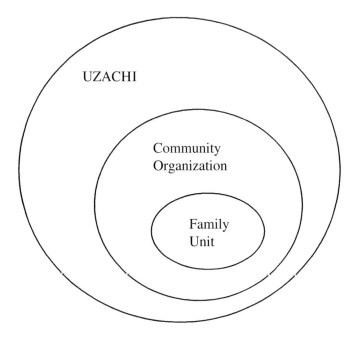

Figure 5.1 Organization levels and interdependence.

ous families engage in labor exchanges that may include food or cash for the most demanding agricultural work.

The basic forest management decisions are made by each community's General Assembly. Such decisions may include the definition of those areas of the community territory that are devoted to agriculture, commercial forestry, and wildlife, along with rules to regulate the collection of firewood, the grazing of livestock, and other land uses. The General Assembly also determines forest management issues such as reforestation practices and CFE issues such as how much of the annual authorized volume to cut and decisions concerning the sawmill. Figure 5.2 shows the structure of relationships of the CFE within the community and the external relationship with ERA, the NGO that has supported them since the late 1980s.

In the majority of issues related to natural resource management, the local community governance structures have been effective, making decisions efficiently on issues such as the definition of rules governing access to forest resources, the planning and construction of road networks, the production of sawnwood, and the obligation of community members to participate in forest protection. A form of community labor service known as the *tequio* is the vehicle whereby community members contribute to the maintenance of community infrastructure such as libraries, health clinics, and potable water systems. It is now also used to maintain logging roads.

Today, UZACHI is composed of the four communities of La Trinidad, Santiago Xiacuí, Calpulalpam de Méndez, and Santiago Comaltepec. As is shown in Table 5.1, the four communities together have 23,125 hectares of their total surface area of 28,978 hectares in permanent forest estates for the sustainable management of forest production.

It is the responsibility of the technical team of UZACHI, headed by the university-trained forest technical director (a community member since 1990), to develop forest management plans for each community, following the guidelines of each assembly and of Mexican law. UZACHI has also developed a regional training program and has begun another program to support the development of agroforestry systems. In addition, it has started a research program with the participation of various academic institutions, along with a biodiversity and carbon sequestration development program.

The organizational chart of UZACHI is shown in Figure 5.3. The most important union decisions are made in the Asamblea de Delegados. Each community names four delegates to participate in this Union Assembly. In addition, the president of the Comisariado de Bienes Comunales joins the participants. In both the union and the communities, representatives and delegates are elected every three years, with no consecutive terms. The

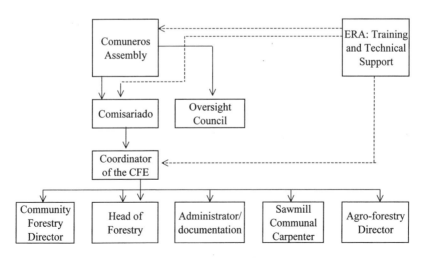

Figure 5.2 Organization of a community member of UZACHI.

Table 5.1. Area of the UZACHI (ha)

	Total	Agriculture/ livestock*	Forest
La Trinidad	913	189	724
Santiago Xiacuí	2,229	462	1,767
Calpulalpam de Méndez	7,470	2,083	5,387
Santiago Comaltepec	18,366	3,119	15,247
Total	**28,978**	**5,853**	**23,125**

Source: UZACHI 1993.
*Note: Area includes zones under temporary agriculture, pastoral zones, and secondary forest created through rotation agriculture or the extraction of firewood and building materials.

personnel responsible for technical areas, like the forest technical director and the union's program coordinators, along with the forestry chief or manager of each of the community's sawmills, are kept on or changed depending on the decisions of the newly elected representatives.

Developing New Resources

The natural and social capital–forming strategy is yielding clear dividends for UZACHI members. On the one hand, an emphasis on profitable logging has kept the CFEs in business in spite of the very harsh economic environment during the last two decades. On the other hand, a lot of effort has been directed to increasing other monetary and nonmonetary values as well, such as food self-sufficiency and the development of new sources of natural resource income.

Mushrooms provide an especially interesting case. As a result of traditional restrictions, only a few people in each community had knowledge of mushroom ecology and uses, and this knowledge was vanishing. UZACHI, with technical assistance from ERA, started a project to restore mushroom knowledge (Chapela and Massieu 2001). Mushroom samples and information about uses were stored in UZACHI facilities. Mushroom collections are accessible to UZACHI members and the information collected was compiled in a handbook that was distributed as a draft. The handbook has not been published for lack of funds, but the project greatly increased mushroom knowledge in the communities. As a result, many mushroom production and collection initiatives have appeared in UZACHI communities and elsewhere in Oaxaca, and wild mushrooms are more frequently found in local marketplaces. Forest areas not used for logging because they were not appropriate have now gained new value as wild mushroom production areas.

The search for new resources led UZACHI to a very innovative project in which community members used wildlife refuge areas to participate in a study that quantitatively analyzed the relationship between microbiological diversity and several management environments in an attempt to gain understanding of what drives chemical innovation in nature. This was a joint project between the Swiss-based pharmaceutical company Sandoz (which later merged with Ciba to form Novartis) and UZACHI, and it involved the challenge of undertaking high-quality technical work in the field. In structuring the collaboration, UZACHI put as conditions that the agreement would not guarantee Sandoz researchers access to communal lands, that all fieldwork would be done by UZACHI members under the direction of the UZACHI technical director and executive council; that under no circumstances would the agreement involve the selling of indigenous traditional knowledge, that the terms of the agreement should be in alignment with Mexican legislation, current or future; that the agreement should increase equipment and capacity on UZACHI's premises; that the agreement should leave trained people in UZACHI; and that UZACHI communities should receive sufficient payment to keep their wild areas management programs running during the agreement and some years later (Chapela and Massieu 2001).

Sandoz, convinced of UZACHI's technical capacity and reliability, accepted these conditions, making it unnecessary to hire professional biologists since community members were trained to conduct field research activities on their own. The project opened a window for rural organizations to engage in bioprospecting, keeping control of the process, and taking a reasonable share of the benefits (Kissling et al. 2002). This agreement ended in 1999 because Novartis and UZACHI felt that the legal framework was still too weak to engage in further collaboration. However, the laboratory which had been dedicated to producing microbial samples turned to producing mushroom mycelia, and is now the largest producer of mushroom mycelia in Oaxaca.

UZACHI has also been exploring the potential to use their forest areas to develop carbon sequestration activities. This initiative has led to the formation of a statewide organization called Servicios Ambientales de Oaxaca (SAO; Oaxaca Environmental Services), which organizes the main

Table 5.2. Carbon capture area and sequestration costs

| Community | Area devoted to sequestration activities (ha) | | | | Total by community | |
	Communal protected areas	Timber production	Shade coffee	Agroforestry systems	Area	Sequestration cost
Santiago Teotlaxco	80	300	37	180	597	24,362
San Juan Metaltepec	110	250	338	500	1,198	48,908
Santiago Comaltepec	10,004	4,210		120	14,334	585,424
San Miguel del Puerto	120	700	45	230	1,095	44,722
San Miguel Aloapam	980	490		160	1,630	66,572
Capulalpam de Méndez	873	1,500		80	2,453	100,185
Santiago Xiacuí	382	1,500		80	1,962	80,131
La Trinidad	84	1,500		120	1,704	69,594
San Juan Yagila	40	1,000	61	150	1,251	51,093
Totontepec, Villa de Morelos	80	900	65	120	1,165	47,581
Nvo. Zoquiapam	88	1,500		100	1,688	68,941
San Bartolomé Loxicha		1,000	110	290	1,400	57,178
La Merced el Potrero		1,000	130	310	1,440	58,812
Santa María Huatulco		1,200	200	240	1,640	66,980
Santa María Xadani	60	900	120	250	1,330	54,319
San José el Paraíso	20	500	90	218	828	33,817
Cuajinicuil	10	450	80	150	690	28,181
Total	**12,931**	**18,900**	**1,275**	**3,298**	**36,404**	**1,486,800**

Source: SAO 2003.

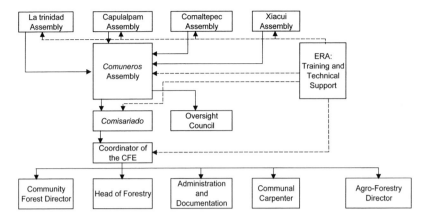

Figure 5.3 UZACHI organization.

forestry and coffee production groups in Oaxaca to offer carbon sequestration services to polluters in Mexico using domestic schemes and to polluters elsewhere using the Clean Development Mechanism (CDM), set up
by the UN Framework Convention on Climate Change.

As can be seen in Table 5.2, SAO has already developed a *sink* on 36,404
hectares managed by communal organizations, with an expected yearly
income of 1,486,800 pesos (about US$148,680), proceeding from the cap-
ture and sequestration of 123,900 carbon tons per year by enhanced community forestry activities (SAO 2003). In the carbon project, the availability of a staff of community technicians able to manage sophisticated
concepts such as carbon sequestration and trained to do baseline and
follow-up studies is crucial. Once again, the accumulation of investment
in social capital in the previous years, coupled with an effective stewardship of communities' natural capital, seems to have begun yielding dividends for UZACHI and other communities in Oaxaca.

The union has served as an effective regional organization that is able
deal with natural resource management issues that the communities cannot attend to individually because of the scale, cost, or complexity involved. The current structure of UZACHI is shown in Figure 5.3. Technical Forest Services, which is a professional team with occasional external
consultancies, is one of the few instances of a new organizational structure that has been grafted onto traditional governance mechanisms. Other
examples have been specialized committees that have dealt with biodiversity management and the sale of services related to it, as happened in the
carbon sequestration and bioprospecting projects described above.

The Restoration of Natural Capital and Impacts on Social and Human Capital

In this section, I will evaluate the impacts of logging on natural capital during the concession and community forestry period; I will also comment on the contributions to social and human capital that have arisen from community forest management. To discuss the impacts on natural capital, I will draw principally on a 1974 forest inventory carried out by FAPATUX (Escárpita et al. 1994) in what would become the UZACHI communities, and compare it to the first UZACHI forest inventory carried out 18 years later, in 1992 (Chapela and Lara 1993).

During the FAPATUX period, with its 25-year concession, there was little incentive to make long-term investments in the forest to increase natural capital. After a period of reflection and experimentation, the communities have taken steps to safeguard their natural capital. Their analysis of the situation revealed that after some two decades of management under MMOM, stocks of pine had fallen by 7%, but oak and other non-commercial species had increased by 68%. As explained earlier, this is the typical response of tropical pines to MMOM. When the 1974 and the 1992 forest inventories were compared, effects on the productivity levels of pine were also observed. The annual average increase of the commercial forest stands fell by 16.26%, from 30,104 cubic meters per year in 1974 to 25,210 in 1992. In 1974, the UZACHI forests were valued at 30 million pesos (1994 equivalent rate). After the concession scheme, the communities received forests valued at 25 million pesos. The concession scheme led to a loss in timber stocks of 16%. That is to say that the UZACHI communities lost almost 5 million pesos (1994 equivalent rate) during the 1974–1993 period, which means a loss of 258,000 pesos (US$772,737 at 1994 rate) every year (Chapela and Lara 1993).

The underlying logic of concessionaires versus that of the communities is simple. The concessionaire's access rights expire after a period of time; therefore it makes no economic sense to invest in anything that will only pay beyond the 25-year concession period. In contrast, for the CFE, the ownership of the forest is for the long term, and it clearly makes sense to make capital investments, such as forest improvements or long-lasting infrastructure, that will pay dividends 20, 30, or 40 years from now, making sustainable forestry the most rational choice for them. Communities believe they will be compensated for the higher investments required by sustainable forestry through the maintenance of forest value and the increased productivity of both the forest and the CFE itself.

Table 5.3. State of marginalization: Rankings of UZACHI communities

Key	Municipality	Population	Degree of marginalization[b]
20458	Santiago Comaltepec	1,972	405
20496	Santiago Xiacuí[a]	2,333	535
20247	Capulalpam de Méndez	1,427	555
	Total	**5,732**	

Source: Consejo Nacional de Población 1990.
[a] La Trinidad community is part of Xiacuí municipality.
[b] Oaxaca has 570 municipalities. Therefore, the most marginalized has a marginalization degree of 1. The least marginalized (or wealthiest) has a degree of 570.

In addition to the increases in natural capital which community forestry has yielded, there has also been a notable formation of social and human capital and a consequent impact on levels of poverty and marginalization. UZACHI itself is a form of social capital, which has brought significant economic benefits to the member communities. Policies of job rotation have spread forest management skills throughout the community, and investments have been made in agricultural training and infrastructure as well. It is also apparent that the UZACHI communities are relatively prosperous in the context of Oaxaca, and while in some cases this may be due to other factors, clearly community forest management has made a significant contribution to this relative prosperity. The National Population Council has ranked all 570 municipalities of Oaxaca as to their degree of economic and social marginalization (i.e., a ranking of relative poverty, with 1 being the most marginalized and 570 being the least marginalized, or most prosperous). Table 5.3 shows that some UZACHI communities rank among the least marginalized in Oaxaca.

Discussion

The UZACHI model of family, community, and regional organizational interdependence has allowed for the integrated management of 28,978 hectares of community territory. This scale of management is sufficiently large to talk about the management of forest ecosystems at a regional scale. The communities control significant watersheds and areas that sustain large areas of habitat for viable populations of trees, other plants, and fauna. Without a system of communal management, forest areas might well be fragmented among the 1,000 families that make up the four UZACHI communities. If the land area of UZACHI were to be evenly divided among the families, this would lead to 28-hectare properties, each one with its own plots of agricultural land and pasture. In such a situation, the chance of protecting habitats from fragmentation would be very low. However, under the common property system, there are forest areas that extend for more than 12 kilometers without interruption.

The experience of UZACHI shows that even small forest communities like Santiago Xiacuí, with an annual timber production of 2,000 cubic meters and sales on the order of US$120,000 a year, are able to rent road-building machinery and to purchase cranes, chainsaws, and trucks. If there were no organized forest management, each family would have to face the problem of paying for the cost of managing its 28-hectare property. Without community organization, it is quite easy to imagine properties being dedicated to the rearing and grazing of livestock, to orchards or agriculture, but forestry activities and the maintenance of wildlife conservation areas would be practically impossible.

The high level of community organization has meant that community land use planning activities have been relatively easy to carry out, and it has clearly established the objectives of forest management, with well-defined priorities (UZACHI 1993). UZACHI's principal strategic planning objectives include (1) ensuring the availability of firewood and wood for other domestic uses for community members; (2) ensuring the permanence of forest habitat in which processes of species diversification are maintained and ensuring a supply of genetic material for the maintenance of forest biodiversity; (3) maintaining indefinitely the production of forest timber from the forest production area and generating local employment; (4) maintaining indefinitely the production of processed wood in Oaxaca and generating regional employment; (5) advancing our knowledge of current commercial tree species and of non-timber forest product species that are of potential commercial importance; (6) preserving watersheds, in particular, the Río Valle Nacional and Rio Grande watersheds; (7) maintaining the scenic value of the most important recreational areas; and (8) increasing the level of forest production through the restoration of areas that previously were dedicated to nonforest use.

These objectives reflect the need to give top priority to the economic needs of families and communities as well as to forest and ecosystem service conservation. This is in line with UZACHI's principal mission, which is to make the forest a permanent source of benefit for its member communities. The objectives linked to sustainable production have also been given a high priority, which corresponds to the idea that the forests should serve as a strategic base within the regional economy. Finally, consideration is also given to the provision of regional and global environmental services, and their contribution to the economy and development of the state of Oaxaca.

The communities of the Sierra Norte have received significant support over the years from the state and federal governments, although there have also been periods of conflict and opposition. But UZACHI is unique in that it has had consistent long-term support from student advisors who later organized themselves into ERA and who are able to help arrange for external subsidies from foundations and other sources of support. If society has decided that it needs to maintain its forests, and if community forestry can preserve these forests, how can Mexican or global society finance the formation of the capital that is needed to do this, not only in the four communities of UZACHI, but in most of the 570 municipalities of Oaxaca and nationally? The promise and the challenge of UZACHI is that appropriate investments in human, social, and natural capital produce a stream of economic and environmental benefits for local communities and for the planet.

Note

1. GATT was the General Agreement on Tariffs and Trade, which became the World Trade Organization (WTO).

References

Alatorre Frenk, G. 2000. *La construcción de una cultura gerencial democrática en las empresas forestales comunitarias.* Mexico City: Casa Juan Pablos, Procuraduría Agraria.

Bray, D. 1991. The struggle for the forest: Conservation and development in the Sierra Juárez. *Grassroots Development* 15(3):13–25.

Castaños, L. J. 1999. Written interview. 6 June.

Castro, H. 1985. *La Jornada.* 8 October, p. 8.

Chapela, F. J., and Y. Lara. 1993. *Impacto de la política forestal sobre el valor de los bosques: El caso de la Sierra Norte de Oaxaca, México.* Oaxaca: Estudios Rurales y Asesoría Campesina—World Wildlife Fund Project; Impacto Ecológico y Económico de las Unidades de Administración Forestal en el Estado de Oaxaca.

Chapela, F. J., and Y. Massieu. 2001. Acceso a recursos genéticos y biopiratería en México. Paper presented at the third meeting of the Asociación Mexicana de Estudios Rurales. Zacatecas.

Consejo Nacional de Población. 1990. *Sistema atomatizado de información sobre la marginación en México.* Mexico City: Consejo Nacional de Población.

Daly, Herman E. 1993. The perils of free trade. *Scientific American* 269(5):50–57.

Díaz, U. 1985. *Uno más Uno.* 21 December, p. 5.

Escárpita, J., et al. 1994. *Inventario forestal de las secciones de ordenación III y IV.* Tuxtepec, Oaxaca: FAPATUX.

Kissling, I., U. Baruffol, S. Biber-Klemm, and L. Merino-Pérez. 2002. *The Contractual Regulation of Access to Biological Resources and Genetic Information: An Agreement between Mexican Communities and a Multinational Bio-Prospecting Concern.* Bern: Swiss Academy of Sciences.

Ley Forestal 1986. *México, diario oficial de la federación,* 30 May.

Ostrom, E., and T. K. Ahn. 2001. A social science perspective on social capital: Social capital and collective action. A report prepared for the Bundestag-Enquete Comission.

SAO. 2003. Resumen del proyecto de manejo integrado de recursos comunitarios para la captura de carbono. Unpublished manuscript. Oaxaca, Oaxaca.

SARH-SFF. 1980. *Programa nacional de desarrollo forestal por proyectos.* Mexico City: SARH-SFF.

UZACHI. 1993. Programa de manejo forestal persistente. Internal document. Capulalpam, Oaxaca.

CHAPTER 6

Empowering Community-Based Forestry in Oaxaca: The Union of Forest Communities and *Ejidos* of Oaxaca, 1985–1996

RODOLFO LÓPEZ-ARZOLA

In Oaxaca's recent history (1982–2002), indigenous forest communities have been able to combine a conservationist vision with increased efforts to take advantage of production opportunities offered by a globalized world.[1] The Unión de Comunidades y Ejidos Forestales de Oaxaca (UCEFO) was one of the pioneer organizations in Mexico and in Oaxaca in the effort to create a new form of forest organization for local communities. Their efforts placed Oaxaca in a global leadership position in community forestry and provided an early model for how local and indigenous communities could assume direct stewardship of their forest resources. Although UCEFO succumbed to internal and external tensions after 11 years of existence, it is important to remember its achievements and the lessons to be learned from both its rise and its fall.

The state of Oaxaca has a population of some 3 million and covers an area of 95,364 square kilometers, with a population density of 31.2 inhabitants per square kilometer. The most important forest management communities are found in the branches of the Sierra Madre known as the Sierra Norte (or Sierra Juárez) and the Sierra Sur. These two mountain ranges vary in altitude from 800 to 3,500 meters above sea level, and feature climates ranging from cold-temperate to temperate and warm subtropical. Annual precipitation is from 800 to 1,600 millimeters, depending on the altitude and geographical orientation. Topography is characterized by slopes with gradients greater than 30% (UCEFO/WRI 1991).

Oaxaca has 14 of the 54 ethnic groups found in Mexico, with 40% of the state's population speaking an indigenous language. Sixty-eight percent of the *ejidos* and indigenous communities are forest communities, laying the basis for the successful development of community forest enterprises

(CFEs) in the state. Oaxaca has the eighth largest forest area in Mexico, with 3 million hectares covering 31% of its total area. It has been estimated that the potential productive timber capacity of the state is 2 million cubic meters annually but, in contrast, timber production in 1990 was 400,000 cubic meters.

These forest riches attracted loggers to Oaxaca from a very early period. In 1948 the private logging company the Oaxaca Forest Company (Compañía Forestal de Oaxaca, or CFO) began logging in the Sierra Sur Zapotec community of San Pedro el Alto for the first time under a concession, building logging roads into San Pedro's forest, while the community had to build the access road to the community itself with picks and shovels. CFO began logging in the neighboring community of Santiago Textitlán in 1956 and in Santa María Zaniza in 1961, but it was not until 1964 that they received the formal concession for logging in the area. Various smaller logging companies began working in the 1970s in other communities in the region, such as San Andrés el Alto and San Antonino el Alto. In the Sierra Norte, the parastatal Tuxtepec Paper Factory (Fábricas de Papel Tuxtepec; FAPATUX), created to make the paper for Mexico's school textbooks, began logging in 1956 under a 25-year concession in Santa Catarina Ixtepeji, San Juan Atepec, Ixtlán de Juárez, and others, while the private company Timber Company of Oaxaca (Compañía Maderas de Oaxaca; CMO) logged in Pueblos Mancomunados from 1970 to 1976.

In exchange for the increasing flow of timber coming out of their communities, they received only a stumpage fee (*derecho de monte*) that was deposited in a government trust fund which they had difficulty getting access to, and only a very few jobs. This was because in the beginning most of the lumberjacks came from Michoacán, which had a longer history of logging. These years of exploitation of the communities' forests deeply affected the dignity and integrity of the communities, creating a system of corruption of community authorities through gifts and bribes that influenced decisions with reference to volume, cutting areas, length of contracts, and timber prices. Various government institutions were complicit in the corruption, such as the Secretaría de Reforma Agraria (SRA) and the Secretaría de Agricultura y Recursos Hidráulicos (SARH).

The failure to comply with community contracts that obligated companies to open up tracks and roadways, pay fair salaries, and build local schools, as well as abuses such as missing *derecho de monte* payments, led to a series of strikes and protests and to demands for increases in the stumpage fee and for fulfillment of the contracts (see also Chapela, this volume). In

1964, the communities of Recibimiento and Río Humo in Santiago Textitlán suspended logging and blocked the roads in protest over damage to the forest and illegal extraction, with women taking a leadership role in protecting the men when the army intervened on behalf of the logging companies. In 1967 in the Sierra Norte, 15 communities, led by San Pablo Macuiltianguis, refused to sign the logging contracts; they continued the work stoppage for six years before FAPATUX finally ceded to some of their demands. At this early stage, the demands still revolved around labor issues and stumpage fees rather than the goal of having their own CFE. However, this would not be far behind. In 1973 another production strike was launched in Santiago Textitlán that led to the complete suspension of logging, and by 1976 the community had begun to organize its CFE, later called Zapoteco Cárdenas because they received support from Cuauhtémoc Cárdenas when he was forestry subsecretary in the late 1970s. Other work stoppages took place in San Pedro el Alto in 1974 and in Santa María Zaniza in 1976. In 1976 Pueblos Mancomunados held logging equipment belonging to CMO hostage in protest of illegal logging and used this as the basis for launching the first autonomous CFE in Oaxaca in 1977, followed by Santiago Textitlán in 1977.

Pueblos Mancomunados, an alliance of neighboring communities with the same collective landholding, had more freedom because they had not been included in the FAPATUX concessions, which meant there was less political pressure on them. Santiago Textitlán, on the other hand, was under the CFO concession and, despite launching its own CFE, was forced to sell its timber exclusively to CFO at the price they set. After operating for two years (1978–80), they ceased operations in 1981 because of administrative problems which stemmed in large part from operating in a hostile environment without outside support. Conflicts also continued elsewhere, with yet another equipment capture by San Pedro el Alto in 1979, which led to the jailing of community authorities. A common complaint was that the communities did not know how much timber was being taken out. As a community member from Santiago Textitlán complained, "The community members only saw the logging trucks leaving loaded with timber, from 25 to 30 trucks a day."

The cumulative effect of these protests and work stoppages and the approach of the end of the concession period in the late 1970s and early 1980s led the companies to begin ceding more responsibilities in some areas to some communities, with more community members rising to greater positions of responsibility in the logging operations. In 1980, in the Sierra Norte, the Organization for the Defense of Natural Resources of the Sierra Juárez (Organización para la Defensa de los Recursos Naturales y el Desarrollo Social de la Sierra Juárez; ODRENASIJ) was formed to work against the renewal of the FAPATUX concession, scheduled to end in 1981.

In this troubled context, a group of government forestry extension agents from the General Office of Forest Development (Dirección General de Desarrollo Forestal; DGDF) in Mexico City arrived to begin working in Oaxaca in 1981. Since 1976, extension agents from the DGDF had been forming CFEs—then called Unidades de Producción de Materia Prima Forestal (UPMPF; Forest Raw Material Production Units)—and using a forest community organizing strategy they called socioproduction in Tlaxcala, Puebla, and Veracruz, with considerable success. At the national level, León Jorge Castaños led the DGDF, and in Oaxaca, I led the DGDF team. Oaxaca was the first time DGDF had entered an area where concessions were important. They first began working in 1982, with Pueblos Mancomunados, which had been struggling alone with its CFE since 1977. In the meantime, the parallel efforts of the DGDF team, ODRENASIJ, and its external advisors were challenged when the government announced in November 1982 in the official government newspaper the granting of new forest concessions to the parastatal and private companies in the Sierras Sur and Norte that would continue them for another 25 years. The communities responded by filing suit (*amparo*) against the government, and due to extensive public pressure and interest in the issue, government courts found in the communities' favor, officially ending the concession period in Oaxaca by 1983 and freeing the communities to begin developing their own CFEs.

The DGDF team moved quickly to take advantage of this new opening, and in 1983 established a new UPMPF in the former concession community of Santa Catarina Ixtepeji, followed quickly in the same year by San Miguel Aloapam, San Juan Bautista Atepec, and Nuevo Zoquiapam. By 1984 the establishment of UPMPFs, or CFEs, spread into the Sierra Sur in San Pedro el Alto, Santiago Textitlán, and in the Sierra Norte, La Trinidad, and San Miguel Cajonos.

In the period of transition from the concession period to the CFE period, there was an inevitable drop in timber production, and by 1984 production had dropped by 30%, creating new pressures from industry that the CFEs retake the levels of production that had been achieved in the concession period. This focused the attention of the DGDF team on exactly how to promote CFEs in the community and what form they should take.

The CFEs at the Heart of UCEFO

After the initial organizing work done by the DGDF team in 1982–1984, the next step of its work was the organization of UCEFO, S.C., which was formed on 30 December 1985 by the Zapotec communities of San Pedro el Alto and Santiago Textitlán from the Sierra Sur and Pueblos Mancomunados, Santa Catarina Ixtepeji, and San Miguel Aloapan from the Sierra Norte. They were later joined by the communities of San Andrés el Alto, San Antonino el Alto, Santa María Zaniza, Santiago Xochiltepec, and San Miguel Mixtepec. The creation of UCEFO was in response to the strategic vision that the DGDF team glimpsed when it first arrived in the Sierra de Juárez: the need to make community-based forest organizations a political force in the state. Although UCEFO was focused on forest management and logging as a strategic and necessary step at the time, the communities themselves continued with their strong agricultural traditions, including subsistence agriculture, small-scale livestock rearing, and fruit orchards, as well as carpentry and bakery shops. The total area covered by the communities of the UCEFO was 122,000 hectares, of which 88% was forested by conifers and broad-leaved species, 8% was under cultivation, and 3% devoted other uses. In 1988, the potential forest productivity of the UCEFO was considered to be 160,000 square meters, with the state's total production at around 400,000 square meters. But with all this potential, and after these important victories, now the hardest part began: how to lay the groundwork for a new culture of sustainable community development.

As we have seen, the first CFEs were actually established in the late 1970s, but they were isolated, struggling, and were not always able to continue operating. There were few models for how a community could operate a logging enterprise, but these first CFEs did not have a defined structure or clear plan on how the CFE should relate to traditional community governance structures. However, the DGDF promoters had their prior experiences in the promotion of UPMPFs as part of the then-current National Forest Development Program, as well as experience in rural organizing in Chiapas by some members of the team. The model developed by the DGDF had an enterprise-oriented vision with an emphasis on administration and accounting, as well as management schemes that were based on the social and collective traditions of the communities, as well as a training approach based on democratic, educational principles designed for the concrete situation in Oaxaca.

The challenge was how to graft a CFE onto the existing community

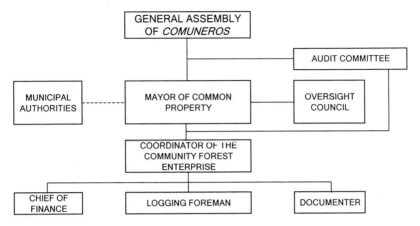

Figure 6.1 Structure of an indigenous community with CFE.

governing structures, since the UPMPF model had not developed in communities with such large timber volumes and in the context of the traditional *cargo* system in Oaxaca. Thus, the base for organization was the indigenous community structures or agrarian organization authorized by the SRA. This included the General Assembly as the main decision-making authority; the Comisariado de Bienes Comunales (Mayor of Common Property), who was traditionally in charge of all communal assets; and the Oversight Council (Consejo de Vigilancia). Under these levels of authority, there was a coordinator, a documenter, a logging foreman (*jefe de monte*), and a chief of finance. The last three would be with or without assistants, depending on the volume of timber (see Figure 6.1).

To these positions was also added another oversight body, the Community Audit Committee (Comisión Revisora), to deal with the specialized demands of the CFE on community governance. In addition, the Review Committee was incorporated into the community as part of the cargo system. Thus, traditional internal community mechanisms were used to elect the management team of the CFEs, which unfortunately also led to the selection of people who had fulfilled community service well rather than those with specialized knowledge of forest issues.

As a result of traditional community democratic practices, most important decisions with respect to the CFEs were made by the General Assembly of *comuneros*. These included decisions on salaries, staffing, and timber sales. However, in some cases the General Assembly mechanism did not guarantee participation for the majority of community members, as smaller groups within it dominated the assembly itself.

Forest Management

In the period when the DGDF team organized and advised the CFEs and UCEFO was formed, the communities still worked with the existing administrative structures for the provision of forest technical services, the so-called Forest Administration Units (Unidades de Administración Forestal; UAF), which by law were responsible for forest inventories and marking of trees to be logged each year, plague control, reforestation, and everything related to the protection and growth of the forest. The UAFs promoted the traditional silvicultural method in Mexico, the Mexican Method of Forest Management (Método Mexicano de Ordenación de Montes; MMOM) in Oaxaca's forests, which led to the forest becoming increasingly dominated by oaks. In written feedback to the DGDF team from the CFEs, there were frequent expressions of discontent that the only services the communities received from the UAFs were the marking of trees and the filling out of the forms at the end of the logging year, and that the foresters were never seen otherwise. The CFEs also expressed concern about what they perceived to be the high pay for foresters and their lack of attention to plagues and other problems that were affecting the forest. This lack of compliance became one of the main reasons for creating the UCEFO. Thus, the technical forestry aspects, along with other issues such as the laborious paperwork to get access to the stumpage fee deposits, were what later led the DGDF team to mobilize the communities to get their own concessions for the forest technical services, and take it out of the hands of the UAFs.

As a first step toward gaining greater control of the technical aspects of forestry and focusing on areas not attended to by the UAFs, in 1985 the first Plague Control Center run by the communities themselves was established in Santa Catarina Ixtepeji with the support of the DGDF team. Communities from the Sierra Norte and Sierra Sur participated in a training program on forest pest control for young men and women. However, the challenge to the traditional authority of the forest engineers in the UAFs was not taken lightly, and generated problems with official forestry agencies in the state.

The Workings of UCEFO

The first challenge that UCEFO had was to establish a legal status that would allow it autonomy in decision making. This would not have been possible under the legal forms offered by SRA and SARH, since these agencies would then have had considerable influence over the operations of the organization. Advisors such as Héctor Hernández and I suggested civil society legal registry, which would enable them to make decisions without interference from SRA or SARH on forest management or commercial and industrial issues. After much negotiation and pressure from SARH, in the middle of 1986 an agreement was reached which allowed UCEFO to conduct forest technical services in operative and administrative terms, but without full legal rights. Such rights were sanctioned by a new 1986 law, but did not go into effect until the regulations for the law were finally approved in 1989. Thus, in practice UCEFO was given the leeway to contract its own forestry professionals and technicians even before the law allowed it.

In 1987 the UCEFO commissioned Jonas Ortíz Avendaño, Manuel Jesús Góngora Turriza, and me, all original members of the DGDF team, to function as part of the staff of UCEFO, and we in turn contracted with a forestry engineer recommended by the DGDF to direct the forest technical services, since the law did not allow a campesino, despite rich experience in forest management, to perform this function.

The structure of UCEFO was modeled after the governance structures of the communities. The main form of authority was the Assembly of Representatives, made up of the communal authorities of the member communities, the coordinators of the CFEs, the Oversight Council, and the delegates elected by their communities to represent them before the union (see Figure 6.2). The Assembly of Representatives also elected the Executive Committee, composed of a president, a secretary, and a treasurer each year, with these positions rotating among the member communities.

There were two operative divisions: (1) the Forest Management Division, on which the CFEs depended for technical forestry support and studies as well as support for sawmills and other processing industries, and (2) the Support and Services Division, entrusted with the financial, commercial, administrative, and accounting training for the Executive Committee, the Review Committees of the CFEs, and the UCEFO delegates, as well as the estimation of production costs, the determination of salary scales, bookkeeping, and reports to the assembly. Training activities were constant because the one- to three-year rotation of the delegates and authorities, consistent with community practices, ensured that inexperienced people were constantly assuming leadership positions.

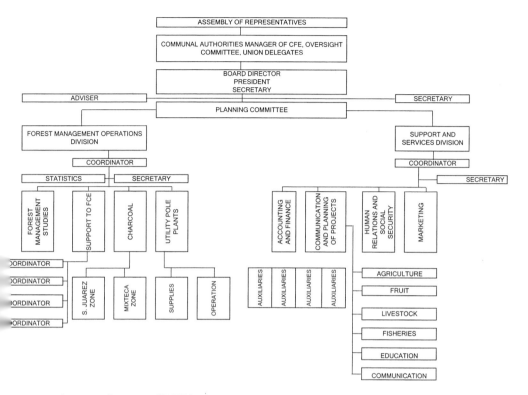

Figure 6.2 Structure of UCEFO.

Forest Technical Services and Its Central Role

The communities that formed UCEFO had little experience with reference to forest management decisions or how to run a CFE, since the concession system had given them few opportunities to learn. The Forest Law of 1960 had established the exclusivity of SARH's forest technical services through government concessions, as in the UAFs, with the stumpage fee payments administered by the SRA through the now defunct National Trust Fund for *Ejido* Development (Fideicomiso del Fondo Nacional de Fomento Ejidal; FIFONAFE), whose funds could only be accessed by the communities by submitting proposals for its use. Likewise, the SRA had to approve all timber contracts made by the CFEs. This all began to change once UCEFO was established. For example, as mentioned earlier, the administration of the forest technical services (FTS) now came under the practical control of UCEFO, with the fee for FTS now being paid directly by UCEFO on the basis of the authorized volume of timber extracted per year. UCEFO also took quick steps to improve forest management. The first integrated forest management study, which introduced the Método de Desarrollo Silvicultura (MDS; Method of Silvicultural Development) to southern Mexico, was carried out in 1987, with Finnish support, in San Pedro el Alto. MDS was a more flexible silvicultural system than MMOM that by opening larger spaces in the forest assured a regeneration of pine. The study also served to strengthen forest management by establishing soil and riparian zone protection areas. The study was carried out over a period of three years and involved the training of 10 community technicians.

The first community forestry technicians were trained in this way. In partnership with the forest technical director and contracted forest specialists, they made up UCEFO's technical team. This team was in charge of carrying out integrated management studies, planning the construction and maintenance of roads, applying silvicultural treatments, monitoring cutting sites, planning protection and restoration programs, and issuing regulatory forest documentation. The responsible person to SARH continued to be the forest technical director.

However, even after 17 years, it is questionable whether genuine community silviculture really exists except in a few cases, such as La Trinidad. It is in these few communities that more than 50% of the adult population and their children have access to information, field data, and theory regarding forestry activities. The majority of communities lack such information even when they have forestry engineers and technical staff. There should be a permanent and well-established training program as part of each community's development strategy.

UCEFO, as the first major forest management organization in Oaxaca and one of the most important in Mexico, was always beset by internal and external tensions that would eventually result in its dissolution, although its legal shell still exists. Some of the external tensions included the following:

- Discomfort on the part of the established forest engineer interests with the increased autonomy of UCEFO in forest management
- Hostility of the economic actors in the Oaxaca forest sector that were threatened by UCEFO
- Fear among the established forest interests that the UCEFO model could spread to other forest communities, further affecting their economic interests

In 1989, in order to stop the spread of the UCEFO model of forest community autonomy, the SRA and the National Campesino Federation (Confederación Nacional Campesina; CNC) began promoting multiple *ejido* unions and a statewide confederation called the Rural Collective Interest Association (Asociación Rural de Interés Colectivo; ARIC), using World Bank and Inter-American Development Bank funds, in order to co-opt the emergence of more independent associations. However, since these government-created organizations did not benefit from the kind of careful and patient organizing work that gave birth to UCEFO, almost all of them were very short-lived. The only exception was the Ixtlán-Etla Community Union (IXETO), which has survived to this day.

Some of the internal tensions included the following:

- Too much power within the CFEs of forest technical services, which made all decisions with respect to the forest. This was a reproduction of the UAF scheme inside UCEFO. The forest technical director did not understand, or want to understand, the difference between being part of a community organization and being in the service of a company or government institution.
- Constant proposals by the Support and Services Division to increase the participation of community members in decision-making and to ensure that CFE staff were well trained in administrative and accounting skills, and that community authorities were encouraged to diversify production activities in agriculture and integrated development.

Unfortunately, from my point of view, many community leaders supported the forest technical director in the diversification debate, since the forest was considered a community concern, but agriculture, educational, and training issues were considered individual matters. This support was also strengthened by a traditional respect for legal authority figures such as the forest technical director. Because of the significant economic resources that flowed from the forest management activities, there was little interest on the part of the communities in changing existing policies.

The Support and Services Division, which I headed, urged broader discussion and actions regarding the needs of the communities, and a more integrated vision of development, one not just confined to forestry. With this in mind, the division developed the first initiative in carbon sequestration in Mexico in association with a North American energy company. Unfortunately, the idea was not carried through because the international context was still not favorable to such projects and because of the internal tensions between the forest technical director's office and the Support and Services Division.

In this dispute, UCEFO finally opted to focus only on forest management issues, in opposition to the proposal to facilitate greater participation of the population in general over the operation and control of UCEFO. As a result, the Support and Services Division was limited in its actions, its functions were easily obstructed, and it slowly distanced itself from some of the communities. This situation was exacerbated by the fact that the division was outside the economic structure of UCEFO and did not receive a direct income, as did forest technical services. Faced with this situation, the Support and Services Division, which had been the founding team of UCEFO, resigned, noting the difficulties in continuing their work due to the opposition of the forest technical director and the Executive Committee of UCEFO. The staff of the Support and Services Division made known its interest in continuing to work independently on its vision with some of the member communities of UCEFO such as San Pedro el Alto, San Andrés el Alto, San Miguel Mixtepec, and San Antonino el Alto. This technical team would continue its work with forest community enterprises and alternative development strategies as the nongovernment organization Technical Assistance to Oaxacan Communities (Asistencia Técnica para las Comunidades Oaxaqueñas; ASETECO, A.C.).

In subsequent years more communities left UCEFO and it was decided to divide up the assets, such as vehicles and other equipment, and lay off most of the staff. All that was left was a small forest technical services staff providing services to a few communities.

Conclusions and Lessons Learned

The guiding concept that enabled the formation of UCEFO as an independent and self-managed organization was the transfer of knowledge, not only in forest management, but also in administration, accounting, and finance. This transfer of knowledge destroyed the myth that only those who had formal academic study could learn these disciplines. The Support and Services Division eschewed the teacher-student relationship, supporting the process of learning by doing. This meant that traditional training courses were substituted with practical learning. The establishment of the Social Audit Committees in both the CFEs and in UCEFO was an example of this practice, as was the elaboration of the regulations of the CFEs. This conception of advising and training required great flexibility and consciousness-raising, as well as the development through time of specialized pedagogical and communications materials.

With these principles and actions, an effort was made to promote a model of integrated development, carrying out studies and diagnoses on other economic activities in the communities, launching projects that encouraged the financial flows from the CFEs to go toward the entire population, including women, children, and senior citizens, through programs that benefited them. The capitalization that the CFEs generated in the communities required planned and participatory investments that were at least partially achieved at times through intense consciousness-raising efforts in the community General Assemblies and the leadership of the CFEs and UCEFO, who sought to promote more integrated and equitable development.

Although UCEFO finally collapsed as an organization, it achieved many important industrial and political goals. These included the following:

- Being the first forest community union in Oaxaca and one of the first truly autonomous ones in the country
- Being the first community forest organization in the country to use the legal organizational category of the Civil Society, which allowed for independence from SRA and other federal and state government agencies
- Being the model for many of the elements in the 1986 Forest Law, which formally ended the concession period and allowed communities to directly administer their own FTS
- Being the first community forest organization in the country that obtained the concession of FTS
- Carrying out the first study of integrated silvicultural management in the state and in the country, which introduced MDS to Oaxaca (it is also significant that the study was carried out with trained community forest technicians)
- Winning the National Forest Merit Award in 1986 (in later years, the same award was given individually to the communities of San Pedro el Alto, San Miguel Mixtepec, Santa Catarina Ixtepeji, and Pueblos Mancomunados, all former members of UCEFO)

However, despite these achievements, the historical impact in more recent years is less certain. Since 1985, it is not possible to see, in my view, substantial changes in some forest communities with reference to community silviculture and the real appropriation of the forest by the communities. In addition, although there have been clear improvements in community infrastructure, it is less clear that there have been improvements in the quality of life of families and communities. A symptom of a lack of vision among some of the leaders in the communities and UCEFO is the absence of industrial development other than sawmills and drying ovens over the last 20 years. Nonetheless, UCEFO was an important pioneer in Oaxaca and nationally, and served as an inspiration for many other efforts throughout Mexico. It is important that its achievements be remembered, but also that we learn from its failures. UCEFO achieved much in forest management, but it failed to take full advantage of these accomplishments to use the CFEs as an engine to drive more diversified community development.

Note

1. This article draws on personal archives of the author and an extensive study of the historical development of UCEFO (ASETECO 2002).

References

ASETECO. 2002. *Una caminata de 20 años en los bosques comunales de Oaxaca: Historia del acompañamiento de un asociación civil (ASETECO) a las comunidades indígenas con recursos forestales del estado de Oaxaca, México.* Oaxaca: ASETECO.
UCEFO/WRI. 1991. *La organización comunal indígena como alternativa en la protección, fomento, y aprovechamiento forestal de los bosques en Oaxaca, México: El caso de la unión de comunidades y ejidos forestales del estado de Oaxaca, S.C.* Oaxaca: UCEFO/WRI.

CHAPTER 7

New Organizational Strategies in Community Forestry in Durango, Mexico

PETER LEIGH TAYLOR

Neoliberal organizing principles of globalization today are overtaking modernist evolutionary paradigms of development. Nation-states now seek first to position themselves in the global economy rather than maximize national welfare (McMichael 1996:26). Trade liberalization policies worldwide promote a model of economic growth in which markets allocate resources via individual actors making rational decisions about privately owned resources. Given the pervasiveness of this powerful neoliberal vision of growth propelled by individual economic rationality, concern expressed for the future social and ecological sustainability of collectively owned and managed natural resources (Ostrom and Schlager 1996) is well justified. This paper discusses indirect impacts of globalization and its underlying neoliberal policies on community forestry in the Mexican state of Durango. Community forestry is a common property management regime, which pursues sustainability by linking the social and economic interests of local people with forest conservation (Fortmann and Bruce 1988; Peluso 1992; Richards 1997). In Mexico in general and in Durango in particular, community forestry has been a significant feature of forest management.

Global market and neoliberal policy pressures on the social institutions of community forestry are particularly visible in Mexico, where the 1910 Revolution set into motion over 70 years of land redistribution and significant collectivization of rural resource tenure. Nearly two decades of economic restructuring, including entry into the GATT in 1986 and NAFTA in 1994, as well as profound changes in rural land tenure regimes, have transformed the framework of agrarian production (Beaucage 1997; Cornelius and Myhre 1998; Gómez Cruz and Schwentesius

1997). Campesino (peasant) timber producers today struggle to develop new strategies to survive in an increasingly competitive global market. Nevertheless, it would be a mistake to view Mexico's community-based timber producers as passive objects of structural forces. Mexican agrarian change is shaped not only by external structural pressures such as neoliberal policy reform, but by adaptation, resistance, and appropriation by rural producers defending and pursuing their interests (see, e.g., Cockcroft 1998). As social agents, campcsino producers are making and remaking the social institutions that underlie their common pool resource management regimes.

This paper explores community-based forestry in the northern state of Durango and focuses on new forms of social organization pursued by timber peasants in the face of structural change. In the first instance, peasants are taking advantage of post-1992 changes in Mexican agrarian law to establish smaller organizational units to work with the communal forest ιesource as alternatives to collectively organized forestry. In the second instance, campesino producers are developing new forestry-sector alliances with industry and state agencies to pursue timber certification in an effort not only to improve their competitiveness in timber markets but also to revitalize local economies. Below, I discuss strengths of both organizational forms and strategies and identify some of their current and potential problems. I suggest that these and similar innovations in the social institutions of community forestry be evaluated with reference to one of community-based forestry's basic principles of sustainable management: that is, whether they promote viable communities of producers who benefit from the forest resources and have a collective stake in sustainable resource management, or whether they bypass such stakeholder communities in favor of individual beneficiaries.

Collective Governance, Privatization, and Forest Policy in Mexico

Mexican forestry is in many ways an exemplar of a common property resource management regime. Because of Mexico's postrevolutionary land tenure system, some 80% of forests are held in common by two types of collective property communities: *ejidos* and agrarian communities (see Chapter 1).[1] Up to 40% of timber production has been carried out by the organized community forestry sector (Bray 1997).

The policy vacillations represented by the forest laws of 1986 and 1992 are discussed in Chapter 3. Here, it can be noted that major neoliberalism-inspired constitutional and legal reforms in 1992 moved decidedly away from the collective ownership traditions from which community forestry emerged, and toward privatization, which privileged the individual economic actor. Article 27 of the 1917 Mexican Constitution was modified in 1992 to effectively end the revolutionary project of land redistribution. Affecting more than 28,000 agrarian reform communities, nearly half of Mexico's grazing, agricultural, and forestland, and 3 million campesinos and their dependents, the new reforms set into motion the privatization of Mexico's collectivized agrarian sector (DeWalt et al. 1994:4).[2] A new agency, PROCEDE (Programa de Certificación de Derechos Ejidales y Titulación de Solares, or Certification Program for *Ejido* Parcels and for Titling of Urban Plots), was established to map *ejidos* and certify individual parcels, which could then be legally sold, rented, sharecropped, or mortgaged. *Ejidatarios* were no longer required to personally work their parcels to maintain their ties to the land. New economic associations among *ejidatarios* and with outside investors were authorized. New provisions allowed parcels to be concentrated, within legal limits, for more economical exploitation (Cornelius and Myhre 1998:1–3).

Critics of the post-1992 reforms feared that a privatized rural sector would experience a concentration of property reminiscent of prerevolution *latifundias* (large estates) (Bartra 1991b). Nevertheless, a growing literature on the new agrarian reform suggests that neither the hopes of neoliberal policy architects nor the fears of their critics have been fully realized (Gordillo et al. 1998). With the possible exception of *ejidos* in densely urbanized or tourism areas, land sales and concentration have been slow to emerge (Cornelius and Myhre 1998). Perhaps more significantly, researchers have found that *ejidatarios* have not rushed to privatize, as policy makers expected but have instead tended to appropriate the PROCEDE program critically according to locally specific conditions (Cornelius and Myhre 1998). As will be seen below, campesino forest producers in Durango have similarly appropriated the new agrarian reforms in strategic fashion.

Early critics of the new agrarian reform feared that changes first introduced into *ejido* law would eventually be applied to agrarian communities and even forests. Bartra wrote in 1991 that

> the same arguments with which one attempts to justify the "liberation" of parcelized *ejido* lands (that in practice they are already sold and rented and that full property rights will encourage the investment of capital) can be applied to indigenous communities, to *ejido* forests and pastures

and even the lands of population centers. If today these arguments are accepted as valid, then nothing will prevent their extension tomorrow, in an act of congruency, to all "imperfect" property. (1991a:26–27)

Today, forested *ejidos* and agrarian communities are commonly understood to be unaffected by the post-1992 privatization. First, because of their status as a national heritage, all forests and rainforests (including those belonging to *ejidos* and agrarian communities) are exempted by Articles 29 and 59 of the new agrarian law (López Nogales and López Nogales 1999). Moreover, because of their distinct origin, all agrarian communities are exempt regardless of whether they have forests (Chávez Padrón 1999). Nevertheless, though the formal privatization of indigenous and forested communities and *ejidos* has not occurred as once feared, the new agrarian reform has profoundly affected Mexico's forested *ejidos* and agrarian communities.

First, neoliberal policies since 1992 have rewritten the rules of forestry production along free market lines. The 1992 Forestry Law definitively moved away from the 1986 Forestry Law's commitment to community-based forestry (Chapela 1997:47). It aimed to eliminate "excessive" state intervention in the forestry sector, promoting private investment and free markets for products and services (Wexler and Bray 1996:243). The new law reduced the 1986 law's extensive paper trail of extracted timber to a harvest permit and the authorization stamped on authorized trees. The system of regional forestry technical service providers was eliminated and turned over to the market, where communities were free to negotiate service contracts with any certified forestry engineer (Cabarle et al. 1997:28; Snook 1997:30).

The post-1992 legal framework made no mention of the organized community forestry sector (Bray 1997:13; SEMARNAP 1997). The turning over of forestry technical services to the open market promoted a decline in their quality because competing service providers lowered costs by reducing services related to the logging permit. The new system also triggered the disintegration of some secondary peasant organizations, which had focused heavily on the provision of technical services to members (Merino-Pérez and Alatorre 1997; Merino-Pérez and Madrid 1997; Taylor and Zabin 2000; Zabin 1998). Deregulation of timber transport contributed to a significant increase in illegal felling and contraband activities (personal interviews in Durango, 1999; also see Taylor and Zabin 2000). In 1997 and 1999, a new forestry law and its forestry regulation established new procedures for tracking legally cut timber, including the reintroduction of obligatory documentation for transport of timber aimed at combating clandestine harvesting. Moreover, interviewees in 2001 and 2002 observed that Durango now has more effective monitoring and enforcement by federal and state authorities in organized collaboration with owners and their representatives.

Second, though the modification of Article 27 is often invoked as the principal explanation for changes in rural land tenure and resource organization, the new agrarian law has more direct significance for resource management in forest *ejidos* and agrarian communities today. The new law includes several key ambiguities that open up space for experimentation with new forms of local organization. For example, Article 23 recognizes the autonomy of the internal life of *ejidos* or agrarian communities,[3] empowering their assemblies to define who is and is not a member. Assemblies may develop internal regulations to govern the acceptance of new members or the expulsion of existing ones. On the other hand, Articles 14, 17, and 18 protect the rights of individual *ejidatarios* or *comuneros* to use and dispose of their shares of collective resources as they wish. These individual rights can be lost, according to Article 20, but unlike the previous law, the new one does not specify what may cause an individual *ejido* to lose its communal rights (López Nogales and López Nogales 1999:72).

Regarding collectively held natural resources, Articles 73 and 74 prohibit division of communal lands important to the community's sustenance. Additionally, the prohibition against dividing forests and rainforests promotes keeping the natural resources of forest *ejidos* and agrarian communities under collective control. Yet other articles of the new law now promote less collective forms of resource management. Prior to 1992, for example, any activity employing communal resources had to be open to all *ejidatarios* and *comuneros* and administered directly by the village authorities. Article 75 now states that *ejido* common lands can be exploited by joint ventures among subgroups of *ejidatarios* and outside business entities. Article 105 expressly empowers agrarian communities to divide into internal groups to work with common pool resources (López Nogales and López Nogales 1999:241).

The new law is unclear on how exactly these new internal groups are to possess and control resources, of particular import in forest *ejidos* and agrarian communities, where forests cannot be physically subdivided. For example, are volumes of timber or harvest area to be divided for harvest and sale by each internal group? How are management decisions about the forest holding as a whole to be handled if new organizational units are created within the community? According to some commentators (López

Nogales and López Nogales 1999:86), the liberal spirit of the new law suggests that the *ejido* or community should settle such ambiguous issues using their internal regulations. Unfortunately, many *ejidos* and communities have not developed internal regulations adequate to the new legal regime.

The new law's lack of clarity regarding individual versus collective control over natural resource use offers space for local experimentation. This ambiguity does not necessarily reflect poorly conceived law, but rather may mirror the complexity of Mexican rural realities. Indeed, legal scholar James Boyd White (1984) has argued that law represents less a set of clearcut rules than a framework for argument. Ambiguity can be an important characteristic of effective law because it establishes a ground upon which parties may argue their cases, developing interpretations adequate to a particular context. According to forestry technical staff and representatives of the agrarian solicitor interviewed in 1999, many of the practical details of the implementation of the new agrarian law are being decided by policy makers in response to questions and experimentation by the peasants themselves. As will be seen below, in Durango, producers are exploiting the agrarian reform's ambiguities to experiment with organizational forms that deal not only with forestry, but also with broader social and political problems.

Forestry in Durango

Durango is Mexico's most important timber-producing state, with about 10% of the nation's forests (SEMARNAT 2001) and nearly 29% of national timber production in 1991, mostly pine and oak (INEGI 1994:37). Durango has about 15% of the nation's inventory of commercially exploitable timber, with 422 million cubic meters. In 2000, the state produced about 1.6 million cubic meters (in log form) of pine and 125,000 cubic meters in oak (Gobierno del Estado de Durango 2001). In 1998, the primary sector (including agricultural and animal husbandry, forestry, and fishing) contributed 16% of the state's economic production. Together, the timber and wood products industry represented about 21% of the state's industrial manufacturing (INEGI 2000:239, 243).

Durango has a total population of about 1.4 million inhabitants, with about 40% living in rural areas (Gobierno del Estado de Durango 2001). In 1995, *ejidos* represented about 48% of the state's territory. Agrarian communities represented 22% and private property accounted for 25%

Table 7.1. Timber and wood industry in Durango's urban areas, 1993–1998

	Economic units		Jobs	
	1993	*1998*	*1993*	*1998*
Sawmills	233	235	9,668	7,514
Wood packaging and others	169	242	1,868	3,769
Wood furniture	367	469	2,180	3,604
All timber and wood industry	769	946	13,716	14,887
All industry in Durango	3,940	4,720	47,723	71,519

Source: INEGI 2000:325.

(INEGI and Gobierno del Estado de Durango 1996:31). Although Durango is one of the potentially richest states in natural resources, in 1991 it was below the national average in about half of 21 standard-of-living indicators (UNECOFAEZ 1992). Not surprisingly, deforestation driven by poverty, as forests are cleared for subsistence agricultural use, has been a serious problem (UNECOFAEZ 1992:59).

With Mexico's entry into NAFTA in 1994, the prospect of elimination of tariffs awoke fears that the forestry sector would be flooded with cheap foreign timber. In reality, imports decreased during the early years of NAFTA because of the economic crisis in 1993 and the gradual devaluation of the peso, which made the price of Mexican timber competitive (Zabin 1998). Nevertheless, structurally the Mexican forestry sector does not enjoy a competitive position. Mexican forests have been 3.5 times less productive than those of the United States and 2.3 times less productive than those of Canada (Téllez Kuenzler 1994:266). With the exception of its modern cellulose sector, most timber firms in Mexico are small scale, lacking up-to-date technology and insufficiently dedicated to value-added activities (World Bank 1995:17, 18).

Durango's timber industry firms had an average size of 16 employees in 1998 (see Table 7.1). This is similar to the rest of Durango's industrial manufacturing firms, which had in 1998 an average size of 15 employees, with 79% having fewer than 6 employees (INEGI 2000:326). Durango's forest-related industry, as indicated in Table 7.2, is concentrated in relatively low value-added productive activities. Lumber (*escuadria*) production represents nearly 88% of total forest industry in Durango, with the cellulose and veneer and plywood production accounting for only 7% of total industrial production.

Table 7.2. Forest industry production in Durango, 2000

Product	Volume (m³)[a]
Lumber	1,554,950
Cellulose	126,112
Veneer and plywood	4,450
Posts and piles	46,605
Domestic firewood	41,530
Charcoal	1,162
Railway ties	1,656
Total	**1,776,465**

Source: Gobierno del Estado de Durango 2001.
[a] Logwood.

In general, the timber industry of Durango suffers from an over-capacity of sawmills and insufficient value-added processing. Production plants have in the past been largely oriented toward primary processing and suffer from chronic raw material shortages (Chapela 1991:141). According to interviews with Durango-based technical foresters, as large-diameter trees have become scarce in recent years and as more accurate inventories are completed, government-authorized harvests have been reduced. Yet many sawmills employ technology appropriate for logs with larger diameters than those available today, making much of the current infrastructure of Durango's timber industry uncompetitive. The crisis of supply of many sawmills in Durango has encouraged illegal felling as many small firms struggle to survive.

In interviews in 2001, officials in the State Forestry Department and researchers at the University of Durango spoke of a new crisis of competition in the last two years precipitated by the entry of Chilean plantation-grown pine. Although of lesser quality, Chilean wood was reportedly cheaper in the City of Durango than wood from the state's own forests. Current statistics were not yet available at the time of fieldwork, but interviewees concurred in observing that because of international competition, the decrease in inventories of large-diameter wood, and the obsolescence of much of the industry's technology, many small firms and some large firms in Durango's forestry sector have been disappearing. The closure of sawmills and other processing plants represents the loss of many jobs, not only in Durango's cities, but also in rural *ejidos* and agrarian communities. One local historian observed that the resulting economic crisis is encouraging a dramatic increase in migration to the state's cities, to other cities elsewhere in Mexico, and abroad.

Producers' Responses to Structural Change: Work Groups and Certification

Forestry Work Groups

A new form of community-based forestry organization has emerged in recent years within the forest communities of northwestern Durango, commonly known as work groups (*grupos de trabajo*) (Taylor 2000, 2001, 2003; also see Armijo Canto 1999 on work groups in Quintana Roo). Made possible both directly and indirectly by the above-discussed changes in the Constitution and its related agrarian law, the forestry work groups in some ways appear to embrace neoliberal principles. The groups aim to enhance producers' participation in forestry and improve its efficiency. The groups nevertheless may in some cases undermine a community's political unity and fragment forest management. At the same time, the forestry work groups often appropriate external structural change for objectives internal to the community, as they take on political and cultural attributes beyond what neoliberal reformers intended. The groups suggest that the situation of forestry communities is not being completely determined by larger structural forces, but is shaped by local action, in local context.

Since the 1992 reform, forestry work groups have appeared in numerous *ejidos* and agrarian communities in Durango. The following discussion is based on fieldwork between 1996 and 1999 in two agrarian communities with work groups, Canelas and Santa Marta (Taylor 2001, 2003).[4] Interviewees were unanimous in characterizing the use of groups in timber production as a post-1992 phenomenon.[5] The work groups are, nonetheless, not entirely the top-down product of neoliberal reform. They also emerge from peasants' frustration with long-standing problems of inefficiency and corruption in forestry organized collectively at the *ejido* or community level. The work groups, organized on a smaller scale within the *ejido* or community, provide instruments to *ejidatarios* and *comuneros* for dealing with internal social and political conflicts.

Below, I briefly discuss how in Canelas and Santa Marta, local struggles over how to manage collective natural resources emerged from struggles over community identity and who should benefit from communal natural resources, what Zendejas and Mummert describe as "the construction and redefinition of boundaries between 'us' and 'them', between 'those of us who have rights over this kind of land' and 'those who do not' " (1998:197). I then discuss some of the technical and political impacts of the groups in both communities and explore some of the work groups' implications for the relationship between forestry and community development.

WORK GROUPS AND CONTESTED COMMUNITY IDENTITY

Both Canelas and Santa Marta are relatively large, each with over 600 *comuneros* and with 74,000 and 20,000 cubic meters of annual pine and oak timber harvest, respectively. As mentioned above, most agrarian communities in Durango are not indigenous, but mestizo. Both Canelas and Santa Marta were originally formed in the early 1970s from land held by large private owners seeking to protect their property from federal expropriation for distribution as *ejidos* and to gain access to significant fiscal benefits. In Canelas, for example, the original owners converted their private property holdings into agrarian communities by organizing relatives, friends, employees, and "clients" to join in petitioning the government for agrarian community status. As one forester put it, "they simulated a community and protected their property." In both cases, the conversion to a common property agrarian community created intractable problems. The original establishment of Canelas joined together eight settlements that had actually been seeking to become individual agrarian communities. Santa Marta's membership rolls at the outset were supplemented by federal authorities with outsiders unrelated to the original applicants in order to obtain the required number of participants.

The problematic conversion to agrarian communities has been vastly complicated by the contemporary migration of half or more of both communities' original members. In Canelas, most migrants are considered to have abandoned *comunero* status. "They left and were not going to come back. . . . And now that there is timber money, they appear again, demanding a share," complained one *comunero*. Similarly, more than half of Santa Marta's titled *comuneros* live outside of the community. Most residents who were born in the community and helped care for the forest had until recently no legal right to share in timber returns. Long-standing conflicts between nonresident titled *comuneros* and resident non-*comuneros* without resource rights erupted into violence in the 1980s and halted timber harvesting for several years.

The reorganization in the 1990s into smaller units has given both communities opportunities to address long-standing struggles over community membership and access to common property resources. In its version of "work groups," Canelas divided into 8 "annexes" representing the original settlements, which later were further divided into 11 annexes. Common property physical assets were divided among the annexes. "All we have in common now is the *directiva* [legal agrarian community administrative council]," explained one *comunero*. Each annex has its own salaried representative who meets periodically with other annex representatives and the *comisariado* (agrarian community council president), whose participation is still required by law. In Santa Marta, inspired by the suggestion of an agrarian solicitor representative in 1992, four work groups were formed, two "below" groups that represented migrated *comuneros* (living in Durango City and other urban areas) and two "above" groups that represented non-*comunero* residents (living in mountainous Santa Marta).

Beyond forestry, the restructuring of timber production in Canelas and Santa Marta involves redefining who remains an active member participating in timber extraction and its benefits and who does not. In Canelas's annex system, many forests have been informally parcelized, each with an individual *posesionario* (possessor). This form of organization goes beyond work groups into individualized production, though some communal management practices remain in place. Some annexes have begun mapping these parcels, and at least one annex has fenced its *posesionarios'* parcels, despite the legal prohibition against physically dividing the forest. PROCEDE has also been invited to map annexes' lands.[6] Canelas's annexes serve as vehicles for purging inactive members, who are generally not as well organized as in Santa Marta. *Comuneros* expect the PROCEDE process to bring residents greater tenure security, discourage migrated *comuneros* from claiming timber benefits, and even help purge their rolls of inactive migrated community members. Eventually, many *comuneros* want their individual annexes to become legally independent agrarian communities;[7] some hope for an eventual conversion to private property.

The work groups in Santa Marta have evolved in similar fashion into political instruments for viable and arguably more democratic community administration. Part of the compromise that led to the creation of the groups involved granting formal legal status to most adult residents of the community. Important assembly decisions are now controlled by "below" representatives who wield the numerical power of proxy votes from more distant but well-organized members. Nonetheless, *comuneros* of the "above" groups exercise practical veto power over many decisions through their control of physical access to the community and its forests.

WORK GROUPS' IMPLICATIONS FOR RESOURCE GOVERNANCE

Canelas's annex-organized forestry has individualized timber activities to a degree unusual among other forest agrarian communities and *ejidos* in Durango. Virtually all of the land has individual possessors. Each possessor (often referred to internally as a *dueño*, or owner) coordinates with contracted forest technicians to mark trees on "their" parcels for harvest and coordinates with annex representatives to find buyers for the timber. The annual cut may involve several individual possessors and buyers. One annex representative asserted that "Canelas works because it's managed as if it were private property."

Canelas's forests are still governed according to a single management plan developed by the local forest technical services bureau and approved by SEMARNAT, the environmental ministry. Treating the forest as a single ecological unit allows technical staff to deal effectively with fire prevention, timber health, natural regeneration, and other aspects of forest management. Nevertheless, technical staff also observed that when each parcel is exploited individually, greater pressure exists toward overexploitation. Individual possessors sometimes pressure foresters to mark more trees since trees will not be harvested again from "their" land for 15 years or more. One technical person argued that "in Canelas, most people are now thinking only in terms of their immediate benefits. I see a pine. I cut a pine. I sell a pine."

In Santa Marta, the forest had never been subdivided, even informally. The groups negotiate each year a division of timber *volumes* rather than forested land areas. Group chiefs, chosen for three-year terms, work with contracted technical staff to mark trees for harvest, negotiate buying agreements on behalf of their groups, and attend when the *comisariado* signs contracts. Group chiefs also receive timber profits directly and are responsible for distributing them to group participants.

Santa Marta's forests are also managed as a single unit, with a single harvest permit. Its technical services director stated that his technicians work willingly with groups authorized by the assembly. However, staff end up making multiple trips to coordinate with group leaders and to negotiate harvest procedures—an expensive and potentially conflictual process. "It would be better to work as a united community, but the groups were the only way we could agree to work the forest," said one *comunero*. Despite their internal conflicts, according to technical staff, the community as a whole supports the sustainable harvest of their resource.

Though both Canelas and Santa Marta had sawmills and other extraction and processing equipment, after restructuring into smaller organizational units, their secondary industries were abandoned and sold. The annexes and groups now sell their trees standing in the forest, a situation that allows outsiders to appropriate most of the value-added.

WORK GROUPS AND FINANCING COMMUNITY DEVELOPMENT

A central tenet of community forestry has been that ecological sustainability can best be promoted by explicitly linking the social and economic interests of forest dwellers with conservation (Peluso 1992). As one Mexican rural activist put it in an interview, "We can't talk about forest conservation in Mexico without talking about poverty." Because Canelas's annexes and Santa Marta's work groups affect the relationship between timber production and community development, they reshape the stakes *comuneros* have in the timber, both as individuals and as a collective.

Mexico's 1992 agrarian reform eliminated the legal requirement that at least 20% of profits from communally owned resources be reinvested in an *ejido* or agrarian community's social fund. Thus, each of Canelas's annexes now decides how to dispose of forest-related benefits. In one annex, 50% of timber profits are destined to social works, administrative costs, or outright distribution to all titled *comuneros*. In another annex, by contrast, the individual possessors whose "parcels" are being harvested retain 90% of timber profits. Ten percent is held back for the representative's expenses; social expenditures each year are negotiated ad hoc from possessors' 90%. Several interviewees observed that individual possessors often oppose costly communal projects during their year of harvest because of community "taxes" on their timber returns.

In Santa Marta, by contrast, interviewed *comuneros* consistently reiterated their assumption that the forest is still considered a communal resource. Timber benefits accrue to the community as a whole, to be divided among the four groups. Sixty percent of profits go to the "below" groups because of their greater numbers and 40% to the "above" groups. Each group, including those "below," pays a quota for the community's social and administrative expenditures. One "below" group member explained: "We want them to prosper up there. They are the ones who live there, take care of the forest, fight fires. We don't."

In Santa Marta, timber profits have been used recently to install a 7-kilometer-long potable water system. Both "below" groups invested 10% of their share that year to help pay for the project. All four groups collaborated equally to purchase land and build and fence a school in the community. Most recently, the four groups planned an ambitious electrification project using funds provided by a mining company in exchange for opening a breach in Santa Marta's forest.

Relative to Santa Marta, Canelas has less possibility for future development as an overall community. First, it no longer really functions as an aggregate unit. Each annex is responsible for its own development, and the more timber-wealthy annexes are reluctant to subsidize the poorer ones. Within many individual annexes, development projects are based largely on the economic investment strategies of individual *comuneros.* For example, one *comunero* used his social connections and profits from his timber to establish a box factory in a nearby town. Whether this individual control of most of such annexes' timber profits generates lasting benefits for the annex as a whole is not clear.

Both agrarian communities have formed smaller organized units below the level of the community as a whole. Both continue to manage their forests with a single management plan. Canelas, however, has significantly individualized community members' stake in the resource by informally parcelizing the forest. It assigns most direct economic benefits to the individual possessor, making it more difficult to harness community-owned resources for community development and arguably, potentially undermining support for decisions in support of effective management of the forest as a whole. By contrast, Santa Marta's strategy strengthens a community of beneficiaries of the collective resource and helps ensure that members maintain a stake in sustainable management.

Timber Certification

The current problems of Durango's forestry sector have encouraged the emergence of unusual alliances within the sector in the last three years. Producers, timber industrialists, and state-level authorities have joined together to pursue timber certification by the Mexican Civil Council for Sustainable Silviculture, an independent certifying entity accredited by SmartWood and the Forest Stewardship Council (FSC).[8] Forest owners seeking FSC certification must satisfy 10 sets of FSC principles and criteria that deal with legal tenure issues, local resource rights and responsibilities, indigenous peoples' rights, community and worker relations, distribution of forest-related benefits, forest management practices, monitoring, and other standards (see Chapter 4). The certification process includes consideration of the interests of a diverse range of stakeholders in the production and commercialization process, including non-owning neighbors, employees, and others. Once certified, owners can bring their timber to market as "certified" wood, qualify for any market premiums that might exist for this certification, and can use the FSC trademark logo (FSC 2003).

According to FSC data available in February 2003, 27 privately and collectively owned forests had been certified in Mexico, representing a total of 588,561 hectares. Sixteen forests totaling 219,696 hectares had been certified in Durango. Twelve of those forests, representing 192,325 hectares, were collectively owned by *ejidos* or agrarian communities (FSC 2003).

AN UNPRECEDENTED COLLABORATION

The participants interviewed explain their pursuit of certification as part of a coordinated strategy to confront both the economic problems of the forest sector and the more general problem of regional development. In interviews and meetings, peasant and private owners, timber industrialists, and state officials expressed their hope that certification will one day yield more favorable prices and more secure markets, although most interviewees appeared to understand that certification currently guarantees neither.

Industry representatives and state authorities remarked that price is not the only basis of a successful competitive strategy in Durango. Certification also represents a vehicle for diagnosing and improving product quality and addressing technical and organizational problems. Certification will demonstrate to buyers and external stakeholders in Durango's forestry sector that the state produces a high-quality product under sustainable conditions.

Interviewees described several unprecedented meetings in which representatives of state agencies, industry, and private and "social sector" forest owners met to discuss the problems of Durango's forestry sector. These meetings aimed to help participants identify the true costs of each link of the extraction, transport, processing, and commercialization chain. One objective of the meetings was to determine what costs participants at each link of the commodity chain would be willing to reduce in order to increase the general competitiveness of Durango timber. Not surprisingly, the participants have had diverse, sometimes conflicting, notions of what costs are truly necessary, yet interviewees described these meetings as a positive step toward addressing the forestry sector's competitiveness problems.

CERTIFICATION AND REGIONALIZATION STRATEGIES

Producers, industrialists, and state authorities concurred that timber certification is part of a more general strategy of "regionalization." This strategy represents an effort by the state to enlist diverse economic actors in cooperation to improve not only the forestry sector but also the general conditions of development in a given region. As part of the regionalization strategy, by late 2002, almost 220,000 hectares of *ejido*, agrarian community, and privately owned forests in contiguous geographic areas of the state had already been certified (FSC 2003), and more were in the process of certification. Once certified, each region is to be marketed as a source of well-managed, sustainably developed timber. In the first years of the certification effort, in addition to having their own portion of the "chain of custody" of timber certified, at least two prominent forest industry firms contributed financial support toward the costs of *ejido* and agrarian community certification. In other cases, *ejidatarios* and *comuneros* committed themselves to covering the costs of the process. In 2002, the state government was collaborating with the National Forestry Commission (Comisión Nacional Forestal; CONAFOR) to support the costs of certification for *ejidos* and agrarian communities in Durango.

PERSPECTIVES ON CERTIFICATION

One state official explained his agency's support of certification as a medium-term strategy to respond to the competitive pressures of Chilean timber. The state is also trying to help counter what he referred to as the "social fragmentation" that has occurred within some forest *ejidos* and communities since the agrarian reform of 1992. Several interviewees, including state officials, industrialists, and *ejidatarios*, reported cases of *ejidos* and communities in which the formation of multiple internal groups to work the forest has undermined effective forest management.

One timber industrialist I interviewed explained his support of certification as part of an effort to promote the competitiveness and security of his region's timber supply. While this industrialist openly seeks long-term, 10-year contracts with some of the certified communities, he emphasized that his firm's support of certification is not contingent on the signing of such contracts. He cited an example of his efforts to promote and facilitate certification within one *ejido* that had no contract with his firm. "I have an interest in this region's development, as a businessman, and also as someone who lives here," he said.

In interviews and community meetings in two *ejidos* seeking certification, community leaders and members explained that they saw certification as a path out of depressed local forest economies. Both *ejidos* had long histories of organized forestry production. In both cases, the contribution of timber to their community economies has decreased dramatically in recent years. Both had had at one time sawmills and small processing plants that were recently abandoned because of internal administrative problems and market difficulties. As a result, both *ejidos* are currently selling their trees standing in the forest, a situation which makes them highly vulnerable to fluctuating prices.

Both communities have suffered an exodus of their populations as *ejidatarios* and their children have migrated to Durango City and other urban areas in Mexico and abroad in search of employment. In both cases, new social divisions have emerged between titled *ejidatarios* with rights to forestry economic benefits, on the one hand, and their children and unrelated *avecindados* (non-*ejidatario* neighbors) without formal resource rights, on the other. Interviewees in both communities spoke of the urgent need to provide jobs and income for their children and *avecindados* who are steadily being obligated to migrate. While *ejidatarios* and *avecindados* consistently stated that they knew certification could not guarantee higher prices or secure markets, it was clear that much of their motivation to enter the process stemmed from the hope of both. Leaders of both communities reported that they currently plan to pay the costs of their own certification, though the possibility exists of subsidy from industry and official sources. *Ejido* leaders interviewed also spoke of the regionalization strategies and the role that certification is to play in it. *Ejidatarios* have participated in meetings with industry and state officials through representatives in their *ejido* unions.

This unusual state-level alliance in Durango has been shaped by several factors that have created a congruence of interests among various actors. The state's forestry sector has suffered from a crisis of competitiveness rooted in problems with its existing productive infrastructure and exacerbated in recent years by an influx into its markets of cheaper, plantation-grown Chilean lumber. Durango's state natural resources agency has supported certification as part of a broad strategy to improve Durango's competitiveness in forestry and to support regional development in general. Actors within the state's private timber industry have supported certification as a means of improving their own competitiveness by ensuring the continued availability of reliable sources of high-quality timber from well-managed forests. Forest owners, both collective and private, have sought via certification more stable, favorable outlets for their timber. *Ejidatario* and *comunero* owners, in particular, are wagering that certification will be an important component of a strategy to confront the deepening unemployment crisis in the countryside. It is still too early to assess the long-term sustainability and effectiveness of this alliance of forestry actors in Durango. Nevertheless, it represents an important innovation in organizational strategies for community-based forestry.

Conclusion

The Durango case suggests that much of the impact of globalization's neoliberal policy orientation may be indirect, as it promotes changes in the rules of the game by which people make, remake, or discard social institutions governing use of common pool resources. In the two cases discussed, these rule changes have related to individual and collective access to natural resources, resource management organization, the distribution of benefits, and the link between collectively owned resources and community development.

Nevertheless, more attention needs to be paid to the role social agency plays in institutional change. Although restructuring does constrain the choices available to social groups, through organization, people mediate the impact of external forces. As local people struggle to pursue forestry activities which are more efficient, less corrupt, have a fairer distribution of benefits, and are more democratic, as in the case of the work groups, they exercise social agency. They also engage in social agency as they seek to improve their position in a difficult, rapidly restructuring market via investment in new kinds of collaboration and management models, as in the case of certification. Local actors involved in these new forms of social organization of forestry in Durango demonstrate that change is not completely determined from above, but is largely shaped by local agendas, each with its own historical context.

More research is needed on specific experiences, and their context, to discover the conditions under which local action represents progress toward sustainable management of natural resources. How are such instances of local social agency to be evaluated? One way to pursue this line of inquiry would be to consider them in terms of community forestry's principle that sustainable management is more likely when viable communities of stakeholders in sustainability exist. To what degree are the relevant stakeholders involved in decisions about resources? To what extent do those decisions take into account stakeholders' material needs and other interests so that the community benefits from forest development? Can the forest continue to be managed as an ecological unit, or is management fragmented?

From this perspective, the experience of work groups in Durango is mixed. In Canelas, the annex scheme has clearly resulted in more participation in forestry at the annex level, where inhabitants exercise greater oversight than when harvests were controlled by concessionaires or the *comisariado*. Nevertheless, the annexes deal with identity problems posed by the imposition of the agrarian community structure and by out-migration, both of which narrow the boundaries of the community of stakeholders in forestry. Within each annex, participation in forestry has actually decreased as the principal actors have become individual possessors of the parcels harvested each year. Second, Canelas's restructuring aims to exclude migrated *comuneros* from participation in decisions about the community and its resources, and ultimately from the community itself. "We want to update the community rolls so the people who live there are the ones benefiting, not those who want to fill their pockets and leave again," explained one annex representative.

Santa Marta's work groups, by contrast, significantly expanded participation in forestry as the pool of forestry stakeholders grew to include non-*comunero* residents. "The groups have their drawbacks," said one member of an above group, "but they allow us to work the forest where we didn't before." The groups both delivered formal legal status to disenfranchised residents and made it possible for migrated *comuneros* to continue to participate in community affairs and benefit from community resources. The work groups operate in a context of considerable conflict, yet the conflict predated their emergence. The groups actually provide an important channel for working through these conflicts and making progress toward what, in Santa Marta, remain largely collective goals.

Santa Marta's forests have never been subdivided, formally or informally. The forest continues to be seen as a communal resource, to be used in support of community needs as well as to provide direct benefits to individual *comuneros*. Its work groups, then, operate to strengthen the community of stakeholders in communally owned natural resources. By contrast, Canelas's annex system aims to individualize access to the community's resources. The forest has been informally parcelized, with individual stakeholders given priority in resource-related decision making. While both communities' forests continue to be managed as ecological units, over the longer run, coherent, integrated management is likely to face greater pressures toward fragmentation from Canelas's annex system.

Forest certification aims explicitly to promote participation by relevant stakeholders in forest management and in the distribution of its diverse benefits. Aside from the benefits pursued by certification participants (the possibility of higher prices and more secure markets, improvements in forest management stimulated by the certification process, and the potential market advantages of providing a high-quality, environmentally sustainable product), there are likely other benefits to forest certification. The certification process promotes greater transparency and accountability at each level of production, processing, and commercialization, making it possible for the owners of Durango's forests to learn about and potentially improve their position in the timber production chain. Certification in Durango, moreover, is promoting an unprecedented degree of coordination and collaboration among quite diverse actors in the forestry sector. To have a chance of bringing sustained benefits, certification in Durango virtually requires collaboration among these actors: the *ejidatarios, comuneros,* and private owners who most directly control the forested land; the timber industry, whose part of the "chain of custody" must also be certified for commercialization; and state government officials, who can help offset high financial costs of certification and otherwise provide a supportive policy environment.

Nevertheless, the promise of certification in Durango currently appears to be exactly that: a promise that it will serve the needs of its participants as well as the world's need for sustainably managed forests. The peasant, industry, and state government participants in the process are investing their scarce time and resources in timber certification in the hope that it will help them address their forestry problems. Certification recognizes the central role the global market currently plays in how forests are managed and represents an effort to help producers in the global South compete more effectively in that market. It remains to be seen whether the unprecedented collaboration among these groups can be sustained over the longer run. Much will depend on whether returns come from the marketing of certified timber that are sustained, concrete, and visible to each of the different groups of participants.

In the Mexican agrarian sector, neoliberal constitutional changes have created a "legal framework for a redeployment of institutional power that seeks to bypass existing rural organizations by dealing directly with the individual (usually male) *ejidatario*" (Harvey 1996: 152). In the forestry sector, policy reform has encouraged economic associations in communities based on the interests of individuals rather than collectives. Yet community-based forestry in Mexico survives; it is undergoing change but still represents significant local management of the resource. The forestry work groups and new collaboration around certification discussed here show clearly the capacity of forest campesinos to organize effectively to manage their natural resources. Outside support could be directed to these producers in ways which recognize the autonomy of local organization yet encourage the basic social and ecological principles of community-based forestry. The forestry groups could be assisted with technical support to reinforce their positive tendencies and to discourage tendencies that may undermine the social and economic sustainability of the community. Instead of being seen as an alternative to community cooperation, the work groups could become one of several organizational options encouraging broad participation in forestry.

The national and international community of stakeholders in Mexico's forests can help insure that forest certification in the future represents a viable alternative for its participants. Financial and technical support could be directed toward communities interested in obtaining and maintaining forest certification, a process which is time-consuming and costly. Attention also needs to be given to increasing consumer demand in the industrial North for certified timber. Specialized markets for certified timber produced by peasant communities might be developed, perhaps in coordination with the rapidly growing fair trade movement sponsored by the Fair Trade Labeling Organization (see Raynolds 2000).

The powerful insight of community forestry has been that for conservation to be possible, the genuine participation of those with a stake in sustainable use of those forest resources is required. Ironically, despite strong outside interest in forests in the global South, today the campesino producer carries nearly the entire cost of forest conservation. State financial support of community-based forestry is customarily referred to pejoratively as "subsidy," currently anathema in a neoliberal policy milieu. The term *subsidy* is possibly appropriate in cases of private appropriation of privately owned and utilized resources. It is arguably inappropriate with regard to Mexico's forests, which represent important means for community livelihood, a constitutionally protected national heritage, and a source of vital ecological services to regional, national, and international communities (Taylor and Zabin 2000).

If Mexico's forestry sector is to be based on principles of sustainable development, those outside of the *ejidos* in national and international communities who care about the forest should also participate with resources to help pay for conservation. Rather than seeing assistance to community-based producers as subsidies, the state and the international community should consider sharing the cost of conservation as a co-investment with the forest's owners. Moreover, they should take seriously the lessons of local campesino communities in Durango and elsewhere in Mexico. They experience most directly forestry's economic, social, and environmental problems. They may also well be where the solutions emerge which best deal with the multifaceted dimensions of sustainability.

Notes

AUTHOR'S NOTE: I would like to thank Sergio Madrid, Dawn Robinson, the editors of this volume, and participants in Durango's forestry sector for helpful comments on previous versions of this paper. I have full responsibility, nevertheless, for all errors of fact or interpretation.

1. *Ejidos* and *comunidades agrarias* are rural collective property regimes with roots in the land redistribution begun after Mexico's 1910 Revolution (see Chapter 1). Unlike the situation in southern Mexico, in Durango most agrarian communities are not indigenous, but actually have roots in individual private property titles held by mestizo owners.

2. The post-1992 reforms are often viewed as affecting only *ejidos* within Mexico's collectivized social sector, with agrarian (indigenous) communities exempted. As will be described below, however, the privatization reforms are also reshaping agrarian communities' use of collectively held resources.

3. Article 107 provides that all provisos applying to *ejidos* also apply to agrarian communities unless expressly provided otherwise (López Nogales and López Nogales 1999:242).

4. Agrarian community names are pseudonyms.

5. Elsewhere in Mexico, *ejidatarios* have long formed smaller groups to work with non-timber resources such as *chicle* (gum) (see Taylor and Zabin 2000). In Durango, new intracommunity economic associations build on preexisting social forms such as kinship and political networks.

6. Strictly speaking, PROCEDE will not survey internal agricultural and forest plots "belonging" to Canelas's possessors. According to a Durango-based agrarian attorney, in practice forest peasants have access to land for food production. Nevertheless, in strictly legal terms, "agricultural land" does not exist in forest *ejidos* and agrarian communities and forests cannot be legally physically divided (personal communication, 1999). In forest agrarian communities, PROCEDE delineates external boundaries and "urban" parcels upon which *comuneros* have houses.

7. Agrarian communities can admit more members but cannot legally divide. Under Article 104, an agrarian community could vote to convert to an *ejido* and then vote to subdivide into two *ejidos* (López Nogales and López Nogales 1999:240). According to one agrarian attorney interviewed, this has not yet happened in northwest Durango.

8. I participated on Mexican Civil Council for Sustainable Silviculture certi-

fication teams in 2001 and 2002. The following discussion of certification in Durango is based on my contribution to those studies. While the information presented is available in public certification documents, here the anonymity of local participants is preserved in keeping with the discussion of the work group cases.

References

Armijo Canto, N. 1999. Las sociedades civiles de productos forestales en Quintana Roo. In *Creación de alternativas en México*, ed. D. Cazes, 85–101. Mexico City: UNAM/Centro de Investigaciones Interdisciplinarias en Ciencias y Humanidades.

Bartra, A. 1991a. Pro, contras y asegunes de la "apropiación del proceso productivo." In *Los nuevos sujetos del desarrollo rural*, ed. A. Bartra, 3–22. Mexico City: ADN Editores.

———. 1991b. El 27. *Cuadernos agrarios* 3(September–December):24–29.

Beaucage, P. 1997. The third wave of modernization: Liberalism, Salinismo, and indigenous peasants in Mexico. In *The Third Wave of Modernization in Latin America: Cultural Perspectives on Neoliberalism*, ed. L. Phillips, 3–27. Wilmington, DE: Scholarly Resources.

Bray, D. B. 1997. La reconstrucción permanente de la naturaleza: Organizaciones campesinas y desarrollo popular sustentable. In *Semillas para el cambio en el campo: Medio ambiente, mercados y organización campesina*, ed. L. Paré, D. B. Bray, J. Burstein, and S. Martínez Vázquez, 3–17. Mexico City: UNAM, Instituto de Investigaciones Sociales, La Sociedad de Solidaridad Social 'Sansekan Tinemi y Saldebas, Servicios de Apoyo Local al Desarrollo de Base en México, A.C.

Cabarle, B., F. Chapela, and S. Madrid. 1997. Introducción: El manejo forestal comunitario y la certificación. In *El manejo forestal comunitario en México y sus perspectivas de sustentabilidad*, ed. L. Merino-Pérez, 17–33. Cuernavaca: UNAM, SEMARNAP, CMSS, WRI.

Chapela, G. 1991. De bosques y campesinos: Problemática forestal y desarrollo organizativo en torno a diez encuentros de comunidades forestales. In *Los nuevos sujetos del desarrollo rural*, ed. A. Bartra, 135–184. Mexico City: ADN Editores.

———. 1997. El cambio liberal del sector forestal en México: Un análisis comparativo Canadá-México-Estados Unidos. In *Semillas para el cambio en el campo: Medio ambiente, mercados y organización campesina*, ed. L. Paré, D. B. Bray, J. Burstein, and S. Martínez Vázquez, 37–56. Mexico City: UNAM, Instituto de Investigaciones Sociales, La Sociedad de Solidaridad Social 'Sansekan Tinemi y Saldebas, Servicios de Apoyo Local al Desarrollo de Base en México, A.C.

Chávez Padrón, M. 1999. *El proceso social agrario*. Mexico City: Editorial Porrúa.

Cockcroft, J. D. 1998. *Mexico's Hope: An Encounter with Politics and History*. New York: Monthly Review Press.

Cornelius, W. A., and D. Myhre. 1998. Introduction. In *The Transformation of Rural Mexico: Reforming the Ejido Sector*, ed. W. A. Cornelius and D. Myhre, 2–21. San Diego: Center for U.S.-Mexican Studies, University of California.

DeWalt, B., M. W. Rees, and A. D. Murphy. 1994. *The End of Agrarian Reform in Mexico: Past Lessons, Future Prospects.* San Diego: *Ejido* Reform Research Project, Center for U.S.-Mexican Studies, University of California.

FSC. 2003. http://www.fscoax.org/principal.htm. Accessed 20 February 2003.

Fortmann, L. M., and J. W. Bruce, eds. 1988. *Whose Trees? Proprietary Dimensions of Forestry.* Boulder, CO: Westview Press.

Gobierno del Estado de Durango. 2001. *Durango forestal.* Durango: Secretaría de Recursos Naturales y Medio Ambiente.

Gómez Cruz, M. A., and R. Schwentesius, eds. 1997. *El campo mexicano: Ajuste neoliberal y alternativas.* Mexico City: Centro de Investigaciones Económicas Sociales y Tecnológicas de la Agroindustria y la Agricultura Mundial.

Gordillo, G., A. de Janvry, and E. Sadoulet. 1998. Entre el control político y la eficiencia: Evolución de los derechos de propiedad agraria en México. *Revista de la CEPAL* 66:149–166.

Harvey, N. 1996. Impact of reforms to Article 27 on Chiapas: Peasant resistance in the neoliberal public sphere. In *Reforming Mexico's Agrarian Reform,* ed. L. Randall, 151–171. Armonk, NY: M. E. Sharpe.

INEGI. 1994. *Durango: Panorama agropecuario VII censo agropecuario 1991.* Mexico City: INEGI.

———. 2000. *Anuario estadístico Durango, edición 2000.* Mexico City: INEGI, Gobierno del Estado de Durango.

INEGI and Gobierno del Estado de Durango. 1996. *Anuario estadístico del estado de Durango.* Mexico City: INEGI, Gobierno del Estado de Durango.

López Nogales, A., and R. López Nogales. 1999. *Ley agraria comentada.* Mexico City: Editorial Porrúa.

McMichael, P. 1996. Globalization: Myths and realities. *Rural Sociology* 61(1):25–55.

Merino-Pérez, L., and G. Alatorre. 1997. Las condiciones de los aprovechamientos forestales en los casos de distintas comunidades de Mexico. In *El manejo forestal comunitario en México y sus perspectivas de sustentabilidad,* ed. L. Merino-Pérez, 35–56. Cuernavaca: UNAM, SEMARNAP, CMSS, WRI.

Merino-Pérez, L., and S. Madrid. 1997. *Forestry and Conservation Policies in Mexico.* Mexico City: Department for International Development.

Ostrom, E., and E. Schlager. 1996. The formation of property rights. In *Rights to Nature: Ecological, Economic, Cultural, and Political Principles of Institutions for the Environment,* ed. S. S. Hanna, C. Folke, and K.-G. Mäler, 127–156. Washington, DC: Island Press.

Peluso, N. 1992. *Rich Forests, Poor People: Resource Control and Resistance in Java.* Berkeley: University of California Press.

Raynolds, L. 2000. Re-embedding global agriculture: The international organic and fair trade movements. *Agriculture and Human Values* 17(3):297–309.

Richards, M. 1997. Common property resource institutions and forest management in Latin America. *Development and Change* 28:95–117.

SEMARNAP. 1997. Ley Forestal. In *Anuario estadístico 1995.* Mexico City: SEMARNAP http://www.semarnap.gob.mx/ Accessed August 1997.

SEMARNAT. 2001. Estadísticas forestales. Mexico City: SEMARNAT http://www.semarnat.gob.mx/estadisticas_ambientales/estadisticas_am_98/forestales/forestales09.shtml. Accessed August 2001.

Snook, L. K. 1997. Uso, manejo, y conservación forestal en México: Implicaciones de la tenencia comunitaria y los recientes cambios en las políticas. In *Semillas para el cambio en el campo: Medio ambiente, mercados y organización campesina*, ed. L. Paré, D. B. Bray, J. Burstein, and S. Martínez Vázquez, 19–35. Mexico City: UNAM, Instituto de Investigaciones Sociales, La Sociedad de Solidaridad Social 'Sansekan Tinemi y Saldebas, Servicios de Apoyo Local an Desarrollo de Base en México, A.C.

Taylor, P. L. 2000. Producing more with less? Organizational problems of social forestry in Durango, Mexico, in an era of trade liberalization. *Rural Sociology* 65(2):253–274.

———. 2001. Community forestry as embedded process: Two cases from Durango and Quintana Roo, Mexico. *International Journal of Sociology of Agriculture and Food* 9(1):59–81.

———. 2003. Reorganization or division? New strategies of community forestry in Durango, Mexico. *Society and Natural Resources* 16(7):643–661.

Taylor, P. L., and C. Zabin. 2000. Neoliberal reform and sustainable forest management in Quintana Roo, Mexico: Rethinking the institutional framework of the forestry pilot plan. *Agriculture and Human Values* 17(2):141–156.

Téllez Kuenzler, L. 1994. *La modernización del sector agropecuario y forestal*. Mexico City: Fondo de Cultura Económica.

UNECOFAEZ. 1992. *Plan de desarrollo y conservación en la región noroeste de Durango 1992–1995*. Santiago Papasquiaro, Durango: UNECOFAEZ.

Wexler, M. B., and D. B. Bray. 1996. Reforming forests: From community forests to corporate forestry in Mexico. In *Reforming Mexico's Agrarian Reform*, ed. L. Randall, 235–245. Armonk, NY: M. E. Sharpe.

White, J. B. 1984. *When Words Lose Their Meaning. Constitutions and Reconstitutions of Language, Character and Community*. Chicago: University of Chicago Press.

World Bank. 1995. *Mexico: Resource Conservation and Forest Sector Review*. Report no. 13114–ME. Washington, DC: Natural Resources and Rural Poverty Operations Division.

Zabin, C. 1998. Free markets and forests in Mexico: Community-based forestry in the era of neoliberal reform. In *The Transformation of Rural Mexico: Reforming the Ejido Sector*, ed. W. A. Cornelius and D. Myhre, 401–425. San Diego: Center for U.S.-Mexican Studies, University of California.

Zendejas, S., and G. Mummert. 1998. Beyond the agrarian question: The cultural politics of *ejido* natural resources. In *The Transformation of Rural Mexico: Reforming the Ejido Sector*, ed. W. A. Cornelius and D. Myhre, 173–201. San Diego: Center for U.S.-Mexican Studies, University of California.

CHAPTER 8

Community Adaptation or Collective Breakdown? The Emergence of "Work Groups" in Two Forestry *Ejidos* in Quintana Roo, Mexico

PETER R. WILSHUSEN

In February of 1997 approximately 125 representatives of government agencies, nongovernmental organizations, academic institutions, community forestry associations, and others met for four days to discuss the complex challenges facing the forestry sector in Quintana Roo, Mexico. The Agenda Forestal de Quintana Roo was organized by state agencies and nongovernmental organizations (NGOs) with support from the United Kingdom's Department for International Development (DFID). In addition to topics such as industrialization, marketing, technical services, and public support, participants examined what they perceived to be worrisome trends regarding the capacity of land grant communities (*ejidos*) to consolidate community forest enterprises (CFEs). One of the main concerns centered on the apparent breakdown of CFEs into multiple independent producer groups. Several analysts suggested that such internal divisions might lead to a free-for-all in which individual groups would claim tracts of forest commons and abandon collective management and harvesting (DFID et al. 1998; Zabin and Taylor 1997). The move toward internal division within *ejidos* appeared to stem from broad legal reforms instituted by the Mexican government in 1992.

In line with the actions of states across Latin America and other regions during this period, the Mexican government transformed the legal structure of the agrarian sector, promulgating constitutional and statutory reforms designed to promote economic liberalization and political decentralization. These institutional reforms included shifts in economic policy that lowered trade barriers and allowed for the privatization of state-owned industries. They also produced revisions to the federal Constitution that ended agrarian reform and altered the legal underpinning of the *ejido* system. Whereas collective lands were inalienable prior to

1992, the legal changes made it possible for community assemblies to dissolve their communal landholdings and obtain private property titles to the individual plots of land that had been governed collectively since the 1930s. Changes to the Constitution also allowed foreign corporations to own land in Mexico and enter into commercial partnerships with *ejidos*, both of which were illegal before 1992 (Cornelius and Myhre 1998; Key et al. 1998). As with all agricultural policies, the national forest law was rewritten to fall in line with liberal designs (see Merino-Pérez and Segura-Warnholtz, this volume). Beyond the legal changes regarding land tenure and foreign partnerships, revisions to the agrarian code permitted *ejidatarios* to form internal groups for commercial production. This subtle but important legal change allowed registered producer groups within *ejidos* to operate as independent commercial entities separate from the executive committee (*comisariado ejidal*), which had previously administered communal enterprises (see Taylor, this volume).

This chapter explores how the formation of independent subgroups — known locally as work groups (*grupos de trabajo*) — has affected forest management, local economies, and community governance in two of Quintana Roo's most prominent forestry *ejidos:* Caoba and Petcacab. In the majority of large forestry *ejidos* in southern Quintana Roo, work groups have replaced *ejido* executive committees in the administration of most forest management responsibilities. This organizational shift constitutes a de facto dissolution of the CFE as originally conceived in the early 1980s under a program known as the Plan Piloto Forestal. Each work group administers timber profits from a percentage of the *ejido*'s authorized annual harvest volume. While the work groups in both communities coordinate their forest management activities, they each decide how to use timber-based income.

Since work group formation is not unique to Quintana Roo (see Taylor, this volume, for a discussion of the same phenomenon in Durango), it is worth exploring implications of these groups not just for communal forest management but also for collective governance under the *ejido* structure. What impact do work groups have on forest management and, by extension, forest protection? How do they affect the local economy, generally, and the distribution of timber profits, specifically? Finally, what impacts have work groups had on local governance? Do they represent the de facto breakdown of forestry *ejidos* in Quintana Roo?

The chapter's first section provides a descriptive overview of Caoba and Petcacab. While the two *ejidos* are similar in many ways, they differ in terms of forestry production potential. Interestingly, Petcacab, the *ejido* with the higher production potential, and thus presumably greater economic incentives to cooperate, faced stiffer governance challenges compared to its less endowed counterpart, Caoba. The second section presents a comparative analysis of work group formation in Caoba and Petcacab. Caoba had seven groups in 2000, although two of these commanded a significant majority in local decision making. In contrast, Petcacab subdivided at two levels between 1996 and 2000, including 11 groups and another 18 group "sections." In the third and fourth sections, I examine the evolving collective rule systems that govern multigroup forest management in the two communities. While groups in Caoba mostly adhered to new rules, their counterparts in Petcacab frequently deviated from norms. The fifth section explores how work groups have affected local forest management and politics by focusing on changes in governance practices, participation, and informal economies. The final section of the chapter summarizes what work groups might mean for the future of community forestry in Quintana Roo.

Portrait of Two *Ejidos:* Caoba and Petcacab

Caoba and Petcacab are two of eight *ejidos* in central and southern Quintana Roo that established viable CFEs by the early 1990s.[1] The two communities share similar political and economic histories. Both Caoba and Petcacab were created during the first wave of agrarian reform in Quintana Roo in the 1930s and 1940s, comprising large, forested land grants intended for timber and chicle harvesting. The *ejidos* participated actively in the regional chicle economy into the 1970s and also fell under the MIQROO concession beginning in 1957. The state-owned timber company MIQROO (Maderas Industrializadas de Quintana Roo) was integral to a federal government strategy aimed at encouraging colonization and economic development in Quintana Roo. The company held a 25-year concession for harvesting mahogany and other species from both *ejido* and federal lands. With the expiration of the MIQROO concession in 1982, both communities opted to participate in the Plan Piloto Forestal (1983–86) and later became founding members of the state's first community forestry association, the Sociedad de Productores Forestales Ejidales de Quintana Roo (SPFEQR, or as it is more commonly known in the region, and the term that will be used here, the Sociedad Sur) in May 1986 (see Figure 8.1 for a map of members of the Sociedad Sur).

In the wake of the 1992 changes to Mexico's forest law and agrarian code, Caoba and Petcacab decided in 1996 to manage their forest resources in independent subgroups rather than continuing to operate collectively under a regime administered by the *ejido* executive committee. While the legal reforms facilitated the division into work groups, long-standing internal rifts within both *ejidos* prompted the creation of new organizational and procedural arrangements.

The *ejido* Caoba is located in southwestern Quintana Roo along the border with the state of Campeche (see Figure 8.1). It includes 68,553 hectares of forest, open grassland, inland lakes, and seasonally flooded areas of which the *ejido* assembly has designated 32,500 hectares as a permanent forest reserve. Caoba had 311 registered *ejidatarios* in 2000 and a population of 1,535, including 749 men and 786 women. Eighty-nine percent of Caoba's population lived in the main settlement of the same name, while the remaining 11% resided in a smaller village called San José de la Montaña (INEGI 2000). Historically, the *ejido's* economy has been dominated by the harvest of forest products, principally chicle and timber. While timber harvesting remains an important activity, it is no longer the principal source of income. Moreover, with the disappearance of the chicle market in the mid-1990s, residents no longer tap chewing gum resin. As a result of government-sponsored agricultural development programs beginning in the 1960s, community members began raising cattle, producing honey, and cultivating commercial crops such as corn and chile peppers. Since the late 1990s, many community members have been harvesting and selling locally abundant grasses used for constructing thatch roofs on open pavilions (*palapas*) in tourist areas. At approximately the same time, a significant number of residents began migrating to the United States in search of employment. During the first half of 2000 at least 30 people made the trip north, including the *ejido* president and treasurer (Robinson 2000).

At 46,000 hectares, the *ejido* Petcacab covers less area than Caoba but maintains the same amount of its land as a permanent forest reserve (32,500 hectares). The full extent of Petcacab's forest commons contains commercially valuable timber stands. Petcacab is located in central Quintana Roo, southwest of the town of Felipe Carrillo Puerto (see Figure 8.1). The *ejido* had 206 members in 2000 and a population of 947, including 484 men and 463 women. Of this total, 751 residents lived in the village of Petcacab and the remaining 196 were located in Polinkín (INEGI 2000).

Like Caoba, Petcacab has historically relied on chicle and timber extraction. In contrast to Caoba, however, Petcacab and its neighbor Noh-Bec have the state's richest mahogany forests. As a result, the *ejidatarios* of

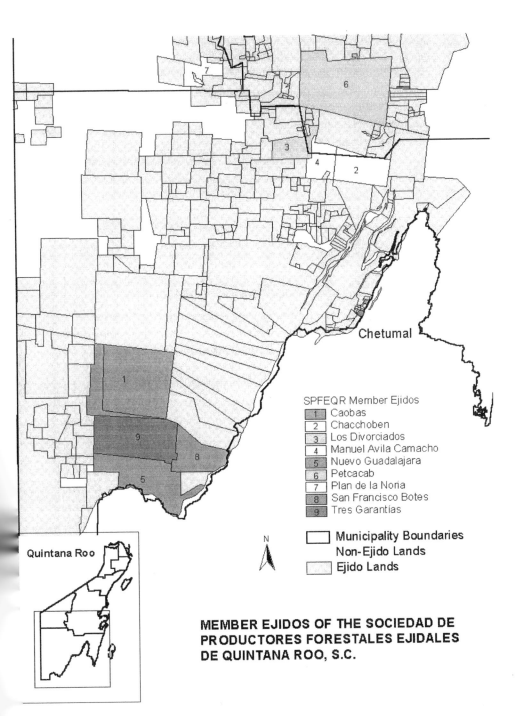

Figure 8.1 *Ejido* members of the Sociedad Sur (SPFEQR).

The following labels appear within the figure:

- 7
- 6
- 3
- 4
- 2
- Chetumal
- 1
- 9
- 8
- 5

SPFEQR Member Ejidos
1 Caobas
2 Chacchoben
3 Los Divorciados
4 Manuel Avila Camacho
5 Nuevo Guadalajara
6 Petcacab
7 Plan de la Noria
8 San Francisco Botes
9 Tres Garantías

N

☐ Municipality Boundaries
Non-Ejido Lands
☐ Ejido Lands

Quintana Roo

MEMBER EJIDOS OF THE SOCIEDAD DE PRODUCTORES FORESTALES EJIDALES DE QUINTANA ROO, S.C.

Petcacab focus most of their efforts on timber harvesting, although cattle raising and commercial agriculture are also important economic activities. Unlike Caoba's residents, most residents of the *ejido* Petcacab do not migrate further than Quintana Roo's tourist areas in search of employment. Many younger community members spend part of the year working on hotel construction in Cancún and Playa del Carmen. New tourism development along the southern coastal areas extending from Mahaual to Xcalak has generated further employment opportunities for construction workers.

With respect to forest management, the most important difference between Caoba and Petcacab is per capita harvest volume. After its neighbor Noh-Bec, Petcacab had the second highest annual mahogany harvest volume in Quintana Roo in 2000 (1,499 cubic meters) and thus enjoyed significantly higher per capita incomes from forestry vis-à-vis other *ejidos* in the state.[2] Compared to Caoba, Petcacab had both higher harvest volumes and fewer *ejidatarios* (206) such that each member was guaranteed the equivalent of at least 7.3 cubic meters in timber-based income. Given an average market price of 2,000 pesos (US$222) per cubic meter of roundwood mahogany during 2000, members grossed some 14,600 pesos (US$1,622). In contrast, Caoba had an annual harvest volume for high-value timber (mahogany and cedar) of only 301 cubic meters divided among 311 *ejidatarios*, which translated to just under 1 cubic meter per member each year. Thus, community members in Caoba grossed but 1,940 pesos (US$216) in 2000.[3]

In addition to income earned from forestry, commercial agriculture, and wage labor, *ejidatarios* from Caoba, Petcacab, and other forestry communities receive significant federal and state government financial support including development projects, agricultural extension programs, and subsidies. Between 1994 and 2001, forestry *ejidos* associated with the Sociedad Sur received assistance from the Secretariat of Social Development (Secretaría de Desarrollo Social; SEDESOL) in the form of community development projects related to forest plantations, a timber-marketing fund, a wood-drying kiln, and artisan workshops, among others.

In addition to SEDESOL, the Secretariat of Environment, Natural Resources, and Fisheries (Secretaría del Medio Ambiente, Recursos Naturales, y Pesca; SEMARNAP) provides financial support to forestry *ejidos* across Mexico via two financial support programs: the Forest Development Program (Programa de Desarrollo Forestal; PRODEFOR) and the National Reforestation Program (Programa Nacional de Reforestación;

PRONARE).[4] The forest development fund, PRODEFOR, is a small grants program jointly funded by federal and state governments. The fund has operated in Quintana Roo since 1998 and provides monies to *ejidos* annually for forest inventories, management plans, training workshops, and silvicultural experiments. Since the *ejidos* associated with the Sociedad Sur already had management plans in place prior to the start of the program, most funds were directed toward updating forest inventories between 1998 and 2001. Under PRONARE, *ejidos* received support for producing mahogany and cedar seedlings for subsequent enrichment planting in harvested areas. In 2001, the nine forestry *ejidos* associated with the Sociedad Sur received 2,128,810 pesos (US$226,469) from these three federal support programs (Wilshusen 2003).

Regarding federal agricultural subsidies, the most important during the 1990s in terms of family income was PROCAMPO, which was initiated in 1993 to buffer lower income Mexican farmers from price drops in staple crops precipitated by the North American Free Trade Agreement (NAFTA). *Ejidatarios* in both Caoba and Petcacab received annual PROCAMPO payments amounting to 832 pesos (US$92) per hectare for 2001–02, generating income only second to timber profits for most households (Wilshusen 2003).

In summary, despite their similarities in terms of size, economic history, and internal organization, Caoba and Petcacab differ considerably with respect to forestry production potential. Whereas Petcacab currently has Quintana Roo's highest authorized harvest volume for mahogany, Caoba's volume has declined over the last 10 years. Petcacab's per capita distribution of mahogany volume was almost seven and a half times higher than Caoba's in 2000. As of the 2002 harvest season, the differential increased to nine to one. In spite of these advantages, however, Petcacab faced stiffer governance challenges than Caoba.

Internal Reorganization in Caoba and Petcacab

Although CFEs in Quintana Roo faced collective action problems such as internal conflict, elite domination, and petty corruption as early as 1983, external support programs, agrarian law, and histories of collective organization encouraged *ejido* assemblies to maintain operations administered by the local executive committee. By the mid-1990s, members from mahogany-rich *ejidos* like Petcacab began questioning the organization of timber-harvesting operations given chronic inefficiencies and conflicts over administration of funds. Petcacab was the first *ejido* to divide into multiple work groups during the 1996 harvest season, followed a year later by Caoba and another member *ejido* of the Sociedad Sur called Tres Garantías. The remaining Sociedad Sur *ejidos* did not divide into work groups given low mahogany harvests and dominance of other agricultural activities.

The work group model devolves decision-making power over production and sale of timber to independent subgroups of *ejidatarios*. In both Caoba and Petcacab, the *ejido*'s total authorized harvest volume is divided among registered members. During 2000, this amounted to 0.968 and 7.276 cubic meters per *ejidatario* in Caoba and Petcacab, respectively (in 2002, Petcacab's per capita mahogany volume increased to 8.7 cubic meters).[5] In both cases, the main motivation for forming subgroups was to overcome chronic infighting over administration of communal funds. Each group manages its own finances and is responsible for contributing proportionate amounts of labor and payments to cover timber-harvesting costs. While *ejidatarios* have divided into groups that vary in size, annual cuts continue to follow previously established management plans. Thus, both Caoba and Petcacab have maintained their community forest reserves, and work groups coordinate their actions with the resident technicians of the Sociedad Sur during all phases of planning and harvesting. How the groups coordinate their actions differs, mainly as a function of the size and extent of each *ejido*'s timber harvest.

WORK GROUPS IN CAOBA

Starting in 1997, the *ejido* Caoba divided into three forestry work groups, including two in the main settlement (Caobas) and a third representing families in the village of San José. By 1999, one of these groups had subdivided, spawning three new groups. Since then Caoba has maintained seven work groups ranging in size from 137 to 10 *ejidatarios*. Given a per capita distribution of mahogany volumes of just under 1 cubic meter, the largest group managed timber with a gross value of approximately 239,000 pesos (US$26,555), or about 1,744 pesos (US$194) per member. In contrast, the smallest group administered timber valued at just over 17,400 pesos (US$1,933), although per capita yields are the same (see Table 8.1).

In addition to size, work groups in Caoba differed in their development strategies and material resources. The two largest groups, Chichan Há and Pinos Caribe, both formally registered their organizations as Sociedades de Producción Rural (SPRs) with the National Agrarian Registry (Registro Agrario Nacional; RAN) and thus could receive credit and loans without working through the *ejido* executive committee. In addition to

Table 8.1. Work group timber volumes and income in Caoba, 2000

Group	No. members	Volume (m³)ᵃ	Gross per group ($)ᵇ
Chichan Há, S.P.R.	137	132.616	$238,709
Pinos Caribe, S.P.R.	65	62.920	$113,256
Plan de Ayala	30	29.040	$52,272
Centenario	27	26.136	$47,044
La Ceiba	26	25.168	$45,302
Pro Selva	16	15.488	$27,878
Lol-Ché, S.P.R.	10	9.680	$17,424
Total	**311**	**301.048**	**$541,885**

Source: Wilshusen 2003.
ᵃ Harvest volume for mahogany and cedar (high-value species).
ᵇ Based on $1,800 pesos (US$200) per m³ in 1999–2000 (avg. internal community exchange rate). The denomination "S.P.R.," or Sociedad de Producción Rural, indicates that the group is formally registered with the National Agrarian Registry (Registro Agrario Nacional; RAN).

financing, the SPRs could independently buy and sell timber and other products and could emit invoices. The smallest work group, Lol-Ché, also acquired SPR status but focused its efforts mostly on beekeeping rather than forestry. None of the remaining four groups was registered with RAN in 2000. For members of small groups, the costs of registration and the low per capita income from timber made investment in forestry production unattractive. Lol-Ché presented an exception because the ratio of startup investments to income was more favorable for honey production.

Beyond size, the differences in development strategies were, to a large degree, the result of varying technical and administrative capacities. The two largest groups—Chichan Há and Pinos Caribe—had members with experience in managing the CFE. Both group leaders had served as president of the *ejido* executive committee. By 2000, both Chichan Há and Pinos Caribe had leveraged government loans to purchase an agricultural tractor/skidder and woodworking machinery. Both groups also established small (under 500 hectares) timber plantations. In addition, each group successfully solicited grants from SEDESOL for carpentry equipment. Chichan Há further invested in a wood drying kiln that involved purchase of a lot within the main settlement and construction of a storage building. The two largest groups distributed lower cash payments to their members as a result of these investments. These individual payouts ranged from 800 to 1,000 pesos (US$89–$111) per season for 1999 and

2000. Each group expected that the investments would pay off by the third or fourth season in terms of employment and increased profit sharing. While the two groups coordinated forestry planning and harvesting with the other groups, they opted not to collectively manage a community tree nursery, as had been the case prior to 2000. Rather, the two largest groups established separate nurseries to produce a sufficient number of seedlings for annual reforestation activities. The five remaining smaller groups continued to collectively manage what had been the *ejido* nursery.

In contrast to Chichan Há and Pinos Caribe, the other work groups had no development strategies with respect to forestry. Some groups, such as Plan de Ayala and Lol-Ché, made alternative investments in a vanilla plantation and beekeeping, respectively. The group Plan de Ayala is illustrative of the challenges faced by the smaller groups. Members of Plan de Ayala expressed an interest in becoming more involved in forestry production by formally registering their group and investing in equipment. However, they also indicated that the small size of their group in combination with the low per capita harvest volumes made such investments difficult. In addition, members had not formerly participated in forestry and thus lacked many of the technical skills necessary to develop further. With the exception of ProSelva—the work group comprised of members from San José—the smaller groups were initially a part of Pinos Caribe but left between 1998 and 1999 because of disagreements about management of group funds. None of the small groups made collective investments in forestry or any other activities. For these groups, timber income represented a small cash injection on the order of 1,400 pesos (US$155) that complemented earnings from agricultural production and government subsidies such as PROCAMPO.

WORK GROUPS IN PETCACAB

Petcacab was the first forestry *ejido* in Quintana Roo to subdivide into work groups in 1996. In contrast to Caoba, which initially divided into two groups consisting of rival factions, Petcacab experienced multiple levels of subdivision corresponding to family clans and later individual families. By 2000, Petcacab featured 11 work groups, most of which had further subdivided into a total of 18 sections. Whereas groups collectively administered most of the costs associated with their portion of the timber harvest (including labor), sections individually managed timber profits. In all, there were 28 representatives including both groups and sections, although only group leaders had voting power in work group assemblies.

During 1996 and 1997, groups collectively managed their profits, but many members distrusted their leaders and expressed dissatisfaction with how finances were managed. Most sections represented small family groups of between 4 and 10 *ejidatarios*. One of the groupings—the *desvalagados*, or "disengaged"—included 17 young *ejidatarios* who did not have an affiliation with any group or section and sold almost all of their volume to local buyers (see Table 8.2). In some cases, individual *ejidatarios* decided to form sections, including those who became timber buyers within the community. Moreover, differences in gross group or section income varied not just by size (combined per capita volumes), as in Caoba, but also by relative accumulation of timber volume from local purchases and sales. This is reflected in Table 8.2, where it can be seen that one individual accrued 90 cubic meters of mahogany, worth a minimum gross of 162,000 pesos (US$18,000), while a section composed of eight *ejidatarios* previously sold their entire combined volume and thus had no timber income corresponding to that harvest.

As in Caoba, work groups in Petcacab had varying development strategies and capacities. Three groups—Machiche, Sufricaya, and Zapote Negro—registered as SPRs in 1999 and thus administered their own credit, grants, and timber sales. All three of these groups shared similarities with Chichan Há and Pinos Caribe in Caoba. First, they chose to reinvest significant percentages of their timber incomes from 1999 and 2000 on collective goods such as agricultural tractors, pickup trucks, and woodworking machinery. Their stated goal was to purchase equipment to reduce production costs and develop small industries to generate employment and add value to wood products. Second, of the three groups that demonstrated an interest in economic development, two—Machiche and Sufricaya—obtained special government loans to help finance some equipment acquisitions. These two groups also met on a regular basis during 2000 in order to discuss and make decisions on harvest planning and economic development. By comparison, the group Zapote Negro met less frequently but maintained strong internal cohesion because of family and religious ties. Third, Machiche and Sufricaya had members with experience in forestry, including planning and harvesting. Zapote Negro's members showed interest in learning about forest management but had no prior experience with the CFE.

The remaining small groups and sections in Petcacab presented trends similar to those of their counterparts in Caoba, with one important difference. As in Caoba, none of Petcacab's smaller groups invested timber

Table 8.2. Work group timber volumes and income in Petcacab, 2000

Group	Section	No. members	Volume (m³)[a]	Gross per group[b]
Machiche, S.P.R.[c]	—	17	131.692	$237,046
Tankasché	—	7	127.916	$230,249
	Poot Medina Family	5	18.104	$32,587
	Francisco Poot M.[d]	0	77.208	$138,974
	Emilio Poot M.[d]	0	90.000	$162,000
	Uc Chan Family	6	9.552	$17,194
	Sinanché	4	35.104	$63,187
	Secc. Tankasché	3	14.828	$26,690
	Canul Family	8	0.000	0
Yaití	—	3	18.828	$33,890
	Sección Yaití	4	17.828	$32,090
Zapote Negro	—	??	135.796	$244,133
	Gongora I	5	20.828	$37,490
Sufricaya, S.P.R.	—	31	234.556	$422,201
	Rodríguez Family	10	69.088	$124,358
Pech Family	—	4	35.380	$63,684
	Reyes Poot Family	4	29.104	$52,387
Selva Tropical	—	10	77.036	$138,665
	Verdes	8	42.932	$77,278
	Dzul Family	6	43.036	$77,465
Botan	—	3	46.380	$83,484
	Botanes	7	37.380	$67,284

profits in equipment or other collective goods but rather retained monies for personal or family use. Indeed, the sections broke off from groups so that certain heads of families could directly manage timber income. The emergence of local timber buyers generated important political dynamics in Petcacab that did not appear in Caoba. Comparatively wealthy individuals who had purchased large timber volumes claimed disproportionate decision-making power even though they did not represent a work group. In contrast, those small groups and sections with low mahogany volumes (0–45 cubic meters) participated in work group assembly meetings but had less influence in decision making. Those groups and sections that sold most of their standing volume to local buyers participated minimally.

Table 8.2. Continued

Group	Section	No. members	Volume (m³)ᵃ	Gross per groupᵇ
Cruzché	—	4	26.104	$46,987
	Tzalam	2	46.932	$84,478
Quebrahacha	—	3	9.552	$17,194
	Quebrahacha 2	3	16.828	$30,290
	Gongora 2	4	32.104	$57,787
	Nicolas	1	24.552	$44,194
Caracolillo	—	5	29.104	$52,387
"Desvalagados"ᵉ		17	0.552	$994
Total		**206**	**1498.304**	**$2,696,947**

Source: Wilshusen 2003.
Note: Individual and family names are pseudonyms.
ᵃ Harvest volume for mahogany and cedar (high-value species). Group volumes show totals managed during harvest year including internal sales of individual timber volumes, not just per capita distributions.
ᵇ Based on 1,800 pesos (US$200) per m³ in 1999–2000 (avg. internal community exchange rate).
ᶜ The denomination "S.P.R.," or Sociedad de Producción Rural, indicates that the group is formally registered with the National Agrarian Registry (Registro Agrario Nacional; RAN).
ᵈ Indicates an individual timber buyer whose membership and individual volume are counted under the family section.
ᵉ Desvalagados translates as "disengaged" or "unaffiliated." It does not represent a group per se but rather a grouping of individuals not affiliated with other groups.

An Evolving Modus Operandi

With the organizational shift from the *ejido* executive committee to work group leaders, most formal decisions regarding forest management and harvesting took place in meetings of work group representatives rather than *ejido* assemblies. This change led to the creation of new rule systems in an attempt to fairly distribute rights and responsibilities among groups. Yet, the rule systems in place during 2000 were the product of experimentation carried out during the three previous years. Caoba and Petcacab had varying degrees of success in maintaining and enforcing rules. In general, groups in Caoba adhered to collectively established rules while their counterparts in Petcacab deviated from norms such that potential economic gains decreased. In both cases, groups tended to cooperate to the minimum extent necessary to extract and mill timber rather than to work proactively to increase economic efficiency. In this sense, groups success-fully increased individual timber profits by circumventing chronic mis-management by *ejido* executive committees but were unable to improve the overall efficiency of community forestry production.

CAOBA

Despite the shift to work groups, forest planning and timber harvests in Caoba followed much the same organization and management practices as those employed by the *ejido* enterprise. At the beginning of the harvest season, the heads of each group met to select members to fill key positions, including head woodsman (*jefe de monte*), record keeper (*documentador*), head of the sawmill (*jefe del aserradero*), and timber volume measurer (*cu-bicador*), among others. Each appointee received a salary based on a costs table (*tabulador*) that group representatives agreed upon prior to the start of harvesting activities. Those selected to fill technical posts had to have the requisite experience. In addition, work group leaders divided salaried positions proportionately so that larger groups' members were hired to fill more posts. At the same time, the larger groups had members with the greatest technical skills. The positions rotated on an annual basis. The one exception to this set of rules was the head of the community sawmill and machinery. Work group representatives decided that the president of the *ejido* executive committee would manage the sawmill and *ejido*-owned ma-chinery as a means of generating income to cover authorities' salaries and administrative costs.

With respect to timber harvesting, work group leaders drew lots at the beginning of the season to determine the order in which each group would receive and saw its wood. The head woodsman and resident forestry tech-nician from the Sociedad Sur coordinated the delineation of the annual cutting area, marking of harvestable trees, felling, skidding of logs to land-ings, de-limbing, removal of diseased sections (*saneo*), and calculation of timber volume. The work group leader or his delegate oversaw *saneo* and volume measurement to ensure wood quality. The *ejido* president then co-ordinated the transportation of logs to the sawmill and milling of logs into rough-cut boards. Buyers then picked up the sawnwood and trans-ported it to market. In 2000, all of Caoba's forestry work groups sold their wood through a timber-marketing fund (*fondo de acopio*) established in conjunction with the Sociedad Sur. In addition to the salaried positions, groups provided a proportionate number of day laborers. These workers were mostly unskilled (in terms of forestry), although some were hired for their abilities as chainsaw operators, truck drivers, and so on.

For collective activities such as community development, serious illness, or death, each group made contributions that were administered either by the *ejido* president or the municipal delegate.[6] Prior to the formation of groups, the *ejido* assembly approved collective expenditures from the *ejido* account managed by the executive committee. The communal account often became overdrawn from frequent personal loans that were never repaid and some misuse of monies by *ejido* authorities. Although the assembly retained the authority to approve or disapprove collective expenses following internal reorganization, in practice work group leaders made these decisions. *Ejidatarios* then pooled resources to cover the costs of hospital or burial fees, public works, and the like.

PETCACAB

Like Caoba, forestry work group leaders in Petcacab appointed fellow *ejidatarios* to the main salaried positions, including head woodsman, record keeper, head of the sawmill, and timber volume measurer. Candidates needed to have the technical capacity to effectively carry out the job. Work group leaders were not eligible for salaried positions. However, groups in Petcacab did not establish quotas for the distribution of posts, like the groups in Caoba. Moreover, although the *ejido* president performed a coordination and oversight role for group activities, he did not have special responsibilities for managing the community sawmill. Petcacab also established a costs table at the beginning of the harvest season in order to establish fixed expenses for all groups.

Because of its high timber harvest volume and numerous groups and sections, the rule system for timber harvesting in Petcacab was more complex than in Caoba. In Caoba one forest management team worked the annual cutting area and delivered logs to the sawmill crew, which handled secondary processing in conjunction with the *ejido* president. Work group leaders oversaw this process. In Petcacab all aspects of planning and harvesting were coordinated with work group leaders. As in Caoba, Petcacab's work groups organized a lottery in which leaders drew lots to determine the order of extraction. Beyond the lottery, however, two resident forestry technicians from the Sociedad Sur worked in conjunction with the head woodsman to divide the annual harvest area into lots, giving each a number. Following the lottery among groups and sections, the forestry technicians divided the 25-hectare lots based on the results of the lottery and assigned the number of lots estimated to cover a group or section's volume.

Technicians estimated harvestable volume for each lot based on previously completed inventories and on a process of lot delineation and tree identification that also required coordination and proportional division of labor among groups and sections. For example, in order to divide the cutting area into lots, the Sociedad Sur technicians established the distribution of labor responsibilities of each group and section by calculating the number of meters each would have to clear. A group with 17 members was required to clear underbrush along transect lines for 3,995 meters and complete lot delineation totaling another 2,703 meters. The next group in line picked up where the previous one left off until the entire cutting area was subdivided. Once the technicians assigned individual lots, each group or section assumed responsibility for the next phase, which included tree spotting, felling, and skidding logs to a central logyard. Given the number of groups and sections, the Sociedad Sur technicians played a key role in organizing work teams and maintaining lines of communication among group leaders.

During this second phase of the harvesting process, group leaders established temporary proprietary claims to the trees located in their assigned areas. They hired crews to mark, stamp, and later fell their mahogany trees.[7] A separate crew removed logs with a skidder and yet another team transported the logs from the landing to the sawmill. Some groups had trucks and made use of *ejido*-owned machinery such as a skidder. Other groups, particularly individual buyers with high volumes, hired additional logging teams from outside the *ejido* that brought their own machinery. In summary, timber extraction in Petcacab followed a complex rule system that emphasized group separation rather than collaboration. While groups coordinated their actions through the technicians, they collaborated minimally.

Timber management in Petcacab differed from Caoba in yet another way that had a significant impact on local power relationships. A vibrant "free" market developed in which local elites purchased timber volume from cash-poor or needy community members. Only *ejidatarios* from Petcacab could purchase wood (although some local buyers served as surrogates for nonlocal interests). Table 8.3 shows a breakdown of mahogany buyers for 2001. Fully 57% of the *ejido*'s authorized mahogany volume for that year was actively traded. Of this total, three individuals controlled 29% of Petcacab's high-value timber. All three were historically dominant leaders with well-established networks for securing capital and later marketing wood.

Petcacab's internal timber market generated significant additional coordination and mediation activities for local authorities and the two resi-

Table 8.3. Mahogany buyers in Petcacab, 2001

Buyer	Volume (m³)
Eleuterio May	168.140
Francisco Poot Medina	156.468
Emilio Poot Medina	104.052
Dzul Family	45.828
Evaristo Rodríguez	41.380
Pedro Rodríguez	39.244
Nestor Canche	33.000
Bernardo Canul Cau	32.468
Martin Pech	27.776
Antonio Coh	27.500
Aurelio Canto	19.000
Machiche	17.000
Carlos Yama	17.000
Raul Canul Che	16.828
Ernesto Gongora	13.656
Evaristo Poot Medina	13.000
Daniel Noh	9.000
Epifanio Pool	8.276
Vicente May	8.104
Rafael Noh	7.828
Paulino Yam May	7.328
Valerio Coh Ucan	7.328
Sufricaya	7.000
Pablo May Canul	5.276
Efrain May	5.000
Agustin Poot	3.276
Marcial Ucan	3.000
Lorenzo May Yam	3.000
Rufino Gongora	3.000
Juan Canul Cau	2.000
Julian May Cruz	1.000
Miguel Uc Canul	1.000
Cristobal Canul Canul	0.552
Total	**854.308**

Source: Wilshusen 2003.
Note: All names are pseudonyms.

dent forestry technicians employed by the Sociedad Sur. A single cubic meter of mahogany might change hands two or three times before harvest, and the resident technicians took on the responsibility of tracking sales. Moreover, members sold timber volume as much as two years in advance such that wood corresponding to 2002 was traded in 2000. Individual *ejidatarios* reported sales by presenting handwritten receipts, whereupon a forestry technician logged the transaction for future reference. However, many members waited to report sales until the forestry team registered final volume allocations for the harvest season. Since the total annual harvest volume for mahogany could not surpass 1,499 cubic meters, buyers accepted some risk in that certain sellers sold more than their 7.3 cubic meters. As a result, work group leaders decided that all receipts from timber exchanges had to be dated such that any late sales surpassing an individual's annual volume would be transferred to the next year's harvest cycle.

Although buyers faced some financial risks, they stood to make strong profits from acquiring the standing volumes of fellow *ejidatarios*. In 2000 most timber buyers paid an average of between 1,000 and 1,200 pesos (US$111–133) per cubic meter of standing volume. In some cases they paid as little as 800 pesos (US$89). In general, the exchange value of a cubic meter of mahogany in most forestry *ejidos* during 1999–2000 was 1,800 pesos (US$200). Most sellers sold 1 or 2 cubic meters of mahogany (out of a total of 7.3) as a source of cash. Some families needed cash quickly to cover unexpected medical expenses and thus sold their entire annual volume and sometimes more (a family might have multiple *ejidatarios* selling volume for more than one season). Still other community members sought cash to purchase beer, which many consumed on a daily basis. Despite the extraction and secondary processing costs incurred, buyers profited handsomely. Once sawn, a cubic meter of mahogany was worth on average between 3,000 and 3,800 pesos (US$333–422). This translated to a minimum gross profit of 1,800 pesos and a maximum gain of 2,800 pesos (US$311) per cubic meter.

Beyond the economic gains experienced by some buyers, the timber market in Petcacab affected local power relationships. The three timber buyers with the most volume in 2001 controlled nearly a third of the *ejido's* total annual cut and thus heavily influenced decision making. Two of the three top buyers were members of sections while the third was a group leader. All three were long-standing leaders with reputations for maximizing their economic interests at the expense of the *ejido*. As a result they maintained low levels of trust with other community members and operated individually rather than in groups. Had the two section members not controlled such high volumes, they would not have had a strong voice in work group assembly meetings. The third buyer nominally represented a group of 10 members and so had formal voting power in assemblies. Thus the internal market allowed historically powerful leaders to maintain their influence over timber management even though they did not form economic coalitions with other *ejidatarios*. This stands in contrast to Caoba, where decision-making power was linked to group size since individual timber volumes did not change hands.

Rule Making and Rule Breaking

In general, Caoba's forestry work groups adhered to collectively established rules for timber harvesting and processing during 2000. Despite achieving a certain level of cooperation, however, Caoba continued to face problems of maintenance and capitalization of collective investments. In effect, work groups cooperated to the extent necessary to harvest and mill timber but otherwise worked independently. While the formation of separate small enterprises allowed some groups to make capital investments and others to receive comparatively higher per capita timber incomes, it did not resolve a long-standing inability to maintain or improve community goods such as the sawmill or logging roads. Indeed, the establishment of two new tree nurseries in 2000 by the largest groups suggests that *ejidatarios* were willing to incur additional overhead costs rather than expend time and energy on expanding intergroup cooperation. Further, the agreement by which the *ejido* president managed the sawmill and machinery provided incentives for short-term operational efficiency but did not encourage long-term investment in collective goods. Since *ejido* authorities serve three-year terms, it is unlikely that they would have sufficient time to recover up-front costs for maintenance and improvement (Robinson 2000).

In contrast to Caoba, Petcacab faced recurring deviations from collectively established norms. In general, groups cooperated with initial financial and labor commitments that were necessary for the harvest to occur. For example, all groups completed their portion of stand lot delineation, allowing individual groups and sections to identify their harvestable trees for removal. In addition, groups respected the cutting order and took trees only from assigned lots.

Chronic rule breaking occurred in those phases of production that required the use of collective goods. In contrast to the Caoba groups, each

Petcacab group removed its assigned trees and milled its wood for later sale. In an attempt to avoid an open-access scenario in which individual groups could maximize their economic interests at the expense of fellow *ejidatarios*, group leaders established a quota system to cover maintenance and repair costs for the sawmill and other community-owned machinery, such as a skidder. Using the annual costs table, leaders created a payment schedule based on the number of cubic meters of wood transported or board feet milled. Groups were to pay 50% at the beginning of the harvest season to establish a collective fund that would cover most costs for all groups. They were to deliver the remaining fraction after selling their wood. While a majority of groups contributed at least part of their quotas, certain individuals who had purchased high timber volumes did not.

Similar patterns of defection emerged in relation to road maintenance. During 2000, several points along the access road developed deep ruts that hampered transport of work teams to and from the cutting area. Group leaders attempted to reach an agreement on repairing the road but were unable to sort out financial and labor responsibilities before the harvest season began. The road continued to deteriorate, and some groups were forced to use an alternative route to transport their logs to the mill following a series of early rainstorms. Just as importantly, the poor state of the road reduced the efficiency of the harvest. Chronic noncompliance also arose with respect to maintenance of tree nurseries and reforestation of harvest areas.

In analyzing the different degrees of cooperation in Caoba and Petcacab, the question arises: why did Caoba cooperate more effectively than Petcacab if the latter had significantly greater economic incentives to follow collectively agreed upon rules? Beyond individual differences presented by work group and other leaders in the two communities, four structural factors help to explain Caoba's relatively more successful rule system.

First, Caoba featured a concentration of power in two of its seven groups, whereas in Petcacab, power was dispersed among groups, sections, and individual timber buyers. The two largest work groups in Caoba joined two thirds of community members while the biggest included just under half of all *ejidatarios*. These two groups controlled most aspects of collective decision making and otherwise operated independently. Petcacab presented a broad distribution of power among representatives and timber buyers where groupings included four to seven members, usually from the same nuclear family. Only three groups had enough members to warrant investments in machinery and infrastructure for small enter-

Table 8.4. Comparison of work group dynamics in Caoba and Petcacab

	Caoba	Petcacab
Decision-making power	Concentrated	Dispersed
Timber extraction/processing	Collective	Multigroup
Collective investment (vehicles, tools, machinery)	Medium	Low
Local economic importance of timber	Medium-low	High
Rule enforcement	Untested	Weak
Maintenance/improvement of collective goods (logging roads, sawmill)	Low	Low

prise development. In addition, three timber buyers, who were interested mainly in maximizing individual profits, controlled nearly a third of the *ejido*'s mahogany volume. In sum, divergent interests and a lack of political alliances characterized decision making in Petcacab.

Second, the organization of timber extraction and secondary processing presented fewer opportunities for rule defection in Caoba. Because of Caoba's relatively low harvest volume vis-à-vis Petcacab, work groups in Caoba established one crew to remove wood from the forest and another to produce sawn boards. In Petcacab, work groups also hired fellow *ejidatarios* to administer harvesting and sawing, but each group or section took on a percentage of pre-harvest activities and, once individual lots were delineated, managed their respective timber volumes. Moreover, each individual, group, or section used the *ejido*'s sawmill to process its wood. Although a sawmill manager oversaw secondary processing, each party hired its own crew, so that maintenance problems or equipment failure became the financial liability of the group whose wood was in the mill at the time (see Table 8.4).

Third, the timber economy has decreased in importance in Caoba while it has remained the dominant economic activity in Petcacab. As a result, many *ejidatarios* in Caoba—even those affiliated with one of the two largest groups—had a falling interest in forestry and thus focused on diversifying their sources of income. In contrast, forestry-related earnings comprised over 50% of annual income for *ejidatarios* in Petcacab. This amount almost certainly increased in 2002, when Petcacab's annual mahogany harvest increased from 1,499 to 2,000 cubic meters. In Petcacab, timber harvests and sales occupied *ejidatarios* full time from January to July.

Fourth, rule enforcement was relatively weak in Petcacab. Cooperation broke down in the latter phases of production there because no effective enforcement measures existed. During the early phases of planning and felling, the technical director of the Sociedad Sur could threaten not to stamp a particular group's trees for harvest if it did not adhere to the rules. Once the wood was cut, however, neither the Sociedad Sur nor the assembly of work group leaders had political leverage points. Prior to the formation of work groups, when the *ejido* executive committee administered forest production, the *ejido* assembly could decide to withhold an *ejidatario*'s share of timber profits for major violations such as misuse of communal funds. With the shift in decision making to work group leaders and direct control of timber profits by individual *ejidatarios*, the assembly had yet to develop a workable enforcement system by 2002.

While work groups in Caoba and Petcacab experienced different degrees of success in cooperating on forest management, neither was able to maintain or improve collective goods such as the sawmill unless a breakdown completely impeded production. In Caoba, group leaders experimented with a system of incentives whereby the *ejido* president managed the sawmill and derived his salary from the profits attained. While effective for increasing short-term efficiency, this model did not encourage long-term, up-front investments for preventive maintenance or improvements since elected authorities serve three-year terms. In Petcacab, rules for the use and care of collective goods broke down to the point that it significantly affected production efficiency. Most prominently, a system of quotas for maintaining the *ejido*-owned sawmill and timber extraction machinery failed to generate sufficient revenues to cover running expenses since several leaders did not fully pay their dues. Similarly, groups in Petcacab proved unable to pool resources to repair portions of an access road, which significantly increased the time needed to ferry work crews to and from the annual cutting area.

While work groups in both *ejidos* had difficulties improving collective forestry operations, the organizational changes in local management did not produce net losses in either economic efficiency or forest protection. Rather, the formation of work groups brought important economic advances for individuals and groups but failed to overcome long-standing barriers to collective action.

Impacts of Work Group Formation

The formation of forestry work groups in Caoba and Petcacab between 1996 and 2000 precipitated new power relations at the community level, including a realignment of decision-making authority. In this sense it represented a process of local decentralization. The shift in local organization helped to overcome long-standing domination by *ejido* executive committees of forest management and timber profits under the CFEs. Individual *ejidatarios*, particularly those from Petcacab, received greater timber-based income and participated more directly in forestry operations and decision making than ever before. At the same time, historically dominant *ejidatarios* adapted to the new organizational arrangements by controlling decision making either through large groups (Caoba) or through accumulation of timber stocks (Petcacab).

Governance

The most obvious changes that emerged with the formation of work groups involved *ejido* governance structure. Prior to the appearance of work groups, an elected executive committee administered *ejido* affairs on behalf of the communal assembly. The assembly also chose a three-person oversight committee to monitor officials' performance and report any wrongdoing. While the *ejido* assembly was conceived as a democratic body, in practice local elites tended to dominate decision making, and *ejido* presidents often acted unilaterally or employed authoritarian tactics to advance personal interests or those of political allies. In contrast, with the appearance of work groups, the locus of decision-making authority shifted from the *ejido* president to group leaders. In this sense, it represented an adaptation to recurrent problems with petty corruption and informal lending by elected authorities in which political power was dispersed among several leaders instead of just one. The change in political power marginalized the position of *ejido* president. The assembly still elected an executive committee but it played only a minor role, performing certain administrative tasks that still needed to carry the *ejido*'s name.

Similarly, the *ejido* assembly diminished in political importance. In both Caoba and Petcacab, assemblies met once or twice during 2000. All matters related to timber production or other economic activities were decided in work group assemblies. In effect, work groups became a type of representative governing council that supplanted the *ejido* assembly and executive committee. Groups differed in how they represented their members, however. Some, such as Sufricaya in Petcacab and Chichan Há in Caoba, established formal bylaws and held regular meetings to discuss and debate operations. Other groups operated informally. The small groups in Caoba and most of the groups in Petcacab fell into this category. The majority of groups in Petcacab, for example, did not meet on a regular basis, and leaders often did not inform members of decisions and activities. Thus while *ejido* assemblies in both communities did not function as democratically as intended, the representative council of work group leaders did not necessarily represent community members any better.

Participation

Despite uncertainties regarding the ability of groups to represent all *ejidatarios* and to cooperate in forest management, most *ejidatarios* in both communities indicated that reorganization worked better than when the forestry enterprise was managed by the *ejido* executive committee. Table 8.5 lays out some of the perceived advantages and disadvantages of each system. One advantage of reorganization was that it allowed wider participation in forestry activities than ever before. Under *ejido* executive committee control, a core group of members rotated among positions of power in the CFE. After dividing internally, work groups managed their own timber volumes.

Moreover, division in groups allowed *ejidatarios* to establish their own affiliations and control individual timber revenues. Under *ejido* management, some members typically would advocate for reinvesting part of annual timber income in new equipment and upkeep of existing machinery, while others would favor receiving the highest direct payments possible. Inevitably the *ejido* assembly would vote for maximizing individual payments, leading to a progressive decline in operating efficiency as machinery broke down due to a lack of continuous maintenance. Under the new structure, certain groups opted to develop small enterprises, including carpentry workshops, while others decided not to reinvest in forestry but rather to apply timber income to other uses. In the case of Petcacab, numerous *ejidatarios* chose to sell their standing volume and thus not to participate in timber production.

A third component of increased participation was a rise in local monitoring and whistle blowing regarding illegal timber harvesting. Under *ejido* control, many members knew little about how their forests were managed and simply expected a portion of the profits produced by timber sales. Although timber theft was uncommon in Caoba and Petcacab prior to reorganization, some marginalized groups felt justified in removing trees illegally as a way of circumventing elite control of the forestry enterprise. With the division of timber volume among *ejidatarios*, most members developed a stronger sense of ownership of the forest commons. As a result, internal monitoring increased so that community members who wit-

Table 8.5. Comparison of community forest enterprises (CFEs) and work groups

	CFEs	Work Groups
Governance		
Locus of decision-making authority	*Ejido* executive committee	Work group leaders
Role of *ejido* assembly	Stronger	Weaker
Participation		
Direct involvement in forest management	Weaker	Stronger
Direct management of timber revenues	Minimal	Complete
Monitoring and oversight of timber resources	Lower	Higher
Informal Economies		
Source of cash loans	*Ejido* executive committee	Work group leaders
Collateral	Undefined	Per capita timber volumes

nessed illegal cutting reported it to other members. In Caoba internal vigilance was important in overcoming tensions caused by two *ejidatarios* who claimed that the annual cutting area overlapped with land that they had claimed for agricultural use five years earlier. In Petcacab, *ejidatarios* in the village of Polinkín denounced fellow residents who illegally cut and attempted to transport polewood used in making open pavilions in tourist areas. In both cases internal monitoring helped to halt illegal cutting and land use.

Informal Local Economies

In addition to shifts in the locus of decision-making authority and increased participation, the formation of work groups transferred lending power from the *ejido* president to group leaders. As administrator of most aspects of political and economic affairs, the *ejido* president, and to a lesser extent the *ejido* treasurer, commanded a wide array of resources for rewarding political allies and isolating opponents. Beyond distribution of jobs, the executive committee had wide latitude in doling out personal loans in line with long-standing informal economies. Indeed, *ejido* authorities typically felt strong pressure to provide loans for fellow members both out of a sense of obligation and as a means of avoiding possible future retaliation. Ultimately, loaning practices limited the availability of cash supply and hindered maintenance and improvement of *ejido*-owned machinery and other communal investments.

Two significant changes in lending practices followed reorganization in Caoba and Petcacab. First, the leaders of larger groups such as Chichan Há in Caoba filled the role of the executive committee by offering loans to its members. Second, and just as importantly, the distribution of each *ejido*'s timber volume meant that individual members had collateral that leaders could use to recover loans. Thus in Caoba, for example, work group leaders provided loans to members against their individual timber volumes. In Petcacab a similar dynamic emerged, although exchanges were framed as timber purchases, not as loans. Cash-poor or needy *ejidatarios* sold their standing volume at below-market rates, thereby transferring both production costs and additional profits to timber buyers. While lending within Caoba's groups was limited in 2000, internal exchange of timber volume in Petcacab comprised over half of the *ejido*'s annual total. Interestingly, community members from both *ejidos* used surrogate sources for cash loans that allowed them to avoid repayment, such as the Sociedad Sur and the associated timber-marketing fund (*fondo de acopio*), thus reproducing earlier lending practices.

The More Things Change . . .

The experiences of Caoba and Petcacab at the close of the twentieth century illustrate how forestry *ejidos* in Quintana Roo have responded to the wide-ranging institutional reforms of the early 1990s as well as long-standing internal challenges such as elite control, petty corruption, and informal lending (Wilshusen 2003). With respect to work groups and their impact on *ejido* governance, forest management, and local economies, the cases in this chapter point to important changes as well as continuities. While *ejidos* remain intact, the role of the executive committee and general assembly has diminished. While decision-making power over forestry operations has shifted from the executive committee to work group leaders, the same local elites continue to dominate, much as they did prior to the formation of groups. While forestry profits are more equitably shared under groups, most *ejidatarios* remain cash poor and thus depend on government subsidies like PROCAMPO as well as cash "loans" from a variety of sources. And despite the ability of some groups to make capital investments to improve local employment options, an increasing number of younger *ejidatarios* are seeking work either in the coastal tourism corridor or the United States.

In general, the diverse political, organizational, and economic changes at the local level have resulted in minimal changes in the core community forestry activities in the two *ejidos*. This can be interpreted as both good and bad news. On one hand, collective forest management continues in accord with federal forest and agrarian law, which requires that forest commons remain intact and that harvesting be carried out by *ejidos*. At the same time, however, just as with the CFEs under the administration of *ejido* executive committees, management by work groups in the two communities has so far been unable to improve the overall efficiency of operations. While forest management continued to follow existing plans, *ejidatarios* collectively continued to minimize their cooperation to get wood to market. They were unable to reduce extraction costs, maintain sawmills, or improve access roads. In effect, *ejidatarios* in both communities have successfully decentralized control of financial management and some aspects of community development but have been unable to overcome barriers to proactive cooperation among groups that would allow all groups to increase profits and potentially improve management techniques and forest protection. Thus, despite its potential, community forestry in southern Quintana Roo will likely continue to "muddle through" unless an alliance of community leaders emerges that can successfully develop and enforce collective rule systems, allowing all forestry operations to achieve their full potential. What, then, is the future of community forestry under work groups in *ejidos* like Caoba and Petcacab?

Although division into work groups has not produced a complete breakdown in community forest management, as some predicted, it has generated significant internal reorganization that could lead to further transformation of community forestry. Since work group formation represents a grassroots response to internal and external factors like corruption and institutional change, it could lead to unprecedented collaboration among *ejidatarios*. In this sense, local decentralization could precipitate stronger rule systems within the context of carrying out each *ejido*'s forest management plan. With continued support from second-tier organizations like the Sociedad Sur, even *ejidos* like Petcacab, with its complex internal politics and many groups, could institute enforceable rule systems for all aspects of forest management.

At the same time, however, the internal changes could lead to further specialization, where certain groups take on the role of forest managers on behalf of all *ejidatarios*. Community members might contract these groups to harvest and sell timber, providing a share of profits. Alternatively, following the example of Petcacab, *ejidatarios* might sell their timber volumes up front, leaving individual and group buyers the responsibility of forest management. Either of these latter scenarios could reduce direct participation in forestry, but might also increase operational efficiency. While, as of mid-2003, it is unclear what the formation of work groups will ultimately mean in terms of sustainable forestry in Caoba and Petcacab, trends suggest that group specialization is more likely than strengthened collaboration.

Notes

1. The other six forestry *ejidos* are Tres Garantías, Noh Bec, X-Hazil, Laguna Kaná, Naranjal Poniente, and Felipe Carrillo Puerto. For discussion on this assessment see Wilshusen 2003.

2. As of the 2002 harvest season, Petcacab's authorized annual harvest of mahogany had increased to 2,000 cubic meters (SPFEQR technical director, personal communication, 20 June 2002).

3. Note that non-*ejidatario* residents do not receive cash income from timber harvesting. For an analysis of distributions of forestry benefits in five *ejidos* in Quintana Roo, see Armijo Canto and Robertos Jiménez 1998.

4. In January 2001, the Secretariat of the Environment, Natural Resources, and Fisheries (Secretaría del Medio Ambiente, Recursos Naturales, y Pezca; SEMARNAP) changed its name to the Secretariat of the Environment and Natural Resources (Secretaría de Medio Ambiente y Recursos Naturales; SEMARNAT).

5. In 2002, Petcacab's total mahogany harvest volume rose from 1,499 to 2,000 cubic meters. By internal agreement, each *ejidatario* donates 1 cubic meter to a community development fund to be used for collective works such as community infrastructure. Thus, the total divided among the 206 *ejidatarios* is 1,794 cubic meters.

6. The municipal delegate is a locally elected official responsible for services to all residents (*ejidatarios* and non-*ejidatarios*) of "urban" settlements. In contrast, the *ejido* executive committee represents the assembly of *ejidatarios* and manages affairs associated with the collective rights and responsibilities of members (the scope of which has changed with the formation of work groups).

7. Under the Mexican forest law, a registered forester must stamp the base of harvestable trees with a small sledge hammer upon verifying that its diameter at breast height (dbh) is at or above the legal minimum of 55 centimeters.

References

Armijo Canto, N., and J. Robertos Jiménez. 1998. Distribución de los beneficios socioeconómicos del bosque: Estudio realizado en cinco ejidos forestales del centro y sur de Quintana Roo. Chetumal: DFID.

Cornelius, W. A., and D. Myhre, ed. 1998. *The Transformation of Rural Mexico: Reforming the Ejido Sector.* San Diego: Center for U.S.-Mexican Studies, University of California.

DFID, SEMARNAP, SIMAP, and UNOFOC. 1998. *La agenda forestal de Quintana Roo.* Chetumal: DFID.

INEGI. 2000. *XII Censo general de población y vivienda, resultados por localidad.* Aguascalientes: INEGI.

Key, N., C. Muñoz-Pina, A. de Janvry, and E. Sadoulet. 1998. Social and environmental consequences of the Mexican reforms: Common pool resources in the *ejido* sector. Unpublished manuscript, University of California, Berkeley.

Robinson, D. 2000. An analysis of different forms of organization for forest production in three communities in Quintana Roo, Mexico. In *Study for Increasing Marketing Opportunities of Lesser Known Species and Secondary Wood Products in Tropical Central America and Mexico,* ed. R. Forster. Draft report to the United States Forest Service. Chetumal: Universidad de Quintana Roo.

Wilshusen, P. R. 2003. Negotiating devolution: Community conflict, structural power, and local forest management in Quintana Roo, Mexico. PhD diss., University of Michigan.

Zabin, C., and P. L. Taylor. 1997. Quintana Roo forestry management project: Consultants' report. Chetumal: DFID.

PART III

ECOLOGY AND LAND USE CHANGE IN COMMUNITY FORESTRY

Ecological Issues in Community Tropical Forest Management in Quintana Roo, Mexico

HENRICUS F. M. VESTER AND MARÍA ANGÉLICA NAVARRO-MARTÍNEZ

The question of whether commercial logging can be carried out in tropical forests without inflicting serious ecological damage has been one of the most contentious issues in tropical forest ecology. Some authors proclaim that management should be left to a minimum (Rice et al. 1997), while others argue that sustainable management systems are feasible (Brünig 1996; de Graaf 1986; Johns 1997; Wadsworth 1997).

The tropical forests of the Mexican state of Quintana Roo have been marked by well over 100 years of commercial logging of mahogany (*Swietenia macrophylla*) and Spanish cedar (*Cedrela odorata*), as well as major deforestation in earlier centuries by the ancient Mayan civilization (Turner 1978), thus making it a useful laboratory for evaluating the impact of contemporary logging on forest structure and composition. For most of the last hundred years, logging was concentrated in the southern part of the state along the Río Hondo, the border with Belize. From 1953 to 1983, logging spread into the interior of the southern part of the state under the aegis of the parastatal Maderas Industrializados de Quintana Roo (MIQROO), one of the first logging companies in tropical America to operate with a management plan (Flachsenberg and Galletti 1999). Beginning in the early 1960s, small-scale contractors began logging in the central part of the state, the area of particular interest in this study. Finally, beginning in 1985, a good portion of the forests of southern and central Quintana Roo came under the direct management of the communities themselves, supported by the Forestry Pilot Plan (Plan Piloto Forestal; PPF), a joint project of the Mexican federal and state governments and German foreign assistance (Flachsenberg and Galletti 1999). The PPF, in silvicultural terms, was characterized by the establishment of permanent forest areas (PFAs) where management plans were developed and wherein

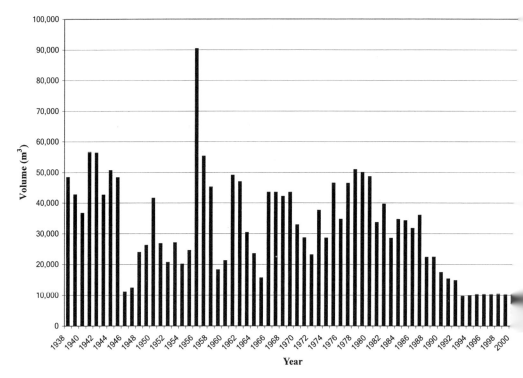

Figure 9.1 Total harvested volume of mahogany and Spanish cedar in Quintana Roo, 1938–2001. *Source:* Bray forthcoming.

agriculture was prohibited. The transition from parastatal and private contractor logging to community logging coincided with a dramatic drop in the annual logging volume in the state, as Figure 9.1 indicates.

However, the very notable decline and subsequent stability in logging volume in the state in recent years does not mean that the elusive goal of "sustainability" has been reached. Most of the communities have continued to operate under management plans adapted from the one used by MIQROO, with particular assumptions about the regeneration and growth rates of mahogany and other species of interest. These assumptions have been vigorously debated (Flachsenberg and Galletti 1999; Negreros-Castillo 1995; Snook 1993, 1996, 1998), as will be further discussed below.

In this paper we will present new research on the forest ecology of logging in general and on the impact of logging on mahogany in particular. Specifically we will estimate the number of different tree species in the forest (species richness) and assess the risks for loss of species due to logging. We will then provide an overview of the natural spatial variation and the principal ecological processes that condition the presence of mahogany in the forests of Quintana Roo and the limitations and the possibilities that this presents for more sustainable management. We will also present new data on growth increments of mahogany and other species. We will argue that the premise that mahogany requires large clearings to regenerate (Snook 1993, 1996, 1998) needs to be reexamined in light of research results that show that mahogany can also regenerate in smaller clearings, under certain conditions. Based on the data presented we will make suggestions for modifications in the silvicultural practices in the mahogany forests of Quintana Roo.

The Eco-systems and Ecology of Mahogany

The peninsula of Yucatán, where the state of Quintana Roo is found, is a karst plateau that arose from the sea in at least three different periods (Lugo-Hubp and García-Arizaga 1999). The limestone mother material causes features that determine land use and human presence. There are few superficial water flows on the peninsula, with most water filtering directly into the substrate, dissolving part of the calcium carbonate. This dissolution process is the origin of landforms like *cenotes*, or sinkholes; *bajos*, or seasonally inundated, sometimes permanently wet large depressions; and *rejolladas*, which are smaller depressions, 2 to 10 meters in diameter. *Cenotes* and *rejolladas* are mostly found in the north, and *bajos* more in the center and the south.

The landscape in general is gently sloping. Toward the center of the peninsula there are pronounced hills. The coast of Quintana Roo is characterized by large wetlands covered with low mangrove forest. Moving away from the coast the landscape is characterized by low and long sloping hills and depressions. In some parts, as in the area northwest of Felipe Carrillo Puerto, the hills are small and pronounced, varying between 2 and 5 meters in height.

The climate in the center and south of Quintana Roo is warm: subhumid with summer rains (Orellana Lanza et al. 1999). The dry period extends for about five months, from December to April, with another dry period in August. The mean annual amount of precipitation varies from about 1,000 (Xpichil) to nearly 1,500 millimeters (Limones, 80 kilometers

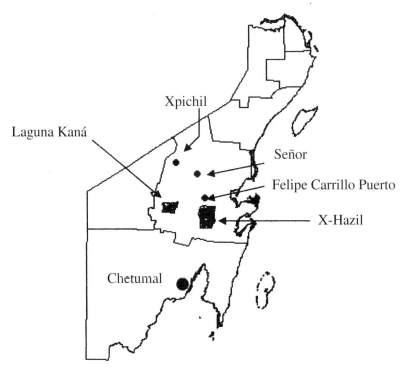

Figure 9.2 Map showing the Quintana Roo study areas, X-Hazil and Laguna Kaná, and some localities referenced in the text.

north of Chetumal) and varies enormously across years, 1,000–2,000 millimeters in Limones and 600–2,300 millimeters in Felipe Carrillo Puerto (Orellana Lanza et al. 1999; see Figure 9.2).

The mean annual temperature is about 25°C in Quintana Roo. The maximum mean annual temperature is about 35°C near the coast (Chetumal) and about 40°C inland (Limones, Señor). The minimum mean annual temperature is higher near the coast, about 20°C in Chetumal and 10°C in Limones and Señor (Orellana Lanza et al. 1999). Between August and November is the hurricane season, with a long history of hurricanes impacting forests and infrastructure. Among the most severe hurricanes that struck Quintana Roo in recent decades are Janet (1955), Carmen (1974), Gilbert (1988), and Roxanne (1995).

The soils, mostly Rendolls, are related to the geomorphology of the landscape. On hills, the soils are shallow, stony, relatively poor in organic material, and dry, whereas in the lower parts they are deeper, often rich in organic material, and with better water-holding capacity. In the *bajos*, the soils remain inundated from October to January. In times of hurricane impact there is increased inundation and temporary formation of rivers.

The main vegetation types in the study area are related to the geomorphology, soils, and climate. Along the coast there are large areas of mangrove forests and wetlands, and just inland a strip of low semideciduous dry forest (SDF), or *selva baja subcaducifolia* (Durán Garcia 1986). Further inland the semi-evergreen forest (SEF) (Rzedowski and Rzedowski 1989), considered by Holdridge et al. (1971) as tropical dry forest, and the major focus of our interest here, is interspersed with *bajos*, with their low inundated forest (LIF). The semi-evergreen forest is characterized by two abundant canopy species, *Manilkara zapota* (chicle) and *Brosimum alicastrum* (ramon).

Mahogany is considered the leading species in Quintana Roo forest management. Together with Spanish cedar (*Cedrela odorata*), mahogany is a high-value timber, getting substantially higher prices than most lesser-known species (LKS). Most of the management practices are directed to this species. Mayhew and Newton (1998) recently reviewed the main ecological issues of mahogany (but see Lugo et al. 2003). They suggest that the optimal growth environment for mahogany seems to be the dry forest, implying that it should be abundant in Quintana Roo, although they also note that the influence of environmental factors on the growth of mahogany is not investigated in detail. In this respect the recent study of Medina et al. (2003) on the *Swietenia* hybrid *macrophylla* × *humilis* shows that height and volume of seedlings under medium light (32.9% of full sunlight) was higher than under full or low light, and plants survived in all treatments, stating that the hybrid has a higher shade tolerance than pioneer and early successional species.

In most of the forests where mahogany grows there are relatively few seedlings and saplings (Snook 1996), raising questions about the ecology of seedlings. It has been found that light is not a limitation for its germination, but the restriction of light strongly diminishes its growth and may influence seedling mortality. Moreover, other factors such as humidity and seed predation also play a role in seedling establishment, and in many cases may be more important (Medina et al. 2003). Mahogany prefers soils that are medium well drained (Mayhew and Newton 1998). This coincides with Miranda's (1958) observation for the Yucatán that mahogany grows preferably in the transition between *bajos* and semi-evergreen forest in long sloping landscapes, and both on slopes and in valleys where the landscape has short, low hills.

Mahogany trees are long-lived organisms that start reproducing when they are big trees. They are insect pollinated, outcrossing, and trees flower in the beginning of the rainy season in March or April, producing fruits 9–11 months later (Loveless and Gullison 2003; Snook 1993). Small trees with diameters less than 75 centimeters usually produce few fruits (Camara and Snook 1998), and maximum fecundity is only reached in trees with dbh[1] of 90–130 centimeters (Gullison et al. 1996). At this size the crown of the tree reaches its maximum height and extension and allocation of sugars to the fruits is larger than in smaller trees that invest more in vegetative growth. Production of fruits is yearly, but there are probably mast years[2] (Grogan et al. 2003). Seed dispersal of mahogany is by wind, but the seeds are fairly heavy, so only strong winds can cause large dispersal distances. The distances over which seed dispersal has been observed vary between 30 and 90 meters (Mayhew and Newton 1998). This means that for a sufficient seed cover by natural seeding, a forest needs to have at least one seed-producing tree per every 2 hectares. Moreover, mahogany does not form part of the seed bank, and thus regenerates from recently fallen seeds (Snook 1998).

Two levels of forest dynamics in mahogany forests play a role in its ecology and organization: large-scale impacts and small-scale impacts. Snook (1993) argues that there are two major forms of disturbance which determine mahogany ecology and organization, and both are large-scale impacts (>1 ha): hurricanes followed by fires and shifting corn cultivation, which has been practiced intermittently in these forests for millennia. Dickinson (1998), in a study of the forests of the community of Noh Bec, found that the dynamics of small-scale impacts in these forests are naturally low in comparison to those in tropical rainforests, with gap formation that is frequent and of small size (<200 m²). Gaps created by logging were usually as large as, but sometimes larger than, the naturally created gaps, and characterized by the opening of upper soil horizons due to the activity of skidders (Dickinson 1998).

It is precisely the effect of the impact of logging on mahogany and LKS that provides the major focus of this study. It has been argued that forest management in Quintana Roo is not based on the ecology of the species and the characteristics of the ecosystem. For example, the annual harvest volume was determined by dividing the standing stock by 25 for the duration of the MIQROO concession because of the lack of data about growth rates. In addition, the original 60-centimeter minimum diameter, later revised downward to 55 centimeters, was established based on sawmill criteria, not on growth rates or ecological function criteria (Snook 1998). These criteria have not significantly changed since 1983. With a polycyclic system of three 25-year cutting cycles, and the new minimum diameter limit of 55 centimeters, it is assumed, for example, that it takes 75 years for a mahogany to reach that minimum (Gómez-Pompa and Burley 1991). However, it has been argued that it actually takes much longer, over a hundred years (Snook 1993, 1998, 2003). Further, concern has been expressed that the indiscriminate logging of all large trees affects fauna (Fimbel et al. 2001; Johns 1997), genetic diversity of the logged species (Newton et al. 1993), and biodiversity in general (Johns 1997; Rice et al. 2001). Moreover, selective logging may deplete a population of its most favored genotypes, causing genetic erosion. This is already the case with *Swietenia mahagoni* (Newton et al. 1993), and for the same reason *Swietenia macrophylla* is included in the CITES (Convention on International Trade in Endangered Species of Wild Fauna and Flora) Appendix II (CITES 2003).

The PPF management plans are based on forest inventories covering 1–2% of the total area and determining the volume of each species to be cut in the first cycle (trees of mahogany >55 cm dbh, LKS >35 cm dbh) and designates the stock for the second cycle (mahoganies between 35 and 54 cm dbh and of LKS between 25 and 34 cm dbh) and the third cycle (mahoganies between 15 and 34 cm dbh and of LKS between 10 and 24 cm dbh). These diameter classes are based on an assumed annual growth rate of 0.8 centimeters for mahogany and 0.4 centimeters for other species. A total of 18 species are logged according to the management plan of a typical community, such as Laguna Kaná (Carreón-Mundo et al. 1990). After logging, which usually takes place in the dry period, logging gaps, skid trails, and logyards are replanted with seedlings of mahogany and Spanish cedar, although concerns have been raised about their survival rates, as will be discussed later.

Snook (1998) has argued that because mahogany has a preference for the infrequent large open places in the forest caused mainly by fires and agriculture, and because the advent of the PPF and the permanent forest areas prohibited agriculture in the logging areas, this has removed one possible source of vigorous mahogany regeneration. She thus suggests there is probably insufficient regeneration of this species to assure a future stock after the third harvest cycle. Moreover, selective logging of large trees in the annual logging area eliminates the most important seed sources, also severely affecting the regeneration of this species in the forest.

Apart from concerns about silviculture in the region, there is a more general concern that logging affects biodiversity because of its impact on forest soils and forest structure (Rice et al. 2001; Vincent et al. 1997).

Logged forests are more prone to the impact of hurricanes (Everham and Brokaw 1996) and during droughts are more receptive to forest fires (Siegert et al. 2001), which may cause local extirpation if they occur on a large scale or are frequent.

Species loss in the Maya Zone has not been recorded, and it is here argued that future loss due to timber extraction is not very likely under current management plans. We base this prediction on Dinerstein et al. (1995), who analyzed the conservation status of terrestrial eco-regions in Latin America and the Caribbean region. They classified the semi-evergreen forests of the Yucatán as vulnerable, which means that there is a certain fragmentation of the habitat, but with conservation measures most of the biodiversity can be maintained. The distinctiveness of the biodiversity is third most important within a scale of four levels classified in the report to be of bioregional importance. Also, according to Hawthorne and Hughes (1997) and other reports (Lynch 1991; Whigham et al. 1991), the ecosystems of the Yucatán Peninsula are highly resilient, having adapted through more than 3,000 years to the frequent impact of hurricanes (Whigham et al. 1991), fires, and agriculture (Turner 1978). Hawthorne and Hughes (1997) remark that most of the species found on the peninsula have wide distribution patterns and are represented in local reserves.

Questions Raised

The community forest managers of Quintana Roo are under the same pressures as other forest managers throughout the world, having to balance needs for income with increasing demands from society for the conservation of natural resources and biodiversity. Although there have been many recent studies of the impact of logging on wildlife (Fimbel et al. 2001), here we will focus on the maintenance of arboreal population structure, tree species diversity, and productivity of economically important species, specifically mahogany.

The dilemmas of conservation and timber production in tropical forest discussed above lead to the following questions:

- What is the effect of logging on tree species in the forest? This question will not be answered directly because there are few areas without logging and scant data on the structure of the forest before logging began. Our analysis will be restricted to tree flora and based on knowledge of the ecology of the species and the dynamics of the forest and its changes through management.

- How can population structure be maintained? In order to guarantee the existence of sufficient large trees for logging every 25 years, the population structure should show a sufficient stock of undersized trees to replace the logged ones. It is supposed that opening up of the forest by logging initiates natural regeneration and stimulates the growth of young trees in the understory. But studies of natural regeneration and seedling planting of commercial species in these gaps have not been encouraging, with very low rates of survival observed (Negreros-Castillo 1995; Negreros-Castillo and Mize 1993, 2003).

- Can the growth rate of species of commercial interest be increased without affecting ecological function, especially species diversity? Apart from a sufficient number of trees, a sufficient growth rate is necessary to obtain the desired timber production. In many silvicultural systems stimulation of growth of some tree species affects the populations of others (e.g., de Graaf 1986).

These questions have not been previously raised with reference to silviculture in the area. In order to answer them we use data from two case studies. These data are analyzed with respect to the impact of logging on biodiversity, the population structure of different tree species populations, and forest architecture and temperaments.

The Case Studies

Research was carried out in two *ejidos* in the Maya area: Laguna Kaná and X-Hazil (Figure 9.2). Laguna Kaná was a founding member of the Organización de Ejidos Productores Forestales de la Zona Maya (OEPFZM), which has been administering its management plans since 1984, while X-Hazil withdrew from the OEPFZM in 1994 and has had privately contracted foresters developing its plans since then. Some additional data was compiled from studies in the *ejidos* of Naranjal Poniente (south of and bordering Laguna Kaná) and Petcacab (south of X-Hazil and bordering Naranjal). Two studies were carried out in each of these ejidos: a transect study and a vegetation composition study. The research was informed by the theory of hierarchy of forest organization by Oldeman (1990; see also Rossignol et al. 1998). In this theory, each climatically and geomorphologically delimited forest type is a mosaic of patches, named eco-units, each grown up after clearing by natural or human intervention. From its start as a gap, in eco-unit terms the innovation phase, an eco-unit passes through a growth phase (aggradation) to a mature phase (biostasis), after which it loses its integration (degeneration phase). Degeneration of the canopy trees may also lead to a transition phase in which the subcanopy and understory trees have the potential to form a new biostasis. These phases can be recognized in the forest by the architecture of the trees that compose it and their organization in the forest (Vester 1997). By analyzing the architecture of a tree through its branching pattern, development phases can be recognized which are indicative of the development phases of the eco-unit (Oldeman 1990).

The transect study in both communities consisted of four 1-hectare transects (20 × 500 m), in which all trees of dbh >30 centimeters were mapped and measured. Also a map of the eco-units (see Oldeman 1990) was made and stumps of logged trees and extraction trails were mapped. Within the transects, forest profiles on short transects were made on selected sites, depicting all trees to scale.

The vegetation study was carried out in order to find out if there were differences in species composition within the forest. Thus, trees of dbh >10 centimeters were inventoried in 29 plots of 472 square meters each in each *ejido*. Plots were deliberately located in eco-units in biostasis. Within these plots, subplots of 3.2 square meters were established for the counting of regeneration.

Biodiversity and Impact of Logging

Species richness in SEF in general is relatively low (69 spp. per 0.1 ha, including all plants with dbh >2.5 cm) when compared with tropical rain-forests (TRFs) (152 spp. per 0.1 ha) (Gentry 1995). Diversity at the family level is very similar between SEF and TRF, but Gentry (1995) also remarks that endemism is relatively high in SEF. With respect to endemism on the Yucatán Peninsula, Ibarra-Manríquez et al. (1995) mention 54 endemic tree species, with 9 restricted to Quintana Roo. Most of these endemic species are found in ecosystems that are not attractive for forestry or agriculture: dry areas, sand dunes, and some inundated systems.

In this section, the analysis of species diversity in the Maya area is based on the findings in the *ejidos* X-Hazil and Laguna Kaná. Our goal is two-fold: to describe the diversity of tree species in the managed forests in order to increase understanding of the logged ecosystems and to evaluate the possible effects of management on persistence of species in the forest, with special attention to endemic species.

The data for Table 9.1 are from the transect study and vegetation studies. The regeneration was counted in 58 subplots of 3.2 square meters in the center of each vegetation plot. A total of 8,422 individuals were counted. In vegetation plots in each of the two case studies, we found that the diversity for small trees, most of which are not typically considered in forest management, is much higher than that for large trees. Among large trees (dbh >30 cm), about 30 different species were found. When we include smaller trees (dbh >10 cm), this number doubles, which means that there are probably twice as many subcanopy species as tree species which reach diameters of >30 cm. This relation of twice as many small as large tree species was found in an earlier forest inventory in X-Hazil, where we found up to 164 different species among 20,416 individual trees with dbh >10 centimeters, and about half of that among trees >30 centimeters dbh (Navarro-Martínez, unpublished data).

When the area of forest increases, the number of species increases. The total area covered by the vegetation plots, where we found 33 species of trees, was 1.4 hectares. On 4 hectares, considering only large trees (dbh >30 cm), the number of species increased to about 50, which is 60% more species on a surface three times larger, indicating that many species are relatively scarce. These species may be much more vulnerable to management than abundant species.

In addition to tree species, we found about 26 species of epiphytes[3] in these forests. Species overlap between the two *ejidos* was nearly 100%, except for two species, which were only found in X-Hazil. These plants are vulnerable to the intensification of the gap frequency and size, because a population of epiphytes is best maintained on old trees.

The species richness in the two *ejidos* of our survey was very similar. In total we found 82 species of trees and epiphytes in Laguna Kaná and 86 species in X-Hazil. The number of species shared between the two *ejidos* and based on these plots is 52. On the one hand, this suggests that the sample was still too small to register the complete biodiversity of the two *ejidos;* on the other hand, there are differences in composition between the two forests (see below).

The total richness in tree species in these *ejidos* is probably somewhat higher than the 164 species yielded in forest inventories (Navarro-Martínez, unpublished data). For the whole peninsula, Ibarra-Manríquez et al. (1995) found 437 species of trees among the 2,477 species of plants

Table 9.1. Richness of trees and epiphytes in the vegetation study

Ejido	Regeneration (including lianas and palms) (0.0093 ha)		All trees >10 cm dbh (1.4 ha)		Only trees >30 cm dbh (1.4 ha)		Trees on large surface >30 cm dbh (4 ha)		All trees		Epiphytes (1.1 ha)		Trees, regeneration, and epiphytes	
	Ind.*	Sp.**	Ind.	Sp.	Ind.	Sp.	Ind.	Sp.	Ind.	Sp.	Ind.	Sp.	Ind.	Sp.
Laguna Kaná	1,498	51	1,218	72	199	32	399	52	1,620	82	149	24	3,259	129
X-Hazil Sur	2,446	68	1,268	73	213	33	410	45	1,666	86	85	26	5,163	147

Note: Twenty-nine plots of 472 m² in each *ejido*; in the transect study, 4 plots of 1 ha in each *ejido*. Regeneration was counted in subplots of 3.2/m².
* No. of individuals.
** No. of species.

Table 9.2. Abundance of tree species in four forest *ejidos* in Quintana Roo

Abundance classification	Class (no. individuals)	No. species	% of total individuals
Very abundant	>1,000	5	41.5
Abundant	500 < X < 1,000	8	19.3
Common	100 < X < 500	30	28.9
Scarce	50 < X < 100	21	5.9
Rare	<50	104	4.3
Total		**168**	

Source: Forest inventories from Laguna Kaná and X-Hazil in Petcacab and permanent plots, in Naranjal were combined for a total of 25,623 trees on 75.4 ha of trees dbh >30 cm and 40.1 ha for trees >10 cm and <30 cm.

registered by Durán Garcia et al. (2000). For comparison, in a botanical garden called "Dr. Alfredo Barrera Marín," in the north of Quintana Roo, on a surface of 65 hectares, 106 tree species were found (Escalante-Rebolledo 2000). On the basis of forest inventories, Hawthorne and Hughes (1997) report up to 220 species of trees with dbh over 10 centimeters. This means that in each *ejido*, between 30% (Laguna Kaná plots) and 50% (Hawthorne and Hughes 1997) of the species richness of the peninsula is represented. Table 9.2 shows species richness in samples from four *ejidos*.

As the table shows, only five species—*Manilkara zapota* (chicozapote, or chicle), *Gymnanthes lucida* (yaiti), *Pouteria reticulata* (zapotillo), *Bursera simaruba* (chacá), and *Brosimum alicastrum* (ramon)—account for more than 40% of the individuals. These five species have uses or potential uses, although *zapotillo* has limited local markets (Argüelles Suárez et al. 1998). Mahogany falls into the class of abundant species, together with *Metopium brownei* (chechem), used for railroad ties and furniture, and six other species. Among the 30 common species are the timber species *Pseudobombax ellipticum* (amapola), *Simira salvadorensis* (chacte kok), *Dendropanax arboreus* (sac chaca), *Piscidia piscipula* (jabin), *Simarouba glauca* (negrito), and *Lysiloma latisiliquum* (tzalam). Scarce species are *Guaiacum sanctum, Platymiscium yucatanum* (granadillo), *Cordia dodecandra* (siricote), and *Caesalpinia mollis* (chacte viga), along with 17 other species. Spanish cedar (*Cedrela odorata*), with 34 individuals, is among 103 other rare species, which account for less than 5% of the individuals.

Rare species with wide distribution areas are probably safe from extinction as long as at least part of the area is maintained as natural forest, such as nature reserves. For rare endemic species, it will be necessary to know their ecology to evaluate the effect of logging on their populations. We found 19 of the 57 endemic tree species mentioned by Ibarra-Manríquez et al. (1995) in the forests of Laguna Kaná and X-Hazil, 7 of them classified as rare and 6 as scarce. Of the 7 rare endemic species, *Sebastiana adenophora, Hampea trilobata*, and *Randia longiloba* are among the 30 most abundant species in the SDF (Durán Garcia 1986). *Bourreria pulchra* is found in drier vegetation than the SEF, though it does not seem abundant there either. This and other evidence suggests that most of the rare endemic species are possibly better represented in other vegetation types than those subjected to logging.

Population Dynamics of Mahogany and LKS

Population dynamics of trees are determined by seed production, germination, mortality, and the growth rates of the individual trees. Forest management is mostly directed to these population characteristics. The presence of seedlings of desired species and the maintenance of growth and survival rates that assure sufficient trees of sufficient diameter are fundamental for the sustained yield of timber.

Seedlings

Seedling densities of mahogany in the managed forest are generally thought to be insufficient (e.g., Argüelles et al. 1998; Brokaw et al. 1999, Negreros-Castillo and Mize 2003; Snook 1993, 1998). In order to compensate for the small stock of seedlings, they are introduced after timber extraction. The planting of seedlings takes place on logging roads and in tree fall gaps, which are in some cases artificially enlarged (Argüelles, personal communication, 2002) with most success in the open spaces (Dickinson 1998). However, planting of seedlings in the forest in gaps and on skid trails is thought to be insufficient, with less then 22% surviving after one to three years (Negreros-Castillo 1995; Negreros-Castillo and Mize 2003). On the other hand, in an artificial seeding experiment, in plots where the overstory was partially removed (0–30%), Negreros-Castillo and Hall (1996) found at least 30% and up to 70% survival of seedlings after one year, irrespective of the percentage of overstory removed. In a survey of mahogany regeneration in gaps in a 9-hectare logged plot in Noh

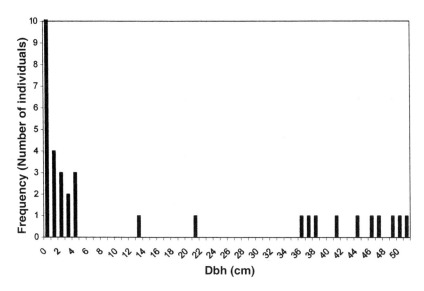

Figure 9.3 Population structure of *Swietenia macrophylla* in part of the permanent forest area in X-Hazil (Navarro-Martínez, unpublished data). The diameter class of 1 cm contains 524 individuals instead of the 10 indicated in the graph.

Bec, Quintana Roo, six years after the event, Olmsted (1990) found 14 mahogany saplings in 2,825 square meters of gaps with a mean surface of 66 square meters per gap, showing that natural regeneration of mahogany takes place in small gaps, although it is not clear if this is sufficient.

Grogan et al. (2003) drew comparable conclusions for mahogany in Brazilian Amazonia forests. They found that germination rates in both closed and logged forest were high, but that survival of seedlings in the closed forest was only 18.2% after 10 months. Of the treelets in gaps created by the logging of mahogany, 63% were suppressed by faster growing species.

This means that mahogany can germinate in the forest and does not depend on the light climate. But for survival as a seedling and growth it needs light, which in dense understory is often too scarce. It is important to recall here that light is not the only limiting factor for growth; water also affects growth, especially of seedlings (Medina et al. 2003).

Given these problems with regeneration, and after over 15 years of community control under management plans, and two to three decades of less controlled logging before then, what is the current population structure of mahogany in these forests? Figure 9.3 shows the results of a study of mahogany distribution in X-Hazil.

The population study was carried out in 100 randomly chosen plots of 500 square meters each from a systematically designed forest inventory in about 1200 hectares (Navarro-Martínez, unpublished data). The inventory data revealed a density of six mahoganies over 15 centimeters dbh per hectare, of which, on average, two trees have dbh over 55 centimeters (Pérez-Palomeque 2000). All mahoganies in the plots were individually marked and counted in 1999 and recounted in 2000 in order to calculate population dynamics (survival, mortality, and growth) and the intrinsic rate of population increase or decrease. The total number of mahogany individuals on these five hectares was 550 in 1999 and 471 in 2000. Of these, 12 individuals were reproductive, producing fruits (Navarro-Martínez, personal observation). The number of deaths between 1999 and 2000 was 185 (66% survival), and the number of new seedlings was 106 in 2000. Mortality was limited to seedlings less than 60 centimeters high except for one larger individual (4.5 cm dbh) which died because of damages due to timber extraction during 2000. As the figure clearly shows, population structure in this forest is discontinuous and possibly reflects the logging history; logging took place respectively, 40, 20, and 2 years before monitoring. These studies prove that natural regeneration of mahogany takes place and that survival is low, but that at least some saplings survive in small gaps, provided a sufficient seed rain.

Annual Growth Increment

The annual growth rate is important because the harvest cycle is determined by the supposition that trees in the diameter class of 35–54 centimeters will reach harvestable diameters in 25 years. In the Quintana Roo community forestry management plans, the estimated annual growth increment for mahogany is usually 0.8 centimeters per year and 0.4 centimeters for the LKS. Are these growth increment estimates accurate? In one recent study, Cambranis-Muñoz (2002) calculated annual growth increments of species in permanent plots from Petcacab (85 plots of 500 m²) and Naranjal Poniente (29 plots of 500 m²). She obtained increments from an initial measurement and a subsequent measurement three years later of species which were represented with at least 20 individuals (see Table 9.3), yielding data which tend to confirm the growth increment assumptions currently used in the forest management plans. The growth of *Piscidia piscipula* is probably underestimated due to measurement errors, and those of *Alseis yucatanensis* and *Pouteria reticulata* due to the measurement of small trees in the subcanopy and understory. These data suggest

Table 9.3. Annual diameter growth per diameter class for forest species in sampling plots totaling 1.5 ha in the *ejido* Naranjal Poniente, Quintana Roo

Species	Annual growth increment	10–20	20–30	30–40	40–50	>50
Swietenia macrophylla	0.8	0.8 (15–25) (6)	1.6 (25–35) (6)	1.2 (35–45) (6)	0.8(45–55) (4)	1.4 (>55) (4)
Alseis yucatanensis	0.1	0.2 (29)	0.1 (10)	—	—	
Bursera simaruba	0.4	0.3 (5)	0.6 (10)	0.3 (7)	—	—
Piscidia piscipula	0.2	0.4 (9)	0.5 (5)	−0.5 (4)	0.2 (2)	—
Pouteria reticulata	0.2	0.4 (29)	0.2 (8)	—	—	—
Brosimum alicastrum	0.7	0.6 (4)	0.4 (10)	1.0 (8)	0.3 (2)	2 (1)
Manilkara zapota	0.4	0.5 (11)	0.3 (20)	0.3 (14)	0.3 (4)	0.5 (3)
Blomia cupanoides	0.3	0.2 (10)	0.3 (10)	0.8 (1)	—	—

Sources: Data for *Swietenia macrophylla* are from the *ejido* Petcacab (4.3 ha) and are calculated over different diameter classes (in parentheses). In parentheses in second line of each cell are the number of trees measured. Measurements were carried out twice, three years apart. Data from Naranjal Poniente from OEPFZM. Data from Petcacab from the Sociedad de Productores Forestales Ejidales de Quintana Roo S.C. (SPEFQR).

that the growth increment assumptions derived from the management plans first formulated by MIQROO as early as the 1950s do have an empirical foundation.

However, other authors have found different growth rates. Juarez (1988) determined an annual growth rate of 0.43 centimeters for mahogany; Snook (2003) determined rates between 0.2 and 1.09 centimeters; and Sánchez Roman and Ramírez Segura (1993) found a rate of 0.72 centimeters. Whigham et al. (1999) showed that the growth rate depends strongly on precipitation, and the graph by Argüelles et al. (1998) shows variance by dbh with a mean growth rate up to 0.66 in the 55–60 centimeter diameter class and a very wide variation in growth rates among individual measurements; this variation is widest in the 30–50-centimeter dbh classes. The maximum growth rate measured by these authors was 1.37 centimeters per year in the diameter class of 30–35 centimeters dbh. This can probably be explained to a large degree by the different social position[4] of trees in diameter classes <50 cm. Above this diameter, trees are usually emergent.

It is probably less important to come up with a single precise measure of the growth rate of mahogany, to which all trees have to conform, than to know that mahogany can obtain the growth rates used in the plans, and what factors affect growth rates. It is clear that mahogany can obtain considerable growth rates (Mayhew and Newton 1998). For example, growth of mahogany in plantations in Quintana Roo after eight years (diameter class 15–25 cm) showed a growth increment of 1.1 (±0.1) centimeters dbh per year (Robinson 1998). It is also clear that ecological factors like moisture (Medina et al. 2003; Whigham et al. 1999) and light (Medina et al. 2003), but also genetic variation (Medina et al. 2003), play a role in the actual growth rates of individual trees.

Forest Architecture

From the previous section, we can draw the following conclusion: mahogany regenerates naturally in logged forest, but only few individuals survive. Those that grow in gaps have the best chances of survival. These seedlings do not need full light to survive but are very sensitive to overshading by fast-growing species.

Their social position and the water-holding capacity of the soil determine growth rate. This means that either the mosaic of different aged eco-units in the forest or the soil characteristics as determined by the geomorphology of the landscape may explain, for example, the population structure as shown in Figure 9.3. This requires a further discussion of these two issues. Knol (2003) made a typification of the SEF in Laguna Kaná and X-Hazil in order to find a relation between geomorphology and vegetation composition. Her analysis clearly shows that X-Hazil had more species adapted to a wet climate than Laguna Kaná, which is further inland. This would be predicted by the higher precipitation nearer the coast (see introduction). Likewise, the higher presence of Spanish cedar in Laguna Kaná, a more drought-resistant species, is explained by the rainfall gradient. These differences in climate probably have an effect on the growth rate of mahogany as well. On a larger scale, classification of the soils within the *ejidos* is not detailed enough to indicate areas preferred by mahogany. A more detailed analysis of the species distribution and growth rates in relation to precipitation, soils, and geomorphology is necessary to adapt forest management to local potentials.

Eco-Unit Dynamics

Maps of gaps in forests near our study area were made by Olmsted (1990) and Brokaw et al. (1999). These maps show the position and size of recent clearings but do not evaluate the remaining forest. In the remainder of the forest, there may be patches that were open 10 years ago, are now in the aggradation phase, and are probably unfit for the establishment of mahogany seedlings. But there may also be patches of degenerating forest which are likely to open up and give space to regeneration. All these aspects can be seen in Figure 9.4, a map of the eco-units (a color version of this map can be accessed at http://www.ecosur.mx/investigacion/divisiones/conservacion/terrestre/arborea/publicaciones). An eco-unit map is a detailed map of part of the forest and should not be generalized. The map presented in Figure 9.4 shows one hectare of forest in X-Hazil where eight stems of mahogany were extracted with diameters of about 70 centimeters dbh in 1998. Five mahoganies with diameters between 30 and 50 centimeters remain in the transect. We also observed regeneration of this species, especially abundant in the eco-unit in innovation at 410 meters.

It is clear from Figure 9.4 that mahogany grows in patches, just like chaktekok (*Simira salvadorensis*). From 30 to 70 meters, 220 to 250 meters, and from 370 to 420 meters in the 500-meter transect, there is a relatively high density of mahogany. It is also clear that these patches were not formed through large-scale deforestation, since the patches are at most 250 square meters. Insight into the structure and dynamics of such a patch can be gained from the analysis of the first patch at 30–70 meters. In this patch there are different eco-units, formed at different moments. The aggradation phase between 30 and 60 meters is the result of logging in the 1960s. Figure 9.5 gives a transect through this aggradation phase. The mahogany trees in the transect have diameters of 13 and 18 centimeters now, but there is also a larger one in the same eco-unit with a diameter of 32.5 centimeters at 45 meters. This means that the regeneration phase started 40 years ago now has trees with dbh between 13 and 32.5 centimeters.

Figure 9.4 shows that a large part of the area is in the transitional phase, an area susceptible for canopy opening by high wind velocities because of its irregular surface. About 24% of the surface is in the aggradation

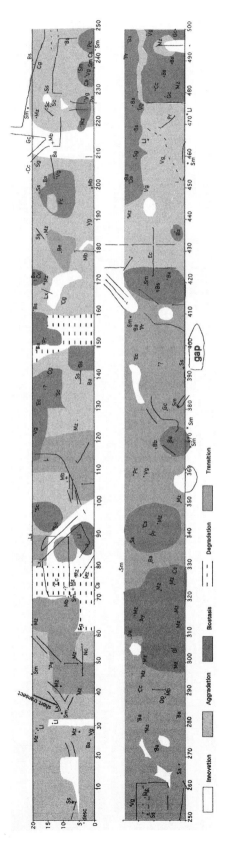

Ay — *Alseis yucatanensis*
Ba — *Brosimum alicastrum*
Bb — *Byrsonima bucidaefolia*
Bs — *Bursera simaruba*
Cg — *Caesalpinia gaumeri*
Ca — *Coccoloba acapulcensis*
Cc — *Coccoloba cozumelensis*
Cs — *Coccoloba spicata*
Da — *Dendropanax arboreus*
Ec — *Eugena capuli*
Gc — *Guettarda combsii*
Ll — *Lysiloma latisiliquum*
Ls — *Luhea speciosa*
Lx — *Lonchocarpus xuul*
Mz — *Manilkara zapota*
Nc — *Nectandra coreacea*
Op — *Ottoschulzia pallida*
Pr — *Pouteria reticulata*
Pc — *Pouteria campechiana*
Pe — *Pseudobombax ellipticum*
Sc — *Swartzia cubensis*
Sg — *Simarouba glauca*
Sm — *Swietenia macrophylla*
Ss — *Simira salvadorensis*
Vg — *Vitex gaumeri*

Transition

Degradation

Biostasis

Aggradation

Innovation

phase. Trees in this phase are mainly less than 30 centimeters dbh, many <10 cm and thus not included in forest inventories (see also Figure 9.5). These areas were gaps about 40 years ago. The innovation phase, the most important for regeneration, covers about 12% of the surface. The biostasis phase, in which the forest can be considered mature, covers 20% of the total surface. The largest part of the surface is in transition to a new biostasis after the death or damage of canopy trees. In this transition, the

Figure 9.4 *(opposite page)* Map of transect 1 in X-Hazil (see color version of figure at http://www.ecosur.mx/investigacion/divisiones/conservacion/terrestre/arborea.html), showing eco-units (dark green: in biostasis, middle green in transition, light green in aggradation, yellow in innovation and brown in degradation phases), skid trails (black lines), stumps (*), dead trees (+) and fallen trees (> —— <), and trees with dbh >30 cm (.). The transect is 500 m long and 20 m wide. The eco-unit in aggradation phase (see also Figure 9.5) between 0 and 40 m originated from logging in approximately 1960. The two eco-units in innovation phase within it were caused by the fall of two *Manilkara zapota* and the logging of a mahogany tree at 34 m and a chacte kok (Ss). Extraction trails from 1960, the 1980s, and 1998 are not clearly differentiated. At 60 m just beneath the extraction road there is a patch of fallen branches of mahogany which affected in its fall some other trees. At 60 m there was a mahogany cut in 1998 with an estimated diameter of 80 cm. Between 60 and 80 m there is an eco-unit in degeneration, with dead or dying LKS. Another *Manilkara zapota* lost a branch during the fall of the mahogany. Between 80 and 100 m there are two eco-units in biostasis formed each by a pair of trees of the present. One of them formed by two trees of katalox (Sc) of which one was affected by a hurricane. The area around these trees has been influenced heavily by the extraction, while there are various extraction tracks. Part of this area is in innovation and part in aggradation. At 200 m a chechem (Mb) of 40 cm dbh was cut in 1998. At 250 m just outside the transect a mahogany of 70 cm was cut in 1998. Near to this site at 240 m in the transect there is a group of 3 mahoganies in the range of 40 to 50 cm dbh. Between 210 and 250 m tracks of extraction have opened up the under forest mainly, leaving a transitional eco-unit while many potential trees still form a closed canopy, broken at two sites. At this site (up to 270 m) chacte kok (Ss) was harvested in 2000. Between 300 and 330 m there is an eco-unit in biostasis of mainly *Manilkara zapota*. The eco-unit in innovation phase at 350 m was formed by the fall of the mahoganies at 370 m, these were cut in 1998 and had dbh of about 70 cm. At 410 m another mahogany was cut in 1998 with an estimated dbh of 70 cm. In the eco-unit in innovation phase just right from the stump a lot of regeneration of mahogany was found. The mahogany cut at 470 m in 1998 had a dbh of about 70 cm. It fell in the direction of 450 m and formed the eco-unit in innovation between 435 and 450 m. The eco-unit in innovation phase between 450 and 480 m is caused by the logging of two big trees of tzalam (Ll) of 40 and 60 cm dbh which were cut in 1999. They left a heap of branches near the Yaxnik (Vg) in the center of the eco-unit.

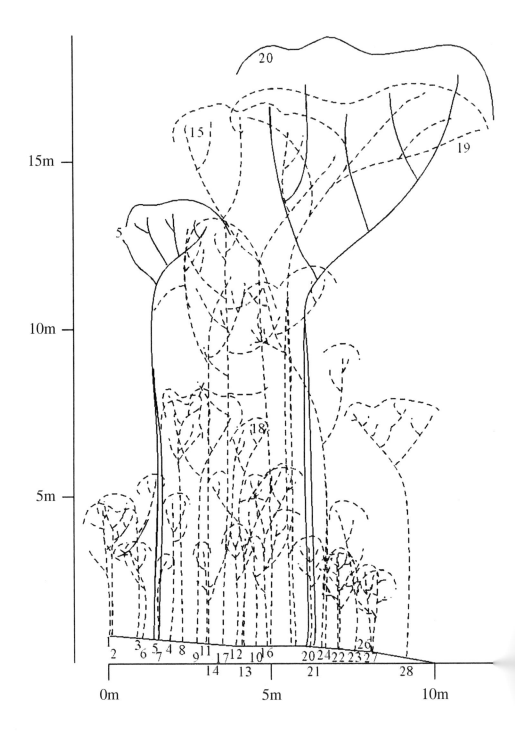

suppressed trees of the mid- and understory are regaining strength to take position and form a new canopy. Many of these trees have bent or forked stems, since they have been suppressed for most of their lives.

Table 9.4 gives an idea of the representativity of these surface distributions by showing the eco-unit surfaces in eight transects in the two case studies. From this table it can be seen that the largest surface is covered in each one of the transects by the transition phase, and that the other development phases are variable in surface area.

Table 9.4 shows that canopy openings over the last three years (innovation phase) vary between 0 and 12% of the surface of the transect. In transects with recent logging, the minimum was 2%. This is similar to data from other studies, except for transect X-Hazil 1, which was relatively heavily logged. For example, Dickinson (1998) found that natural gaps opened up about 0.1% of the canopy per year during 1993–1995. In a given logging area logging will open up 2% of the canopy: with the logging cycle of 25 years, 0.08% per year. Macario Mendoza (1991) found that 1.2% of the canopy was opened in X-Hazil in one year, and an average of 1.4% (0.05–3.75% range) along inventory lines in Noh Bec (Dickinson 1998). In heavily logged parts in Noh Bec, 6.7% was opened (Roque Alamina 1991). In Belize, Whitman et al. (1997) found that 2.8% was opened. Olmsted (1990) reports that a mean of 4% of the canopy was eliminated after logging in Noh Bec.

Seedlings grow best in innovation phases and juveniles should be found in aggradation phases. Both these forest development phases are less abundant than the transition and biostasis phases, where large trees grow. This means that a forest sampling based on the surface of the mosaic as a whole can be representative for large trees but not for smaller trees, particularly when the surface for sampling juveniles and seedlings is reduced. These should be sampled in reduced but specific areas of the forest.

Figure 9.5 *(opposite page)* Transect of forest in aggradation phase of which its position is indicated in Figure 9.4 at 35 m. All trees are potential trees, or trees which are still extending their crowns. Trees 5 and 20 are mahoganies. Other trees: 1, 3, 12: chacni (*Eugenia* sp.); 2, 17, 28: yaxche (*Vitex gaumeri*); 4: chacte kok (*Simira salvadorensis*); 6: chac kax (no scientific name available); 7: poom (*Protium copal*); 8: Chaca (*Bursera simaruba*); 9, 11, 18: Chocche (*Zygia stevensonii*); 10, 13: laurel (*Nectandra coreacea*); 14: kanisté (*Pouteria campechiana*); 15: sac chaca (*Dendropanax arboreus*); 16: yaiti (*Gymnanthes lucida*); 19: tzalam (*Lysiloma latisiliquum*); 21, 23, 26: Chechem (*Metopium brownei*); 22: chauche (*Ficus* sp.); 24: tzol (*Exothea paniculata*); 25, 27: zapotillo (*Pouteria reticulata*).

Table 9.4. Surface areas (m²) of different development phases in eco-units

Plot	Innovation	Aggradation	Biostasis	Transition
X1	1,184 (12%)	2,398 (24%)	2,174 (22%)	4,188 (42%)
X2	732 (07%)	234 (02%)	2,003 (20%)	6,860 (69%)
X3	488 (05%)	1,847 (18%)	264 (03%)	7,425 (74%)
X4	147 (01%)	0	1,606 (16%)	8,246 (82%)
LK 1	334 (03%)	203 (02%)	2,313 (23%)	7,119 (71%)
LK 2	198 (02%)	110 (01%)	495 (05%)	9,196 (92%)
LK 3	0	284 (03%)	407 (04%)	9,197 (92%)
LK 4	207 (02%)	151 (02%)	4,142 (41%)	5,529 (55%)

Note: Large transects were established in X-Hazil (X) and Laguna Kaná (LK), and calculation of surface is based on maps (e.g., Figure 9.4 is plot X1). The surface of degradation phase in this table is included in the transition phase.

The eco-unit map illustrates the mosaic of the forest. It shows the areas where different dynamics take place and thus forms an instrument that foresters can use for their decision making and for a reorientation of the forest inventories. However, these maps are still very elaborate, and not readily available.

Conclusions

As only small fractions of tropical forests will ever be placed in protected areas, the question for most tropical forests is not, "Do we use them or not?" but rather, "How do we use them in a responsible and sustainable fashion?" We have to conclude for now, as in 1988 (Gómez-Pompa and Burley 1991) and in 1996 (Sabogal et al. 1997), that we still know too little about tropical forests to be able to propose sustainable management systems because of the sheer diversity of these forests. However, we can begin to understand more clearly some of the trade-offs between conservation and income generation for poor, rural peoples of carefully managed logging in tropical forests. From the data presented and reviewed in this paper we can conclude that tree species richness is not endangered by community logging in Quintana Roo as it takes place now, especially since most endemic species occur in vegetation types which are not used for logging. We did not evaluate faunal biodiversity. For a discussion of the impact of logging on fauna, see Fimbel et al. (2001).

Contrary to the conclusions of Snook (1998) that mahogany can only be maintained in the forest by opening large areas, our conclusion is that mahogany populations *can* be maintained by small gaps like the ones made by logging (see Figures 9.4 and 9.5). Several studies presented here have shown that juvenile trees survive in natural gaps and logging gaps in the forest (Grogan et al. 2003; Olmsted 1990; Navarro-Martínez, unpublished data). We suggest that the scarceness of saplings and juveniles is probably due to a combination of sampling method and forest architecture, which make it difficult to record regeneration with current inventory methods.

We do think that management plans need to be modified in order to assure viable populations, with sufficient seed trees being of utmost importance for providing seeds in both naturally formed and logging gaps. In order to do this, one mature tree per hectare would suffice. This would reduce the need for costly seedling planting.

This does not contradict the finding that mahogany regenerates profusely in large open spaces, provided seed trees, and we agree that in many areas of the Maya forest, existing stands of mahogany were probably established in this way (Snook 1993, 1998). Rather, this finding complements that research by presenting an alternative for maintaining mahogany populations. We argue that this alternative, which would be easier to implement than planned larger clearing, is a part of the natural forest dynamics and will maintain floral diversity in the forest.

We have seen that the growth rate of mahogany is quite variable according to ecology (soil, rainfall) and history (hurricanes, agricultural openings), and we think that it can be regulated to a certain degree. In order to do this, it is necessary to stratify the forest for areas with favorable conditions (soil, precipitation) and areas with less favorable conditions. Monitoring the growth rate in these different areas could lead to the adjustment of management plans, with longer cycles than currently in some areas and shorter cycles in others. This also suggests that the system of permanent monitoring plots should be revived. Many *ejidos* have permanent plots established in their PFAs, but there is not enough money and infrastructure to monitor them.

The importance of the question of growth rates is clearly illustrated by Figures 9.4 and 9.5, where an eco-unit formed 40 years ago produced trees with dbh between 13 and 32 centimeters. If these trees are to reach their logging diameters in another 35 years, their growth rates should be between 0.66 and 1.2 centimeters per year. According to the data shown in the section on annual growth increments, this should be possible. On a smaller scale, management can be made more precise by mapping and monitoring eco-units, thus adapting forest inventories to the forest mosaic. The identification of juvenile potential trees can also lead to specific management measures, for instance in selectively liberating these potential trees and thus increasing their growth rate.

These recommendations follow from the analysis of the current forest management plans, which we find, in general, to be in accordance with the dynamics of the ecosystem. Adjustments would have to be made when social and economic constraints are considered.

Notes

AUTHORS' NOTE: We have learned a lot about mahogany and its silviculture during our many discussions with Patricia Negreros Castillo, for which we are very grateful. Also the comments of Laura Snook were of great value for improving the text. We stress however that opinions in this chapter are the sole responsibility of the authors.

1. Dbh, or diameter at breast height, is the diameter of the stem of a tree measured at 1.30 meters above the soil level. This is the standard unit of measure that foresters use for estimating wood volume in a forest and growth increments.
2. Mast years are years in which all trees of a species produce abundant fruits. These mast years occur about every three to 7 years, depending on the species. For mahogany this periodicity is not well known, partly because it is obscured by a yearly production of at least some fruits.
3. Epiphytes are plants which grow on other plants without damaging them. They are adapted to grow in this resource-limited environment and usually grow very slowly. They are indicators for old trees and well-conserved forests.
4. The "social position" (Dawkins 1958) of a tree is its relation with surrounding trees. Dawkins (1958) developed a scale of five social positions, ranging from trees in the understory completely covered by other trees to emergent trees that have their crowns towering over all other vegetation.

References

Argüelles Suárez, L. A., F. Sánchez Román, A. Caballero Rodríguez, and E. Ramírez Segura, 1998. Programa de manejo forestal para el bosque tropical del ejido Noh Bec. Chetumal: Tropica Rural Latinoamérica.

Bray, D. B. Forthcoming. Community forestry as a strategy for sustainable management: Perspectives from Quintana Roo, Mexico. In *Working Forests in the American Tropics*, ed. D. Zarin, J. Alavalapati, F. E. Putz, and M. C. Schmink. New York: Columbia University Press.

Brokaw, N. V. L., A. A. Whitman, R. Wilson, et al. 1999. Hacia una silvicultura sustentable en Belice. In *La selva maya. Conservación y desarrollo*, ed. R. B. Primack, D. B. Bray, H. A. Galletti, and I. Ponciano. Mexico City: Siglo Veintiuno Editores.

Brünig, E. F. 1996. *Conservation and Management of Tropical Rainforests: An Integrated Approach to Sustainability.* Wallingford, UK: CAB International.

Camara, L., and L. K. Snook. 1998. Fruit and seed production by mahogany (*Swietenia macrophylla*) trees in the natural tropical forests of Quintana Roo, Mexico. *TRI News*:18–21.

Cambranis-Muñoz, D. 2002. *Evaluación del crecimiento diamétrico en árboles tropicales en la zona maya de Quintana Roo.* Chetumal: Instituto Tecnológico Chetumal.

Carreón-Mundo, M., H. Galletti, and V. Santos-Jiménez. 1990. *Plan de manejo forestal integral de los bosques del ejido Laguna Kaná.* Felipe Carrillo Puerto, Mexico: Organización de Ejidos Productores Forestales de la Zona Maya.

CITES. 2003 (http://ww.cites.org/eng/append/latest_append.shtml).

Dawkins, H. C. 1958. The management of natural tropical high forest with special reference to Uganda. Imperial Forestry Institute Paper 34. Oxford: University of Oxford.

De Graaf, R. 1986. *A Silvicultural System for Natural Regeneration of Tropical Rain Forest in Suriname.* Wageningen, The Netherlands: Agricultural University Wageningen.

Dickinson, M. B. 1998. Tree regeneration in natural and logging canopy gaps in a semideciduous tropical forest. PhD diss., Florida State University.

Dinerstein, E., D. M. Olson, D. J. Graham, et al. 1995. *Una evaluación del estado de conservación de las eco-regiones terrestres de América Latina y el Caribe.* Washington, DC: World Bank.

Durán Garcia, R. 1986. Estudio de la vegetación de la selva baja subcaducifolia de *Pseudophoenix sargentii.* Bachelor's thesis, UNAM.

Durán Garcia, R., G. Campos, J. C. Trejo, P. Simá, F. May Pat, and M. J. Qui. 2000. *Listado florístico de la península de Yucatán.* Mérida, Mexico: CICY.

Escalante-Rebolledo, S. 2000. Flora del jardín botánico. In *El jardín botánico Dr. Alfredo Barrera Marín, fundamento y estudios particulares*, ed. O. Sánchez Sánchez and G. A. Islebe, 27–46. San Cristóbal de las Casas, Mexico: El Colegio de la Frontera Sur.

Everham, E. M. III, and Brokaw, N. V. L. 1996. Forest damage and recovery from catastrophic wind. *The Botanical Review* 62:113–185.

Fimbel, R. A., A. Grajal, and J. G. Robinson, eds. 2001. *The Cutting Edge: Conserving Wildlife in Logged Tropical Forests.* New York: Columbia University Press.

Flachsenberg, H., and H. A. Galletti. 1999. El manejo forestal de la selva en Quintana Roo, México. In *La selva maya: Conservación y desarrollo*, ed. R. B. Primack, D. B. Bray, H. A. Galletti, and I. Ponciano, 74–97. Mexico City: Siglo Veintiuno Editores.

Gentry, A. H. 1995. Diversity and floristic composition of neotropical dry forests. In *Seasonally Dry Tropical Forests*, ed. S. H. Bullock, H. A. Mooney, and E. Medina, 146–194. Cambridge: Cambridge University Press.

Gómez-Pompa, A., and F. W. Burley. 1991. The management of natural tropical forests. In *Rain Forest Regeneration and Management*, ed. A. Gómez-Pompa,

T. C. Whitmore, and M. Hadley, 3–18. Man and the Biosphere series. Vol. 6. Paris: UNESCO and Parthenon.

Grogan, J., J. Galvao, L. Simoes, and A. Veríssimo. 2003. Regeneration of big-leaf mahogany in closed and logged forests of southeastern Pará, Brazil. In *Big-leaf Mahogany: Genetics, Ecology and Management*, ed. A. E. Lugo, J. C. Figueroa-Colón, and M. Alayon, 193–208. Ecological Studies 159. New York: Springer-Verlag.

Gullison, R. E., S. N. Panfill, J. J. Strouse, and S. P. Hubbell. 1996. Ecology and management of mahogany (*Swietenia macrophylla* King) in the Chimanes Forest, Beni, Bolivia. *Botanical Journal of the Linnean Society* 122:9–34.

Hawthorne, W. D., and C. E. Hughes. 1997. *Bioquality of the Forests of Quintana Roo.* Oxford, UK: DFID.

Holdridge, L. R., W. C. Grenke, W. H. Hetheway, T. Liang, and J. A. Tosi Jr. 1971. *Forest Environment in Tropical Like Zones: A Pilot Study.* Oxford: Pergamon Press.

Ibarra-Manríquez G., J. L. Villaseñor, and R. Durán Garcia. 1995. Riqueza de especies y endemismos del componente arbóreo de la Península de Yucatán. *Boletín de la Sociedad Botánica de México* 57:49–77.

Johns, A. G. 1997. *Timber Production and Biodiversity Conservation in Tropical Rain Forests.* Cambridge: Cambridge University Press.

Juarez, B. C. 1988. Análisis del crecimiento periódico de caoba (*S. Macrophylla* King) y cedro (*Cedrela odorata* L.) en un relicto de selva en el estado de Campeche. Bachelor's thesis, Universidad Autónoma Chapingo, Chapingo, Mexico.

Knol, S. 2003. The mapping and definition of forest types in the Mexican Maya-region. Master's thesis, University of Wageningen, Wageningen, The Netherlands.

Loveless, M. D., and R. E. Gullison. 2003. Genetic variation in natural mahogany populations in Bolivia. In *Big-Leaf Mahogany: Genetics, Ecology and Management*, ed. A. E. Lugo, J. C. Figueroa-Colón, and M. Alayon, 9–28. Ecological studies 159. New York: Springer-Verlag.

Lugo, A. E., J. C. Figueroa-Colón, and M. Alayón. 2003. *Big-Leaf Mahogany: Genetics, Ecology and Management.* Ecological studies 159. New York: Springer-Verlag.

Lugo-Hubp, J., and Ma. T. García-Arizaga. 1999. Geomorfología. In *Altas de procesos territoriales de Yucatán*, comp. P. A. Chico Ponce de León, 155–162. Universidad Autónoma de Yucatán.

Lynch, J. F. 1991. Effects of hurricane Gilbert on birds in a dry tropical forest in the Yucatan Peninsula. *Biotropica* 23:488–496.

Macario Mendoza, P. A. 1991. La repoblación natural en una selva mediana subperennifolia en Quintana Roo bajo aprovechamiento forestal. Master's thesis, Institución de Enseñanza e Investigación en Ciencias Agrícolas, Chapingo, Mexico.

Mayhew, J. E., and A. C. Newton. 1998. *The Silviculture of Mahogany.* Wallingford, UK: CAB International.

Medina, E., H. Wang, A. E. Lugo, and N. Popper. 2003. Growth-, water-, and nutrient-related plasticity in hybrid mahogany leaf development under contrasting light regimes. In *Big-Leaf Mahogany: Genetics, Ecology and Management*, ed. A. E. Lugo, J. C. Figueroa-Colón, and M. Alayon, 146–168. Ecological studies 159. New York: Springer-Verlag.

Miranda, F. 1958. Estudios acerca de la vegetación. In *Los recursos naturales del sureste y su aprovechamiento.* Ediciones del Instituto Mexicano e Recursos Renovables. Vol. 2, 215–271.

Negreros-Castillo, P. 1995. Enrichment planting as a silvicultural technique for sustaining Honduras mahogany (*Swietenia macrophylla*) and Spanish cedar (*Cedrela odorata*) production: An evaluation of experiences in Quintana Roo, México. Paper presented at the conference Conservation and Community Development in the Selva Maya of Belize, Guatemala, and Mexico. Chetumal, Quintana Roo, 8–11 November.

Negreros-Castillo, P., and R. B. Hall. 1996. First year results of partial overstory removal and direct seeding of mahogany (*Swietenia macrophylla*) in Quintana Roo, Mexico. *Journal of Sustainable Forestry* 3(2/3):65–76.

Negreros-Castillo, P., and C. W. Mize. 1993. Effects of partial overstory removal on the natural regeneration of a tropical forest in Quintana Roo, Mexico. *Forest Ecology and Management* 58:259–272.

———. 2003. Regenerating mahogany (*Swietenia macrophylla* King) from seed in Quintana Roo, Mexico: The effects of sowing method and clearing treatment. In *Big-Leaf Mahogany: Genetics, Ecology and Management*, ed. A. E. Lugo, J. C. Figueroa-Colón, and M. Alayon, 278–287. Ecological studies 159. New York: Springer-Verlag.

Newton, A. C., R. R. B. Leakey, and J. F Mesén. 1993. Genetic variation in mahoganies: Its importance, capture and utilization. *Biodiversity and Conservation* 2:114–126.

Oldeman, R. A. A. 1990. *Forests: Elements of Silvology.* Berlin: Springer-Verlag.

Olmsted, I. 1990. Untersuchung der natürlichen Verjüngung der Caoba (*Swietenia macrophylla*) auf Hiebslöchern (claros). Unpublished report.

Orellana Lanza, R., M. Balam Ku, I. Bañuelos Robles, et al. 1999. Evaluación climática. In *Altas de procesos territoriales de Yucatán*, comp. P. A. Chico Ponce de León, 163–182. Universidad Autónoma de Yucatán.

Pérez–Palomeque, R. 2000. Representación cartográfica de un inventario forestal del ejido X-Hazil y anexos. Bachelor's thesis, ITA 16, Chetumal, Mexico.

Rice, R. E., R. E. Gullison, and J. W. Reid. 1997. Can sustainable management save tropical forests? *Scientific American* (April):44–49.

Rice, R., C. Sugal, P. C. Frumhoff, E. Losos, and R. Gullison. 2001. Options for conserving biodiversity in the context of logging in tropical forests. In *Footprints in the Jungle: Natural Resource Industries, Infrastructure and Biodiversity Conservation*, ed. I. A. Bowles and G. T. Prickett, 168–179. Oxford: Oxford University Press.

Robinson, D. 1998. Evaluación de una plantación de caoba de 8 años de edad, establecida por el programa de COPLAMAR, ejido Buenavista, Quintana Roo, México. DFID Forestry Project Report.

Roque Alamina, J. G. 1991. Aspectos silvícolas para promover la regeneración de *Swietenia macrophylla* King y otras especies comerciales en la empresa forestal ejidal Noh Bec, Quintana Roo. Bachelor's thesis, ITA no. 16, Juan Sarabia, Quintana Roo.

Rossignol, M., L. Rossignol, R. A. A. Oldeman, and S. Benzine-Tizroutine. 1998. *Struggle of Life, or the Natural History of Stress and Adaptation*. Heelsum, The Netherlands: Treemail.

Rzedowski, J., and G. Rzedowski. 1989. Transisthmic Mexico (Campeche, Chiapas, Quintana Roo, Tabasco and Yucatan). In *Floristic Inventory of Tropical Countries*, ed. D. G. Campbell and H. D. Hammond, 271–294. New York: New York Botanical Garden.

Sabogal, C., M. Camacho, and M. Guariguata, eds. 1997. Experiencias prácticas y prioridades de investigación en silvicultura de bosques naturales en América Tropical. Turrialba, Costa Rica: CIFOR, CATIE, and INIA.

Sánchez Roman, F., and E. Ramírez Segura. 1993. Informe interno PPF (Plan Piloto Forestal).

Siegert, F., G. Ruecker, A. Hinrichs, and A. A. Hoffmann. 2001. Increased damage from fires in logged forests during droughts caused by El Niño. *Nature* 414:437–440.

Snook, L. K. 1993. Stand dynamics of mahogany (*Swietenia macrophylla* King) and associated species after fire and hurricane in the tropical forests of the Yucatan peninsula, Mexico. PhD diss., Yale University.

———. 1996. Catastrophic disturbance, logging and the ecology of mahogany (*Swietenia macrophylla* King): Grounds for listing a major tropical timber species in CITES. *Botanical Journal of the Linnean Society* 122:35–46.

———. 1998. Sustaining harvests of mahogany (*Swietenia macrophylla* King) from Mexico's Yucatán forests: Past, present and future. In *Timber, Tourists and People*, ed. R. B. Primack, D. B. Bray, H. A. Galletti, and I. Ponciano, 61–80. Washington DC: Island Press.

———. 2003. Regeneration, growth and sustainability of mahogany in Mexico's Yucatan forests. In *Big-Leaf Mahogany: Genetics, Ecology and Management*, ed. A. E. Lugo, J. C. Figueroa-Colón, and M. Alayon, 169–192. Ecological studies 159. New York: Springer.

Turner, B. L. 1978. Ancient agriculture land use in the central Maya lowlands. In *Prehispanic Maya Agriculture*, ed. P. D. Harrison, and B. L. Turner, 163–183. Albuquerque: University of New Mexico Press.

Vester, H. F. M. 1997. The trees and the forest: The role of tree architecture in canopy development: A case study in secondary forests (Araracuara, Colombia). PhD diss., University of Amsterdam.

Vincent, L. W., L. E. Rodríguez, O. Noguera, E. Arends, and J. Losada. 1997. Evolución y desarrollos recientes de la silvicultura del bosque tropical alto. In *Experiencias prácticas y prioridades de investigación en silvicultura de bosques naturales en América Tropical*, ed. C. Sabogal, M. Camacho, and M. Guariguata, 25–43. Turrialba, Costa Rica: CIFOR, CATIE, and INIA.

Wadsworth, F. H. 1997. *Forest Production for Tropical America*. Agricultural handbook no. 710. Washington, DC: USDA.

Whigham, D. F., J. F. Lynch, and M. B. Dickinson. 1999. Dinámica y ecología de los bosques naturales y manejados en Quintana Roo, Mexico. In *La selva maya: Conservación y desarrollo*, ed. R. B. Primack, D. B. Bray, H. A. Galletti, and I. Ponciano, 312–327. Mexico City: Siglo Veintiuno Editores.

Whigham, D. F., I. Olmsted, E. Cabrera Cano, and M. E. Harmon. 1991. The impact of hurricane Gilbert on trees, litterfall, and woody debris in a tropical forest in the northeastern Yucatan Peninsula. *Biotropica* 23:434–441.

Whitman, A. A., N. V. L. Brokaw, and J. M. Hagan III. 1997. Forest damage caused by selection logging of mahogany (*Swietenia macrophylla*) in northern Belize. *Forest Ecology and Management* 92:87–96.

CHAPTER 10

Land Use/Cover Change in Community-Based Forest Management Regions and Protected Areas in Mexico

ELVIRA DURÁN-MEDINA, JEAN-FRANÇOIS MAS, AND ALEJANDRO VELÁZQUEZ

The rapid deterioration of global forest cover in recent years has been well documented (Lambin et al. 2001). Although patterns of change in natural vegetation cover do occur due to natural causes (e.g., hurricanes, volcanic eruptions), it is widely accepted that the majority of today's environmental degradation is induced by human actions (Cincotta et al. 2000; Vitousek et al. 1997). Human beings are commonly considered the principal agents responsible for increased levels of desertification, deforestation, habitat fragmentation, and loss of biodiversity (Noble and Dirzo 1997). This is particularly the case in tropical regions, where patterns of land conversion from natural conditions to human-dominated conditions prevail (FAO 1996).

As a response to this process of environmental deterioration, conservation policies have been adopted at the global level that promote, among other measures, the establishment of protected areas (PAs; known in Mexico as ANPs [Areas Naturales Protegidas]). However, the effectiveness of PAs is extremely variable, depending on the specific sociopolitical situation in a particular country, demographic conditions, and on the country's level of dependency upon natural resources. Bruner et al. (2001), evaluating the effectiveness of a global sample of PAs, concluded that this system represented the best model to guide future conservation policy. In response, Vanclay (2001) argued that the evidence that PAs represent the best conservation model is not convincing. Especially in the tropics, with some exceptions, PAs do not seem to ensure the permanence of natural capital (Hansen et al. 1991; Velázquez et al. 2001a). In regard to the effectiveness of PAs, it is important to search for alternatives or complementary strategies to guide both conservation policy and the rational use of natural resources that can generate income for poor, rural peoples (Liu and Taylor 2002; Mangel et al. 1996). This is of particular importance for those tropical regions that are major sources of genetic resources, which are also the areas suffering the most significant losses in native vegetation cover (Bocco et al. 2000; FAO 2001; Kiernan 2000).

Mexico is a good example of a country that is home to a large chunk of the planet's biodiversity and that is also experiencing accelerated rates of environmental degradation (Velázquez et al. 2002). An alternative that has developed in Mexico over the last several decades as a strategy to deliver both conservation and increased rural incomes is community-based forest management. The reasons for this are varied, but two of the main ones are that (1) the greater part of the country's forests, and therefore biodiversity, is found in areas of the common property *ejido* and agrarian community land tenure systems (Alcorn and Toledo 1998; Thoms and Betters 1998); and (2) this land tenure reality laid the basis for historical community struggles and policy initiatives that led to a relatively successful sector of community forest enterprises (CFEs), more widespread in temperate forests than in rainforests (Bray and Merino-Pérez 2003; Merino-Pérez 1997; Merino-Pérez and Segura 2002; Negreros-Castillo et al. 2000; Velázquez et al. 2001a). These CFEs are carrying out logging of natural forests and creating community jobs, while also adopting strategies to conserve and increase forest areas. However, there have been few studies that have quantified the effectiveness of community-based logging in the key conservation indicator of forest cover, or compared them with the more conventional PA-led conservation model as a strategy for forest cover conservation (Berry et al. 1996; Kiernan 2000).

Land use/cover change (LUCC) is an important indicator for quantifying the effectiveness of different land use and land management strategies (Kiernan 2000; Masera et al. 1999). It also generates a spatial-temporal model of the processes taking place (Lambin et al. 2001; Turner and Meyer 1994), which can support policy makers in their efforts to slow down and hopefully reverse environmental deterioration (Velázquez et al. 2002).

This study provides evidence to support the hypothesis that areas under a common property regime and characterized by solid social organizational structures maintain forest cover areas just as effectively as PAs. It should be noted, however, that forest cover is only one indicator, and does not address possible changes in forest structure or composition for either community forests or PAs. Specifically, the study analyzed the land cover change processes that took place over two decades in the forests of two organizations of *ejidos* dedicated to community-based forest management. The results were then compared with those from a large sample of PAs in Mexico.

Area of Study

The study was carried out in two regions of Mexico (Figure 10.1). The first was in the state of Guerrero, where temperate forests dominate, and the second took place in Quintana Roo, a state where tropical rainforest, or *selva*, is the dominant forest cover. In both cases community-based forest management is taking place, *ejidos* are the main form of land tenure, and the *ejidos* have formed second-level, or intercommunity, organizations to help govern forest management. Thus, this study focuses on changes in native vegetation cover in *ejidos* that are members of forest management organizations in the two different states. These organizations are the Unión de Ejidos Forestales "Hermenegildo Galeana" (UEFHG), in Tecpan de Galeana, Guerrero, and the Organización de Ejidos Productores Forestales de la Zona Maya (OEPFZM), in Felipe Carrillo Puerto, Quintana Roo. In the case of the UEFHG, 10 of its member *ejidos* were analyzed, and in the OEPFZM, 12 were analyzed. Not all *ejidos* in each organization have significant logging activities, so this sample represents those communities with significant authorized volumes for logging in annual management plans.

Profile of the Organizations and the Regions

The main function of these organizations is to provide technical assistance, to represent the *ejidos* to government authorities, to negotiate funding and logging permits on their behalf, and, finally, to take part in regional negotiations to regulate timber prices and develop timber markets.

Even though the two organizations operate in different cultural, social, and environmental conditions (see Table 10.1), they share the activity of management of natural forest areas for logging under management plans based on selective cutting. With respect to their management plans, most of the *ejidos* in Guerrero employ the Mexican Method of Forest Management (Método Mexicano de Ordenación de Montes; MMOM), a selective method that focuses on the largest, healthiest specimens (SEMARNAP

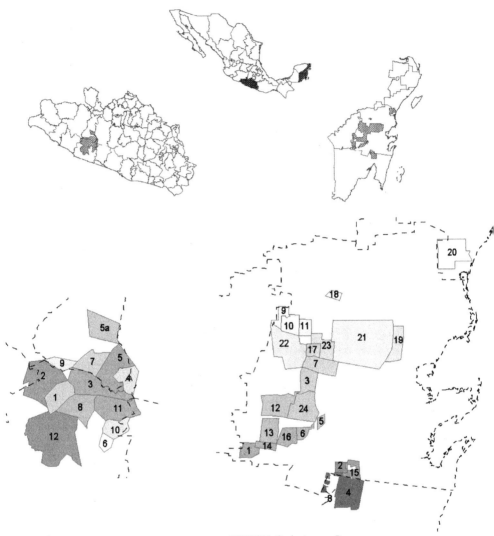

OEFHG-Guerrero

1.- Bajitos *
2.- Bajos de Balzamar *
3.- Cordon Grande *
4.- Cuatro Cruces *
5.- EL Balcón *
6.- El Moreno
7.- Fresnos de Puerto Rico *
8.- Humedades *
9.- La Trinidad *
10.- Pitos, Pitales y Letrados *
11.- Platanillo *
12.- Santa Lucía.

OEPFZM-Quintana Roo

1.- Altamirano
2.- Andres Quintana Roo *
3.- Betania *
4.- Cafetal-Limones *
5.- Chanca Derrepente
6.- Chan Santa Cruz *
7.- Chunhuaz *
8.- Cuauhtemóc *
9.- Dzoyola
10.- Filomeno Mata
11.- Kampokolche
12.- Laguna Kana *

13.- Naranjal Poniente *
14.- Nueva Loria
15.- Reforma Agraria *
16.- Santa Maria Poniente
17.- Tabi
18.- Trapich
19.- Tres Reyes *
20.- Tulum
21.- X-Maben
22.- X-Pichil
23.- Yaxley
24.- Yoactun *

1998). El Balcón *ejido* (part of the UEFHG-Guerrero) recently switched to the System of Conservation and Silvicultural Development (Sistema de Conservación y Desarrollo Silvícola; SICODESI), a highly flexible logging plan which seeks to maintain the present structure of the forest (Bray and Merino-Pérez 2003). In the OEPFZM-Quintana Roo, the management plan focuses on mahogany (*Swietenia macrophylla*) and uses a polycyclic system of three 25-year cycles and a 75-year turn, with a minimum diameter limit of ≥55 centimeters cutting minimum, on the assumption that it takes mahogany 75 years to reach this diameter. Although this assumption has been questioned, it remains the standard in management plans (Snook 1998; see also Vester and Navarro-Martínez, this volume).

In Guerrero, logging activities began in the mid-1970s with a parastatal enterprise, the Vicente Guerrero Forest Company (Forestal Vincente Guerrero; FOVIGRO). Beginning in the mid-1980s, the *ejidos* formed their own CFEs and began logging their own lands, organized within the UEFHG (Bray and Merino-Pérez 2003; Wexler 1995). In most of central Quintana Roo, commercial logging did not begin until around 1960, and the communities did not take charge of their own CFEs until the mid-1980s, although they had been logging tropical hardwoods for railroad ties since the 1970s without a management plan (Bray 2001). The logging companies operating in the state were responsible for the removal of huge volumes of timber, but generated few benefits for the owners of the forest resources. In Quintana Roo, the initiation of a more responsible form of forest management began with the Plan Piloto Forestal (PPF), a joint effort between Mexican federal and state government, German assistance, and the local communities (Santos et al. 1998), although the parastatal Maderas Industrializados de Quintana Roo (MIQROO) had the first management plan for logging of tropical forests in the Americas, which was largely adopted by the PPF (Snook 1998).

Since the mid-1980s the *ejidos* have been directly responsible for timber extraction carried out under authorized management plans. The *ejidatarios* have tried to organize themselves to conduct sound management of their forests and to secure markets and better prices for their timber.

Figure 10.1 *(opposite page)* The LUCC study sites. Asterisks (*) indicate the forest *ejidos* that were included in the land use cover change processes from each *ejido* organization. Twelve of the 24 OEPFZM member *ejidos* and 10 of the 12 UEFHG member *ejidos;* other *ejidos* in each organization have only minor amounts of logging. The area 5a of the "El Balcón" *ejido* (UEFHG-Guerrero) was not included in the change analysis either since no forest practices are carried out in it.

Table 10.1. Summary outline of the organization of *ejidos* where the LUCC analysis was conducted

Characteristic	UEFHG-Guerrero	OEPFZM-Quintana Roo
Total surface	115,494 ha	131,842 ha
Ejidos analyzed	10	12
Beginning of organization for forest management	mid-1980s	mid-1980s
Management plan	MMOM	Selective Treatment Method (polycyclic system)
Human settlements[a]	102	22
Population[a]	5,161	6,538
Climate	Temperate, semihumid with summer rains. Annual mean temperature 14 to 22° C. Annual precipitation 1,500 to 2,000 mm	Warm, semihumid (A(w)), with summer rains. Annual mean temperature is 22 to 26° C. Annual precipitation 1,100 to 1,500 mm
Geology	Metamorphic and extrusive igneous rock	Sedimentary rock (limestone)
Geography and topography	Region: Southern Sierra Madre Mountains; Subregion: Coastal Range	Region: Yucatán Peninsula; Subregion: Yucatán karst (plains with rocky or cemented ground and shallow dips)
Elevation (m above sea level)	1,000 m (peaks close to 3,000 m)	<30 m

[a] *Source:* INEGI 2003.

Although these *ejidos* have been faced with various problems, the success of a number of *ejidos* (from both organizations) has led them to be regarded as models for sustainable forest management (Arriaga et al. 2000; Bray and Merino-Pérez 2003; Kiernan 2000). The benefits generated by these CFEs have included direct benefits such as local job creation and social stability, as well as indirect ones such as creating new areas of study of natural resource management alternatives.

Methodology

The Analysis of Conversion Processes

LUCC analysis consists of comparing two or more sets of data from re-mote sensing from different dates. In this study we made comparisons of spatially explicit data displayed as digital map sets. Use was made of data related to land use and vegetation (t_1), generated by the National Institute of Statistics and Geography (Instituto Nacional de Estadística, Geografía e Informática; INEGI) and designated "Series I" (generated over the period 1968–86). The second database (t_2) was developed by the National Forest Inventory 2000 (Palacio-Prieto et al. 2000). Before the LUCC analysis began, the scale of the work (1:250,000) and the minimum mappable area (1 km^2 = 100 ha) were determined, and the vegetation cover legend was homogenized for both dates in order to make them compatible and comparable (Velázquez et al. 2002).

It was also necessary to carry out field verification to validate reliability of the maps derived from the NFI-2000. As such, a random sampling system was designed with a minimum number of sample units (20 for each region) in the categories with the highest chance of inaccuracy at the vegetation community level (Velázquez et al. 2001a). In Guerrero, the major inaccuracy corresponded to the primary and secondary condi-tions in pine forests, pine-oak forests, oak forests, and tropical deciduous forests. For Quintana Roo, the main discrepancies were found between the high and medium evergreen and semi-evergreen tropical forests (*selva alta*, *mediana perennifolia*, and *subperennifolia*) and the medium deciduous and semideciduous tropical forests (*selva mediana caducifolia* and *subcaducifolia*), as well as the primary and secondary conditions of both communi-ties. The fieldwork was carried out with the help of maps, satellite maps, and images (generated in color from geo-referenced satellite images) and a global positioning system (GPS). A fieldwork sheet that included iden-tification of dominant species, geomorphology, soil characteristics, and the degree of vegetation disturbance was used to characterize the sam-pling sites. Additionally, at each site observations were made in order to compare the maps and the in situ vegetation. Sampling took place over the territory of all the *ejidos* involved in the study, with at least 12 days of fieldwork for each region.

The analysis of land use change largely consisted of crossing and com-paring the corrected maps from two different dates: for the UEFHG-

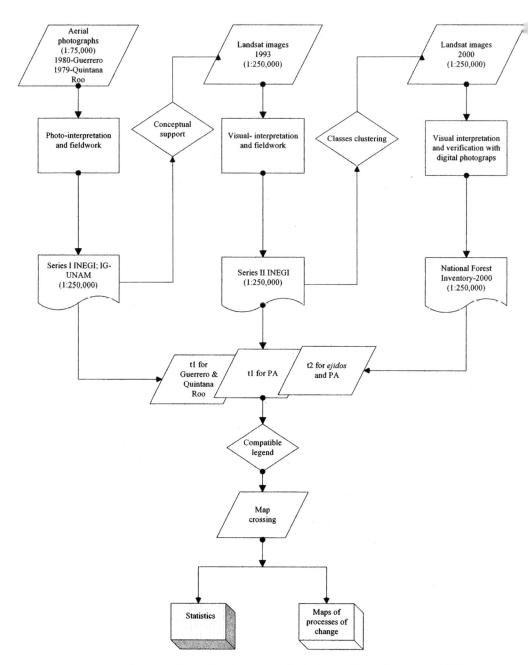

Figure 10.2 Flowchart illustrating the methodological steps followed to produce LUCC analysis and derived statistics and maps.

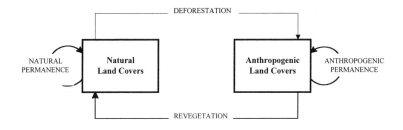

DEFORESTATION	Conversion of natural land covers (in primary or secondary conditions) to anthropogenic land covers
REVEGETATION	Conversion of anthropogenic land covers to natural land covers (in secundary or primary conditions)
ANTHROPOGENIC PERMANENCE	No change in anthropogenic land covers between two dates
NATURAL PERMANENCE	No change in natural land covers (in primary or secondaryconsitions) between two dates

Figure 10.3 Flows depicting processes of land cover conversion and permanence analyzed.

Guerrero $t_1 = 1979$ and $t_2 = 2000$, and for the OEPFZM–Quintana Roo $t_1 = 1980$ and $t_2 = 2000$. As mentioned earlier, the LUCC analysis was carried out in a subgroup of all *ejidos* in the organizations where logging is a central economic activity (10 *ejidos* in the case of UEFHG-Guerrero and 12 for OEPFZM–Quintana Roo). The *ejidos* included in the analysis are shown in Figure 10.1, and the subgroups chosen for the LUCC analysis are noted with asterisks.

For a more detailed look at the methodology used, see Palacio-Prieto et al. (2000) and Velázquez et al. (2002). A general outline is given in Figure 10.2. To identify the principal processes of forest conversion (Figure 10.3), the study made use of a simplified model (FAO 2001) that looked at two main land covers: those considered "native forest" or as existing in t_1 (temperate forests, tropical forests and other forms of natural vegetation cover) and those defined as anthropogenic (including crops, grassland, and human settlements), but did not include secondary succession.

This model also allowed the reduction of possible inherent errors and confusion among similar categories, resulting in an increase in the level of confidence in the statistics. The model specified the permanence of land use change (either through deforestation or revegetation). The rates of

$$t = \left(\frac{A_2}{A_1}\right)^{1/(t_2-t_1)} - 1$$

Where:

  t = rate of change

  A_1 = area at date t_1

  A_2 = area at date t_2

  t_2-t_1 = number of years between the two dates

Figure 10.4 Rates of change calculated according to Puyravaud (2002).

change were calculated according to the equation shown in Figure 10.4 (Puyravaud 2002).

The rates of change obtained are expressed in percentage values multiplying the result by 100. By comparing the maps taken from the dates t_1 and t_2 we constructed a matrix of changes made up of the areas transformed in each category from t_1 to another category in t_2. The different conversion processes were identified and spatially represented in a map showing land use cover change for each region.

Comparison between *Ejidos* and PAs

The rates of change that were observed in the LUCC analysis of the 10 *ejidos* of the UEFHG-Guerrero and the 12 *ejidos* of the OEPFZM–Quintana Roo were then compared with the rates of change observed during analysis (using the same sources of information) for 67 Mexican PAs established before 1993. The reference database (t_1) for the PAs was taken from INEGI (Series II); the technical information for the analysis is described by Smith (2002) and summarized in Figure 10.2. The PAs excluded from the analysis are those in marine environments, those decreed after 1993, or those too small in area to allow for meaningful analysis. The PAs that were analyzed represent about 60% of the total protected area established up to June 2002 in Mexico (www.conamp.semarnat.gob.mx; Mas et al. 2003). A complete list of the PAs analyzed can be found in the appendix at the end of this chapter.

The rate of land use change was compared statistically between the two case study regions (taken as one) and the PAs (Fisher accuracy test; Zar 1984). The hypothesis suggested that there would be no significant difference between the two rates of change.

Results

Changes in the *Ejidos* of the OEFHG-Guerrero

The 10 forest *ejidos* analyzed in Guerrero occupy a total area of 115,494 hectares. In 2000, approximately 92% of this area was recorded as being covered by natural land cover (mainly forest and other forms of natural vegetation). The LUCC analysis documented two change processes: deforestation and revegetation (Figure 10.5). Analysis also identified the extent to which areas of natural vegetation cover had remained. In the OEFHG-Guerrero, the study showed that deforestation had affected 8,986 hectares between 1979 and 2000, representing 7.78% of the original forested area (see Figure 10.6 at http://indy2.igeograf.unam.mx/ua_morelia/_private/2004/prensa.pdf). The annual rate of change from natural to anthropogenic was 0.97%, but began from a very low base of 1,282 hectares in t_1 and resulted in 9,896 hectares for t_2. The opposite process, regrowth of vegetation, had taken place in 29% of the 1,282 hectares originally occupied by anthropogenic land cover. Thus, 92% of original forest area was retained over a 20-year period, and the net annual loss of forest cover was -0.4%, including all the land use change dynamics.

Changes in the *Ejidos* of the OEPFZM-Quintana Roo

Analysis involved 12 forest *ejidos* that occupy an area of 131,842 hectares. In 2000, approximately 95% of this area was covered by native forest. The LUCC analysis carried out in this region showed that deforestation affected 5,364 hectares between 1980 and 2000, representing 4.9% of the original forest area (t_1; Figure 10.5b). The opposite process, regrowth of vegetation, took place in 94.8% (20,763 hectares) of the area originally occupied by forms of anthropogenic land cover. As a result, only 5.2% of such land use areas remained for t_2, while 94.8% of native forest remained (see Figure 10.7 at http://indy2.igeograf.unam.mx/ua_morelia/_private/2004/prensa.pdf). Thus, there was a net annual gain in forest cover of 0.63%. In contrast, areas of anthropogenic land cover decreased at an annual rate of 5.8% with respect to original coverage (Figure 10.7a). However, it should be noted that these figures might change if a more detailed study (at finer scales and on an annual basis) were carried out in order to understand the dynamics of slash-and-burn agriculture in this landscape, where every year both fallow and forestlands are converted to agriculture while other areas are left for secondary succession. Some of the large-

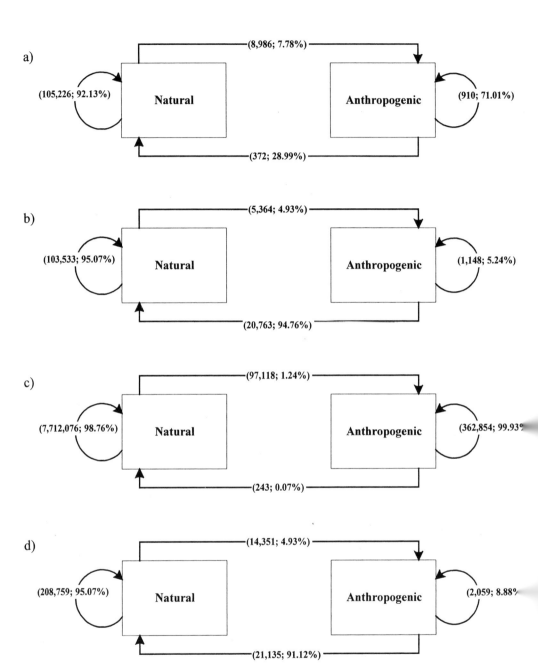

Figure 10.5 Trends of change between anthropogenic and natural cover for the *ejidos* of UEFHG-Guerrero (a); the *ejidos* of OEPFZM–Quintana Roo (b); the protected areas (c); and both groups of *ejidos* (Guerrero–Quintana Roo) (d).

scale shift from anthropogenic to forest could also be accounted for by several thousands of hectares that were opened for pasture by government programs in the late 1970s, much of which was apparently abandoned to secondary succession because the promised cattle never arrived.

Changes in PAs

The 67 PAs included in the analysis cover an area of 8,834,201 hectares, approximately 79% of the total area covered by PAs in Mexico. In 2000, approximately 93.8% of the lands held by these PAs had natural land cover. The LUCC analysis (Figure 10.5c) indicated that deforestation affected 97,118 hectares, or 1.24% of the original area (t_1), an annual rate of growth in anthropogenic areas of 0.38%. With regard to revegetation, the analysis showed that 0.07% (243 hectares) of the original area occupied by forms of human land cover had been converted to a form of natural land cover. Thus, it was deduced that 99.9% of the areas of human land use remained for t_2, while 98.8% of areas of natural land cover remained. The annual conversion rate (-0.2%) also demonstrated a minimal loss of natural land cover.

Comparison between PAs and *Ejidos*

Figure 10.8 shows two sets of comparisons between rates of change in natural cover and anthropogenic cover. Figure 10.8a compares PAs with the Guerrero and Quintana Roo regions separately, while Figure 10.8b compares PAs with the *ejidos* in both regions grouped together. The *ejidos* have managed to conserve, for more than 20 years, approximately 95.1% of the original forest cover (t_1). In comparison, PAs have maintained 98.8% of such covers between 1993 and 2000. On the other hand, if we compare past and present areas of anthropogenic land cover, *ejidos* as a group have decreased by 29.3%, with appropriate caveats about slash-and-burn agriculture in the case of Quintana Roo, while PAs have seen an increase in anthropogenic land cover of 26.7% (both percentage figures are in relation to the original anthropogenic areas). Further, the *ejidos* showed a net annual gain in forest cover of 0.14%; that is, conversion from anthropogenic to natural land cover occurred at a higher rate than forest to anthropogenic land cover, while in the PAs there was an annual net loss of -0.18%; see Figure 10.8b. With rates of change for areas of anthropogenic land cover, the PAs showed an annual increase of 0.38%, while in the *ejidos* a negative rate of change was observed (-0.17%). Statistical

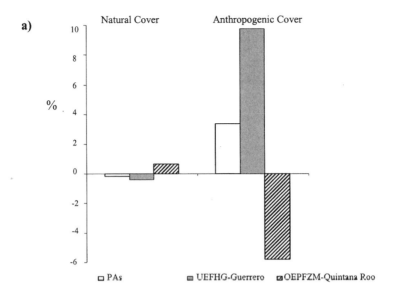

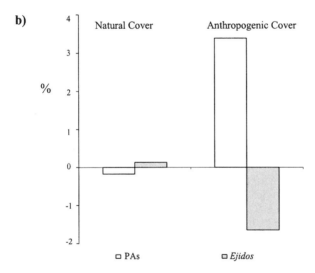

Figure 10.8 Annual rate of change (a) for the *ejidos* analyzed in each region independently and the PAs; and (b) for the *ejidos* combined and the PAs.

analysis (Fisher accuracy test; Zar 1984) did not show significant differences between the rates of change in the *ejidos* and the PAs ($Z = 81.45$, $p < .05$). However, the balance between regrowth and deforestation in the *ejidos* and the PAs (Figure 10.5d) suggested that the PAs had a slightly greater tendency to lose natural land cover, while such areas were more likely to increase in *ejidos* (see Figure 10.8b). Although a large part of the areas with regrowth of vegetation are in a secondary condition, those areas are recovering their ecological functionality and acting as a buffer to connect the patches with forest in prevailing primary states. In *ejidos*, as noted, most of the net gain in forest cover and decrease in anthropogenic areas occurred in Quintana Roo, while Guerrero showed net losses in forest area, although at a low rate.

Discussion

Processes of Change (*Ejidos* versus PAs)

Anthropogenic activities are considered to be one of the major threats to the conservation of biological diversity and the native vegetation covers (Lambin et al. 2001; Mangel et al. 1996). However, the changes in vegetation covers observed in the *ejidos* show that community forest management for the commercial extraction of timber does not necessarily translate into the permanent loss of natural land cover (see Vester and Navarro-Martínez, this volume, for an analysis of the impact of logging on forest diversity and structure in Quintana Roo).

In PAs, the tendency for areas with native vegetation covers to decrease while areas designated for human land use increase contrasts the situation observed in the *ejidos*, particularly Quintana Roo. The contrasting tendencies, however, do not differ significantly considering the rhythm and magnitude by which these changes occur. It is important to consider that the goals and objectives of both conservation and development models are substantially different. The *ejidos* focus on selective logging under regulated management plans and other forms of commercial and subsistence forest use. These are "multiple-use" forests, while PAs are subject to a policy of protection and conservation. The decrease in areas of anthropogenic land cover, observed in Quintana Roo, but not in Guerrero, has taken place despite population growth over the past few decades. In contrast, an increase of 97,118 hectares (1.24%) in the area of anthropogenic land cover in the PAs indicates that despite decrees for their protection, agriculture and livestock activities in particular continue to have a negative impact on native vegetation covers. This tends to occur more in those portions of PAs with characteristics such as easily accessible land, reasonably flat topography, and soil quality suitable for the development of agriculture and livestock (Smith 2002). This suggests that the conservation effectiveness of PAs depends more on the kind of physical characteristics mentioned above than the form of its legal decree or the official management plan to which it is subject (Mas et al. 2003). A similar situation has been documented both in other tropical regions of the world (Hansen et al. 1991; Vanclay et al. 2001) and other regions of Mexico (Ramírez 2002; Velázquez and Romero 1999; Velázquez et al. 2001a).

Deforestation in PAs occurs across all types of original natural vegetation, and principally involves conversion into agricultural plots and pasturelands in equal proportions. In contrast, deforestation in the *ejidos* is the result of a more managed process, with a generally well-observed zoning of land use that prohibits change in the managed forest. In the case of Guerrero, areas of pasture were increased, and in the case of Quintana Roo, the changes from natural to anthropogenic land uses were for agriculture. It should also be emphasized that deforestation in the UEFHG-Guerrero occurred principally in forest areas of less commercial importance (tropical deciduous forest). This suggests that in the UEFHG-Guerrero, the population has geared land use toward the commercially most profitable activities (forestry and livestock rearing). Deforestation in the OEPFZM-Quintana Roo has been confined mainly to areas covered by tropical perennial forests, which have been converted into agricultural areas. In Quintana Roo, in contrast to Guerrero, most of the area is suitable for forest activities. This implies that stakeholders are confronted with a dilemma in defining areas suitable for cropping activities. In some places, unavoidably, there is an overlap in terms of spatial demand. Local stakeholders, as a result, in 1985 delimited specific areas devoted to permanent forest areas where cropping has diminished, whereas areas devoted to agriculture have increased upon remaining forest patches.

The process of regrowth of vegetation is proportionally greater in the *ejidos* than in the PAs (Figures 10.5c and 10.5d). In the PAs, regrowth seems to be part of a natural succession (from anthropogenic land cover to incipient areas with native land cover) taking place in a limited fashion when compared with the total area affected by deforestation. In the *ejidos*, regrowth is observed mainly in those areas that are considered important for commercial forestry activities (pine-oak and pine forests in Guerrero and tropical semideciduous forests in Quintana Roo). The vegetation regrowth patterns in the PAs follow natural processes that are independent of their legal condition, while in the *ejidos* the recovery of forest areas is governed by a social process that promotes forest recovery of commercially valuable areas through the avoidance and control of forest fires, reforestation, and community forestry.

In summary, the *ejidos* use their land in an organized manner under a model of territorial zoning, while processes of change taking place in the PAs, as shown in the study, follow a more unpredictable model and are not directly connected to their standing as PAs. The question needs to be examined with more robust data, but it appears that land inside PAs that is more likely to lose its original cover is land suited to the development of agriculture and livestock activities.

Final Remarks

Evaluating the effectiveness for both conservation and economic development of PAs and community-managed forests must eventually go beyond studies of LUCC, as important as these are. On the basis of our data, we have attempted to suggest the dimensions of some of these contrasting study cases within the framework of the LUCC analysis. Policies shaping PAs in Mexico have become stronger, both operationally and legally, over the past 10 years, thanks to a range of different programs, new decrees, and greater financial support (Melo 2002). To promote conservation in PAs, the government directs human and economic resources through agencies and other stakeholder groups to restrict and regulate human activities within PA boundaries. These resources frequently fail to provide a direct or indirect social and environmental benefit, and on occasions they bring social interests into conflict with conservation interests. In the case of the forest management *ejidos*, the *ejidatarios* are those principally responsible for the actions that determine LUCC. Furthermore, the *ejidos* have managed to translate a great part of their management actions into economic goods that have led to direct benefits for their social communities and the natural environment. From the long-term view, the cost-benefit balance suggests that PAs will be under increasing pressure to demonstrate their economic benefit to society. Well-organized *ejidos* that have developed a community-based forestry plan, on the other hand, must be considered among the conservation strategies with the greatest long-term potential.

When we analyze the financial situations and benefit flows of the two forms of land management, we see some clear differences emerge. PAs, as commonly conceived, are solely the responsibility of government, while forest management can be thought of as a comanagement between the government and the *ejido*, given the strong regulation of logging by the federal government (Klooster 2000). Financial support in the form of investments in PAs must come exclusively from government funds, while most forest *ejidos* invest in their forests with capital generated by the community enterprise. This suggests that the financial viability of PAs depends on the capacity of governments with multiple pressures on them to continue supporting PAs, while CFEs have been demonstrated to be financially viable (see Antinori, this volume). As for benefit flows, although efforts are being made in some cases to involve local communities in the management of PAs, the social and economic benefits from these efforts must be classified as incipient, while the benefit flows from community forest control are multiple and substantial (Antinori 2000; Negreros-Castillo et al. 2000). Thus, PAs and community forests are equivalent in terms of maintenance of forest cover and associated environmental benefits, but the financial situations and benefit flows from PAs are far more uncertain than those from community forests.

However, although issues concerning the financial and social viability of PAs could affect their protective function in the long run, it is also clear that unsuccessful community-based forestry negatively affects the functional integrity of ecosystems (Klooster 2000; Merino-Pérez and Segura 2002). For well-organized *ejidos*, though, these activities translate into multiple benefits that ensure the conservation of their forests and thereby a range of indirect environmental goods and services such as the replenishment of aquifers, the long-term productivity of ecosystems, and the contribution of products to multiple local markets, among others (Daily et al. 1996).

The regions of greatest deforestation found in both PAs and non-PAs coincide with zones where the local social community structure has been seriously weakened, independent of any financial resources assigned. This is the case, for example, in the PAs in the southern part of the Mexican basin (Velázquez and Romero 1999; Velázquez et al. 2001b), the Monarch Butterfly Biosphere Reserve (Ramírez 2002), Montes Azules (Ochoa 2000), and Calakmul (García et al. 2002), among others. In each case, economic, environmental, cultural, and social losses are significantly greater than those experienced in the two *ejido* regions analyzed in this paper.

The environmental costs resulting from social disorganization have been expressed through high deforestation rates in various regions of the country. Nonetheless, throughout history, governmental programs favoring deforestation and the disintegration of social groups have predominated and promoted "productive" and "conventional" activities such as livestock rearing and agriculture (Merino-Pérez and Segura 2002). The social component can be considered as an ally to the conservation of Mexico's genetic resources (Velázquez et al. 2001a). From this perspective, and in view of the results of this study, it is recommended that programs be developed to strengthen the consolidation of environmentally friendly community-based forestry management plans, as a complementary alternative to current conservation programs.

Appendix

Appendix 10.1. List of the protected areas (PAs) studied

	Protected area	Decree date	Area (ha)
1	Bonampak	1992	4,357
2	Bosencheve	1940	14,008
3	Cabo San Lucas	1973	3,996
4	Cajón del Diablo	1937	115,000
5	Calakmul	1989	723,185
6	Cañón del Río Blanco	1938	55,690
7	Cañón del Sumidero	1980	21,789
8	Cascada de Bassaseachic	1981	5,803
9	Cascadas de Agua Azul	1980	2,580
10	Cerro de Garnica	1936	968
11	Cerro de la Estrella	1938	1,100
12	Cerro de la Silla	1991	6,039
13	Chan-Kin	1992	12,185
14	Cofre de Perote	1937	11,700
15	Constitución de 1857	1962	5,009
16	Corredor Biológico Chichinautzin	1988	37,302
17	Cumbres del Ajusco	1947	920
18	Cumbres de Majalca	1939	4,772
19	Cumbres de Monterrey	1939	246,500
20	Desierto del Carmen o Nixongo	1942	529
21	Desierto de los Leones	1917	1,529
22	Dzibilchaltún	1987	539
23	El Chico	1982	2,739
24	El Cimatario	1982	2,448
25	El Jabalí	1981	5,179
26	El Potosí	1936	2,000
27	El Tepozteco	1937	24,000
28	El Triunfo	1990	119,177
29	El Veladero	1980	3,617

Appendix 10.1. Continued

	Protected area	Decree date	Area (ha)
30	El Vizcaíno (Includes El Complejo Lagunar Ojo de Liebre)	1988	2,546,790
31	Gogorrón	1936	25,000
32	Grutas de Cacahuamilpa	1936	1,600
33	Insurg. José María Morelos	1939	4,325
34	Insurg. Miguel Hidalgo y Costilla	1936	1,580
35	Iztaccíhuatl-Popocatépetl	1935	25,679
36	La Michilía	1979	9,325
37	La Primavera	1980	30,500
38	Lacan-Tun	1992	61,874
39	Lagunas de Chacahua	1937	14,187
40	Lagunas de Montebello	1959	6,022
41	Lagunas de Zempoala	1936	4,790
42	Lomas de Padierna	1938	670
43	Malinche or Matlalcuéyatl	1938	45,711
44	Mapimí	1979	200,000
45	Mariposa Monarca	1986	16,110
46	Montes Azules	1978	331,200
47	Nevado de Toluca	1936	46,784
48	Palenque	1981	1,772
49	Pantanos de Centla	1992	302,707
50	Pico de Orizaba	1937	19,750
51	Pico de Tancítaro	1940	23,154
52	Ría Celestún	1979	59,130
53	Ría Lagartos	1979	60,348
54	Selva El Ocote	1982	48,140
55	Sian Ka'an	1986	528,148
56	Sierra de Ajos/Bavispe	1936	184,776
57	Sierra de Álvarez	1981	16,900
58	Sierra de Manantlán	1987	139,577
59	Sierra de Quila	1982	15,193
60	Sierra de San Pedro Mártir	1947	63,000
61	Sierra la Mojonera	1981	9,252
62	Tulúm	1981	664
63	Valle de los Cirios	1980	2,521,776
64	Volcán Nevado de Colima	1936	9,600
65	Xicoténcatl	1937	680
66	Yaxchilán	1992	2,621
67	Zoquiapan y Anexas	1937	19,418

AUTHORS' NOTE: We recognize the support of both organizations for the field-work and information provided. Special thanks go to Victoria Santos and Rosa Ledezma of OEPFZM-Quintana Roo, to Jesús García of *ejido* "El Balcón," and to Leonides Chávez and Jesús Albarrán of UEFHG-Guerrero. We are also thankful for the technical assistance of Rutilio Castro and to Tania Fernández for mapping analysis and the production of the final maps. The financial support for this study was provided by the Instituto de Geografía, UNAM, and the Ford Foundation, through Grant 1010-0595 to the Department of Environmental Studies at Florida International University in Miami, Florida.

References

Alcorn, J. B., and V. M. Toledo. 1998. Resilient resource management in Mexico's forest ecosystems: The contribution of property rights. In *Linking Social and Ecological Systems: Management Practices and Social Mechanisms for Building Resilience*, ed. F. Berkes and C. Folke, 216–249. Cambridge: Cambridge University Press.

Antinori, C. M. 2000. Vertical integration in Mexican common property forests. PhD diss., University of California, Berkeley.

Arriaga, C. L., J. M. Espinosa-Rodríguez, C. Aguilar-Zuñiga, E. Martínez-Romero, L. Gómez-Mendoza, and E. Loa (Coordinators). 2000. *Regiones terrestres prioritarias de México*. CONABIO, México.

Berry, M. W., R. O. Flamm, B. C. Hazen, and R. L. MacIntyre. 1996. The land-use change and analysis system (LUCAS) for evaluating landscape management decisions. *IEEE Computational Science & Engineering* 3(1):24–35.

Bocco, G., A. Velázquez, and A. Torres. 2000. Comunidades indígenas y manejo de recursos naturales: Un caso de investigación participativa en México. *Interciencia* 25(2):9–19.

Bray, D. B. 1991. The struggle for the forest: Conservation and development in the Sierra Juárez. *Grassroots Development: Journal of the Inter-American Foundation*. 15:12–25.

———. 2001. The Mayans of central Quintana Roo. In *Endangered Peoples of Latin America: Struggles to Survive and Thrive*, ed. S. C. Stonich, 3–17. Westport, CT: Greenwood Press.

Bray, D. B., and L. Merino-Pérez. 2003. El Balcón, Guerrero: A case study of globalization benefiting a forest community. In *Confronting Globalization: Economic Integration and Popular Resistance in Mexico*, ed. T. A. Wise, H. Salazar, and L. Carlsen, 65–80. Bloomfield, CT: Kumarian Press.

Bruner, A. G., R. E. Gullison, R. E. Rice, and G. A. B. da Fonseca. 2001. Effectiveness of parks in protecting tropical biodiversity. *Science* 291(5501):125–128.

Cincotta, R. P., J. Winsnewski, and R. Engelman. 2000. Human population in the biodiversity hotspots. *Nature* 404:990–991.

Daily, G. C., S. Alexander, P. R. Ehrlich, et al. 1996. Ecosystems services: Benefits supplied to human societies by natural ecosystems. *Issues in Ecology* 2:1–16.

FAO. 1996. *Forests Resources Assessment 1990. Survey of Tropical Forest Cover and Study of Change Processes*. Forestry Paper 130. Rome: FAO.

————. 2001. *Global Forest Resources Assessment 2000.* Main report. Forestry Paper 140. Rome: FAO.

García G. G., I. March, and M. Castillo. 2002. Transformación de la vegetación por cambio de uso del suelo en la Reserva de la Biosfera Calakmul, Campeche. *Investigaciones Geográficas. Boletín del Instituto de Geografía, UNAM* 46:45–57.

Hansen, A. J., T. A. Spies, F. J. Swanson, and J. L. Omán. 1991. Conserving biodiversity in managed forests: Lessons from natural forests. *Bioscience* 41(6):382–392.

INEGI. 2003. Conteo de Población y Vivienda, 1995. Instituto Nacional de Geografía y Informática, Aguascalientes, Mexico.

Kiernan, M. J. 2000. *The Forest Ejidos of Quintana Roo, Mexico. A Case Study for Shifting the Power: Decentralization and Biodiversity Conservation.* Washington, DC: Biodiversity Support Program.

Klooster, D. 2000. Institutional choice, community, and struggle: A case study of forest co-management in Mexico. *World Development* 28(1):1–20.

Lambin, E. F., B. L. Turner, J. G. Helmut, et al. 2001. The causes of land-use and land-cover change: Moving beyond the myths. *Global Environmental Change* 11:261–269.

Liu, J., and W. Taylor. 2002. *Integrating Landscape Ecology into Natural Resource Management.* Cambridge: Cambridge University Press.

Mangel, M., L. M. Talbot, G. K. Meffe, et al. 1996. Principles for the conservation of wild living resources. *Ecological Applications* 6:338–362.

Mas, J. F., A. Velázquez, A. Schmitt, and R. Castro. 2003. Una evaluación de los efectos del aislamiento, la topografía, los suelos y el estatus de protección sobre las tasas de deforestación en México. *Revista Espacio Geográfico (Ra'ega). Revista de la Universidad Federal do Paraná, Brasil* 6:61–73.

Masera, O., M. Astier, and S. López. 1999. *Sustentabilidad y manejo de recursos naturales: El marco de la evaluación MESMIS.* Mexico City: Mundi-Prensa-GIRA-Instituto de Ecología UNAM.

Melo, G. C. 2002. *Areas naturales protegidas de México en el siglo XX: Temas selectos de geografía de México.* Mexico City: Instituto de Geografía, UNAM.

Merino-Pérez, L. 1997. La heterogeneidad de las comunidades campesinas en México. In *El manejo forestal comunitario en México y sus perspectivas de sustentabilidad*, comp. L. Merino-Pérez, 133–152. Mexico City: CRIM-UNAM-SEMARNAP-Consejo Mexicano para la Silvicultura Sostenible-World Resources.

Merino-Pérez, L., and G. Segura. 2002. El manejo de los recursos forestales en México (1992–2002): Procesos, tendencias y políticas públicas. In *La transición hacia el desarrollo sustentable*, ed. E. Leef, E. Escurra, I. Pisanty, and P. Romero, 237–256. Mexico City: INE-SEMARNAT, UAM, PNUMA.

Negreros-Castillo, P., J. C. González, and L. Merino-Pérez. 2000. Evaluación de la sustentabilidad del sistema de manejo forestal de la organización de ejidos productores forestales de la zona maya de Quintana Roo. In *Sustentabilidad y sistemas campesinos: Cinco experiencias de evaluación en el México rural*, ed. O. Masera and S. López-Ridaura, 83–141. Mexico City: GIRA, Mundi-Prensa, PNUMA.

Noble, I. R., and R. Dirzo. 1997. Forest as human dominated ecosystem. *Science* 277:522–525.

Ochoa, S. 2000. *El proceso de fragmentación de los bosques en los altos de Chiapas y su efecto sobre la diversidad florística.* PhD diss., UNAM.

Palacio-Prieto, J. L., G. Bocco, A. Velázquez, et al. 2000. La condición actual de los recursos forestales en México: Resultados del Inventario Nacional Forestal 2000. *Investigaciones Geográficas: Boletín del Instituto de Geografía, UNAM* 43:183–203.

Puyravaud, J. P. 2002. Standardizing the calculation of the annual rate of deforestation. *Forest Ecology and Management* 177:593–596.

Ramírez, R. 2002. *El ordenamiento ecológico de la comunidad indígena de Yavesía: Distrito de Iztlán de Juárez, Sierra Norte Oaxaca.* Bachelor's thesis, ITAO, Oaxaca, Mexico.

Santos, V., M. Carreón, and K. C. Nelson. 1998. *La organización de la Unión de Ejidos Productores Forestales de la Zona Maya. Un proceso de investigación participativa.* Series: Estudios de caso sobre participación campesina en generación, validación, y transferencia de tecnología. Mexico City: Red de Gestión de Recursos Naturales y Fundación Rockefeller.

SEMARNAP. 1998. *Bases científicas para la elaboración de programas de manejo forestal en los bosques de coníferas con fines de producción.* Puebla: SEMARNAP.

Smith, A. 2002. *Evaluation de l'efficacité du système des aires naturelles protégées au Mexique d'apres l'étude des changements de végétation et d'usage du sol pur deux periodes (1976–1993 et 1993–2000).* Master's thesis, Université Paris XII Val de Marne.

Snook, L. K. 1998. Sustaining harvests of mahogany (*Swietenia macrophylla* King) from Mexico's Yucatán forests: Past, present, and future. In *Timber, Tourists, and Temples: Conservation and Development in the Maya Forest of Belize, Guatemala, and Mexico,* ed. R. B. Primack, D. B. Bray, H. A. Galletti, and I. Ponciano, 61–80. Washington, DC: Island Press.

Thoms, C. A., and D. R. Betters. 1998. The potential for ecosystem management in Mexico's forest *ejidos. Forest Ecology and Management* 103:149–157.

Turner, B. L., and W. B. Meyer. 1994. Global land use and land cover change: An overview. In *Changes in Land Use and Land Cover: A Global Perspective,* ed. W. B. Meyer and B. L. Turner II, 3–10. Cambridge: Cambridge University Press.

Vanclay, J. K., A. G. Bruner, R. E. Gullison, R. E. Rice, and G. A. B. da Fonseca. 2001. The effectiveness of parks. *Science* 293(5532):1007.

Velázquez, A., G. Bocco, and A. Torres. 2001a. Turning scientific approaches into practical conservation actions: The case of Comunidad Indígena de Nuevo San Juan Parangaricutiro, México. *Environmental Management* 5:216–231.

Velázquez, A., J. F. Mas, J. R. Díaz-Gallegos, et al. 2002. Patrones y tasas de cambio de uso del suelo en México. *Gaceta Ecológica INE-SEMARNAT México* 62:21–37.

Velázquez, A., F. J. Romero, H. Cordero-Rangel, and G. Heil. 2001b. Effects of landscape changes on mammalian assemblages at Izta-Popo volcanoes, Mexico. *Biodiversity and Conservation* 10:1059–1075.

Vitousek, P. M., H. A. Mooney, J. Lubchenco, and J. M. Melillo. 1997. Human domination of Earth's ecosystems. *Science* 277:494–499.

Wexler, M. B. 1995. *Learning the Forest Again: Building Organizational Capacity for the Management of Common Property Resources in Guerrero, Mexico.* PhD diss., Boston University.

Zar, J. H. 1984. *Biostatistical Analysis.* 2nd ed. Englewood Cliffs, NJ: Prentice-Hall.

PART IV

THE ECONOMICS OF COMMUNITY FORESTRY

CHAPTER 11

Vertical Integration in the Community Forestry Enterprises of Oaxaca

CAMILLE ANTINORI

Recent studies reveal the prevalence of common property forests (Agrawal 2002; Meinzen-Dick et al. 2001; Scherr et al. 2002; White and Martin 2002). Common property research predominantly focuses on group-level institutions for managing individual extraction. A much less explored question is when and how local stakeholders respond to market opportunities with collective or group-level production. Stakeholders in forest common lands are presented with choices on marketing their non-timber goods, controlling access to possible pharmaceutical discoveries, seeking carbon sequestration credits, and exploiting timber resources. As an indication of the increasing importance of markets in common property management, there are at least 57 examples in 23 countries of community-company forestry partnerships (Mayers and Vermeulen 2002). Community-based enterprises can generate income, but to do so requires competitiveness in the marketplace, which in turn demands management, technical, and sales expertise. At the same time, common property management can provide social, cultural, and other nonmarket benefits to local stakeholders. Examining the institutional solutions that communities have devised for meeting these demands can lead to a better understanding of the sustainability of common property regimes and their developmental role within globalized markets.

Mexican forestry has evolved toward greater local control over forest resources. Despite the land reforms of 1917, the government maintained the right to lease timber in community territory. As a result, a large volume of the timber production in the first half of the century occurred either through private companies contracting directly with the communities or through state-directed firms operating under government-granted leases paying stumpage fees to communities. However, the Forest Law of

1960 (Ley Forestal 1960), and more definitively the Forest Law of 1986 (Ley Forestal 1986), legitimized communal claims to exploit and market their own timber resources. These new economic possibilities fell to preexisting civic governance structures—the *ejido* and agrarian communities, which are the basis for Mexican community forest management (see Chapter 1). While community management faces the challenges of local politics and land disputes, communities have created various strategies from within this nationally mandated governance system.

Industrial organization theory offers an appropriate framework for analyzing community forestry as it focuses on the comparative benefits of contracting options along a chain of production, here realized as the wood products industry drawing raw material from community forests. Using basic concepts from transaction cost economics and contract theory, both components of the extensive industrial organization literature, this paper characterizes the tangible and intangible costs and benefits of a community vertically integrating into the wood products industry, that is, either by selling stumpage rights to private harvesters or by investing in downstream extraction or milling and processing activities. The analysis describes the factors involved in contracting between communities and private companies and objectives of community control over production to explain the current pattern of vertical integration of community forestry in Mexico, under the assumption that the choices communities make reveal their perceptions of risk, cost, and benefit of engaging in the wood products market. The result is a greater understanding of where common property management and the community sector as a whole fits within the overall economy and Mexican society.

The empirical basis of the research is a sample of communities in Oaxaca, Mexico, and their technical forest service providers (*servicios técnicos forestales;* STFs), surveyed in 1997–1998.[1] In Oaxaca, timber production is on common property lands and equipment for producing timber can be owned by communities or private companies. Out of a sample population of 95 communities that produce timber commercially, a random sample of 45 was selected and surveyed. The sample was stratified to mirror the same proportion of communities categorized by end product sold, varying from stumpage to finished wood products like furniture and palettes, as existed among the population.[2] A survey was administered to the elected community leader, or Comisariado de Bienes Comunales (or *Ejidales*), and to the STF provider for each community. Interview questions covered production and contract details, non-timber access and use patterns, and silvicultural information for each community's forest.

Below, a brief historical overview of the evolution of forestry practices and the forestry industry in Oaxaca is provided. In subsequent sections, the political organization of communities and its adaptation to the timber economy are described. Concepts from transaction cost economics and contract theory, both components of industrial organization theory, are applied to community forestry to understand when and why a local community chooses direct ownership and control over the downstream timber processing chain. A section then presents hypotheses to be tested and summarizes survey data. Empirical results of an econometric analysis are discussed, where it is argued that benefits of common property management are not completely contractible in the marketplace, thereby affecting communities' vertical integration decisions and suggesting common property's broader role in local economic development and natural resource management.

Historical Overview

Oaxaca possesses approximately 7 million, or about 13%, of Mexico's 55 million hectares of forest (IBRD 1995), and forests are the largest soil classification group, covering 74% of the state (SARH 1994). The climatic zones of Oaxaca encompass both tropical and temperate forest, including the biologically rich cloud forests that host a number of endangered species (SEMARNAP 2000). An oft-cited figure estimates that 80% of Mexico's forestland is held as common property, while in Oaxaca, a state with the second highest percentage of indigenous population, that figure is closer to 90%. Thus, forests fall mainly within community territory, placing communities at the center of policy efforts in forest conservation and management.

The modern-day institutional link between communities and forest begins with the land reforms adopted after the Mexican Revolution. Article 27 of the 1917 Constitution installs communities as beneficiaries of the state on the land they occupy. The law did not bestow full ownership rights in which the owner can sell land or transfer title, but the communities hold usufructory rights. Individuals have access to individual plots of land for agriculture and livestock, while forestland remains for general community use. The 1992 agrarian reform was a radical departure in that *ejidatarios* became able to privatize land after obtaining community approval. However, common property forestlands may not be subdivided and are to be returned to the government in the case of *ejido* privatization (Bray and Wexler 1996). Further, the law does not apply to agrarian communities (otherwise referred to as *comunidades indígenas* due to their indigenous populations and origin).

Local community populations traditionally used their forests for subsistence and individual harvests of products for sale in local markets or consumption (de la Peña 1950). At an industrial level, Mexico's forest resources have been exploited since at least the early twentieth century, mostly without management plans. In particular, de la Peña (1950) laments the destructive logging practices of sawmill companies in Tlaxiaco, the commercial center of the Mixteca region in Oaxaca, where companies contracting with local communities left land deforested or degraded.

Until 1986, the state maintained the right to issue logging concessions on community land. Prerevolutionary governments granted timber concessions mainly to foreign firms, but a 1926 law prohibited access to forestland by outsiders (Bray and Wexler 1996). The Mexican government again reversed this policy when it implemented a pulp import substitution program during World War II. A number of private companies, often with foreign financial backing, became registered as Unidades Industriales de Explotación Forestal (UIEFs), or Industrial Forest Exploitation Units, and received concessions to forestland by presidential decree with the purpose of developing industrial forestry and ensuring a source of pulpwood. UIEFs had access to large blocks of community forests, and local communities were permitted to sell only to the concession holder and could not transform the wood themselves (Snook 1986). A few companies had a parastatal status in which government officials served on the executive board. To an extent, UIEFs were under a social mandate. Not only did the government direct the companies to provide social benefits such as public infrastructure to the communities, but it also stated that the concession holders had to pay the communities the fair market value of the trees extracted, the *derecho de monte*, or stumpage fee, which the company would deposit in a trust fund for the communities. The final community-UIEF relationship with respect to prices, wages, employment, and other specifics of trade had to be renegotiated yearly. Communities had bargaining power in that they held the right to accept or refuse the contract, but, except for a few communities, they usually accepted it.

Oaxaca's communal forestlands in 1956 were some of the last areas to be concessioned (*Diario Oficial* 1956). In Oaxaca, the UIEFs, Fábricas de Papel Tuxtepec (FAPATUX), and Compañía Forestal de Oaxaca (CFO) held 25-year concessions. Other private companies negotiated one-on-one with the communities without a federal lease.[3] The UIEFs had an advantage over other companies in their ability to secure concessions in forestland of their choice. According to the former chief forester of FAPATUX, concessions were sought in the best quality forest with the easiest access to the market and no internal community conflicts (J. Escarpita, personal communication, 1998).

By the 1960s, however, conflicts had developed between the concession firms and the communities in which they conducted timber operations (López-Arzola and Gerez 1993; Moros and Solano 1995). The basis of conflict is easily interpreted as a misalignment of management incentives and ownership rights. Because the companies had leases with limited life spans, their production practices did not conform to the long-term interests of the communities. Communities complained that firms did not clean the forest after harvest, leaving wood to rot or pose fire hazards (Moros and Solano 1995), and that firms were high-grading (*descremando*), or taking only the large, premium trees. High-grading was prescribed by the federally mandated silvicultural practice of the Método Mexicano de Ordenación de Montes (MMOM), but it left genetically impoverished forests. A main point of contention was hiring practices. The contractors brought in experienced loggers from Michoacán rather than contracting locally and paid them higher rates than local workers. While much logging infrastructure was developed in communities, the firms commonly reneged on promises to invest in public infrastructure like schools and churches. Finally, control over payment was weak. Not only was it unclear what the fair market value of stumpage was at the time, but communities had difficulty in accessing revenues deposited into trust funds held in their names.

A community representative speaking at a meeting to discuss the leases expresses the frustration with the difficulties, constraints, and disadvantages of contracting with the concession firms:

> We want this situation cleared up. The Company [CFO] has always concealed its proposal to the government. They always do everything behind the communities' backs. They have always violated the contract in their operations and payments. We must protest this decree to be free and, if possible, to organize ourselves to establish our own sawmill. If we can't do this, the most important thing is the free market, that every village be free to sell. It's possible to contract with the Company, but we must demand our rights. (Moros and Solano 1995:109)

Protests by community leaders and activists, supported by bureaucratic reformers working within the federal forestry subsecretariat overseeing forestry activities, led to the nullification of the concession system in 1982 and a formal recognition under the 1986 Forestry Law of community rights to produce timber or contract with outside private firms for production services in the open market (Bray and Wexler 1996).[4] Since 1982, communities have either continued to sell stumpage to private firms or have formed *unidades* or *sociedades*, which have the Mexican legal status of community forest enterprises (CFEs), to harvest their own timber resources.[5] A smaller percentage has processing capabilities and sells sawnwood, pallets, tool handles, and house furnishings. Communities with commercially viable forestland have evolved into four categories representing the level of vertical integration into industrial forestry: those where private firms extract timber and pay the community a stumpage fee; those that extract timber themselves and sell roundwood; those that extract and process the timber to sell sawnwood; and, finally, those that extract, process, and finish, selling the range of products from roundwood to wood products (Antinori 2000).

Figure 11.1 shows the significance of this transition within the relatively short period of 11 years, indicating the status of the 44 communities sampled in 1986 versus 1997. A notable feature is that no community sold finished products in 1986, whereas seven did so in 1996, while both roundwood and sawnwood communities increased substantially in percentage terms, displaying a forceful emergence into the wood products market at multiple levels of processing capacity. This "vertical integration transition" in Oaxaca was part of a larger phenomenon which occurred in somewhat different periods in community timber operations throughout Mexico. Today, Mexico probably has the largest community forest sector in the world, as well as the highest percentage of national timber production sourced from state-recognized common property land managed at the local level. Devolution in terms of Mexico's forest policy changes resembles an enhancement of community property rights, rather than a change in title over resources, as well as a liberalization of the timber industry. As such, the community sector illustrates the complexities and possibilities of greater local control over natural resources.

Community-Based Management in Mexico

In what sense is the Mexican forest sector "community-based"? As past history shows, the spatial coincidence of community territory and forests does not guarantee that the community has control over any benefits generated from timber production or forest management or that those

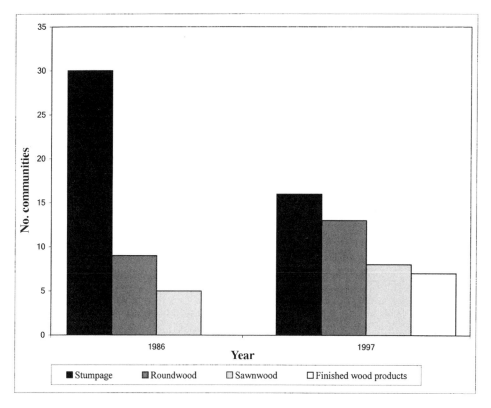

Figure 11.1 Historical comparison of timber processing capability in sample communities, Oaxaca 1986–1997.

benefits are distributed in an equitable fashion. A key to explaining community participation in the industrial forestry sector lies in specifying how community members interact with the market and form a collective, entrepreneurial firm. In Mexico, this interaction occurs through the traditionally and constitutionally defined community governance structure, within which community members can sanction and adapt to commercial activities. This section describes how common property resources and timber production are managed under this system.

The term *community* in this chapter signifies the *comunidades* and *ejidos*, or *colonias*, codified in the Ley Agraria. These three community types are similar in governance structure, with the main differences being in their historical relationship to land. The *comunidad* refers generally to a community of indigenous culture who can legally substantiate that Spanish colonialists or the Catholic Church usurped their ancestral land. Article

27 of the Constitution allows these populations to reclaim their land. The *ejido* was established to entitle landless peasants, giving them the right to petition for expropriation of private estates (formerly *haciendas*) above a given size. Finally, the *colonia* system was created by presidential decree to encourage ranching and new settlements in Mexico's humid tropical areas. Since the Spanish *hacienda* system never took hold in Oaxaca (Spores 1984), *comunidades* rather than *ejidos* predominate in Oaxaca, which has almost half of all *comunidades* found in Mexico.

Within the indigenous *comunidad* form of governance, which comprises the majority of the sample communities studied in this research, lies a system of local governance distinct from state or national political organization, broadly characterized as *usos y costumbres* (Carlsen 1999). While emigration and the advent of diverse religious groups to communities have challenged traditional practices, this system is still much in effect among the communities surveyed.[6] Possibly predating Spanish colonialism, the *comunidad* serves civic and religious functions as well as serving in its role as a political unit. *Usos y costumbres* has many elements that emphasize the idea of service as a basis for individual membership. To be a registered member, one must be a head of household and keep up with civic obligations to contribute labor for community projects (*tequios*) and serve in official offices. In the *cargo* system, every one to three years, members of the community elect members to local offices (Cancian 1992; Kearney 1972; Nader 1990). Positions are unpaid or minimally compensated, and the time spent on official duties limits the person's income-earning activities outside the office; thus it can be a significant financial burden. However, serving one's *cargo* builds prestige in the community, and failure to serve could lead to a suspension of a person's rights within the community and social ostracism. As the supreme governing body, the General Assembly is the primary forum for deciding issues pertinent to the local community. The General Assembly makes major decisions that affect the community as a whole, like elections to local office, distribution of funds to public projects, or, in forestry, accepting a management plan or choosing a buyer. Each registered member has one vote, and votes are by consensus or majority. Women are not usually a presence in assembly meetings and do not participate in the *cargo* system. Therefore, decisions on timber production are usually made by male heads of households. *Usos y costumbres* has achieved growing state-level recognition in national politics despite criticism of its efficacy in linking local to national economies, its religious intolerance, and its exclusion of women (Carlsen 1999; Servicios 2001; Montes 2002). The Oaxacan government in 1998 officially accepted this practice, after which 417 of its 570 municipalities registered votes by *usos y costumbres* (Velásquez 2000). The president of the municipality may be elected according to *usos y costumbres* rather than the party system, although the official must claim a party affiliation once elected (Servicios 2001; Montes 2002).

Community-based commercial timber production has evolved out of this governance system. The General Assembly elects three officers— president, secretary, and treasurer—to serve in the *cargo* of Comisariado de Bienes Comunales (CBC; Mayor for Communal Property), whose purpose is to oversee community property matters, such as patrolling, community representation in territorial conflicts, and enforcement of rules of access to communal forests. The Consejo de Vigilancia (Oversight Council) is elected independently of the CBC to hold the CBC accountable to the community as well as assisting the CBC in his duties. Private firms seeking to contract with the community to extract timber would first contact the CBC, who would present the proposal to the General Assembly. Community members expect the CBC to direct benefits equitably from communal resources to community members. Individual community members usually must obtain permission to extract resources from or clear common areas for personal use, and in some cases must pay a fee to the community for such use. With communities more actively participating in the timber markets since the 1980s, the CBC maintains his role. Several CBCs interviewed during fieldwork expressed awareness of their community obligations, stating that their goals in managing timber operations were to provide local jobs and direct benefits to the community. Abuses of the system occur, as in Mexico's notorious *caciquismo*, or political domination by powerful local elites. The presence of a *cacique* usually represents the breakdown of civic functioning, which in terms of timber production often translates into a shutdown of community operations or forest degradation (Klooster 2000; Merino-Pérez and Alatorre 1997). Even communities with sophisticated timber operations have had experience with power abuses, such as embezzlement of funds. Yet there are enough reasonably well functioning community timber operations to say that the CBC retains his authority over forestry operations as the recognized community representative for common property and that the General Assembly generally has the ability to hold him accountable through elections, dismissal, calls to disclose information in the assembly, and sanctions as might be appropriate.

Major disadvantages for community timber operations are decision-making time in general assemblies and the lack of CBC skills in forestry or marketing. Therefore, as communities have invested in forestry operations, their managerial structure has tended to expand. In communities with extraction and processing capabilities, the CBCs have often appointed additional personnel and formed subcommittees to delegate responsibility. Examples include a logging foreman (*jefe de monte*), general manager (*gerente general*), financial officer (*jefe de finanzas*), or sawmill foreman (*jefe de patio*). These persons remain accountable to the CBC and may have had some prior experience applicable to their job. These posts are outside the *cargo* system in that they are not subject to General Assembly elections, and their term is not for a definite period of time. Further, some permanent employment is emerging. Of the 44 sample observations, 13 had permanent employment, mainly administrative jobs geared toward accounting and sales in finished wood products communities. Finally, some communities are now considering formation of a CBC advisory group whose members are past CBCs who can train the newly elected CBC in forestry matters.

For technical expertise, the STF mediates between the government and community to create and approve the management plan and conduct silvicultural services. The state maintains its role of regulating forestry through its environmental ministry, the Secretaría de Medio Ambiente y Recursos Naturales (SEMARNAT). Any entity, community or private, seeking to harvest timber for commercial purposes must submit a management plan stating technical details (e.g., rotation cycles, soil classifications, and harvest volume) for the ministry's review and approval. Prior to the 1992 Forest Law, STFs worked as government officials with assigned geographical areas under their responsibility or directly for the UIEFs. The 1992 law privatized these services, although many communities retain the services of the STF previously responsible for their area. Some more integrated communities hire STFs as full-time staff. Other than direct hires as staff, communities contract with an STF as a separate transaction from a sales contract, or, in the case of stumpage communities, the private buyer usually pays for STF services.

The STF's role varies broadly across communities. The STF may provide additional services like promotion of non-timber forest projects, budgeting, training in fire control, administration, and so forth. In providing technical advice, STFs can attend General Assembly meetings, but the substance of their participation depends partly on the interests of the community. As one forester explained, he usually reports on broad forestry matters in general assemblies of less integrated communities, while in more integrated communities with a membership familiar with forestry issues, he speaks up only if asked. Over 60% of the sampled communities reported that they sought the STF's assistance to seek financing or suggest investments. However, there seems to be a greater separation of the STF from the community in identifying clients. Less than 40% of the stumpage, roundwood, and finished product communities reported that they engaged the STF in this task. Possible reasons are a level of distrust in combining the technical and marketing side of operations, or clients bringing their own STFs as they seek out contracts with communities (Antinori 2000).

Therefore, Oaxaca's forests are community managed in a strong sense of the phrase. The community governance and territorial land claims have national recognition, and a governance structure is in place where (mainly male) community members can express their views about access to and allocation of forest benefits while the elected authority on common property matters, the CBC, normally has the power to administer decisions on common property forestry matters.

Yet a fundamental question remains as to which factors motivate a community organization to move beyond its traditional activities into collectively investing in its forest resources for commercial purposes. The decision-making process takes organizational effort and time from community members (Bromley et al. 1992; Hardin 1968; Olson 1964; Ostrom, 1990) as well as commitments of current financial resources for future returns. The question is not "Why is production occurring?" since all communities in the sample have commercially viable forest resources, but rather "When does the community invest in the capital necessary to produce and sell value-added goods like roundwood or sawnwood?" The following analysis suggests that significant transaction costs exist because of the role common property plays in these communities, so that market exchanges do not adequately ensure that a stumpage sale fully realizes the objectives that communities have in producing timber. Under conditions to be discussed below, communities prefer to control production at further points along the processing chain to direct production benefits in ways that cannot be fully specified in service contracts. The following section describes the sources of transaction costs and why market contracts do not necessarily address concerns of both buyers and sellers, which in turn leads to particular patterns of production organization in the Mexican community forestry sector.

Transaction Costs, Contractual Hazards, and Vertical Integration: An Application to Mexico

Transaction costs refer to the costs of negotiating, writing, monitoring, and enforcing contracts between a buyer and a seller who are exchanging goods or services. These costs arise in particular when two features of contracting are present: (1) the contract cannot specify every future contingency and (2) the buyer or seller has opportunities to make production choices which diverge from the other party's desired choice (Coase 1937; Demsetz 1967; Williamson 1985). As there are many ways to arrange a transaction, transaction cost economics focuses on determining which institutional structure or governance regime maximizes the net benefits of transactions. For example, labor effort and product quality are difficult for a third party to measure objectively and, therefore, cannot be verified when one is trying to enforce a contract. Knowing of these limitations, the parties to a contract would be reluctant to make investments which are mostly useful, or specific, to that particular contract. Shifting incentives through ownership and control of production can elicit the best possible outcome given the buyer and seller's objectives. If transaction costs are minimal, a firm may choose to avail itself of the specialized skills in the marketplace and hire another firm to provide goods or services. If transaction costs are high, the firm can take on the task of providing those goods and services itself. Characteristics that typically raise transaction costs are uncertainty in the production process; frequency of transactions; presence of durable, transaction-specific, sunk investments; informational asymmetries; and the costs of bearing risks (Joskow 1985; Williamson 1991). Empirical studies using transaction cost analysis typically select variables to represent these characteristics and examine their correlation with the scope of a firm (Klein and Shelanski 1994).[7]

Several transaction cost studies have focused on the timber industry. In the United States, Leffler and Rucker (1991) describe how the value of harvested timber is affected by the care taken in felling the timber, bucking, separating logs from slash, and minimizing stump heights. While timber owners in their sample from North Carolina cannot significantly alter their forestland value in the short run, logging service providers have many opportunities to exploit the difficulty of monitoring behavior. They explain the common industry practice for the timber owner to sell rights to stumpage so that the logging service bears the responsibility of ensuring the highest value for the timber extracted, rather than the timber owner hiring logging services and then selling the logs to a mill. Globerman and Schwindt (1986) found that Canadian pulp and sawmills backward integrated into forest ownership, logging, and transport, most likely because their factories are specialized to the timbershed where they are located, even tailoring the technology to the timber in that location. They also argue that linerboard companies forward integrated into packaging for more control over their markets, as linerboard markets were limited due to transport costs and few exports.

The community members in Mexico, as timber owners, are faced with similar questions when deciding whether to contract in their forest commons. Loggers and other service providers from outside the community control the quality of the harvesting practice, marketing of goods sold, and, to an extent, employment. The size of transaction costs to a community turn on how well it can keep the contract relationship aligned with its monetary and nonmonetary objectives. Can the community monitor a contract relationship successfully? Do outside services interfere with the community's access to the forest and other resources benefits? Does the community place value on non-timber uses of the forest affected by harvesting timber, where harvesting practices are difficult to oversee? The outside logging company also considers costs of contracting with the community, such as the uncertainty in production agreement that would require renegotiation of the contract in the middle of production, after it has invested in the community's forest. The sociolegal context should be considered as well in analyzing community forestry transaction costs (Goldberg 1979). Outside firms investing in the community's forests cannot integrate backward into forest ownership because of the agrarian structure that gives communities rights over forestlands which are not currently marketable. It would be hard to convince a private investor to build a sawmill on community land, as that sawmill would then be highly specific to the surrounding community forest due to transportation costs. In fact, as community rights to commercialize their resources were expanding, private sawmills located next to specific community forests were dismantled (Antinori 2000).

With respect to the transaction costs of community-private firm contracting, vertical integration into extraction and processing could allow community managers to control forestry operations in ways consistent with community welfare beyond payment for material. Vertical integration entails more unified control over organization. In timber production, this includes general coordination of harvesting practices, schedules, hiring practices, and the flow of funds with a community's overall objectives. Therefore, it is argued that as communities become more capable of producing timber goods, they choose greater degrees of control over the production chain, where both transaction cost and community capabilities explain the pattern of a community's investment in the timber industry. It appears possible to direct management under either integration or non-integration, where under the stumpage contracts, the communities are trading access to the communities' timber for jobs and public goods. Of the 16 stumpage communities in the sample, 9 had contract clauses with the private harvester that the harvester hire locally from the community and 5 had additional clauses that specified that the harvester provide training to the persons hired within the community. Forty percent of the communities that sell stumpage require the private firm to invest in schools, electricity, or even paint for public buildings in a community, while the more integrated communities channeled their revenues from the product sales into funding public works on their own. Yet these communities remain vulnerable to opportunistic behavior and hence higher "transaction costs," as has been experienced historically. In recent years, contract breaches have continued to occur across all community types, for example, when a firm did not pay local *comuneros* it hired as loggers, or when another firm did not repair a road.

To assess degree of uncertainty in the timber production process, community authorities were asked the reasons for any harvest less than the amount authorized that year by SEMARNAT. The communities harvesting at 100% authorization levels are a little less than one half the sample. The onset of the rainy season is most often cited, but this may mask a lack of organization that slowed production. However, level of integration is positively correlated ($\rho = .65$) with a stated reduction in harvest due to encountering decayed, diseased, or damaged trees. The second most frequent response, lack of roads to access the timber stand, did not correlate strongly with level of integration, while less integration is correlated with the perceived disorganization of the buyer ($\rho = -.65$). Other stumpage communities blamed either (1) their own disorganization or external territorial conflicts (one case each) or (2) disagreements between themselves and the buyer (two cases). One roundwood community blamed a lack of both labor and a market for their product. Internal conflicts in two finished product communities were blamed for harvests below 100%; thus internal conflicts plague even the more sophisticated operations. Only two finished products communities and one roundwood community made a specific choice in the General Assembly to take a more conservative approach to harvests. Therefore, across the board, shocks occurred that prevented harvesters from obtaining the full authorized volume. Whereas stumpage communities connected the shortfall to the buyer, integrated communities tended to blame their own choices, organization, or natural circumstances.

We look to several indicators to determine when transaction costs influence forward integration of communities into producing roundwood for sawmills or pulp, or transforming the roundwood into finished products. The indicators considered are the community's past experience in the concessionaire era, size and quality of forest holdings, presence of noncommercial timber and non-timber forest product markets, and collective labor skills in extraction and milling. Transaction cost and other possible implications of each variable are discussed, with summary statistics given by integration group in Table 11.1. In this analysis, the focus is on characteristics describing the community as a whole. Political and social conflicts concerning community leadership are addressed only indirectly in the proxy for social capital.

CONCESSION ERA AND SOCIAL CAPITAL

As shown in Table 11.1, the percentage of communities surveyed whose forests were concessioned to the UIEFs increases significantly with levels of vertical integration. Further, the UIEFs harvested for more years, on average, with increasing levels of integration. In contrast, stumpage communities tend to have a history of contracting with private companies without concessions, and non-UIEF companies harvested a lesser average number of years in the communities than the UIEF concessionaires across integration groups. Therefore, more integrated communities today have had exposure to industrial forestry in both a qualitatively and quantitatively different way.

The concessionaire experience may have affected present-day ownership patterns for both constructive and unconstructive reasons. With 25-year leases, the concessionaires invested in extraction and processing infrastructure and human capital, which remained available to communities to begin their own production. In Oaxaca, FAPATUX built a highway connecting the capital city of Oaxaca to Tuxtepec, a town bordering Veracruz state, the site of its pulp factory. The road strategically snakes through the Sierra Norte, with access roads to communities where it held leases. The companies built and maintained logging roads to reach the forest stands in these communities. Sawmills were constructed in some of the communities, which later took over or dismantled machinery and distributed it among communities for their start-up operations. Despite the conflicts over labor, the concession companies hired locally

Table 11.1. Summary statistics and predicted sign of key variables

Variable name	Predicted effect on vertical integration	Mean	Standard deviation
History of concession forestry	+		
Stumpage		13%	.08
Roundwood		31%	.13
Sawnwood		88%	.12
Finished products		86%	.13
Mechanical training index	+		
Stumpage		.23	.06
Roundwood[a]		.35	.07
Sawnwood		.40	.06
Finished products		.61	.09
Forest quality score	+		
Stumpage		3.61	.14
Roundwood		4.13	.15
Sawnwood		4.30	.18
Finished products		4.57	.16
Forested hectares	+		
Stumpage		2,403	482
Roundwood		12,208	7,167
Sawnwood		7,467	2,125
Finished products		11,047	2,827
Initial stock of logging roads (km)	?		
Stumpage		22	7.30
Roundwood[a]		32	12.01
Sawnwood		50	15.82
Finished products		82	26.63
Prior markets in noncommercial timber goods	+		
Stumpage		38%	.12
Roundwood[a]		17%	.11
Sawnwood		38%	.17
Finished products		71%	.17

Note: Number of observations unless otherwise indicated: stumpage, 16; roundwood, 13; sawnwood, 8; finished products, 7.
[a] Number of observations = 12.

to varying degrees, giving at least some community members work experience in the timber industry. Finally, some communities in the first years of community-controlled operations were able to harvest using the same management plans prepared and implemented by the concessionaires, lowering significantly the cost of starting extraction operations.

Besides the physical or human capital created, the concessionaire experience may have shaped and unified community members in their vision of long-term local forestry management and developed their awareness of contractual hazards. Individual stakeholders in a common property resource must overcome organizational hurdles to establish a resource governance system. The coordination to initiate a collective production unit like a CFE demands even further levels of commitment and organization. Exposure to the timber industry as a long-term business may have transformed and motivated the communities' vision of the potential of forests in providing income, skills, and quality of life. Generally, because of the charged nature of the conflict with concessionaires over contracting terms and difficulty of enforcing contracts, all community members were acutely aware of the tensions. Intercommunity alliances formed to lobby government against renewing the concessions. This experience may have contributed to a higher level of social capital—a network of social relations that facilitates collective action (Putnam 1995), rules and institutions (Ostrom 1990), or social capability to substitute traditional social organizations based on kinship and custom with organizations based on rights and responsibilities of citizens in a liberal democracy (Adelman and Morris 1967).

An argument to be explored in the empirical analysis is that the concession era's impact on the pattern of vertical integration goes beyond its creating any existing physical or human capital stock in the communities. The hypothesis is that the concession era experience politicized the communities and changed their expectation of timber extraction in their forests, which contributed to the social capital necessary to organize and form a community forestry enterprise.

Alternative hypotheses also come out of this experience. With greater physical capital infrastructure, concessioned communities might have been encouraged to take over operations because of their lower start-up costs. However, they might also have more easily attracted private harvesters who would pay higher prices for the easier and more convenient access to timber stands. This hypothesis is tested empirically by adding variables for physical and human capital as distinct from the concessionaire variable, which would capture additional social capital effects. Finally, any positive effect on vertical integration in communities could be confounded with higher quality forests, since concessionaires were able to choose high-quality forestland at locations more convenient to their pulp factories or sawmills. The econometric analysis also controls for this possible bias.

MECHANICAL SKILLS

A natural impediment to community forestry is lack of labor skills. Part of the present argument is that community forestry is associated with providing jobs to local residents. For example, the majority of stumpage communities had contract clauses in their stumpage contracts to hire locally. It is hypothesized here that communities with the requisite labor skills would more readily forego the marketplace and forward integrate, leading to a positive relationship between vertical integration and resident labor skills, as indicated in Table 11.1.

During the concession period, community members had opportunities to gain mechanical skills of extraction and processing and, to a lesser extent, technical skills of documentation and accounting. In comparing across community vertical integration levels, no significant differences appear in the reported percentage of people receiving income from alternative activities such as agriculture and livestock, coffee growing, or remittances. It would then appear, by these indicators at least, that community members have relatively similar opportunity costs of time. Distance to the city of Oaxaca, which offers more income opportunities which would compete with local employment in forestry, does vary and is analyzed further in the empirical section.

To create a measure of human capital stock for production, data was collected on past community employment experience in the mechanics of timber operations, such as working with trucks, cranes, chainsaws, and sawmills, and in technical tasks like administrative and documentation skills. "Past" means prior to 1986 or date of vertical integration so as not to confound with skills learned once communities had integrated forward. These measures are combined to create an index of initial skills available to the community as a whole should members collectively decide to invest in timber operations.

A potential source of bias is the negative recollections of community members regarding the concessionaires, which could lead community authorities to underestimate systematically the level of historical hiring by the UIEFs. To reduce bias, the measure of employment experience in each task is a binary variable that takes the value 1 if any member of the community received this experience. Four mechanical tasks and four technical tasks were combined separately, and the community given a percentage for number of areas in each group for which they had some resident experience. For example, a community that claims members experienced in all four mechanical tasks would have a score of 100%, or 1, while a community with member experience in three of four tasks scored 75%, or .75. A positive explanatory effect is predicted for the mechanical skills index, while range of technical experience is not considered as critical a prerequisite skill and is not hypothesized to have explanatory power. As shown in Table 11.1, more integrated communities have a broader range of experience in mechanical tasks—.61 in the index compared to only .23 for stumpage communities.

QUALITY AND SIZE OF FOREST HOLDINGS

Summary statistics in Table 11.1 also show that the quality index and size of forest holdings increase with higher levels of integration. From a transaction cost perspective, a larger extent of commercial quality forested acreage could encourage community forestry enterprises. First, the increase in quality merchantable timber available implies increased frequency of trading in the market and therefore more frequent recurrence of transaction costs that could be minimized by unified governance. Second, a larger forest of commercial quality might increase the extent and scope of both timber and non-timber benefits provided to the local community. The added complexity of managing the forest according to overall community goals could raise transaction costs to encourage community vertical integration. Third, community labor productivity would rise with increased quality and size of the forest as a form of capital, bringing communities into a more competitive position vis-à-vis private loggers and millers. Finally, an outside logging firm might have more to lose if it has invested in the community forest and contract arrangements break apart with the community. Therefore, the predicted effect on community vertical integration is positive.

While the size of forest holdings is in hectares, the measure for the commercial quality of the forest is the average five-point ranking score of three longtime professional foresters in Oaxaca asked to assess the communities' forest quality around 1940 to avoid confounding effects with the location of UIEF concessions.

INITIAL STOCK OF LOGGING ROADS

The primary durable and specific investments in a community forest are logging roads. In addition, refurbishing of roads to the community to connect to transportation routes was required in 13 of the 16 contracts in the stumpage category. Unless outside private firms have long-term secure contracts with the community, it is not in their interest to build quality access roads that will resist runoff the next year, for example. Interestingly, the United States Forest Service provides credits in timber sales to build access roads (Munn and Rucker 1995), and North Carolina nonindustrial private forest owners would attract buyers by building access roads (Leffler and Rucker 1991) because of this disincentive from the buyer's perspective. If the community foresees future timber production, it may be in their interest to invest in infrastructure or own capital to manage and control extraction.

Given the long history of logging in Oaxaca, a network of logging roads in most communities already exists. The network increases from least to most integrated (see Table 11.1), although the logging road density—logging roads per number of forested hectares—does not change significantly among groups (not shown). As building and maintaining logging roads is one of the biggest costs to timber production besides transportation, an existing usable road network would be a substantial cost savings for a community forestry enterprise.

Logging road infrastructure has at least two competing effects on a community seeking to market timber resources, precluding an unambiguous prediction of its effect on integration probabilities. First, existing infrastructure could lower capital constraints for the community. It also represents a stock of physical capital that would remain idle for a period of time if a private harvester backed out of a contract. In this case, the existing stock of logging roads available at the time communities were allowed to integrate forward in 1986 would have a positive effect on integration tendencies. Second, it decreases the amount of specific investments an outside contractor would have to make in the community, thus facilitating a market transaction. So an increase in initial stock of roads, measured as stock existing as of 1986, would encourage contracting. Empirical analysis is needed to determine which tendency is stronger.

PRIOR MARKETS IN NONCOMMERCIAL TIMBER GOODS

A final key variable considered in our model of the community forestry sector is prior existence of markets in noncommercial timber and non-timber forest products. To the degree that noncommercial timber and non-timber forest production are separable from timber production, we should not observe any relationship. Yet, uncertainties and difficulty of monitoring harvest management practices can make contracting with outside services infeasible. Greater noncommercial timber forest and non-timber product collection may raise the importance of monitoring and management of the timber harvest. Therefore, assuming that timber harvests affect the supply of these other forest products, one would expect a positive relationship between where these markets exist and vertical integration, as indicated in Table 11.1.

The survey data contains information on a variety of forest products sold by individuals or groups in each observation unit (community or work group). These include fuelwood, charcoal, wood for domestic use, mushrooms, and an "other" category. A dummy variable takes the value 1 if there was any market in existence in the observation unit for more than 10 years, and 0 otherwise, so that the market predated vertical integration to avoid confounding effects of vertical integration on non-timber production. Thus, the presence of mushroom harvesting activity is omitted from the measure because this market developed substantially during the 10 years previous to the survey.

Quantitative Analysis

Econometric Evaluation of Community Vertical Integration

Econometric regression analysis is used to test the effect of the variables described above on the propensity for community vertical integration. Regression analysis measures how the dependent variable, in this case, vertical integration, varies according to independent indicators, like community and resource characteristics. The ordered logit regression model considers subjects facing a choice with more than two alternatives which have a natural ordering and is applied in this context to test statistically the effects of these independent variables on the probability that a community is at any of the four integration levels described.[8]

The results are presented in Figure 11.2 in terms of their marginal effects on the probability of a particular integration level. For each level, the bar chart shows the average change in probability of being at that level if the independent variable is increased by one unit, holding all other variables equal.

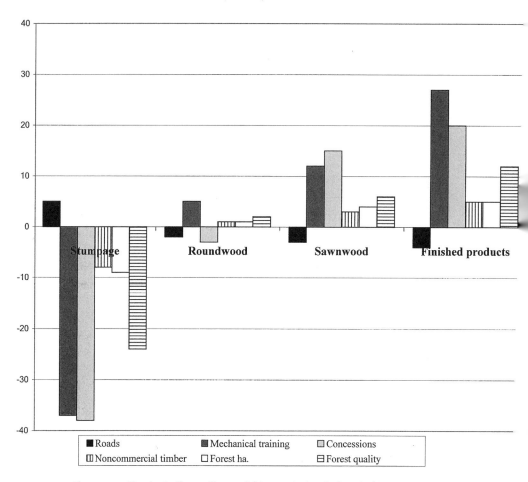

Figure 11.2 Marginal effects of key variables on the level of vertical integration.

The model most successfully explains the highest and lowest levels of integration, that is, the stumpage and finished products groups, as can be seen by the generally higher marginal effects for these groups across independent variables. As predicted, mechanical experience reduces the probability of being a stumpage community and increases the probability of being at any of the more integrated levels. Concession era history, which proxies for social capital, reduces the probability of being either at the stumpage or roundwood level and raises the probability of selling sawnwood or finished products. Prior existence of nonindustrial forest products extraction and sales, forest size, and initial commercial quality all raise the probability that a community is integrated forward to some degree. Initial stock of logging roads is the only variable that reduces the probability of forward integration, supporting the hypothesis that less specific investments required by an outside harvester facilitate contracting rather than serving to relieve capital constraints. In addition, leasing history, mechanically oriented training, forest size, and initial quality are the strongest predictors for community integration. The regression results indicate a standard of statistical significance at the 10% level or better for these variables, meaning that there is at most only a 10% chance that the variable has no explanatory power. Roads and history of marketing nonindustrial timber forest products, while having signs consistent with the transaction cost hypotheses, are less statistically significant, so conclusions cannot be drawn concerning these variables.

Alternative arguments were also considered in the empirical analysis. Variations in percent of community members receiving income from agriculture, livestock, remittances, and other nonforestry related income, as measures of opportunity cost, do not affect the integration level probabilities. In assessing the separate possible effects of concession history, the significant result on the concession dummy variable, even when road infrastructure, employment experience, and the forest quality variables are included, suggests that its impact goes beyond its association with these variables. In addition, correlation coefficients between the concession history dummy and these indicators are low. Further, eliminating from the sample three communities that received substantial sources of credit from the UIEFs for start-up operations did not affect the results. Finally, replacing the concession dummy with a measure of distance of the community from Oaxaca city, a major population and commercial center in Oaxaca, gives a positive result significant at the 10% level, but an inferior model fit, meaning that proximity to the city does not as fully explain the impact of the concession era experience on community enterprises today. The positive sign, however, suggests that proximity to the major commercial center of Oaxaca encourages community members to integrate forward, despite the additional accessibility to employment, markets, and lifestyle opportunities.

Profitability

For additional perspective on community timber operations, survey data was collected on total revenues and costs to estimate profitability. As the goal of fieldwork was to have a general approximation rather than a full disclosure of financial records, a few comments are in order concerning interpretation of the data across the sample. First, the willingness and preparedness to disclose information varied across communities during the survey process. In some communities, we had access to accounting records, while in other communities we relied on the community authorities' stated figures. In a few cases, we calculated revenues and costs from data on volume sold and sale prices by product sold, labor force size and wages, and transportation costs.

Second, it was not possible to verify consistency of accounting practices. For example, capital equipment is usually expensed over time to account for the equipment's services over its "useful life," rather than being expensed all at once in a given year. Silviculture services represent both annual, routine maintenance costs, like thinning, and long-term investments like the design of a management plan, which, from an economic perspective, contributes value to timber operations over the life of the plan. Estimates of profitability largely depend on the treatment of these costs in the communities' financial reporting, and it is highly possible that accounting practices differ across the sample with respect to these costs.

However, the degree of bias due to depreciation cost accounting also likely differs across communities. In stumpage communities, outside harvesters usually own the capital equipment, so there is little capital to depreciate in a community's profit estimation. Only one stumpage community in our sample claimed ownership of a 12-ton truck, used for transport. The age of capital equipment would also affect bias as communities with older equipment would have fully depreciated its costs had they accounted for depreciation. This first approximation of profitability assumes that all equipment is fully depreciated, with less bias expected in the stumpage category and communities employing equipment past its useful life.

With these caveats considered, revenue, costs, and profit are reported in Table 11.2, where the business term *gross profit* refers to sales revenue net sales costs (here, labor and materials). All groups on average generate revenues which cover total labor and material costs, with the sawnwood group having the highest profit margin at 54%. The gross profit margins across groups are quite large, ranging from 32 to 54%, even considering potential underreporting of costs. These profit measures present a different perspective than studies that generally doubt communities' financial viability (e.g., Chapela 1996) and suggest a reevaluation of cash flows generated by community forestry.

A further consideration in analyzing profitability of community forestry activities is the planning time horizon and management goals. Longer rotation periods or conservation plans can lower revenues in any

Table 11.2. Average revenue, cost, and profit by level of integration (new pesos)

	Stumpage (12)	Roundwood (8)	Sawnwood (5)	Finished products (5)
Sales revenue	573,549	1,688,274	3,020,021	9,578,861
Total sales costs	304,125	1,010,740	1,462,620	6,522,042
Gross profit	311,386	870,498	1,557,401	3,056,819
Gross profit, as % of sales revenue	39%	48%	54%	32%

given year. Therefore, a profit calculation for one year can be lower while profit over the length of the planning horizon is higher in a comparison of two separate operations. For example, while the finished products group has the lowest gross profit margin, their average financial returns in the long run could be higher than those of the other groups. The distinctions between long- and short-term profits, as well as accounting practices and management goals, remain for future research.

Conclusion

Common property institutions have a long history in Mexico, where communal land serves social, political, and cultural functions, as well as economic ones. This very complexity makes it unclear how common property institutions fit into the broader market economy, leading to claims that the current agrarian community structure is incompatible with efficient markets. This paper seeks to provide an analysis of how local communities with common property forests approach market opportunities. While difficulties of organizing both within the community and between the community and private sectors pose challenges distinct from solely private-sector operations, we propose a transaction cost analysis as a framework for clarifying these difficulties. This can improve our understanding of not only how the appropriate choice of institutional design can reduce conflicts between local needs and broader policy goals, but also how common property governance performs alongside the private sector in production activities. With varying levels of engagement along the timber extraction and processing chain, the community forestry sector in Mexico has shown an ability to coexist with the private sector, and preliminary evidence suggests that it can yield profitable operations. Access to the market, rather than eroding the basis for common property management, may become another feature of community governance in Mexico.

Treating the community governance structure as a firm, we applied transaction cost economics to the extent that such industrial organization concepts clarify these relationships. The feasibility of production can explain the presence of commercial activities within a community but is not sufficient to explain who carries out which activities. A transaction cost approach interprets vertical integration decisions as a function of contracting problems between private firms and communities that have organized according to traditional norms and customs and have a history of communal forestland tenure. It readily allows consideration of vulnerabilities of both the private firm buyer and community supplier as parties to a contract, how contracts can be structured, and how decision-making control over forestry production matters. A basic argument is that as community productive capabilities become comparable to services available in the market, communities prefer to integrate forward to avoid contractual hazards with outside entities like private logging firms. Common property resources contribute to community welfare. Direct community ownership and control over production ensures community access to these benefits. In addition, private firms take transaction costs into consideration when they contract with communities, affecting the overall governance structures we observe.

The results of the empirical analysis are consistent with a transaction cost explanation of the pattern of vertical integration across the community forestry sector in Oaxaca, Mexico. A range of mechanical skills in forestry available in the community, higher resource endowments, and a history of participation in the federal concession system are the strongest predictors of timber production activities at the community level, where the concession era experience is interpreted as creating the social cohesiveness necessary to facilitate collective action. All of these variables in combination, rather than any one alone, favors the probability that a community will form a community forestry enterprise and invest in downstream production activities. One possibility is that the heightened awareness of potential conflicts between communities and the private sector may have caused formerly concessioned communities to overinvest in downstream activities. However, only three sample communities had moved to a less integrated step in their extraction or processing capacity over the 10-year period prior to the survey. The implications for forestry policy are that policy makers should evaluate the challenges of encouraging joint ventures with the private sector or unions of community forestry enterprises in terms of the variables examined in this research and other transaction cost considerations, including community expectations regarding their common forestland.

An area for further research lies in examining the management of multiple uses of natural resources and local access patterns, where both local and professional knowledge can shape management approaches (Klooster 2002; Peluso 1996). Nontimber resources are receiving increasing attention at the community and state level in Mexico, and diversification of forest uses has frequently been suggested as a strategy for improvement. Enhancing non-timber forest benefits raises questions of how to design plans for separate uses of the forest and develop policy that integrates various sources of knowledge about biological relationships represented in these ecosystems. While the prior existence of noncommercial timber/ non-timber forest product markets, either at the collective or individual level, did not strongly influence the likelihood of vertical integration, the experience of managing timber production might support community efforts by enhancing non-timber benefits. An understanding of community governance and its interaction with STFs as briefly described in this paper could lead to policy that allows useful exchange of information to implement ecosystem management plans.

Second, profitability remains a key issue for the long-term stability of community forestry enterprises. The communities surveyed in this research have the potential to benefit financially from timber production. Further research, plus application of appropriate accounting practices, would improve understanding as to the feasibility of community forestry, either via occasional stumpage sales or ongoing operations.

The present research also has relevance for management issues in other parts of the world. Governments are now more interested in devolving decision making to lower levels of government, local civic groups, and stakeholders. Evidence suggests that this policy reduces poverty and income risk (Jodha 1992), increases community capacity (Kusel and Fortmann 1991), and improves resource management, although no exact formula exists. Local resource management will continue to increase in importance in various forms where market participation is an element of management (Scherr et al. 2002). Close parallels to the Mexican case are Native American Indian tribes in the United States and Canada, where tribes have the right to commercialize forestland on the land they hold under stewardship tenure (UBC 2002). Like Mexican agrarian communities, these tribes have well-defined boundaries, a distinct membership, and a decision-making structure at the local level for timber production for which they have developed forestry enterprises. The enterprises struggle with similar questions of local jobs, expertise, and profitability. The issue of common property rights goes beyond communities with a specific tenure status to communities of interest and the public in general. To name two examples, the Quincy Library Group in the United States demonstrated the influence local residents can play in shaping federal policies in national forests (Duane 1997), and Eastern Europe's land restitution programs will place more general land and forests under common property control to reflect prewar land tenure regimes (Sikor 2002). A transaction cost framework of analysis encompassing the multiple roles of communal resources might identify strategies for long-term resource management and economic development.

Notes

1. *Technical forest services* (*servicios técnicos forestales;* STF) is a term for the professional foresters who draw up the management plans required by Mexican law for logging.

2. Those communities with forests but no commercial production are not included in the sample.

3. The only community-run organization was in San Andrés Cabecera Nueva, the first community to organize for forest production, accomplished by convincing the company Maderera la Mixteca to sell its equipment to the community (F. Maldonado, personal communication, 1998). It is not clear if this organization contradicted laws concerning community commercial operations.

4. The history of and theories about why forest management shifted toward the communities are complex. In brief, there were four major factors in this shift. First, over the time period of the concessions, some community members sought higher levels of education, and in some cases these people provided leadership and management expertise for the transition to community forestry (Klooster 2000; Pego 1995). Second, logging companies and eventually concession companies began hiring from the communities, which led to an accumulation of local technical experience and training in forestry practices (Moros and Solano 1995). Third, the parastatal timber companies supported by the government were inefficient, which made them susceptible to a withdrawal of government backing (F. Chapela, personal communication, 1996). The conflict over the contract renewals may have provided a convenient breaking point. Fourth, bureaucratic and grassroots reformers favorable to community control were a driving force for the 1986 law and for the transition to more environmentally friendly forest policy and community involvement (Bray and Wexler 1996; Klooster 2000).

5. Communities which have vertically integrated into extraction or processing activities will be referred to as *community forestry enterprises* (CFEs) due to the more permanent nature of their timber operations, in contrast to stumpage com-

munities, which may contract intermittently with private loggers. Collectively, the term *community timber operations* refers to all contracting arrangements in which the community has sanctioned production, managed either at the community level or at the subcommunity level (work groups).

6. While supracommunity political organizing in Oaxaca occurs along ethnic lines (Stephen 1997), organizational form at the community level does not exhibit systematic differences across ethnicities (Cohen 1999), nor were the sample communities heterogeneous in ethnicity to any significant degree which appeared to affect forestry operations. Therefore, ethnicity is not a factor in this analysis.

7. Another perspective on transaction cost analysis emphasizes costs of writing contracts and the potential for the "hold-up" problem. Grossman and Hart 1986 and Hart 1995 describe ownership as the residual rights of decision making over an asset. Since contracts are inherently incomplete, the owner decides how to allocate the asset in unforeseen circumstances. Managers who are using the asset but do not ultimately own or control it do not enjoy the full benefit of their specific investments if the contracts are renegotiated and their gains to trade reduced. Since the manager's and owner's interests are likely to diverge, the results are either under- or overinvestment from a first-best optimum.

8. See Maddala 1983 for a complete technical description of the ordered logit model.

References

Adelman, I., and C. T. Morris. 1967. *Society, Politics and Economic Development: A Quantitative Approach.* Baltimore: Johns Hopkins University Press.

Agarwal, B. 2001. Participatory exclusions, community forestry, and gender: An analysis for south Asia and a conceptual framework. *World Development* 29(10): 1623–1648.

Agrawal, A. 2002. Common resources and institutional sustainability. In *Drama of the Commons*, ed. E. Ostrom et al., 41–85. Washington, DC: National Academy Press.

Antinori, C. 2000. Vertical integration in Mexican common property forests. PhD diss., University of California, Berkeley.

Bray, D., and M. Wexler. 1996. Forest policies in Mexico. In *Changing Structure in Mexico: Political, Social and Economic Prospects*, ed. L. Randall. Armonk, NY: M. E. Sharpe.

Bromley, D., et al. 1992. *Making the Commons Work: Theory, Practice and Policy.* San Francisco: Institute for Contemporary Studies Press.

Cancian, F. 1992. *Decline of Community in Zinacantan: Economy, Public Life, and Social Stratification, 1960–1987.* Stanford: Stanford University Press.

Carlsen, L. 1999. Autonomía indígena y usos y costumbres. In *Chiapas* no. 7, 45–70. Mexico City: Editorial Era.

Chapela, G. 1996. La organización de los campesinos forestales en México. In *Antropología política: Enfoques contemporáneos*, ed. H. Tejera Gaona, 545–559. Mexico City: Plaza y Valdés.

Coase, D. 1937. The nature of the firm. *Económica* 4:386–405.

Cohen, J. H. 1999. *Cooperation and Community: Economy and Society in Oaxaca.* Austin: University of Texas Press.

de la Peña, M. 1950. Problemas sociales y económicos de las mixtecas. *Memorias del Instituto Nacional Indigenista* 2(1).

Demsetz, H. 1967. Toward a theory of property rights. *American Economic Review* 57:347-358.

Diario Oficial de la Federación de los Estados Unidos Mexicanos. 23 October 1956.

Duane, T. 1997. Community participation in ecosystem management. *Ecology Law Quarterly* 24(4): 771-798.

Globerman, S., and R. Schwindt. 1986. The organization of vertically related transactions in the Canadian forest products industries. *Journal of Economic Behavior and Organization* 7:199-212.

Goldberg, V. 1979. The law and economics of vertical restrictions: A relational perspective. *Texas Law Review* 58:91-129.

Grossman, S., and O. Hart. 1986. The costs and benefits of ownership: A theory of vertical and lateral integration. *Journal of Political Economy* 94(4):691-719.

Hardin, G. 1968. The tragedy of the commons. *Science* 162:1243-1248.

Hart, O. 1995. *Firms, Contracts and Financial Structure.* Oxford: Oxford University Press.

Hoddinott, J., M. Adato, T. Besley, and L. Haddad, 2001. Participation and poverty reduction: Issues, theory and new evidence from South Africa. Discussion paper no. 98. Washington, DC: Food Consumption and Nutrition Division, International Food Policy Research Institute.

IBRD. 1995. Mexico-resource conservation and forest sector review. Report no. 13114-ME, March 31. Washington, DC: IBRD.

Jodha, N. 1992. Common property resources: A missing dimension of development strategies. World Bank Discussion paper no. 168. Washington, DC: IBRD.

Joskow, P. A. 1985. Vertical integration and long-term contracts: The case of coal-burning electric generating plants. *Journal of Law, Economics and Organization* 1(1):33-80.

Kearney, M. 1972. *The Winds of Ixtepeji: World View and Society in a Zapotec Town.* New York: Holt, Reinhart and Winston.

Klein, P., and H. Shelanski. 1994. Empirical research in transaction cost economics: A survey and assessment. Working paper BPP-60. Berkeley: Center for Research in Management Business and Public Policy.

Klooster, D. 2000. Institutional choice, community, and struggle: A case study of forest co-management in Mexico. *World Development* 28(1):1-20.

———. 2002. Towards adaptive community forestry management: Integrating local forest knowledge with scientific forestry. *Economic Geography* 78(1):43-70.

Kusel, J., and L. Fortmann. 1991. *Well-Being and Forest Dependent Communities.* Sacramento: California Department of Forestry and Fire Protection, Forest and Rangelands Resource Assessment Program.

Leffler, K. B., and R. Rucker. 1991. Transaction costs and the efficient organization of production: A study of timber-harvesting contracts. *Journal of Political Economy* 99(5):1060-1087.

Ley Forestal. 1960. *Diario Oficial de la Federación de los Estados Unidos Mexicanos,* 16 January.

———. 1986. *Diario Oficial de la Federación de los Estados Unidos Mexicanos,* 30 May.

López-Arzola, R., and P. F. Gerez. 1993. The permanent tension. *Cultural Survival Quarterly* 17(1):42–44.

Maddala, G. S. 1983. *Limited-Dependent and Qualitative Variables in Econometrics.* Cambridge: Cambridge University Press.

Mayers, J., and S. Vermeulen. 2002. *Company-Community Forestry Partnerships: From Raw Deals to Mutual Gains.* London: International Institute of Environment and Development.

Meinzen-Dick, R., A. Knox, and M. di Gregoria. 2001. Collective action, property rights and devolution of natural resource management: Exchange of knowledge and implications for policy. Proceedings of the ICLARM/CAPRi International Conference, Feldafing, Germany, 2001.

Merino-Pérez, L., and G. Alatorre. 1997. Los impactos del conflicto social en el manejo de los recursos naturales. In *El manejo forestal comunitario en México y sus perspectivas de sustentabilidad*, ed. L. Merino-Pérez, G. Alatorre, B. Cabarle, F. Chapela, and S. Madrid, 57–74. Cuernavaca: UNAM, SEMARNAP, CCMSS, WRI.

Montes, F. D. 2002. Las controversias electorales en usos y costumbres. In *Memoria de justicia electoral en usos y costumbres: Reflexiones sobre legislación electoral en municipios indígenas*, ed. Comisión Diocesana de Pastoral Social de Oaxaca and Servicios para una Educación Alternativa, Oaxaca.

Moros, F. A., and C. S. Solano. 1995. Forestry communities in Oaxaca: The struggle for free market access. In *Case Studies of Community-Based Forestry Enterprises in the Americas*, ed. N. Forster, 99–119. Madison: University of Wisconsin.

Munn, I., and R. Rucker. 1995. An economic analysis of the difference between bid prices on forest service and private timber sales. *Forest Science* 41(4):823–840.

Nader, L. 1990. *Harmony Ideology: Justice and Control in a Zapotec Mountain Village.* Stanford: Stanford University Press.

Olson, M. L. 1964. *The Logic of Collective Action.* Cambridge, MA: Harvard University Press.

Ostrom, E. 1990. *Governing the Commons: The Evolution of Institutions for Collective Action.* Cambridge: Cambridge University Press.

Pego, M. A. Sanchez. 1995. The forest enterprise of the indigenous community of Nuevo San Juan Parangaricutiro, Michoacan, Mexico. In *Case Studies of Community-Based Forestry Enterprises in the Americas*, ed. N. Forster, 137–160. Madison: University of Wisconsin.

Peluso, N. 1996. Fruit trees and family trees in an anthropogenic forest: Ethics of access, property zones and environmental change in Indonesia. *Comparative Studies in Society and History* 38:510–548.

Putnam, R. 1995. Bowling alone: America's declining social capital. *Journal of Democracy* 6(1):65–78.

SARH. 1994. *Inventario forestal periódico* as quoted in *Los aprovechamientos forestales en Oaxaca, subdelegación de recursos naturales*, ed. SEMARNAP. Mexico City: SEMARNAP.

Scherr, S., A. White, and D, Kaimowitz. 2002. *Making Markets Work for Forest Communities.* Washington, DC: Forest Trends.

SEMARNAP. 2000. *Conservación y manejo comunitario de los recursos forestales en Oaxaca.* Oaxaca: Delegación Oaxaca.

Servicios para una Educación Alternativa (Educa A.C.) and Comisión Diocesana de Pastoral Social de Oaxaca. 2001. *La elección en municipios de usos y costumbres.* Durham: University of New Hampshire.

Sikor, T. 2002. The commons in transition: Sustainable agriculture in central and eastern European countries. Discussion paper no. 10. Division of Resource Economics. Berlin: Humboldt University.

Snook, L. K. 1986. Community forestry in Mexico's natural forests: The case of San Pablo Macuiltianguis. In *Current Topics in Forest Research: Emphasis on Contributions by Women Scientists.* Symposium proceedings, 4–6 November, report no. SE-46. U.S. Department of Agriculture, Forest Service, Southeastern Forest Experiment Station.

Spores, R. 1984. *The Mixtecs in Ancient and Colonial Times.* Norman: University of Oklahoma Press.

Stephen, L. 1997. Redefined nationalism in building a movement for indigenous autonomy in southern Mexico. *Journal of Latin American Anthropology* 3(1):72–101.

UBC. 2002. Proceedings of the International Conference on Global Perspectives on Indigenous People's Forestry: Linking Communities, Commerce and Conservation. 4–6 June, Vancouver, Canada.

Velásquez, M. C. 2000. *El nombramiento: Las elecciones por usos y costumbres en Oaxaca.* Oaxaca: Instituto Estatal Electoral.

White, A., and A. Martin. 2002. *Who Owns the World's Forests: Forest Tenure and Public Forests in Transition.* Washington, DC: Forest Trends.

Williamson, O. 1985. *The Economic Institutions of Capitalism.* New York: Free Press.

———. 1991. Comparative economic organization: The analysis of discrete structural alternatives. *Administrative Science Quarterly* 36(2):269–296.

CHAPTER 12

The Managerial Economics of Sustainable Community Forestry in Mexico: A Case Study of El Balcón, Técpan, Guerrero

JUAN MANUEL TORRES-ROJO, ALEJANDRO
GUEVARA-SANGINÉS, AND DAVID BARTON BRAY

The phenomenon of community-based enterprises competing successfully in the marketplace is relatively new, and there is still very little literature on the subject. Community forest enterprises (CFEs) in Mexico represent a particularly interesting example; CFEs are based on the commercial exploitation of timber from common property forests. The economic development literature in general sheds little light on the "community as entrepreneurial firm" (Antinori 2000; see also Antinori, this volume), but it has been suggested that CFEs have a different "logic" from privately owned capitalist enterprises. Community enterprises have multiple goals that may not be shared by noncommunity private enterprises. Private enterprises aspire only to maximize their earnings, while the CFEs seek the generation of income, the conservation of the forests, the production of public goods for community benefit, and the participation of the *comuneros* (Alatorre Frenk 2000). It has also been suggested that Mexican CFEs are at great risk of disappearing entirely because of foreign competition and the lack of profitability in the sector (Chapela 1996). However, Antinori (this volume) maintains that the CFE sector is actually more profitable than has been thought.

It is true that in terms of management structure, distribution of benefits, productive assets, and other dimensions, CFEs are different from private enterprises. Nonetheless, they must also compete and survive in an economic context that demands efficiency and competitiveness in quality and price, and thus will finally be judged by the same harsh terms of the marketplace as any other business. In this paper, we will attempt to do an analytic case study of one CFE in mostly entrepreneurial terms, while taking into account some of its special characteristics as a community-owned enterprise with a unique history.

The CFE we have chosen was, until recently, little known in the literature,[1] but it is emerging as an example of an unusually successful community enterprise which is now exporting much of its production (Bray and Merino-Pérez 2003; see also Bustamante, 1996). We will undertake an examination of El Balcón in the analytic terms presented by Porter (1990) to understand how it has become competitive despite what are often perceived to be the handicaps of community ownership. Through an analysis of the factor and demand conditions, the related and supporting industries, and firm strategy, structure, and rivalry, we explore why El Balcón has become successful. We will also carry out a brief strategic planning exercise in order to make some concrete suggestions on steps El Balcón can take to further increase its international competitiveness. We will also use the example of El Balcón to evaluate the competitive position of CFEs generally, and while we do not argue that El Balcón has been successful solely because of community ownership, the case study certainly shows that an enterprise based on community ownership of a common property asset is no hindrance for gaining competitive advantage in national and international markets.

The historical development of El Balcón is discussed in some detail in the analysis, so here we will just briefly describe the history and setting. El Balcón is located in the Costa Grande region of Guerrero, the Pacific coast north of Acapulco. Situated in the segment of the Sierra Madre Sur known as the Cordillera Costera del Sur, it has an average elevation of 2,200 meters, with a very rugged topography that leaves parts of the area isolated during the rainy season, when some 1,400 millimeters of precipitation fall. It was constituted as an *ejido* in January 1966 with an endowment of 2,400 hectares. In October 1974, it received an additional 19,150 hectares, including most of its current forests, for a total land area today of 25,565 hectares. Its current land area and perimeter were fixed in the resolution of a boundary dispute with the neighboring *ejido* of Cuatro Cruces in 1986, when it ceded 3,085 hectares of forest in exchange for 7,100 hectares of dry shrub forest. El Balcón has a main village, Pocitos, and two outlying population centers, or *agencias* (La Lajita and Mesa Verde), with a total of 136 *ejidatarios* and population of around 600.

The population was formed from small groups of mestizo families who made their living from corn farming and goat herding, and was severely marked by the violent interfamily and intercommunity clashes over land that have shaped Guerrero in general. The violence of the region in El Balcón makes the CFE and the relative peace of the zone today all the more remarkable. In the early 1960s, this region of the Sierra was described as "enmeshed in terror and killing" as El Balcón became embroiled in brutal interfamily and community conflicts over land (Wexler 1995). Reciprocal murders left the region seriously depopulated for a period as families fled to other communities. Community members from El Balcón sought the intercession of the Mexican government in 1961, initiating the application for *ejido* status to fix their land boundaries. The claim was recognized in 1966, but final *ejido* title was not received until 1972. In the late 1960s and early 1970s, the Costa Grande was further roiled by armed guerrilla movements, which brought military incursions and firefights into the area, once again forcing communities to relocate. Some community members from El Balcón fled to a community to the north called La Laguna, which had been operating its own sawmill and logging operation since the late 1950s. When they returned to resettle El Balcón in the early 1970s, they carried with them the realization that their forests were a potential economic resource. Community members began lobbying for a new land grant, which was given in 1974 for 19,150 hectares.

A national small farmer federation, the Central Independiente de Obreros Agrícolas y Campesinos (CIOAC), played a key role in negotiating peace between the communities during the 1970s (Wexler 1995), and commercial logging began in 1980 as a direct result of social peace in the region. When El Balcón first began selling logs in 1980, it sold directly to the state-owned Forestal Vincente Guerrero (FOVIGRO), with about 20 community members working as laborers. Thus, El Balcón never passed through a stage typical in Mexico where the timber buyers come in and take complete charge of extraction, paying only a stumpage fee to the community (*rentismo*).

El Balcón was able to use the significant profits from the first few years of roundwood sales to expand its capital assets. In 1982–1983 El Balcón bought its first logging equipment, and was thus able deliver roundwood directly to the sawmill, capturing more of the value chain. In 1986 El Balcón acquired a new community asset, the sawmill, in a joint investment with a state development-financing agency, the National Trust Fund for *Ejido* Development (Fideicomiso del Fondo Nacional de Fomento Ejidal; FIFONAFE). FIFONAFE dissolved 10 months later, leaving El Balcón with full ownership of the mill. Thus, in six years, members of El Balcón went from their first logging, essentially as employees of the state-owned enterprise, to full control over their own logging business. This short-term growth confronted serious human capital deficiencies in terms of training and experience in managing a complex industrial enterprise. Due to economic difficulties and managerial problems, in 1989 the *ejido* turned management of the CFE over to an outside professional manager. This included outside staff as well. The *ejidatarios* created a "Council of Principles" as a community oversight committee whose purpose was to approve investment and policy guidelines. After the accumulation of productive assets in the enterprise, the enterprise slowly began to hire *ejidatarios* again in the early 1990s, and today the labor force is over 70% *ejidatarios*. El Balcón's professional management has also achieved important efficiency gains, such as using logging trucks with double trailers, significantly lowering transportation costs. All this has led to what is reported to be a relatively healthy financial profile. The enterprise reports a 20–35% profit margin in recent years, with an average of around US$1 million annually in net profits.

El Balcón has established a successful commercial relationship with a Washington-based timber marketing company called Westwood Forest Products. Westwood is currently importing both sawnwood and moldings to the United States from El Balcón. From late 1995 to late 2001, El Balcón exported approximately $19 million worth of timber to Westwood. Westwood has been crucial in financing both capital assets and operating costs over the last several years. Other important features of El Balcón are discussed below.

Analytical Framework

Due to its history and evolution, the CFE of El Balcón is one of the most interesting and instructive examples of common property forest management in Mexico. El Balcón might be considered a result of a superior phase of an evolutionary economic process (Nelson and Winters 1994), and thus one to which other rural communities involved in forestry can aspire; or it might be thought of as an organization where a particular crisis led to innovative solutions. Or in Bryson's (1995) managerial terms, it might also be considered an organization in which a crisis becomes precisely the origin of a continued strategic impulse that leads to success.

All of these are viable explanatory frameworks for understanding El Balcón's success. However, we argue that a modified interpretation of Porter's "diamond" (1990) offers the most powerful explanatory framework for understanding El Balcón's success. The diamond explains the determinants of economic success of nations and their distinct industrial sectors. The determinants are the factors that are considered necessary to reach and maintain competitive advantage. The determinants, composed of the four vertices of competitive advantage, constitute a system through

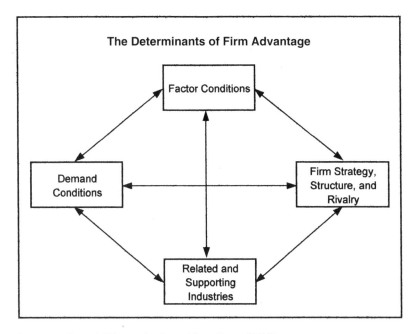

Figure 12.1 Porter's Diamond, adapted from Porter (1990)

which many characteristics influence competitive success. This system is an evolving one in which each vertex of the diamond is mutually reinforcing in that each is subject to the changes of the others and the effects of one determinant often depend on the state of the others. Although the diamond system excludes both chance and government, these also play a major role in his theory. The four determinants that make up the vertices of the diamond are shown in Figure 12.1.

In this chapter, we apply the analytic framework at the level of the firm to help understand both the general and specific enterprise characteristics of a common property CFE that have helped make El Balcón nationally and internationally competitive. Just as Porter (1990:69) asks what makes a particular nation a more or less desirable "home base" for competing in an industry, so, by extension, we will be asking if there are any special characteristics of a community as the literal "home base" that may hinder or help competitiveness.

Factor Conditions

This analytic framework includes all of the inputs necessary to create and sustain an industry and can be divided into basic and advanced factors. The basic factors are natural resources, climate, location, unskilled and semiskilled labor, and debt capital. Advanced factors include advanced communication infrastructure, highly educated personnel, and university research institutes in sophisticated disciplines. These advanced factors are the most important in gaining competitive advantage. The trade theory is based on the understanding that every industry and/or enterprise is endowed with different stocks of factors of production. An industry's endowment of factors plays a key role in the competitive advantage of firms, and the continual sophistication and renovation of the production factors within industries is important in gaining and maintaining competitive advantage.

Demand Conditions

Porter (1990) suggests that home demand's influence on competitive advantage can be categorized into three broad attributes: (1) the composition of home demand, (2) the size and pattern of growth of home demand, and (3) the mechanisms by which an industry's local preferences are transmitted to foreign markets. He defines the first element as a basis for national advantage, while the second amplifies this advantage by affecting investment behavior, timing, and motivation. The assumption underlying his claim is that a large and demanding group of local consumers pose a powerful incentive for firms to strive for excellence in production and marketing, which in turn grants a competitive advantage at the international level. We believe that in the context of globalization, the competitive advantage of a sector or firm is also strongly stimulated by international demand, and that, even if a firm lacks all the necessary elements to take complete advantage of this demand, joint ventures with other firms can complement the missing attributes to develop such an advantage.

Related and Supporting Industries

The next determinant of competitive advantage in an industry is the presence in the country of supplier industries or related industries that are internationally competitive. Here, "related industries" refers to firms and industries that have similar activities in the "value chain" in competitive markets, as well as firms and industries that provide complementary goods and services. Competitive advantage in some supplier industries bestows potential advantages of firms in many other industries, or for internationalization.

Firm Strategy, Structure, and Rivalry

This last determinant refers to the context in which firms are created, organized, and managed, as well as the nature of domestic rivalry. Competitive advantage is in part a result of a good combination of goals, strategies, and ways of organizing firms in industries. This, along with the rivalry within industries that gives rise to innovation and prospects of international success, is the foundation for maintaining competitive advantage and is closely tied to the previous determinant of related and supporting industries. In the following section, we will examine these factors as they are applied to El Balcón; at the end of the section we will summarize the competitive advantages or disadvantages of the community as entrepreneurial firm.

Analysis of El Balcón's CFE

Factor Conditions in El Balcón

In this section we consider five fundamental production factors of El Balcón: natural resources, human capital, physical capital, social capital, and road and communications infrastructure.

NATURAL RESOURCES, CLIMATE, AND LOCATION

El Balcón's 25,565 hectares is composed of 15,190 hectares with forest cover; the rest (40%) is a mixture of dry shrub and grazing areas. Only 72% of the forest area of El Balcón is under timber production; the rest is saved for conservation purposes and restoration, with 163 hectares under forest plantations. As noted, El Balcón's major forest resource was granted to it by the Mexican government in 1974. This transfer of a valuable natural asset was part of Mexico's ongoing process of agrarian reform, but the land was also given to create a new source of supply for a state-owned timber company and to pacify political unrest in the region in the late 1960s and early 1970s.

The forest cover is characterized by pine (81% of the forest cover) and mixed stands of pines, oaks, and other hardwood species.[2] Timber production is the main use of the forest area. Logging is concentrated in pine (46%), oak (21%), fir (16%), and other hardwoods and dead trees (17%) (Ejido El Balcón 2000). The harvest of additional species is limited; oaks and other hardwoods are removed for firewood and tools. Given the location of El Balcón, the existence of highly commercial non-timber forest products (such as mushrooms and medicinal plants) is very likely, but they are not currently harvested for subsistence or sale.

The forest stock is composed mostly by overmature forest with low growth rates. The last forest inventory shows that the current growth rate averages 2.54 m³/ha/year, although there are some places where the mean annual increment can be 3.2 m³/ha/year, still very low considering the growth potential in the area. The forest inventory shows that 87.4% of the forest area is composed of old growth stands with an average of 309 m³/ha.

HUMAN CAPITAL

The counties in which El Balcón is located are among the most marginalized in the country (CONAPO 2001).[3] The degree of marginalization of El Balcón, expressed in two indicators that reflect the level of human capital, is actually low relative to the municipality. However, the three villages that compose the *ejido* show that there is still a large degree of marginality by national standards. The main town, Pocitos, has a kindergarten, a basic school, and a "telesecundaria."[4] Despite these facilities, El Balcón shows a 15% illiteracy rate in the population over the age of 15, and 35% with less than a primary education. This is a low level of literacy by national standards and poses serious restrictions in successful firm management.

The forest production system of El Balcón is divided into three phases: forest maintenance, logging, and industrialization, with each phase demanding different levels of labor specialization. Forest maintenance is still dependent on outside forest technicians, with *ejido* members only participating in reforestation activities. However, the *ejido* has been successful in the management of logging, possibly due to the human capital inherited from the FOVIGRO period. In contrast, the industrialization phase is still far from being totally acquired by the *ejido*, since barely 20% of the workers in the mill are *ejido* members. However, the low percentage is significantly due to the fact that the sawmill is in Técpan, far from the community, but *ejido* members also occupy only a few of the technical and managerial positions in the sawmill.

FORMAL EDUCATION AND TRAINING From 1991 to 1996 the *ejido* launched a program to support secondary school studies for children of *ejido* members. However, this support was terminated after a decision that this should be the responsibility of each household. Despite the termination of the scholarship program for high school scholars, there was still some funding directed to help university students. As a result of that program some *ejido* members now work in technical and managerial positions as accountants, lawyers, and forest technicians. Only two *ejido* members who obtained a scholarship to continue a university education failed to return to the *ejido*. El Balcón does not currently have a systematic training program, but some *ejidatarios* have learned some of the more sophisticated mill operations. For example, the young operator of the highly sophisticated automated saw is from El Balcón. Training by practice among the *ejido* members is a goal in the mill administration. The current professional manager, while not from El Balcón, learned management from the previous professional manager while he was forest technical director. No other activity requires formal training. Some important logging and planting activities are still performed with traditional and inefficient methods.

HEALTH ISSUES   Since the beginning of the forest operations, resources have been directed to installing the water distribution system and to providing health benefits. Before 1997, all the expenses for direct medical care in Técpan or Acapulco were covered by the CFE, for workers and all *ejido* members. Currently, there is a small medical clinic attended by two doctors who provide medical services three weeks a month. These services are now only partially subsidized by the *ejido* (medicines and transportation costs) because medical services have been provided from the state budget since 1999. However, major medical care is still covered by the CFE.

PHYSICAL CAPITAL

Contrary to conventional wisdom in the development literature, it is not lack of physical capital but the relative abundance of it that is a major concern for El Balcón. For example, the sawmill capacity is many times superior to the harvest capabilities, operating at only about one-sixth of its potential, resulting in additional sunk costs. The overcapacity problem could be confronted by buying logs from neighboring *ejidos*, an activity which El Balcón has begun. Additional problems are that logging activities are impossible during the rainy season and the logyard is too small to store a larger amount of logs.

The sawmill is totally equipped with shops for sharpening and mill maintenance. Additionally, the sawmill is used for storing the logging trucks and other equipment for road construction and maintenance. The plant also has a chip mill, as well as two front-end loaders, seven winches, and six tractors. The main shop for repairing trucks is located within the sawmill facilities. Clearly, the current logging and industrialization equipment of El Balcón surpasses that required by timber harvest levels. And, even though the plant has safety equipment, most of it is not used. Workers in the mill are not used to wearing hardhats, gloves, or other protection equipment.[5] The processing infrastructure includes four drying ovens. These ovens use sawdust and other waste material from the sawmill to operate, which introduces significant environmental efficiencies and a reduction in costs. In addition, these ovens are equipped with pollution-reducing chimneys, and the dry kiln schedules are totally automatic. Most of the lumber is dried, and occasionally the ovens are used to dry lumber from other mills. This activity represented between 6 and 7% of the gross income in the mill during 1999 and 2000. The drying ovens and the sawmill represent an investment of US$2.3 million; the loan from Westwood that financed their purchase has been largely repaid.

In 1997 a fire burned down the sawmill. Fortunately, this loss was covered by insurance, which, with commercial credit, was used to rebuild a more modern plant with a higher capacity and greater efficiency. The new sawmill has one main saw and two parallel saws for small boards. A major bottleneck is the fact that the logyard is small compared to the sawing capacity. If the sawmill is working three shifts, the yard can just store logs for a maximum of 6 days. However, given the low log volumes, the sawmill works only one shift a day with only one line out of the two sawing lines. In addition, sawmill activities occur during the dry season, from the middle of November to the middle of May. The rest of the year the sawmill is closed.

SOCIAL CAPITAL

To the traditional factor endowments we would like to add the concept of "social capital," which is particularly pertinent in the case of a community enterprise. Social capital may be thought of "those forces that increase the potential for economic development in a society by creating and sustaining social relations and patterns of social organization" (Turner 2000). These forces may include norms, family structure, and informal and formal organizations. The basic concept is that there are certain social relations that may increase economic competitiveness in the marketplace as well as collective action in the public interest (Fox 2000). El Balcón clearly started out with a very low social capital endowment. The community does not have the communal institutions of many indigenous communities or a history as a self-governing *ejido* stretching back decades. It was formed out of violently quarrelling families with extremely low levels of trust who began learning how to govern themselves under *ejido* structures and practices only in the late 1960s. This makes the relatively rapid accumulation of social capital particularly noteworthy. Sources of social capital accumulation can be traced to the participation of several communities in the Técpan region in a national small farmer federation, the Central Independiente de Obreros Agrícolas y Campesinos (CIOAC). In the 1970s, local CIOAC leaders negotiated social peace between the neighboring communities, although the final agrarian solution did not occur until 1986 with the land exchange previously mentioned. Nonetheless, the social peace established in the late 1970s led directly to the beginning of commercial logging in 1980. The *ejido* president at the time was a "visionary leader who saw community organizing and regional peace as necessary precursors to the establishment of a community forestry enterprise"[6] (Wexler 1995:54).

As they struggled to form their CFE in 1986 they journeyed to San Juan Nuevo Parangaricutiro in Michoacán, already established as a national model in community forestry. One of the most important lessons they took away from the visit was the need to create new organizational structures that would separate the management of the timber business from the politics of the *ejido*. In 1989, as a part of the dramatic decision to turn forest enterprise management over to an outsider, El Balcón finally created its own Council of Principals, modeled after San Juan Nuevo's Communal Council. The Council of Principals functioned as a community oversight committee over the professional manager, approving general investment and policy guidelines, but leaving day-to-day management to him. It represents a further accumulation of social capital, both as an organizational innovation and as a new space to build accountability, mechanisms for forest monitoring, and experience in conflict resolution. Finally, El Balcón's participation in the second-level organization, the Unión de Ejidos Forestales "Hermenegildo Galeana" (UEFHG; see below) represents another source of social capital.

ROADS AND COMMUNICATIONS

One of the greatest challenges for the firm is the distance and difficulty of road access between the forest and the sawmill. The road is in service only during the dry season. During the rainy season the communication between the *ejido* and the mill is cut off. In this season the *ejido* members can reach larger towns only by the road through Ajuchitlán del Progreso, located in the opposite direction from the sawmill. The main road is maintained by the road committee, a group composed of members of different *ejidos* that use the road. Financing for road maintenance comes from a quota for each cubic meter of log transported along the road. The *ejido* machinery is rented to the road committee to perform the rehabilitation activities. Radio communication is available in the mill, three basic camps in the *ejido*, the logging camp, and the three towns.

Demand Conditions in El Balcón

Since the mid-1990s (especially after the North American Free Trade Agreement (NAFTA),[7] demand for El Balcón products can be characterized as a dual system, a regimen that exports higher quality, higher value added products, while leaving those of lesser quality to the internal market. El Balcón's logs are of high quality given the relative abundance of old growth, and it is common to find large-diameter logs of species such as *Pinus michoacana* or *P. pseudostrobus*. From 1996 to 2001, El Balcón exported 40–45% of its volume, which represented 65% of total sales, with all first-class timber exported through Westwood. From late 1995 to late 2001, El Balcón exported approximately US$19 million worth of timber to Westwood.

Eighty percent of the lumber produced is sold dried; only hardwood species like oaks and some pines are not dried, although there is no reported problem in selling undried lumber. The drying system is very efficient; the losses because of bad drying kiln schedules have been minimized and variance of the dried lumber in each load is low. The percentage of premium lumber is relatively high (between 10 and 15%) by Mexican standards, basically because of the high-quality logs and the sawing strategy.

Most of the production comes from third- and fourth-grade lumber, which fetches a higher price when dried. Table 12.1 shows the evolution of prices of different species, grades, and sizes of lumber. It can be observed that real prices have been falling (except for fourth-grade classes) since the 1995 economic crisis, and they have not recovered to the levels held at the beginning of the 1990s.[8] For the highly commercial grades, prices recovered slightly during 1997–1998 (a year of high demand in the American market), but they fell again, and although the *ejido* exports a great percentage of its production, the prices do not follow the lumber price cycle in the U.S. market, but keep falling. Comparing real prices of El Balcón at a regional level, it is evident that the prices are very competitive, especially since the lumber is kiln dried. This advantage guarantees that the *ejido* keeps a very low inventory of lumber during the year and ensures sales of third- and fourth-grade class at prices slightly higher than the regional market.

Export prices usually are 8–10% above domestic prices (nominal base),

Table 12.1. El Balcón products and sale (real) prices (domestic market)

Species	Grading	Size	Mexican pesos/board feet (base year = 2000)									Average price decline (1992–2001)
			1992	1993	1994	1995	1997	1998	1999	2000	2001	
Pine	Premium and first class	3/4"	13.56	13.27	8.66	11.26	10.18	10.48	9.78	8.00	8.55	−36.95%
	Third class	3/4"	8.53	8.50	5.08	6.61	5.92	6.89	6.49	5.50	5.58	−34.58%
	Fourth class	3/4"	7.43	7.47	3.46	4.16	4.25	5.54	5.18	4.50	4.50	−39.43%
Ayacahuite pine	Premium and first class	3/4"	14.87	14.52	9.47		10.94	12.73	11.48	9.50	9.99	−32.82%
	Third class	3/4"	8.97	8.92	5.08	6.61	6.08	7.11	6.86	5.80	6.21	−30.77%
	Fourth class	3/4"	7.87	7.47	3.70	4.16	4.40	5.54	5.30	4.95	5.22	−33.67%
Fir	Premium and first class	3/4"	n.d.	n.d.	n.d.	9.24	8.35	9.43	8.86	7.50	7.43	−19.59%
	Third class	3/4"	n.d.	n.d.	n.d.	5.54	4.86	5.54	5.12	4.30	4.50	−18.77%
	Fourth class	3/4"	n.d.	7.05	3.23	3.88	3.49	3.97	3.81	3.20	3.60	−48.94%

Source: El Balcón price lists, 2002.

which has been a great support for El Balcón during this period of price depression; however, the trend of these prices follows the same path as the domestic prices and for some years does not compensate the lost due to exchange and inflation rates. Nonetheless El Balcón exports represent the base of their market since most of the profits derived from lumber sales come from exports, although this share is not equally proportional in terms of volume. Without the market relationship with Westwood Forest Products, El Balcón would have faced a different and more depressed market scenario. However, in the last two years the share of sales in the domestic market has increased a lot, especially in the third and fourth classes, whose prices have recovered substantially.

Related and Supporting Industries in El Balcón

As already mentioned, the presence in the country of supplier and related industries that are internationally competitive, like Westwood Forest Products, is important for the development of competitive advantages. In our opinion, not only private industries like Westwood but also other institutions have been instrumental in the successful economic performance of El Balcón, namely (1) regional or national farmer organizations, (2) government, and (3) other sources of financing.

MEMBERSHIP IN FARMER ASSOCIATIONS

In the period when El Balcón began establishing its CFE, it also began organizing a negotiating front for prices with other communities. In 1986, this loose coalition became the Unión de Ejidos Forestales "Hermenegildo Galeana" (UEFHG), with seven founding members (Wexler 1995). The relationship has varied, depending on the level of interest of the El Balcón–elected *ejido* authorities. Unlike other forest *ejido* unions, where the most powerful members typically withdraw from the organization after a period because they are subsidizing the forest technical services for smaller members, El Balcón has always remained in the union, although it hired its own forest technical director early on. Through the *ejido* union, El Balcón has been able to get access to regional development projects by government agencies such as the Secretariat of Social Development (Secretaría de Desarrollo Social; SEDESOL) and the Secretariat of the Environment and Natural Resources (Secretaría de Medio Ambiente y Recursos Naturales; SEMARNAT), which prefer to work with second-level organizations rather than individual *ejidos*.

WESTWOOD AS A SOURCE OF TECHNICAL AND FINANCIAL ASSISTANCE

Westwood invested considerable time and effort in building the relationship with El Balcón and providing technical assistance and financing. Its representative spent one week a month at the Guerrero site for a couple of years. Westwood is currently importing both sawnwood and moldings to the United States from El Balcón, shipping to their warehouse in El Paso, Texas. Westwood has also been crucial in financing both capital assets and operating costs over the last several years. Westwood loaned El Balcón US$200,000 to put in dry kilns in addition to helping to arrange for a 6% interest loan from the manufacturer. In 1999 and 2000, Westwood loaned El Balcón US$400,000 to $500,000 in start-up operating capital, all of which was repaid within months. In 2001, only $100,000 was loaned because by then El Balcón had sufficient operating capital (Chris Cooper, personal communication, 2002).

GOVERNMENT SUPPORT PROGRAMS

El Balcón has been very successful in getting financing from government forestry programs such as the Program for the Development of Forest Plantations (Programa para Desarollo de Plantaciones; PRODEPLAN) and the Forest Development Program (Programa de Desarrollo Forestal; PRODEFOR). From PRODEPLAN they obtained support for building the forest nursery and for engaging in reforestation activities. The *ejido* is about to stop asking for this support given that the amount is lower than the costs involved in the paperwork and funding requirements. They have obtained some financing from PRODEFOR for precommercial thinning, forest fire equipment, and development of the forest management plan. Some members of the community receive benefits from other programs, such as PROGRESA and PROCAMPO.

SOURCES OF FINANCING

The first assets were acquired from savings and governmental support. Recently, assets have been obtained by private financing, a very rare source of financing for most *ejidos* in Mexico. The main sources of private financing have been clients like Westwood as well as the commercial banks. El Balcón's new sawmill was financed by the insurance obtained from the loss of the first mill, plus commercial financing. Current financing is obtained from different banks and is used for operating costs, annual start-up costs, and replacement of heavy equipment.

Firm Strategy, Structure, and Rivalry in El Balcón

Appropriation of Common Property Resources

In order to understand the firm's strategies and structure, it is important to recognize the nature of the ownership and distribution of their main forestry asset, the forest itself. This is an aspect that, combined with community governance arrangements, makes CFEs in Mexico unique as firms. Many common property forests in Mexico have been informally divided up, but El Balcón's common property has remained held by the community as a whole. However, there have been major struggles over the allocation of the flow of benefits from the common property. Flows of benefits can be categorized into capital investment in the enterprise, employment in the enterprise, investments in community enterprise, and direct cash distribution (a form of profit sharing). For example, in 1987, as El Balcón was struggling to get its forest enterprise off the ground, the *ejido* bought five trucks on credit, to be paid for with forest proceeds and envisioned as an investment in the enterprise. However, the *ejido* truck drivers began assuming private possession of the vehicles. A period of severe internal conflict followed, but the *ejido* authorities were eventually able to reclaim the vehicles as community property, stopping the private appropriation of a common resource (Wexler 1985). A more dramatic example of struggle over employment in the enterprise followed. As the CFE tumbled into disorganization and debt in 1988 after the initial period of direct community management, the community made the controversial decision to turn the operation of the enterprise over to a professional manager, a dramatic dilution of community self-management. The professional manager had to consult on his investment decisions with the emerging Council of Principals (mentioned earlier), but one of his first decisions was to entirely cut off the community from the benefit flow as employees, hiring all staff from outside. However, significant benefits continued to flow into the community as profits that were channeled into community benefits and profit sharing. Beginning in 1995, the community slowly began integrating itself back into the community enterprise as employees, primarily in the logging operation, reclaiming employment as a benefit flow from the forest common stock. In recent years, the amount of investment in capital expenses in the CFE has declined and investment in social infrastructure and benefits has increased. Figure 12.2 shows the trend of shares of rents derived from the whole process directed to social investments, direct forest investments, debt, and capital investments. As can be observed, social in-

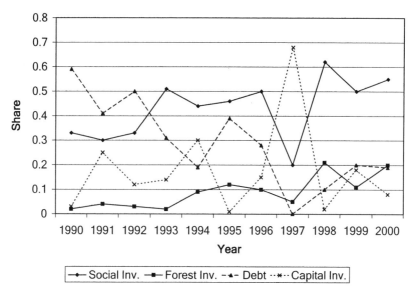

Figure 12.2 Trend of the distribution of profits in El Balcón. *Source:* El Balcón sawmill accounting books, various years.

vestments have increased in recent years, as well as the investments in the forest stock, although social investments have usually been much higher than any of the other categories.

Most of the social investments are distributed among different community requirements such as direct subsidies of material for construction (20%), church infrastructure (25%), religious activities (10–15%), *ejido* management expenses (8–10%), and medical assistance (10–15%). As noted, from 1991 to 1996, 25 high school students were supported, but now only small scholarships for university-level education are given. Direct distribution of profits was a common practice before 1993. Thereafter, no direct profit shares have been distributed among *ejidatarios*, although some direct financial support for housing and special medical care has been distributed. Direct payments in the form of pensions are given to widows and elderly *ejido* members.

Community Enterprise and Forest Management Plan

When the professional manager was hired in 1989, El Balcón created its own Council of Principals, modeled after San Juan Nuevo Parangaricutiro's Communal Council (Bray and Merino-Pérez 2003). The Council of Principals functions as a community oversight committee over the professional manager, approving general investment and policy guidelines, but leaving to him the day-to-day management. This is also a unique feature of a CFE, although it could be said that this council operates in a similar way to a board of directors in a private-sector firm.

The Council of Principals reports to the *ejido*'s General Assembly and is said to represent each family in the community. It is made up of young people, seniors, men, and women; current numbers are reported to be between 26 and 32. The council itself does not make decisions. Rather, it discusses and analyzes enterprise issues and then makes recommendations for new rules or policies to the General Assembly. However, members report that the council's recommendations are invariably accepted by the General Assembly. Since El Balcón has almost no families lacking agrarian rights, community cohesion is aided by the fact that nearly everyone participates in the larger decisions on local resource use.

Labor Profile and Employment

A distinctive mark of the El Balcón CFE is the balance achieved between labor hired from within and outside the community. The entire CFE employs 140–145 people, but only 26 of these are employed for the entire year. For most other employees, the enterprise generates about eight months of work a year. As noted earlier, almost all sawmill employees are from Técpan, although some of the more skilled technical positions are filled by *ejidatarios*. In forest extraction and transportation, about 80% of the employees are from El Balcón, with 70% of all *ejidatarios* now working in the enterprise. November–July is the period of maximum work in the forest. All workers receive benefits, social security, retirement payments, and a Christmas bonus. In addition, the *ejido* administrative positions of *comisariado* (commissioner), secretary, and treasurer are all paid positions. The Oversight Council is also paid, although at a lower rate.

The major roles in the forest production system at El Balcón are partially or totally held by the *ejido* members. A forest technician who is in charge of following the forest management plan coordinates logging. The forest technical director, an outside professional, is responsible not only for overseeing the activities related to silviculture and forest management but also for doing the required paperwork, monitoring the marking of trees selected for logging in the management plan, and defining strategies for scheduling harvest.

The current manager of the logging operations (*jefe de monte*) and his assistants are *ejido* members with long experience in all these activities. They are responsible for the planning and operation of logging and yarding equipment, road construction and maintenance, and the scheduling of trucks and cutting areas. This part of the production system is totally managed by the *ejido*. However, the operation of this activity has much space for improvement. For instance, road and skidding trails construction is not planned to minimize skidding or yarding costs. Most of the trail and secondary roads are not built to minimize sediment production or to protect water flows or important habitats.

Forest Management Plan

El Balcón started logging the forest in 1987 on a 15-year management plan that authorized the harvest of 400,000 cubic meters over the entire period. However, because of the managerial problems in the early years, the annual cuts were far below the authorized volume. Thus, the forest managers made the decision to log at much higher volumes in recent years in order to achieve the full 400,000 cubic meter volume over the period. However, a new 10-year management plan (2001–2010) calls for a significant reduction, down to an annual cut of around 20,000 cubic meters, of which only 55% is pine. Figure 12.3 shows the harvest flows since 1987 and the expected flows derived from the new forest management plan.

Until recently, El Balcón forest management followed the Mexican Method of Forest Management (Método Mexicano de Ordenación de Montes; MMOM), but with the new management plan, it adopted the System of Conservation and Silvicultural Development (Sistema de Conservación y Desarrollo Silvícola; SICODESI), a variant of the Silvicultural Development Method (Método de Desarrollo Silvicultura; MDS). SICODESI is a software program that was developed under the Mexico-Finland Agreement in the early 1990s. The program estimates harvest schedules by using predictive whole stand models, taking into account ecological protection as well as socioeconomic and legal variables. It includes a suite of silvicultural treatments, including liberation and pre-clearing cuts (*preaclareos*), regeneration cuts, small clear cuts (*aclareos*), and selection cuts. The harvest schedules are simulated among different alternatives for a given stand. The simulation follows an ideal condition defined by a silvicultural sequence that would begin with a liberation cut, followed by regeneration cuts, clearing cuts, and selection cuts. Hence if the forest considered under the simulation is an old growth forest, the program provides good estimates for harvest schedules. However, if the

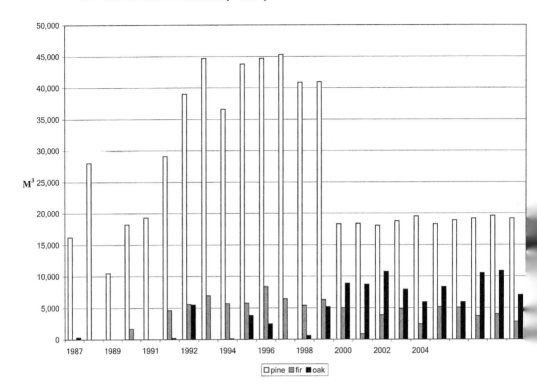

Figure 12.3 El Balcón timber harvest by species, 1987–2000; projected harvest, 2001–2010.

forest is a "surplus forest,"[9] the harvest schedules are limited in the amount of harvest estimated, since harvest is constrained to the maximum yield, which is very low in an old growth surplus forest. This result can be confirmed in the new plan, where the cutting strategy involves a slow removal of larger trees between 60 and 70 years in an effort to maintain the present structure of the forest.

Some 500 hectares of formerly cultivated lands are also being converted to forest plantations of native species. They are planted in fenced areas with seeds of pine species obtained from their own forest. It is expected that the plantations will generate an additional harvest flow estimated at 250 m^3/ha with a rotation age ranging between 40 and 50 years.

The forest brigade, composed of 20 persons, chops up the volume that is left in the forest to reduce the risk of forest fire and hasten decomposition. The brigade has also cut 45 kilometers of firebreaks and carries out forest enrichment activities. Since 1993, the *ejido* has maintained a nursery in the forest that has a annual production capacity of 100,000 seedlings and is composed mainly of *Pinus pseudostrobus*, *P. ayacahuite*, *P. chiapensis*, and *P. patula*. Maintenance of production requires additional investments since the forest cover at El Balcón is over-mature and overcrowded in some areas. This means that activities such as liberation cuts to favor natural regeneration and thinning (perhaps noncommercial) are necessary.

El Balcón places 4,058 hectares of the forested area under complete protection. These include permanent and seasonal watercourses (20- and 10-m strips respectively, called for by Mexican forest law), fringes along roads, forested areas around the population centers, and a forest area with low production potential held as a wildlife reserve. The forested land on the El Balcón *ejido* contains specimens of *P. chiapensis*, a species protected under Mexican law. The *ejido* gives special protection to this species, marking all individually as they are found to prevent their being logged, and is seeking to expand its presence in the forest through reforestation. Other conservation measures include leaving trees with nests in them, or large dead trees suitable for nesting, closing logging roads that are not needed in the short term, leaving piles of branches as wildlife refuges, and segregating important habitat areas from logging areas.

A few years ago, the *ejido* prohibited hunting of any kind, an important measure for mammalian biodiversity conservation. The forest brigades who patrol for fires, illegal logging, and hunting enforce this regulation. It was also reported that members of the community are too busy with paid employment in the *ejido* to hunt.

Cost Structure and Cost-Saving Strategies

At a glance, the forest production system at El Balcón seems efficient. However, the distribution and evolution of the cost structure shows some problems. For instance, until 1992, the proportion of costs was quite regular. After the acquisition of the logging and transportation equipment, logging and transportation costs were reduced from 60% of the total cost to 36% (still very high since current logging and extraction costs are close to US$31.6/m^3).[10] Sawing cost share has remained relatively constant even with the introduction of the new sawmill in 1997. In spite of the improved technology of the new mill and the efficiency in how the activities are performed, the sawing ratio is not higher than 61% and did not improve after the installation of the new sawmill.[11] This might be due to the fact that sawing is performed according to the demand of lumber size instead of

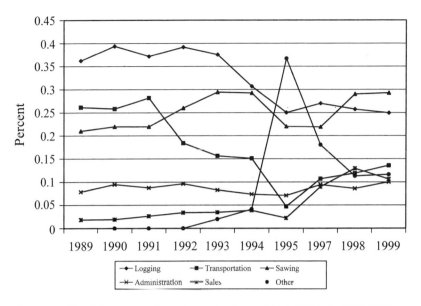

Figure 12.4 Trends in percent of cost by production activity in El Balcón, 1989–2000.

optimizing the maximum amount of lumber that could be obtained from the sawing, which can be a good strategy if the market provides a premium high enough to hide the inefficiencies and losses generated.

As Figure 12.4 shows, the share of administrative and marketing costs has been increasing in the past five years. Most of the administrative costs are due to the increasing necessity of buying timber outside the *ejido*, yielding higher administration costs because of negotiation and other transaction costs. Other sources of administrative costs are the transaction costs derived from the increasing use of government funds and the need to fulfill additional requirements such as the new forest management plan and to meet certification requirements.[12] On the other hand, marketing's higher cost share is mainly due to the loss of profits because of clients who did not pay for product delivered (a serious problem after the 1995 crisis).

On average, labor cost accounts for only 17% of the total cost. Some activities have additional incentives to promote efficiency. Sawing, recycling lumber, or bucking have bonuses according to the efficiency achieved measured in additional first-class lumber or logs. Other activities, especially those performed in the field, have incentives in the form of subsidies for meals or additional holidays.

Profits

Gross profits derived from the three stages of the production system (without accounting for depreciation, debt, and taxes) are about US$1 million yearly (20–30% of gross sales). These relatively high profits must be considered as the accumulated profits from all the stages. If average debt payments as well as average annual depreciation costs derived from the original capital investment (US$2.3 million) are considered, those profits would be severely reduced. Of the three stages, industrialization seems to be very efficient but with high sunk costs, which weigh heavily on profits when depreciation is considered. On the other hand, logging seems to be the most inefficient stage, since, as discussed earlier, average logging costs surpass Mexican and international standards. This means that high nominal profits come mostly from logging. This stage has been the one with the lowest investment level and mostly subsidized by the government. These high nominal profits can be maintained only as long as harvest levels continue to be high, which as we will review in the next section, is not the case.

The strategy of buying roundwood from other *ejidos*, discussed further below, could decrease profits dramatically, since the *ejido* will then have to face the inefficiencies of the other stages of production. Sustainability of profits depends largely on the availability of high harvest levels with extremely low production costs. This suggests that if additional investments in the forest to increase productivity are not made soon (e.g., additional forest plantations, thinning, and upgrading the road standards), profitability will not be sustainable.

Current Production Problems and Future Strategies

We mentioned earlier the drastic reduction in timber harvests called for in the new forest management plan, from around 40,000 to just over 20,000 cubic meters. This reduction could dramatically reduce the efficiency (and sustainability) of the mill and the economy of the *ejido*. However, El Balcón is pursuing an innovative firm strategy in response to this reduction by recruiting other *ejidos* as partners to supply logs for the mill. Thus, El Balcón is prepared to subsidize in other *ejidos* the development of forest management plans, and road construction and maintenance, as well as logging and bureaucratic paperwork, all areas in which they have acquired extensive experience. They believe that this is the strategy that will ensure

Table 12.2. SWOT analysis, El Balcón

	Internal	External
(+)	Strengths	Opportunities
	• Abundance of old growth	• Sawmill overcapacity
	• High levels of social capital	• Governmental funds available
	• Accumulated knowledge in community forestry	• Potential market for certified products
	• Vertically integrated enterprise	
(−)	Weaknesses	Threats
	• Current forest management plan underestimates the harvest potential	• Cheap lumber continues to be imported from other countries (Chile, USA, Canada)
	• Low levels of human capital	

the sustainability of the mill, given its high sunk costs and overcapacity. Before discussing this strategy further, we will present a brief analysis of the environment in which these strategic decisions are being made.

BRIEF SWOT ANALYSIS

In this section, we analyze *ejido* enterprises' strengths, weaknesses, opportunities, and threats, a so-called SWOT analysis (Bryson 1995). This allows an exploration of the range of possible responses to reduction of harvest flows and other problems that pose a challenge for the El Balcón CFE. Table 12.2 summarizes the SWOT analysis.

We suggest that two general strategies are called for to address the issues presented in Table 12.2: (1) improving the forest management plan and (2) reengineering the production, investment, and distribution process.

IMPROVING THE FOREST MANAGEMENT PLAN

According to the current forest management program, total average volume in the *ejido*'s forest area reaches $206.4 \text{ m}^3/\text{ha}$ (the current timber stock reaches $2,122,314 \text{ m}^3$) with a rotation age ranging between 60 and 80 years and concentrations of stock in old age classes. This forest can be generally classified as an old growth and surplus forest. As mentioned earlier, the SICODESI system estimates low harvest schedules for this type of low-growth forest. In addition to the new strategy of buying additional logs from neighboring communities, there remains a possibility of increasing harvest flows. Just by considering the current average yields, the estimated stock in sustained yield[13] might be about 921,340 m^3. Such a stock is very low compared with the current timber stock (more than 2 million m^3); hence it is possible to liquidate some surplus volume, whose amount could reach up to 1.5 million m^3 along the conversion period (60–80 years). Considering the rate of growth of the old growth forest as well as the rate of change of prices, the annual liquidation rate should not be higher than 1.1%, which yields an additional volume for liquidation of nearly 17,000 m^3 a year for more than a rotation period. Such a volume could ameliorate the huge scarcity of logs for the mill. Thus, El Balcón's current management plan could be regarded as overly conservative.

REENGINEERING THE PRODUCTION, INVESTMENT, AND DISTRIBUTION PROCESS

The first social benefits accrued from the enterprise were widows' pensions, much needed after years of violent conflicts. The pensions currently support some 20 widows with about US$150 a month. The forestry business also provides 15 retirement pensions at about US$200 a month each. There is complete medical coverage for both *ejidatarios* and non-*ejidatarios* residing in the community. In 1986–1989, the *ejido* implemented direct profit sharing (*reparto*), but this included the distribution of a loan for working capital and was one of the causes of the financial collapse that led to the decision to hire a professional manager and *repartos* were mostly discontinued. There have only been four *repartos* in the last 15 years; thus almost all profits are reinvested either in the business or in collective community development projects.

The enterprise manager estimates that from 1989 to 1998, the *ejido* invested about 60% of profits in the business and 40% in community infrastructure and social services. In the most recent period, 1998–2001, about 90% has been invested in the community, because the business has not required any further investments. It is estimated that some US$41 million has been spent on roads alone. Other social investments include potable water, solar energy, and housing. As of 2001, the *ejido* had constructed 32 houses, but is now experimenting with a lower cost home that requires participation of the homeowner. The *ejido* has also invested in productive projects such as pig rearing and organic agriculture.

Investment in the forest has been increasing in recent years not only from investment of *ejido* profits but also because the *ejido* has been very successful in obtaining subsidies from government programs such as PRONARE and PRODEFOR. In real terms, investment in direct forest activities accounts for an average of 1.26 million pesos a year (year base = 2000), with an average annual increment of almost 50% a year.

Finally, El Balcón has invested in the human capital of their children, as has already been noted. Currently, they have produced around nine college graduates and three forest technicians, most of whom have returned to the community. The fellowship amounts exceed many of the salaries, and there has been some discussion that with the reduction in logging, this is one of the benefits that would have to be looked at more closely.

Conclusions

This analysis has helped to delineate some of the determinants of El Balcón's relative success in national and international markets and also some of the areas of weakness, which could undermine the prospects for continued success. El Balcón has an excellent forest stock but one characterized by an over-mature forest with low growth rates. It has made significant investments in human capital in both health and education, although there are still very notable deficits in this area that may take another generation to overcome and will require continued investment. The *ejido* has excellent physical capital but is currently burdened with a serious underutilization of the sawmill. It has demonstrated an impressive capacity to build new social capital. The demand conditions for El Balcón are good, with strong sales in national markets and a growing presence in international markets through a successful relationship with a U.S. timber company. The *ejido* has made astute use of other sources of support such as the *ejido* union and government subsidies. El Balcón has effectively developed community institutions for governing the CFE, which can be likened to a board of directors in a private enterprise. The *ejido* demonstrates that common property resources administered by a community enterprise are not necessarily a hindrance in the marketplace, and may be a source of particular strength in delivering greater social equity while also ensuring enterprise survival. The concept of the "community as entrepreneurial firm" is not an oxymoron (Antinori 2000). However, current patterns of reinvestment may be shortchanging the forest in favor of social investments. The forest management plan may be underestimating the volume of timber that can be extracted while still maintaining crucial ecosystem functions. The new firm strategy of financing the development of CFEs in other communities that will then become suppliers to El Balcón is an effective way to address the underutilization of the sawmill but will also involve increased costs that must be carefully monitored.

The case study of El Balcón suggests that a natural asset of substantial value, good community organization, the particular history associated with the professional manager, and the market link with Westwood Forest Products have positioned this community to successfully compete in national and international markets. However, the previous successful record could be jeopardized if the strategic actions suggested here are not taken into consideration.

Notes

1. This case study is based on a number of field visits to El Balcón between March 2001 and May 2002. Information is drawn from documentary research, personal observations, and interviews with Jesús García, manager of the El Balcón enterprise; Chris Cooper, of Westwood Forest Products; Bernadino Ramírez, former president of the Oversight Council, Unión de Ejidos Forestales Hermenegildo Galeana (UEFHG); Alejandro Albarrán, UEFHG forest technical director); Mario Cedillo, forest technical director, Ejido El Balcón; Leónidas Chávez, president of the UEFHG Administrative Council; Fidel López, *ejidatario* of Ejido Bajos de Balsemar; Jorge Villa, forest technician and *ejidatario* of Ejido El Balcón; and Jesús López, *comisariado ejidal* of El Balcón. We are sincerely grateful for the research assistance of Josefina Braña, Mariana Mazón, Melina Villagómez, and Martino Aguilar. Some material for this article has been adapted from Bray and Merino 2003.

2. The main commercial species are *Pinus herrerae, P. teocote, P. pseudostrobus, P. oocarpa, P. michoacana, P. ayacahuite*, and *Abies religiosa*.

3. It is situated in the 14th percentile of the municipalities with the highest degree of marginalization in Mexico.

4. *Telesecundaria* is a broadcasted junior high school system.

5. Most of the accidents occur in logging, not in the mill. On average, every year there is one fatality or serious injury.

6. This president was assassinated in 1986, so the forest enterprise has also been able to survive the loss of a charismatic leader.

7. Commercial tariffs on wood and wood products between Canada, Mexico, and the United States were eliminated in 2003. Nevertheless, before NAFTA, tariffs between Canada and the United States for wood and wood products were virtually zero (CEMDA et al. 2002). On the other hand, Mexico held import tariffs of 15 to 20%, depending on the product (PEF 2001). After NAFTA, differences in tariffs still exist; nevertheless, they are much smaller. Mexico agreed to eliminate quantitative restrictions in favor of tariff rate quotas which allow a certain amount of a product to be introduced. If that quota is exceeded, remaining imports for the product will be imposed a certain tariff. Average tariff reduction by

Mexico on wood and wood products has been significant. By 1998, average tariffs by NAFTA members were as follows: Mexico 11.32%; Canada 3.88%; and United States 1.4%.

8. The crisis is of course an important factor in explaining such decline, but it is also important to recognize that other factors, such as the entrance of cheaper forest products from Chile, Canada, and the United States after NAFTA and other free trade agreements play a significant role.

9. A surplus forest is a forest whose harvest rate can be potentially higher than the long-term sustained yield harvest rate.

10. Average logging costs in Mexico are US$24.60/m^3; in Chile they are around US$15.60, and in Brazil they are around US$18.50 (base year = 2000).

11. The average sawing ratio with the old sawmill (1990–1997) was 59%, while the average sawing ratio with the new sawmill only improved slightly, to 61%.

12. Certification was granted in February 2003 with some constraints.

13. Stock reached when the forest is totally regulated and produces the maximum sustained yield.

References

Alatorre Frenk, G. 2000. *La construcción de una cultura gerencial democrática en las empresas forestales comunitarias.* Mexico City: Casa Juan Pablos, Procuraduría Agraria.

Antinori, C. M. 2000. Vertical integration in Mexican common property forests. PhD diss., University of California, Berkeley.

Bray, D. B., and L. Merino-Pérez. 2003. A case study of El Balcón *Ejido*, Guerrero. In *Confronting Globalization: Economic Integration and Popular Response in Mexico*, ed. T. Wise, H. Salazar, and L. Carlsen, 65–80. Bloomfield, CT: Kumarian Press.

Bryson, J. M. 1995. *Strategic Planning for Public and Nonprofit Organizations.* San Francisco: Jossey-Bass.

Bustamante, T. 1996. Los recursos forestales de Guerrero, su aprovechamiento social y la apertura comercial. El caso de Ejido El Balcón. In *La sociedad rural mexicana frente al nuevo milenio. Vol. 3: El acceso a los recursos naturales y el desarrollo sustentable*, ed. H. Mackinlay and E. Boege, 367–384. Mexico City: Plaza y Valdés.

CEMDA, CESPEDES, and Consejo Coordinador Empresarial. 2002. *Deforestación en México. Causas económicas. Incidencia del comercio internacional.* Mexico City: CEMDA.

Chapela, G. 1996. La organización de los campesinos forestales en México. In *Antropología Política: Enfoques Contemporáneos*, ed. H. Tejera Gaona, 62–78. Mexico City: Plaza and Valdés.

CONAPO. 2001. *Índices de marginación municipales 2000.* Series. *Índices sociodemográficos.* Mexico City: CONAPO.

Ejido el Balcón. 2000. *Programa de manejo para el aprovechamiento forestal maderable persistente (Tomo I).* Técpan de Galeana, Guerrero: Ejido El Balcón.

Fox, J. 2000. The World Bank and social capital: Lessons from 10 rural development projects in the Philippines and México. *Policy Sciences* 33:399–419.

Nelson R., and S. Winters. 1994. *An Evolutionary Theory of Economic Change.* Cambridge, MA: The Belknap Press of Harvard University Press.

PEF. 2001. Plan Estratégico Forestal para México 2020 (Phase I). Análisis económico de la industria forestal y mercados de productos forestales. Mimeo.

Porter, M. E. 1990. *The Competitive Advantage of Nations.* New York: The Free Press.

Turner, J. H. 2000. The formation of social capital. In *Social Capital,* ed. P. Dasgupta. Washington, DC: World Bank.

Wexler, M. B. 1995. Learning the forest again: Building organizational capacity for the management of common property resources in Guerrero, Mexico. PhD diss., Boston University.

PART V

GLOBAL COMPARISONS AND CONCLUSIONS

CHAPTER 13

The Global Significance of Mexican Community Forestry

DAN KLOOSTER AND SHRINIDHI AMBINAKUDIGE

Amid high rates of forests being lost to agriculture and being degraded from cut-and-run logging, and in the context of demands to respect the land rights of traditional forest inhabitants, the central question currently emerging in forest conservation debates is, "Who can save the forests and what are the necessary social arrangements for success?" As the following review makes clear, the emerging answer is often "community forestry," where forest inhabitants benefit from forest management and play active roles in forest conservation on forestlands which they have traditionally used or owned.

In this chapter, we first explore the conceptual justifications and the practical politics behind the worldwide interest in community forestry. Second, we provide an overview of some illustrative community forestry experiences from around the globe. Third, we propose a typology of community forestry and use it to compare and contrast the Mexican model to what is occurring elsewhere. We focus on Mexico both because it is the subject of this volume and because it may have the largest number of forest communities in the world with secure land tenure, and it certainly has the largest number of community forest enterprises (CFEs) oriented toward the commercial production of timber (Bray et al. 2003).

The Global Politics of Community Forestry

Community forestry appeared at the confluence of three interrelated transformations of theory and practice. First, there was the late-twentieth-century context of political change, including the widespread replacement of authoritarian regimes with democracies and an ascendant neoliberal approach to development policy that disparaged the state, lauded civil society, and prescribed decentralized development projects (Cernea 1985; Peet and Watts 1996:27; World Bank 1997). At the same time, proponents of alternative development approaches also called for "empowerment," stressing the importance of organized communities and grassroots action (Friedmann 1992; Hirschman 1993; Redclift 1987). Theoretical underpinnings for a growing interest in local people managing collective resources came from the literature analyzing the role of common property in sustainability (Berkes et al. 1989; Ostrom 1990).

A second stream of support for community forestry springs from the analysis of conservation and forestry projects. International pressure from conservationists long centered on creating national parks and other kinds of preservationist set-asides. However, influenced by work on the grassroots approach to rural development, a growing appreciation for local environmental knowledge, and the promise of slowing habitat destruction by recognizing indigenous land claims, some conservationists began to embrace a wider array of options. A shift toward a decentralized conservation strategy evolved, with interests in sustainable rural development issues outside of parks (Western and Wright 1994).

Meanwhile, in forest policy there were calls to address the "other energy crisis" of fuelwood depletion (FAO 1978). A first generation of fuelwood projects focused on village-level afforestation projects, but researchers came to have a greater appreciation for the multiple values of the common property natural forests. Emphasis shifted toward natural forest management (Arnold 1992; Foley et al. 1997). Forestry researchers also renewed attention to the social aspects of forestry projects (Blair and Olpadwala 1988; Rambo 1984). By the late 1980s, participation was a central instrument of social forestry, based on a better understanding of existing rural institutions (World Bank 1991).

The institutional arrangements for timber production also came under greater scrutiny. A 1990 review noted uncontrolled and destructive logging practices often associated with unsupervised logging concessions[1] (World Bank 1991). Several influential studies showed how concession approaches to forest management led to violent conflict between excluded peoples and forest guards, undermining forest management objectives, squandering rural development possibilities, and violating human rights (Guha 1989; Peluso 1992). An alternative critique suggested that resident communities might be the best agents to take into account the environmental forest values that concessionaires and government forest departments failed to consider. Advocates also expected an important enforcement benefit because communities would craft legitimate local governance and resource management rules, and this would diffuse conflict inherent in state-bureaucratic forestry (Ascher 1995; Johnson and Cabarle 1993).

Social movements of traditional forest inhabitants and their supporters comprise a third stream of support for community forestry. Indigenous peoples have long struggled for greater autonomy and self-determination (Wilmer 1993), but in the 1980s and 1990s indigenous struggles became increasingly visible and influential. On one hand, conservationists seeking pristine forests for conservation set-asides found those forests inhabited by indigenous and peasant communities with long-term histories of occupancy. Some began to argue that indigenous peoples' local technical knowledge made them wise stewards of these forests (Clay 1988). Indigenous peoples successfully used this perception to win environmentalist allies in their ongoing struggles to secure land claims. They were able to leverage the growing body of environmental legislation and international regulations being developed in places like the World Bank to halt large infrastructure and forest colonization schemes (Anderson and Huber 1988; Friedmann and Rangan 1993; Hecht and Cockburn 1990).

In the context of the global politics of empowerment and evolving development theory in conservation and forestry, indigenous social movements have had measurable effects on forest tenure. Most forests in developing countries are still national, but governments already reserve 8% of forests for communities, and they have recognized de jure community ownership over 14% of forests. More than half of those transfers were formalized during the last 15 years (see Figure 13.1). As Figure 13.1 shows, Mexico is second only to Papua New Guinea for the proportion of its forests in the hands of communities, followed by China and Australia as a distant fourth, with most of these Mexican land transfers occurring prior to 1977 (Challenger 1998; Klooster 2003).

A Global Overview of Community Forestry Experience

Significant developments in community forestry have accompanied this discernible shift in forest tenure, with examples found all over the globe (Arnold 1998; International Network of Forests and Communities 2002; Messerschmidt 1993; Stone and D'Andrea 2001). In order to illustrate the diversity of community forestry, we review some of these experiences by region.

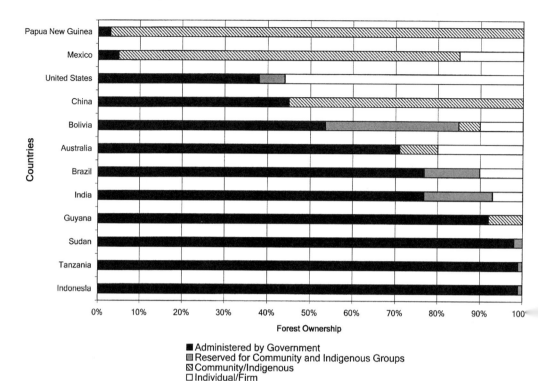

Figure 13.1 Tenure in some forest-rich countries. *Source:* White and Martin 2002.

Asia and Pacific

In most Asian countries, forests comprise an economically strategic tim-ber resource managed by powerful centralized forest bureaucracies that benefit directly from timber revenues. Government forestry agencies fear losing control of these lands and hesitate to recognize local management rights or to transfer authority to local groups. At the same time, tens of thousands of forest communities reside in Asian forests and practice diverse, productive, and ecologically viable agroforestry systems. These communities struggle to demonstrate their customary possession and use of forestlands, sometimes winning collaborative agreements with the state to reestablish access controls over forestlands—especially lands recover-ing from logging (Poffenberger 1994). Asia has a staggering range of varia-tions in community forest management patterns, and here we will only look at three countries that illustrate this diversity.

INDONESIA

In Indonesia, the government administers 99% of forests, with just 1% reserved for indigenous and community groups. Indonesia's biologically diverse tropical forests provide a plethora of non-timber forest products (NTFPs) including several that enter national and international markets. Forests also supply a large-scale logging and timber processing industry that generates employment for hundreds of thousands of Indonesians, creates trade worth several billion dollars, provides a substantial proportion of Indonesia's foreign exchange, and brings enormous wealth to a few hundred tycoons (Colchester 2003). The fourth most populous nation in the world, Indonesia is home to over 300 different ethnic groups, scattered throughout the archipelago. Many are directly dependent on forest resources for subsistence and small-scale commercial products. Most of the indigenous people live in or near forests (Liedtke 1999).

The Indonesian state has been the sole owner of the forestlands since the Dutch colonial period, and by the mid-1980s the forest department, with more than 40,000 employees, controlled 78% of the nation's total land area and about 90% of the territory in the outer islands. Until recently, de facto community-based rights to forest resources were recognized only in areas where the state was unwilling or unable to exploit, reserve, or lease those resources itself (Colchester 2003; Lynch and Talbott 1995). Nearly a third of the country's land area is under concession to a small number of companies. Big logging firms, whose billionaire owners enjoy personal government connections, impose their will on customary forests, using bulldozers and armed guards to clear local people's productive rattan and fruit gardens, remove valuable trees, and often convert the forest to oil palm or pulp plantations (Fried 2000; Liedtke 1999; McCarthy 2000).

In 1997 and 1998, devastating forest fires and the fall of Suharto focused attention on forestry corruption and freed the voices of nongovernmental organizations (NGOs), student groups, and academics to call for a "new forestry paradigm" that would provide for the people's welfare (McCarthy 2000). By 1999, about 92,000 hectares were leased out to communities, mainly to encourage them to rehabilitate degraded forests (Colchester 2003). A subsequent program leased out 66,000 hectares on lands without existing concessions under so-called social forestry schemes. These leases are contingent on the submission of detailed management plans approved by the district-level forestry service, and require the community to register itself as a cooperative. Relevant for the Mexico comparison, a small number of communities have begun to produce timber commercially with support from German foreign assistance (Nolan 2001).

A seesaw of decentralization and recentralization between district authorities and the central Ministry of Forestry have complicated the issue of community-based natural resource management over the past few years (see McCarthy 2002; Thorburn 2002). Although the reformed forestry laws recognize greater community land rights than before,[2] they continue to subordinate community land and forest access rights to the Ministry of Forestry, to the disappointment of community forestry advocates (Colchester 2003; Lindayati 2002). So far, reforms have failed to confront the property rights issue underlying the social inequity and the ecological destruction associated with the state forestry regime as it operated under Suharto (McCarthy 2000).

INDIA

In India, states directly administer 77% of the nation's forests, with 16% reserved for communities and only 7% as private property. Nearly all of India's forests are tropical; Himalayan subtropical forests comprise less than 5% of India's forests (FAO 2002). Since colonial times, Indian governments have regulated forests in favor of the logging industry and the generation of state revenues, granting only limited privileges to local people despite their reliance on forests for building materials, medicines, agricultural inputs, ceremonial goods, grazing, and food. This often led to the alienation of local people and the demise of traditional systems of management (Gadgil and Guha 1992; Guha 1989).

During the 1970s and 1980s, in the face of growing fuelwood needs, social forestry programs attempted to involve local people in tree-planting projects. These projects devolved some rights and benefits to a local government unit, the *gram panchayat*, but this unit did not adequately represent forest users (Sarin 1996). Nevertheless, social forestry projects established a process in which forest departments negotiated with local communities and considered their needs (Poffenberger and McGean 1996).

The forest policy of 1988 and a national Joint Forest Management (JFM) resolution in 1990 marked a paradigm shift in the Indian forest policy. JFM promotes developing partnerships between local communities and the state forest department based on mutual trust and jointly defined roles and responsibilities with regard to forest protection and restoration (Lele and Shrinidhi 1998). As of March 2002, some 140,953 square kilometers of forestlands were being managed under the JFM program through 63,618 Village Forest Committees (VFCs) in 26 of India's 29 states (Government of India 2003).

JFM policy calls for VFCs comprised of villagers, forest department staff, NGOs, and local government officials. These new institutions, however, often reproduce local social relationships that inhibit broad-based participation (Martin and Lemon 2001). In response, states have made provisions for VFCs to include the representation of Scheduled Castes and Tribes,[3] the landless, and other marginalized sectors of the village—especially women (Agarwal 2001; Hildyard et al. 1998; Martin 1999). Involvement of NGOs, meanwhile, is supposed to counteract a tendency for officers of the forest departments to favor village elites and personal contacts (Hildyard et al. 1998; Lohmann 1998). Despite these efforts, landed elites often benefit disproportionately from JFM practices (Lele and Shrinidhi 1998; Saxena et al. 1997).

VFCs, with the help of NGOs, prepare a micro plan for managing the forestland. The forest department usually picks the forest area, however, and often prepares the plan itself. The prime function of the VFC is forest protection, and members have the power to apprehend smugglers, seize the wood illegally cut, and hand the offenders over to the forest department. The forest department has the power to resolve disputes, dissolve committees that are not working well, cancel membership, nominate members of NGOs, and impose a local forest official to a leadership position in the village forest committee (Lele 1998; Poffenberger and Singh 1996).

JFM does not transfer ownership of forests to the village committees; the states still own 94% of Indian forests (White and Martin 2002). Instead, beneficiaries are given recognition of usufruct rights to minor forest products. They are also entitled to get a portion of the proceeds from the sale of forest products, including trees. The proportion of the harvest that goes to the community varies from 100% in a few states to only 20% in others (Sundar 2000; Tata Energy Resource Institute 2002). Furthermore, JFM applies mainly to degraded forests, which minimizes potential local benefits while increasing pressure on the good forests. Recent JFM guidelines direct the states to include up to 100 hectares of good forests per village, but only stipulate a 20% share of harvest proceeds to villagers (Government of India 2000). Indian JFM, in summary, represents an evolving attempt to induce social capital around forest management in a representative village body.[4]

There are also self-initiated forest protection groups in different parts of India. The Van Panchayats in the hills of Uttaranchal and forest protection groups in Karnataka, for example, have been managing village forests since about 1930. In Bihar and Orissa, some village forest protection committees have been functioning for over 100 years (Bhattacharya and Mitra 2002; Gadgil and Guha 1992; Human and Pattanaik 2000; Ravindranath et al. 2000). These self-initiated groups have been recognized by the forest departments in some cases, ignored in others, and actively undermined by JFM policies in others (Shackleton et al. 2002:4).

PAPUA NEW GUINEA

Papua New Guinea (PNG) contains one of the largest remaining expanses of rainforest in the world. These ancient forests are also important to the country's 5 million people from over 700 indigenous cultures that depend on forests to meet subsistence and development needs. Forests are also a source of timber revenues and foreign exchange. The PNG constitution recognizes communal ownership of land and forests, and 97% of PNG's land is customarily owned by traditional groups, clans, lineages, or families (Liedtke 1998; Turia 2001). While the PNG constitution and forestry legislation appear to provide a strong legal basis for landholders' rights, the constitution also allocates responsibility for natural resource management to the state, which retains substantial power to override land rights (Lynch and Talbott 1995).

Forestry in PNG corresponds to two basic models: a concession model with community compensation, and a community forestry model in which communities are more directly involved in forest management and use. In the first and dominant model, foreign companies are the primary actors in logging. A 1989 report described a situation of widespread "malfeasance" among concessions, however, with corruption, extensive violations of landholder's rights, and environmental devastation (Liedtke 1998; PNG Eco-forestry Forum 2002; Turia 2001). In the concession model, customary landholders sell long-term cutting rights to the Papua New Guinea Forest Authority, which then grants timber permits to logging companies. Currently, 6.1 million hectares are under permit to 42 logging companies, with a moratorium on new concessions since 2000 (Hunt 2002).

Concession agreements foreclose alternative forest uses during 35–year rotation periods, and so "community participation in forestry is essentially limited to the requirement that landowners be incorporated before they transfer control of their forest resources to the State" (Hunt 2002:iii). The economic returns from such concessions are very low. The royalties accruing to the landholders are only 6% to at most 12% of the market value of logs (Hunt 2002). Concession forestry disrupts the fabric and integrity of forest communities' social life, increases local reliance on the cash economy, and exacerbates social tensions. For example, negotiations for concessions are often restricted to a few key individuals who undermine the general structure of customary land tenure in return for cash (Liedtke 1998).

In "eco-forestry," the second general forestry model, community groups engage in forest management projects involving small-scale timber harvesting and processing enterprises using portable sawmills. Several Papua New Guinea NGOs and foreign donors provide funds to train these landowner groups in saw operation and forestry management, ensure that a viable forest management plan is in place, and in some cases defray the costs of forest certification. Currently, there are approximately 200,000 hectares of forest and more than 100 such projects (Liedtke 1998; PNG Eco-forestry Forum 2002). The model confronts problems because of the isolation of tribal groups from each other and from the government. Furthermore, the state maintains a strong bias toward large-scale operations and is reluctant to devote resources toward a community-oriented forest management strategy (Liedtke 1998).

Africa

In Africa, several of the most famous community-based natural resource management projects focus on game management in and around national parks, such as CAMPFIRE in Zimbabwe. These are part of a much wider, donor-driven movement toward decentralization of natural resource management in the region (Ribot 2002; Stone and D'Andrea 2001; Western et al. 1994).

Interest in trees and natural vegetation management has been particularly acute in the Sahel,[5] where colonial, national, and international actors have long perceived spreading deserts and fuelwood shortages. In precolonial times, traditional institutions and rulers governed the use of common resources, but colonial authorities declared forests to be national domain and instituted centralized and repressive forest management bureaucracies that continued under national governments. Forest services routinely blamed rural people for degrading forest ecosystems, while ineffective and underpaid forest guards harassed local people and undermined their role in conserving forests (Kerkhof 2000). Political changes in the 1990s have brought about greatly increased recognition of forest management by rural Sahelians, including a kind of joint management approach to firewood and charcoal production. Usually started with external support, these rural firewood market projects typically center on a management plan that partitions the forest into harvesting zones. The national forest service retains most of the power over planning and management, but they sometimes generate substantial income flows to the villages involved (Foley et al. 1997; Kerkhof 2000).

Cameroon provides an example of community forestry in West Africa's humid tropics. Following pressure from the World Bank, a radical overhaul of the forest legislation in 1994 opened the way for community involvement in the management of forests for commercial timber production despite opposition from an established commercial logging sector with tight links to domestic political power structures (Brown and Schreckenberg 2001; Ekoko 2000). The first community forest in Cameroon was established in 2000. As of November 2001, 138 applications had resulted in 64 recognized forests and 39 management plans (Brown et al. 2002). The process is so complex, however, that no community has been able to establish a community forest without extensive external assistance (Ribot 2002).

In Southern Africa,[6] decentralization for natural resource management empowers district-level organizations, traditional authorities, and village-level organizations. In Malawi and Tanzania, forest departments support community-elected Village Forest Committees that can make and enforce conservation rules on state forests, regulate local use of forest products, plan fire patrols, and collect revenues (Campbell and Shackleton 2001).

SENEGAL

The case of Senegal is one of the more carefully analyzed experiences of national participatory forest policies in the region, and it reveals the ease with which forest departments and merchants can subvert the expected rural benefits of joint management arrangements (see Ribot 1995, 2000). In the early 1990s, Senegal adopted a new participatory approach to forestry aimed at redressing a history of excluding villages from the lucrative trade in firewood and charcoal, the major sources of cooking fuel in the cities. However, the law grants very limited control and responsibility for forest use to rural populations. Senegalese forests are a "national domain." As Forest Service personnel see it, "the forests serve the whole nation. They are needed to provide fuel to the cities. The forests don't belong to villagers." The Forest Service oversees harvest rotations, issues licenses to sell wood products, and grants cutting permits (Ribot 2000:142).

Despite appearances, the new participatory law actually grants villages very little power to manage their forests because the Forest Service maintains tight control over woodcutting and marketing products. The law does provide village governments with the rights to cut trees in the forests of their locality, but only if they work with the Forest Service to draw up a forest management plan that includes provisions for reforestation. Villages do not have the legal right to protect their forests from woodcutting, however, because the Forest Service can grant cutting permits to wood merchants without the village's consent. In that case, villagers' only power to exclude outside woodcutters is to withhold their access to the water, food, and lodging available only in villages.

Despite this veto power, the social arrangements of Senegalese forestry severely limit local control and benefit. Villagers have no effective mechanism to participate in the practice or financial benefit from forestry. The participatory forest code grants specific powers to Rural Communities, which are preexisting territorial-administrative units grouping 10 to 15 villages. Villagers elect members to the Rural Council, but they must choose from lists imposed by the national parties. Since independent candidates have no ability to get elected, this institution is neither accountable to nor representative of villagers. At the village level, there are also village chiefs, but these are lifelong, usually hereditary, positions. Chiefs are not necessarily accountable to the villagers either, and often grant access to woodcutters without village consent (Ribot 2000).

Initial cautious optimism that villagers would get greater access to the labor opportunities of woodcutting (Ribot 1995) were not met in practice, because the law did not change the politics of resource control. Forest Service permits and licensing reinforce the power of wood merchants, who control wood markets. Village control over forest access does not give them leverage over the economic benefits that come from producing and selling forest products (Ribot 2000). Even so, the very limited recognition of village power under the law, coupled with an awakening of village interest in forest opportunities and awareness of local power to exclude woodcutters, resulted in some gains. About half the villages in one important forest area were able to exclude woodcutters. More importantly, some villages mobilized around forest issues and began to formulate a vision of participatory forest management with a much greater role for villagers. Nevertheless, better forest management—and improved rural development options—will require additional reforms in the politics of villager representation, leadership accountability, and in the social relationships of forest product marketing (Ribot 2000).

The Americas

UNITED STATES

In the United States, 56% of forests are private, 38% are government lands, and 6% are reserved for indigenous groups. U.S. forests are used for recreation, timber, and a variety of non-timber forest products, with large-scale industrial forest interests frequently dominant. Logging is increasingly embroiled in paralyzing conflict about its impacts on endangered species and other ecosystem attributes, unsustainable timber yields, and industrial restructuring. Forest-dependent communities suffer in this context. Poor, remote, politically weak, resource-dependent but marginalized from the decisions that affect the forests that surround them, these communities share many characteristics of marginalized forest communities around the world, frequently including a strong sense of place and knowledge of the resource that could form the basis of better stewardship (Baker and Kusel 2003; see also Peluso et al. 1994). Community-based collaborative partnerships are increasingly important in U.S. natural resource management as groups of people work together to define and address common resource management issues that affect specific places but cut across government regulatory agencies (Cheng et al. 2003; Colvin 2002; Weber 2000).

In the U.S. national forests, management plans have long required public consultation, but this has not given effective voice to local communities. In the midst of environmental conflict, however, ecosystem management became the official forest management philosophy in the early 1990s, and the Forest Service paid greater attention to the "human dimension" of the ecosystem in forest planning and management. Since then, national forests have entered into isolated collaborative efforts with local communities. Many of these include various kinds of small grants to community action groups. Most of these increased local economic diversification and added value to timber products. Some also include a focus on forest planning. Some forests also experiment with stewardship contracts that bundle restoration activities with timber extraction (Danks 2000; Evans 1999; Frentz et al. 2000; Kusel and Adler 2001). Stressing the idea that healthy forest ecosystems depend on healthy human communities, regional movements of community forest activists are advocating to create wider legal and political openings for increased local stewardship over forests, especially in U.S. national forests, despite opposition from some environmental organizations[7] (Baker and Kusel 2003).

PERU

One of the earliest and most touted community forestry efforts in Latin America was the Yánesha Forestry Cooperative (COFYAL) in the Peruvian Amazon, founded in 1986. It folded in 1993. Although the cooperative had been successful in designing a timber harvesting system that combined scientific and traditional knowledge, it was enormously overfunded by the U.S. Agency for International Development (USAID) and the Peruvian government, was conceived on a larger scale than the Yánesha could appropriately manage, and was not able to overcome marketing problems (Benavides and Pariona 1995; Hartshorn 1989; Lázaro et al. 1993; Stone and D'Andrea 2001). Currently, community forestry is considered counter to the market-oriented economic model of the Peruvian government (Brownie 1998b).

BOLIVIA

Tropical forests cover 53 million hectares of Bolivia—half of the country. Prior to the mid-1990s, commercial loggers exploited these forests under short-term contracts, removing as many valuable trees as they could in as short a time as possible. Forest residents, including many indigenous peoples, used these forests for agriculture, subsistence gathering, and small-scale commercial gathering. They received little benefit from logging, however, which created widespread social conflict over land rights. Meanwhile, in the absence of clear property rights, deforestation helped establish de facto land possession (Contreras-Hermosilla and Vargas Rios 2002).

The 1990s saw a series of legal reforms that included decentralization to *municipios*,[8] a constitutional amendment that gave indigenous communities the exclusive right to their lands and territories, and a new forest law. Together, these reforms favor communal forest management by indigenous peoples (Contreras-Hermosilla and Vargas Rios 2002; Ferroukhi 2003). The Bolivian lowlands are home to some 250,000 indigenous people in 36 ethnic groups who have made claims to 23 million hectares of land. Indigenous peoples can now operate commercial logging operations in legally recognized territories as long as they comply with forest management plans. By mid-2000, the forest department had approved management plans in a quarter of a million hectares of indigenous territories, with 90 more proposals under review (Contreras-Hermosilla and Vargas Rios 2002).

The case of the Chiquitano Lomerio illustrates the situation.[9] Some

5,000 Indians there evicted logging companies and established the right to manage 53,000 hectares of forests on their traditional territory, but have not so far been able to establish title. Operating with the support of Bolivian NGOs tightly linked to international donors,[10] the Chiquitanos log their own forests, operate tree nurseries, and conduct reforestation with valuable species; they earned provisional certification for good forest management under Forest Stewardship Council criteria (McDaniel 2002; Stone and D'Andrea 2001). Some of the resulting economic relationships, however, are culturally problematic. There were disputes over wages between worker/owners and their NGO/managers, for example. Certification also lapsed, apparently because indigenous leaders suspected certification mainly benefited the desire of the NGO intermediaries to gain international recognition and publicity. More recently, the Chiquitanos had to close a sawmill that employed community members (Contreras-Hermosilla and Vargas Rios 2002). These issues underscore the complicated interdependence between the Chiquitanos, the NGO intermediaries, and the donor community[11] (McDaniel 2002). Despite these rather substantial ambiguities, the project generates local economic benefits, implements low-impact logging, and protects the Chiquitano's forest from outside logging companies.

Like the Chiquitano, other indigenous communities also face a shortage of financial resources, a lack of organizational strength, and a lack of technical and managerial knowledge. The management of forest resources for commercial purposes is not part of the indigenous community culture, and they are still in the process of gaining knowledge and experience in managing forests for commercial timber and interacting with markets, NGOs, and the government. The greatest barrier to community forestry in Bolivia, however, comes from continuing land conflicts and a very slow rate of land titling. So far, the government only recognizes indigenous ownership to 2.9 million hectares out of the 23 million hectares claimed. Following the forestry and agrarian reforms of the mid-1990s, the amount of land involved in conflicts declined from some 2.7 million to 628,000 hectares, but loggers continue to operate concessions in indigenous lands. Some indigenous groups face overlapping claims to more than a third of their territories, and illegal logging often occurs in indigenous lands, which decreases prices for logs and boards (Contreras-Hermosilla and Vargas Rios 2002). However, the number of communities that are reportedly managing their forests for the commercial production of timber has gone from 9 to 32 in the last few years (Nolan 2001).

GUATEMALA

In Guatemala, forests are state property, but the state lacks the resources to protect the forest from illegal logging or clearing for agriculture.[12] Community concessions in Guatemala represent an attempt to confront the dynamic of deforestation in the Petén, a significant tract of lowland rainforest that borders Mexico and Belize. Deforestation and forest degradation in the region result from destructive logging, the overharvesting of non-timber forest products by conventional concessionaires and by illegal loggers and extractivists, and the expansion of small-scale agricultural activities, especially by newcomers to the area (Schwartz 1995). Much of the area has been declared a biosphere reserve, but because of the impossibility of relocating the tens of thousands of people who live in the forest, Guatemalan conservation strategy relies on concessions to communities as a way to incorporate local people's needs while meeting conservation goals (Gretzinger 1998).

The Guatemalan community concessions do not concede ownership rights, but they do include the rights to harvest timber, take non-timber forest products, and even to continue farming on previously cleared agricultural lands surrounding long-established villages of chicle tappers and xate palm harvesters. The Community Forestry Organization in the Petén was a crucial actor in this process. It mobilized the communities to participate in the long and complex process of mapping their territories, taking into account traditional uses and assessing the size needed for viable timber and NTFP production. They also mobilized legal support to design proposals and helped coordinate technical assistance coming into the region through NGOs[13] (Deborah Barry, personal communication, 2003; Gretzinger 1998).

Communities must pay fees on their concession, post a performance bond, and pay taxes on the timber and non-timber forest products produced. They must also prepare management plans, species inventories, and environmental impact assessments, usually with the assistance of an NGO. The Guatemalan parks department can cancel concessions for failure to pay the fees and bonds or failure to comply with forest management plans, but unless there are repeated violations, renewal of the 25–year concessions is automatic (Gretzinger 1998).

Community economic benefits can be substantial. One early concession granted 7,039 hectares, three-fourths of it forest, to a village of 33 families. After one year of hiring a contractor, they used their own oxen to extract the timber. This increased local employment and generated enough earnings to buy a small sawmill. Other concessions include a 70,000-hectare area for non-timber forest products and several smaller timber concessions in the 13,000- to 18,000-hectare range (Gretzinger 1998). In the past few years, 11 Guatemalan communities managing 280,000 hectares of communal forests have received certification for sustainable forest management according to Forest Stewardship Council criteria (FSC 2003). Nevertheless, capital shortages limit the ability of communities to add value through local processing, despite studies that indicate this is necessary for logging to pay for conservation in the area (Gretzinger 1998). Villagers seek concessions not only for the economic benefits of timber production, however, but also for legal assurance that they will not be thrown off their land (Sundberg 1998).

MEXICO

As described in greater detail in the other chapters of this book, as much as 80% of Mexico's remaining tropical and temperate forests are in the hands of communities with collective land grants. Historically, these forests have been used for industrial timber production through concession models or locked away in regions of logging bans. Following a series of land reforms ending in 1976, however, and an uneven history of significant support from state agencies, NGOs, and the donor community, Mexican community forestry now appears to have reached a scale and level of maturity unmatched anywhere else in the world. Currently, an estimated 533 to 740 or more of these communities operate community businesses producing timber on their own lands (Bray and Merino-Pérez 2002; Bray et al. 2003; Klooster 2003).

Although they must operate within a framework of restrictive environmental laws, Mexican villages have responsibility for hiring a professional forester to create a management plan, and they are in charge of implementing that plan. Most communities enter into short-term contracts with logging companies, but a large number possess their own logging equipment and many even have their own sawmills. Furthermore, during a history of commercial forestry and external support, villagers developed skills in forest management, so not only do they have the power to manage their forests, they also have the ability to do so (Bray and Merino-Pérez 2002; Bray et al. 2003; Klooster 2003).

A Framework for Comparison of Community Forestry

To compare and contrast the Mexican experience with other examples of community forestry, it is useful to consider four aspects of the relationship between communities, forests, and the state. These include the formal tenure arrangements, the degree of management power, the ability of communities to benefit from forest values, and the governance arrangements within communities and between communities and other actors.

Land Tenure

Formal tenure categories range from full community ownership through several gradations of state ownership. State-owned forests can be granted in full concessions to communities, as in Guatemala; managed jointly between forest departments and local groups, as in India; reserved for state management; or granted as concessions to private businesses. In Papua New Guinea, private companies may gain access to community-owned forests through state-brokered concessions. Many communities still occupy and manage forests without official state sanction, but they risk suddenly finding their forests gazetted for logging or exclusionary preservation. Mexico stands out in this category because of its legally recognized community ownership over the majority of forests. Only Papua New Guinea has a greater proportion of its forests under community ownership (see Figure 13.1).

Forest Economic Benefits

Community forestry also varies greatly in the power communities have to benefit from forests. So far, compensation for environmental services—the holy grail of forest conservation—remains beyond the reach of forest communities (Fearnside 1997; Klooster and Masera 2000). In many countries, timber is one of the few forest values recognized by existing markets, but it is rare for states to recognize community rights to commercial use of this resource. A small number of community-based logging operations do exist in Papua New Guinea, Bolivia, and Guatemala, but only in Mexico is it relatively commonplace for communities to get the full economic benefits of logging, and even milling in many cases. The current JFM model in India, in contrast, only gives communities a share of timber revenues, but even this is an improvement on the Indian "social forestry" practices of the 1980s, which only allowed communities to benefit from the sale of minor forest products. Industrial concession models provide even fewer inputs to rural livelihoods, but instead violently exclude local people from using or protecting their forests, as in most parts of Indonesia.

Management Power

A third way to compare community forestry is through the forest management powers that communities enjoy. At the highest level of management power, communities not only plan the management of their forests, but are also in charge of implementing that management plan. Below that, communities may have the power to participate in the process of planning forest management in significant ways, while the actual implementation of that plan remains the responsibility of a forest department, as is the case in a small number of collaborative forest management agreements in the United States. A lesser degree of management power is the responsibility for implementing some aspects of management plans that were derived elsewhere, such as planting trees, weeding, and coppicing at determined intervals. Finally, the management power of communities may be restricted to merely protecting a forest from encroachment by neighbors or village cattle.

In a surprising number of the experiences reviewed here, communities ostensibly have powers to plan and implement forest management. Nevertheless, such powers are always mitigated by the oversight of forest departments, and their exercise requires a suite of skills usually provided through the technical assistance of NGOs. Thus, the actual role of communities in the exercise of forest management is often minimal, with forest departments retaining tight control over community forestry (Brown et al. 2002; Shackleton et al. 2002). In Mexico, however, communities clearly exercise substantial forest management powers.

Local Social Organization

The ways in which communities are organized to manage their forests varies drastically between countries, but also within them. Some local social organizations may have long histories of occupying a territory and resolving collective action problems to defend it and manage it. Often, they are ethnically indigenous, and many of the most successful experiences with community forestry involve these kinds of communities.

Frequently, community forestry models involve the empowerment of existing local authorities and government units. There are also forms of community forestry in which donor-driven forestry departments effectively imposed a model on local communities, creating new forest management institutions. In either case, the newly empowered local authorities do not always represent the interests of local people, and they may not be accountable to them (Ribot 1999, 2002). Community forestry, therefore, requires attention to the larger context of political democratization and representation. Following unsuccessful experiences working with existing *panchayat* village governments, for example, community forestry policies in India and Nepal now explicitly attempt to engineer local forest management institutions to better represent the caste, gender, and tribal makeup of forest users.

The local social arrangements of community forestry also include vitally important interactions with government promoters, NGOs, and industry. These actors may have interests quite different from the communities they work with, but their services are vital for building the skills communities need to deal with governments, forest management, and markets. As examples from Peru, Guatemala, Senegal, and Bolivia suggest, international agencies, governments, and NGOs can overwhelm local autonomy instead of empowering it. On the other hand, the Mexican experience with community forestry illustrates that local managerial capacity can improve with experience and outside support.

Two Key Axes: Management Power and Benefit

Much of the variation between these four aspects of participatory forestry can be captured by two components: the degree of benefit and the amount of local management control. Community forestry models fall roughly into spaces defined by these two criteria (see Figure 13.2). For example, with a few minor exceptions, most Indonesian communities are excluded from any benefit or participation in logging or logging concessions, even though they have customary claims to the land. In Mexico, in contrast, communities have clear tenure to their lands and forests. Subject to national laws, they control logging operations and keep all the proceeds from logging. Eco-forestry in Papua New Guinea and community forestry in Bolivian indigenous communities also have these characteristics, but compared to Mexico, community forestry is still incipient in those countries; communities there do not have nearly as much experience as Mexican communities do, and they lack access to capital, appropriate extension, and land titling.

Environmental services					
Commercial timber and sometimes milling				Guatemala community concessions	Mexico. Papua New Guinea eco-forestry. Bolivian indigenous communites.
Share of commercial timber, payments from concessionaires, or labor opportunities		Papua New Guinea concessions	Collaborative agreements in U.S. national forests	India JFM	
Minor forest products		Social forestry in Java and 1980s. India Senegalese participatory forestry			
Local exclusion	Most of Indonesia				
	No powers over forests	Power to forests	Participate in planning	Plan and implement on state-owned lands	Plan and implement on community-owned lands

LOCAL BENEFIT (vertical label, left axis)

MANAGEMENT POWER

Figure 13.2 A comparison of community forestry according to characteristics of local management power and local benefit.

Conclusions

Mexico is in the vanguard of the community forest movement worldwide on several fronts. First, community ownership of forests is much more extensive than almost anywhere else in the world, and this tenure is relatively secure. Second, tenure over forested land includes the right to harvest and sell trees. Elsewhere, especially in Asia, powerful forest departments often treat forests as a source of state revenue, but in Mexico the state role over forests is merely regulatory. Third, Mexican communities exercise a significant and central role in forest management. Even though the state strictly regulates forest management, Mexican communities do have central responsibilities in overseeing the creation and implementation of forest management plans. Fourth, Mexican community forestry relies on local governance structures that are often reasonably representative, democratic, and much more autonomous than the norm.[14] Enshrined in the Mexican constitution and codified in agrarian law, the *ejido* and *comunidad agraria* provide recognizable patterns for community governance that are now part of Mexican rural culture and with which the state is accustomed to interact. As the other chapters in this volume make clear, these conditions have resulted in 533 to 740 or more community-managed forest enterprises that compete successfully in national and international markets for timber and value-added wood products and that demonstrate the potential for rural communities to progressively improve their internal organizations and forest management capabilities.

Clear ownership, strong management powers, and significant potential forest benefits transformed opportunities for Mexican communities, led to gains in forest conservation and rural development, and generated powerful motivations for communities to engage in the construction of grassroots social capital. The Mexican experience suggests that community forestry elsewhere is missing opportunities to increase formal community ownership over forests, to enhance community powers to manage forests, and to amplify the benefits communities can get from their forests by allowing them to keep all proceeds from commercial harvests of timber and other valuable forest products. Eventually, as markets for environmental services develop, these benefits should also reach community forest owners.

Mexico also underscores the substantial opportunities that exist for the state, together with NGOs and other actors, to promote local management capacity through appropriate extension strategies. Government extension agents and social activists cultivated community forest organizations during a nascent phase in the 1970s and 1980s, and this experience may hold globally significant lessons for the relationships between internal community organization and external agents, including government promoters, NGOs, and social activists. Furthermore, Mexico is now engaged in an explicit effort to extend and improve community forestry through the provision of training in forest and business management, including innovative community-to-community extension techniques through programs like the Program for Forest Conservation and Management (Programa para la Conservación y Manejo Forestal; PROCYMAF) (Klooster 2003; Klooster et al. 2000). A careful evaluation of this experience should also reveal useful lessons for extension efforts elsewhere.

The Mexican model of community forestry represents a fairly successful answer to the question, "who can save the forests, and what are the necessary social arrangements for their success?" As the other chapters in this volume show, when Mexican villagers have control over forest management and forest benefits, they often achieve substantial gains in conservation and rural development. The case of Mexico, therefore, confirms the expectations of community forestry proponents: greater community participation in forest benefits and greater community power over forest management result in better forest use and protection and improved livelihoods for local people.

Notes

AUTHORS' NOTE: The authors gratefully acknowledge insights from Matthew Taylor, Craig Thorburn, David Bray, Deborah Barry, and an anonymous reviewer.

1. The World Bank continues to identify the problem of governance in forestry, especially the "unscrupulous large private sector loggers operating under weak institutional or legislative controls" (World Bank 2002:3).

2. The Krui region of the island of Sumatra represents an exception to a general rule of community exclusion from forest management. Local communities there have been managing forests of damar (*Shorea javanica*) trees for generations, but they lacked any kind of security over their damar forest gardens until a 1998 decree granted community members the right to manage national forest land for both non-timber products and timber (Liedtke 1999; Michon et al. 2000).

3. The Indian government recognizes Scheduled Castes and Tribes as deserving special privileges in order to overcome a history of social exclusion and discrimination.

4. Indian JFM resembles Nepal's community forest management. Forest ownership remains with the government in both cases, and forest officials have the authority to cancel the village forest groups for failing to adhere to plans. Nepalese forest user groups, however, can fix the price and sell the forest products themselves, an authority Indian villagers lack. By 2001, in Nepal, 10,969 community forest user groups had been established covering 84,7282 ha, which accounts for 23.5% of the potential forest area (Acharya 2002).

5. Cape Verde, Mauritania, Senegal, Gambia, Mali, Burkina-Faso, Niger, and Chad are normally considered the Sahelian countries.

6. Campbell and Shackleton (2001) review 14 cases from Botswana, Namibia, South Africa, Zimbabwe, Tanzania, Malawi, Zambia, and Lesotho covering rangeland, wildlife, and forest management.

7. For an explanation of environmentalist opposition to an early experiment in devolution, see Blumberg and Knuffke 1998.

8. As contiguous political units covering rural and urban areas, *municipios* are more similar to U.S. counties than they are to U.S. municipalities.

9. Other examples include Monte Verde, Yuracares, Yuquis, Territorio Indígena Siriono, Guarayos, and some Guaraní communities (Becker and Leon 1998; Contreras-Hermosilla and Vargas Rios 2002).

10. These include an NGO with Dutch government support that assisted their struggle against outside loggers, and it also includes the Bolivian Sustainable Forestry Project (Proyecto de Manejo Forestal Sostenible Boliviano; BOLFOR), which benefits from funding and support from USAID and a consortium of other international development and conservation organizations, including Conservation International and the Wildlife Conservation Society (see McDaniel 2002).

11. Community forestry is usually portrayed as a win-win-win strategy between the interests of indigenous peoples, conservationists, and development promoters. McDaniel 2002, however, identifies significant tension between indigenous interests and the professionalized NGOs that channel resources to the community. Indigenous leaders did not pursue the forestry project in search of profits, but rather as part of a strategy to protect their lands from logging companies and eventually get title to it. The NGOs, however, are effectively accountable to their funders, not the Chiquitanos. "While forest certification, sustainable forest management, and community-based development may be worthy and important goals, they are being forced upon communities by a 'development community' that takes its orders from above" (McDaniel 2002:383).

12. In one exceptional case, however, the 35,000 indigenous inhabitants living in 63 villages have been able to maintain collective control over a 25,000-ha temperate forest in Totonicapán, the highlands of Guatemala. Relying on local institutions such as village meetings and locally selected forest guards, these villages have been able to protect their forests from unsanctioned logging (Brownie 1998a; Elias Gramajo 1997; Veblen 1978).

13. NGOs play a central role in providing technical support in the concession application and management process. Local promoters of one concession project describe a bitter learning process in which one NGO representative was thought to be misappropriating funds and interfering with the work of other NGOs for his own benefit (Chayax Huex et al. 1998; see also Sundberg 1998). The Community Forestry Organization in the Petén, however, recently negotiated an agreement with criteria for how the NGOs should work with the communities, and community-NGO relationships have improved (Deborah Barry, personal communication, 2003).

14. In some regions of Mexico, such as Oaxaca, indigenous communities have particularly deep stores of social capital and traditions of village democracy to draw on, but village elites are sometimes able to capture forest benefits anyway (Klooster 2000). *Ejidos* in parts of northern Mexico, on the other hand, can be quite exclusionary, with a very small number of rights-holding men operating almost like a corporate board, making forest management decisions that do not necessarily represent and are not necessarily accountable to thousands of excluded residents. Despite these failings, in general the Mexican rural institutions are reasonably representative and accountable, especially when compared to the situation elsewhere.

References

Acharya, K. P. 2002. Twenty-four years of community forestry in Nepal. *International Forestry Review* 4(2):149–156.

Agarwal, B. 2001. Participatory exclusions: Community forestry and gender: An analysis for South Asia and a conceptual framework. *World Development* 29(10): 1623–1648.

Anderson, R. S., and W. Huber. 1988. *The Hour of the Fox: Tropical Forests, the World Bank, and Indigenous People in Central India.* Seattle: University of Washington Press.

Arnold, J. E. M. 1992. *Community Forestry: Ten Years in Review.* Rome: FAO.

———. 1998. *Managing Forests as Common Property: FAO Forestry.* Paper no. 136. Rome: FAO.

Ascher, W. 1995. *Communities and Sustainable Forestry in Developing Countries.* San Francisco: Institute for Contemporary Studies.

Baker, M., and J. Kusel. 2003. *Community Forestry in the United States: Learning from the Past, Crafting the Future.* Washington DC: Island Press.

Becker, C. D., and R. Leon. 1998. Indigenous Forest Management in the Bolivian Amazon: Lessons from the Yuracare People. Paper presented at Crossing Boundaries, the Seventh Annual Conference of the International Association for the Study of Common Property, 10–14 June, Vancouver, Canada.

Benavides, M., and M. Pariona. 1995. *The Yanesha forestry cooperative and community-based management in the central Peruvian forest. Case studies of community-based forestry enterprises in the Americas.* Paper presented at the Symposium Forestry in the Americas: Community-Based Management and Sustainability, 3–4 February, University of Wisconsin, Madison.

Berkes, F., D. Feeny, B. J. McCay, and J. M. Acheson. 1989. The benefit of the commons. *Nature* 340:91–93.

Bhattacharya, P., and B. Mitra. 2002. Lessons from self-initiated forest protection systems in India: An eye-opener to CPR studies. Ninth Biennial Conference of IASCP, 17–21 June, Victoria Falls, Zimbabwe.

Blair, H. W., and P. D. Olpadwala. 1988. *Forestry in Development Planning: Lessons from the Rural Experience.* Boulder, CO: Westview Press.

Blumberg, L., and D. Knuffke. 1998. Count us out: Why the Wilderness Society opposed the Quincy Library Group legislation. *Chronicle of Community* 2(2): 41–44.

Bray, D. B., and L. Merino-Pérez. 2002. The rise of community forestry in Mexico: History, concepts, and lessons learned from 25 years of community timber production (version 2). Report to the Ford Foundation.

Bray, D. B., L. Merino-Pérez, P. C. Negreros-Castillo, G. Segura-Warnholtz, J. M. Torres-Rojo, and H. F. M. Vester. 2003. Mexico's community-managed forests: A global model for sustainable landscapes? *Conservation Biology* 17(3):672–677.

Brown, D., Y. Malla, K. Schreckenberg, and O. Springate-Baginski. 2002. From supervising "subjects" to supporting "citizens": Recent developments in community forestry in Asia and Africa. *Natural Resource Perspectives* 75:1–4.

Brown, D., and K. Schreckenberg. 2001. Community forestry: Facing up to the challenge in Cameroon. Rural Development Forestry Network. Forestry paper no. 25a.

Brownie, K. 1998a. The context for community forestry in Bolivia: Forest legislation and policy. International Network of Forests and Communities. URL http://www.forestsandcommunities.org/Country_Profiles/bolivia.html. Accessed 5 May 2003.

———. 1998b. Peru country profile. International Network of Forests and Communities. URL http://www.forestsandcommunities.org/Country_Profiles/Peru.html. Accessed 30 October 2002.

Campbell, B., and S. Shackleton. 2001. The organizational structures for community-based natural resources management in southern Africa. *African Studies Quarterly: The Online Journal for African Studies* 5(3). URL http://web.africa.ufl.edu/asq/v5/v5i3a6.htm. Accessed 8 May 2003.

Cernea, M. M. 1985. *Putting People First: Sociological Variables in Rural Development.* New York: Oxford University Press and the World Bank.

Challenger, A. 1998. *Utilización y conservación de los ecosistemas terrestres de México, pasado, presente y futuro.* Mexico City: Comisión para el Conocimiento y Uso de la Biodiversidad; Instituto de Biología, UNAM; Agrupación Sierra Madre, S.C.

Chayax Huex, R., F. Tzul Colli, C. Gomez Caal, and S. P. Gretzinger. 1998. The Bio-Itzá reserve: History of an indigenous effort to conserve the Itzá Maya community of San José, El Petén, Guatemala. In *Timber, Tourists and Temples,* ed. R. B. Primack, D. Bray, H. A. Galettim, and I. Ponciano, 317–326. Washington, DC: Island Press.

Cheng, A. S., L. E. Kruker, and S. E. Daniels. 2003. "Place" as an integrating concept in natural resource politics: Propositions for a social science research agenda. *Society and Natural Resources* 16:87–104.

Clay, J. W. 1988. *Indigenous Peoples and Tropical Forests.* Cambridge: Cultural Survival.

Colchester, M. 2003. Bridging the gap: Challenges to community forestry networking in Indonesia, CIFOR, as part of its study of "Learning from International Community Forestry Networks." URL http://www.cifor.cgiar.org/publications/pdf_files/CF/Indonesia_CF.pdf. Accessed 29 April 2003.

Colvin, R. 2002. Community-based environment protection, citizen participation, and the Albany Pine Bush Preserve. *Society and Natural Resources* 15:447–454.

Contreras-Hermosilla, A., and M. T. Vargas Rios. 2002. *Social, Environmental and Economic Dimensions of Forest Policy Reforms in Bolivia.* Washington, DC, and Bogor, Indonesia: Forest Trends and CIFOR. URL http://www.forest-trends.org/whoweare/pdf/BoliviaEnglish.pdf. Accessed 29 April 2003.

Danks, C. 2000. Community forestry initiatives for the creation of sustainable rural livelihoods: A case from North America. *Unasylva* 51(202):1–14. URL http://www.fao.org/docrep/x7273e/x7273e09.htm. Accessed 20 April 2003.

Ekoko, F. 2000. Balancing politics, economics and conservation: The case of the Cameroon forestry law reform. *Development and Change* 31(1):131–154.

Elias Gramajo, S. 1997. *Autogestión comunitaria de recursos naturales: Estudio de caso en Totonicapán.* Guatemala City, Guatemala: FLACSO.

Evans, B. 1999. United States: Forest legislation and policy. International Network of Forests and Communities. URL http://www.forestsandcommunities.org/ Country_Profiles/us.html. Accessed 30 October 2002.

FAO. 1978. *Forestry for Local Community Development*. Rome: FAO.

———. 2002. *Global Forest Resources Assessment 2000 Main Report*. Rome: FAO.

Fearnside, P. M. 1997. Environmental services as a strategy for sustainable development in rural Amazonia. *Ecological Economics* 20:53–70.

Ferroukhi, L., ed. 2003. *La gestión forestal municipal en América Latina*. Bogor, Indonesia: Center for International Forestry Research and IDRC. URL http:// www.cifor.cgiar.org/publications/pdf_files/Books/La_gestion27.pdf. Accessed 29 April 2003.

Foley, G., W. Floor, G. Madon, E. Mahamane Lawali, P. Montague, and K. Tounao. 1997. *The Niger Household Energy Project: Promoting Fuelwood Markets and Village Management of Natural Woodlands*. Washington, DC: World Bank.

Frentz, I. C., D. E. Voth, S. Burns, and C. W. Sperry. 2000. Forest service-community relationship building: recommendations. *Society and Natural Resources* 13:549–566.

Fried, S. G. 2000. Tropical forests forever? A contextual ecology of Bentian Rattan agroforestry systems. In *People, Plants and Justice*, ed. C. Zerner, 204–233. New York: Columbia University Press.

Friedmann, J. 1992. *Empowerment: The Politics of Alternative Development*. Cambridge, MA: Blackwell.

Friedmann, J., and H. Rangan, eds. 1993. *In Defense of Livelihood: Comparative Studies on Environmental Action*. West Hartford, CT: Kumarian Press.

FSC. 2003. *Forest Stewardship Council*. Forest Stewardship Council website. URL http://www.fscoax.org. Accessed 2 May 2003.

Gadgil, M., and R. Guha. 1992. *This Fissured Land: An Ecological History of India*. Oxford: Oxford University Press.

Government of India. 2000. *Guidelines for Strengthening JFM*. New Delhi, Ministry of Environment and Forests, no. 22–8/2000-JFM (FPD). URL http:// www.rupfor.org/jfm_india04d.htm. Accessed 14 May 2003.

———. 2003. *Status of JFM (as of March 1, 2002)*. New Delhi, Ministry of Environment and Forests. URL http://www.rupfor.org/jfm_india.htm. Accessed 11 May 2003.

Gretzinger, S. P. 1998. Community forest concessions: An economic alternative for the Maya Biosphere Reserve in the Petén, Guatemala. In *Timber, Tourists, and Temples*, ed. R. B. Primack, D. Bray, H. A. Galetti, and I. Ponciano, 111–124. Washington, DC: Island Press.

Guha, R. 1989. *The Unquiet Woods: Ecological Change and Peasant Resistance in the Himalaya*. Berkeley: University of California Press.

Hartshorn, G. S. 1989. Sustained yield management of natural forests: The Palcazu production forest. In *Fragile Lands of Latin America: Strategies for Sustainable Development*, ed. J. O. Browder. Boulder, CO: Westview Press.

Hecht, S. B., and A. Cockburn. 1990. *The Fate of the Forest: Developers, Destroyers, and Defenders of the Amazon*. New York: HarperCollins.

Hildyard, N., P. Hegde, P. Wolvekamp, and S. Reddy. 1998. Same platform, different train: The politics of participation. *Unasylva* 194(49):26–34.

Hirschman, A. O. 1993. *Getting Ahead Collectively: Grassroots Experiences in Latin America.* Arlington, VA: Inter-American Foundation.

Human, J., and M. Pattanaik. 2000. *Community Forest Management: A Casebook from India.* Oxford: Oxfam.

Hunt, C. 2002. *Production, Privatisation and Preservation in Papua New Guinea Forestry.* London: International Institute for Environment and Development. URL http://www.iied.org/psf/publications_def.html#cert. Accessed 30 April 2003.

International Network of Forests and Communities. 2002. *International Network of Forests and Communities.* URL:http://www.forestsandcommunities.org/. Accessed 30 October 2002.

Johnson, N., and B. Cabarle. 1993. *Surviving the Cut: Natural Forest Management in the Humid Tropics.* Washington, DC: World Resources Institute.

Kerkhof, P. 2000. *Local Forest Management in the Sahel: Towards a New Social Contract.* London: SOS Sahel International UK.

Klooster, D. 2000. Institutional choice, community, and struggle: A case study of forest co-management in Mexico. *World Development* 28(1):1–20.

———. 2003. Campesinos and Mexican forest policy during the twentieth century. *Latin American Research Review* 38(2):94–126.

Klooster, D., C. Allieri, M. Couffingal, B. Sharbono, S. E. J. Yeo, and G. Segura. 2000. Working with communities to strengthen forest management in Mexico. In *Thinking Out Loud II: Innovative Case Studies on Participatory Instruments*, ed. M. Anderson, 103–112. Washington, DC: Latin America and the Caribbean Civil Society Team of the World Bank. http://wbln0018.worldbank.org/lae/lacinfoclient.nsf/d29684951174975e85256735007fef12. Accessed 29 June 2004.

Klooster, D., and O. Masera. 2000. Community forest management in Mexico: Carbon mitigation and biodiversity conservation through rural development. *Global Environmental Change* 10(4):43–70.

Kusel, J., and E. Adler, eds. 2001. *Forest Communities, Community Forests: A Collection of Case Studies of Community Forestry.* Taylorsville, CA: Forest Community Research.

Lázaro, M., M. Pariona, and R. Simeone. 1993. A natural harvest: The Yanesha forestry cooperative in Peru combines western science and indigenous knowledge. *Cultural Survival Quarterly* 17:48–51.

Lele, S. 1998. Godsend, sleight of hand, or just muddling through: Joint forest management in India. Paper presented at Conference on Crossing Boundaries: The Seventh Common Property Conference, 10–14 June, University of British Columbia, Vancouver, Canada.

Lele, S., and A. S. Shrinidhi. 1998. Indian forest policy, forest law, and forest rights settlement: A serious mismatch. Paper presented at International Workshop on Capacity Building in Environmental Governance for Sustainable Development, 8–10 December, Indira Gandhi Institute for Development Research, Mumbai.

Liedtke, M. 1998. The context for community forestry in Papua New Guinea: Legislation, policy, tenure. Forests and Communities. URL: http://www.forestsandcommunities.org/Country_Profiles/Papua_New_Guinea.html. Accessed 5 May 2003.

————. 1999. The context for community forestry in Indonesia. Forests and Communities. URL: http://www.forestsandcommunities.org/Country_Profiles/indonesia.html. Accessed 5 May 2003.

Lindayati, R. 2002. Ideas and institutions in social forestry policy. In *Which Way Forward? People, Forests, and Policymaking in Indonesia*, ed. C. J. P. Colfer and I. A. P. Resosudarmo, 36–59. Washington, DC: Resources for the Future. URL http://www.rffpress.org/rff/ExternalFiles/chapter2.pdf. Accessed 5 May 2003.

Lohmann, L. 1998. Briefing 4—Same platform, different train: The politics of participation. URL: http://cornerhouse.icaap.org/briefings/4.html. Accessed 14 May 2003.

Lynch, O., and K. Talbott. 1995. *Balancing Acts: Community-Based Forest Management and National Law in Asia and Pacific.* Washington, DC: WRI.

Martin, A. 1999. *Imposing Local Resource Management: Government-Led Development of Community Institutions for Forest Management, South India*, Bedford, UK: De Montfort University.

Martin, A., and M. Lemon. 2001. Challenges for participatory institutions: The case of village forest committees in Karnataka, South India. *Society and Natural Resources* 14:585–597.

McCarthy, J. F. 2000. Forest Property and *Reformasi* in Indonesia. *Development and Change* 31(1):91–130.

————. 2002. Turning in circles: District governance, illegal logging, and environmental decline in Sumatra, Indonesia. *Society and Natural Resources* 15:867–886.

McDaniel, J. 2002. Confronting the structure of international development: Political agency and the Chiquitanos of Bolivia. *Human Ecology* 30(3):369–396.

Messerschmidt, D. A. 1993. *Common Forest Resource Management: Annotated Bibliography of Asia, Africa, and Latin America.* Rome: FAO.

Michon, G., H. Foresta, Kusworo, and P. Levang. 2000. The Damar agroforests of Krui, Indonesia: Justice for forest farmers. In *People, Plants and Justice: The Politics of Nature Conservation*, ed. C. Zerner. New York: Columbia University Press.

Nolan, T. M. 2001. Community-based forest management: Commercial harvesting of the rainforest of Indonesia. *The International Forestry Review* 3(3):231–235.

Ostrom, E. 1990. *Governing the Commons: The Evolution of Institutions for Collective Action.* New York: Cambridge University Press.

Peet, R., and M. Watts. 1996. Liberation ecology: Development, sustainability, and environment in an age of market triumphalism. In *Liberation Ecologies: Environment, Development, Social Movements*, ed. R. Peet and M. Watts, 1–46. New York: Routledge.

Peluso, N. L. 1992. *Rich Forests, Poor People: Resource Control and Resistance in Java.* Berkeley: University of California Press.

Peluso, N. L., C. R. Humphrey, and L. Fortmann. 1994. The rock, the beach, and the tidal pool: People and poverty in natural resource dependent areas. *Society and Natural Resources* 7(1):23–38.

PNG Eco-forestry Forum. 2002. PNG Eco-forestry Forum. URL: http://www.ecoforestry.org.pg. Accessed 30 April 2003.

Poffenberger, M. 1994. The resurgence of community forest management in eastern India. In *Natural Connections: Perspectives in Community-Based Conservation*, ed. D. Western, R. M. Wright, and S. Strum, 53–79. Washington, DC: Island Press.

Poffenberger, M., and B. McGean, eds. 1996. *Village Voices, Forest Choices: Joint Forest Management in India.* Delhi: Oxford University Press.

Poffenberger, M., and C. Singh. 1996. Communities and the state: Re-establishing the balance in Indian forest policy. In *Village Voices, Forest Choices: Joint Forest Management in India*, ed. M. Poffenberger and B. McGean, 56–85. Delhi: Oxford University Press.

Rambo, A. T. 1984. Community forestry: The social view. In *Community Forestry: Some Aspects*, 39–47. Bangkok: FAO Regional Office for Asia and the Pacific, United Nations Development Programme and E.-W. Center.

Ravindranath, N. H., K. S. Murali, and K. C. Malhothra. 2000. *Joint Forest Management and Community Forestry in India: An Ecological and Institutional Assessment.* New Delhi: Oxford University Press.

Redclift, M. 1987. *Sustainable Development: Exploring the Contradictions.* New York: Methuen.

Ribot, J. C. 1995. From exclusion to participation: Turning Senegal's forestry policy around? *World Development* 23(9):1587–1599.

———. 1999. Decentralisation, participation and accountability in Sahelian forestry: Legal instruments of political-administrative control. *Africa* 69(1):23–65.

———. 2000. Rebellion, representation, and enfranchisement in the forest villages of Makacoulibantang, Eastern Senegal. In *People, Plants and Justice: The Politics of Nature Conservation*, ed. C. Zerner, 134–158. New York: Columbia University Press.

———. 2002. *Democratic Decentralization of Natural Resources: Institutionalizing Popular Participation.* Washington, DC: WRI.

Sarin, M. 1996. From conflict to collaboration: Institutional issues in community management. In *Village Voices, Forest Choices: Joint Forest Management in India*, ed. M. Poffenberger and B. McGean, 165–209. Delhi: Oxford University Press.

Saxena, N. C., J. Sarin, R. V. Singh, and T. Shah. 1997. *Western Ghats Forestry Project: Independent Study of Implementation Experience in Kanara Circle.* London: ODA.

Schwartz, N. B. 1995. Colonization, development, and deforestation in Petén, Northern Guatemala. In *The Social Causes of Environmental Destruction in Latin America*, ed. M. Painter and W. H. Durham, 101–130. Ann Arbor: University of Michigan Press.

Shackleton, S., B. Campbell, E. Wollenberg, and D. Edmunds. 2002. Devolution and community-based natural resource management: Creating space for local people to participate and benefit? *Natural Resource Perspectives* 76:1–6. URL http://www.odi.org.uk/nrp/76.pdf. Accessed 5 May 2003.

Stone, R. D., and C. D'Andrea. 2001. *Tropical Forests and the Human Spirit.* Berkeley: University of California Press.

Sundar, N. 2000. Unpacking the "joint" in joint forest management. *Development and Change* 31:255–279.

Sundberg, J. 1998. Strategies for authenticity, space, and place in the Maya Biosphere Reserve, Petén, Guatemala. *Conference of Latin Americanist Geographers Yearbook 1998* 24:85–96.

Tata Energy Resource Institute. 2002. *National Study on Joint Forest Management.* New Delhi: Ministry of Environment and Forests, Government of India.

Thorburn, C. 2002. Regime change: Prospects for community-based resource management in post–new order Indonesia. *Society and Natural Resources* 15:617–628.

Turia, R. C. H. 2001. *Masters of a domain or property owners: An analysis of forest use in Papua New Guinea. From tradition and globalisation: Critical issues for the accommodation of CPRs in the Pacific Region — The Inaugural Pacific Regional Meeting of the International Association for the Study of Common Property.* Brisbane, Australia: Digital Library of the Commons.

Veblen, T. T. 1978. Forest preservation in the western highlands of Guatemala. *Geographical Review* 68:417–434.

Weber, E. P. 2000. A new vanguard for the environment: Grass-roots ecosystem management as a new environmental movement. *Society and Natural Resources* 13:237–259.

Western, D., and R. M. Wright. 1994. The background to community-based conservation. In *Natural Connections: Perspectives in Community-Based Conservation,* ed. D. Western, R. M. Wright, and S. C. Strum, 1–12. Washington, DC: Island Press.

Western, D., R. M. Wright, and S. C. Strum, eds. 1994. *Natural Connections: Perspectives in Community-Based Conservation.* Washington, DC: Island Press.

White, A., and A. Martin. 2002. Who owns the world's forests? Forest tenure and public forests in transition. Washington, DC: Forest Trends and Center for International Environmental Law.

Wilmer, F. 1993. *The Indigenous Voice in World Politics.* Newbury Park, CA: Sage.

World Bank. 1991. *Forestry: The World Bank's Experience.* Washington, DC: World Bank, Operations Evaluation Department.

———. 1997. *World Development Report 1997: The State in a Changing World.* New York: Oxford University Press.

———. 2002. Revising the bank's forest policy: Key questions and answers. World Bank. URL: http://lnweb18.worldbank.org/ESSD/essdext.nsf/14Doc ByUnid/0D92CD541CABDBA485256BD1006AAB62/$FILE/RevisingForest PolicyKeyQandA.pdf. Accessed 30 October 2002.

CHAPTER 14

Community Forestry in Mexico: Twenty Lessons Learned and Four Future Pathways

DAVID BARTON BRAY

As the chapters in this book have made clear, the Mexican community forest sector has made historic strides since the 1970s. Until then, almost all Mexican forest communities that produced timber were considered to be *rentistas*—communities simply "rented" their forests to outside loggers, whether contractors or concessionaires. The term *rentista* referred to (1) communities that did not participate in any way in the extraction process, commonly not even as loggers, since the outside companies would bring their own crews; and (2) communities that received only an administratively set *derecho de monte*, or stumpage fee, which was below the market value of the timber sold on the stump.

Beginning in the 1970s, large numbers of CFEs began to emerge, and the era of the concessions came to a close in the 1980s. Almost all forest communities were allowed to sell their timber and receive the full market price, not a government-set stumpage fee. In this sense, the traditional "stumpage fee" *rentista* communities no longer existed. Nonetheless, the term *rentista* is still used today to refer to communities that sell their timber on the stump for (in theory) full market value, even if they do not participate in the extraction process or form a formal CFE to do so. However, since classical exploitative *rentismo* is a historical stage that has been superseded in many areas of Mexico, it is here proposed that these modern communities be referred to as simply "stumpage communities." Historical forms of *rentismo* may still exist in pockets in states such as Chihuahua and Guerrero, although even here we should perhaps use the term neo-*rentismo*, since they normally do not suffer the worst forms of exploitation of the past. The continued presence of neo-*rentismo* shows that despite historic achievements, there are still many and profound problems in the community forest enterprise sector. Many smaller CFEs continue to struggle with problems of isolation, corruption, lack of capital and technical assistance, and illegal exploitation by outsiders. Many communities are still engaged in intense and violent struggles to gain effective control of their common property forest resources. In 1996, 13 *ejidatarios* of the San Alonso *ejido* in Chihuahua, with the support of a Chihuahuan forest and human rights NGO, filed suit against the International Paper Company for cutting unmarked pine outside of the logging area and for logging a listed species. The suit was settled in favor of the *ejidatarios*, which led to the suspension of the logging permit, the suspension for one year of the license of the forestry engineer, and a fine of 205,000 pesos against the *ejido* authorities, although later protests and negotiations on the part of other members of the *ejido* apparently diluted the impact somewhat. Other *ejidos* have led protests against clandestine logging on their lands, but with little response from government authorities. PROFEPA, the environmental attorney general, has investigated 411 claims of forest violations from 1996 to 2000 in Chihuahua, but there are no comparative numbers from other states to judge whether this is high or not. Exploitative logging by outsiders continues to be widespread in states like Chihuahua and Guerrero, with frequent corruption of *ejido* authorities (Guerrero et al. 2000). The community of San Juan Tierra Negra in southern Oaxaca is another documented example of the kind of abusive exploitation of forest resources which continues in poorly organized communities (Merino-Pérez 1997).

At the same time, however, after an initial year of considerable confusion around the forest policies of the Vicente Fox administration, a clearer and highly promising policy picture has begun to emerge, as Merino-Pérez discusses in Chapter 3 of this book. The first director of the National Forest Commission (Comisión Nacional Forestal; CONAFOR) was a former governor of Jalisco and said to be an intimate of President Fox. As such, he was the highest-ranking political figure to occupy the top forestry policy position since Cuauhtémoc Cárdenas in the late 1970s. This director, Alberto Cárdenas, subsequently became Secretary of the Environment and Natural Resources (Secretaría de Medio Ambiente y Recursos Naturales; SEMARNAT) in September 2004. The significance of this is showing up in the budgets for forestry programs. The Forest Development Program (Programa de Desarrollo Forestal; PRODEFOR), which subsidizes forest management activities in community forests, and the Program for the Development of Forest Plantations (Programa para Desarrollo de Plantaciones Forestales; PRODEPLAN), which supports both industrial and community plantations, have been significantly expanded in resources and broadened in scope (see Merino-

Pérez and Segura-Warnholtz, this volume). According to official government figures, the annual resources for PRODEFOR are now larger than those of both programs in the total of the previous four years, with a budget of 276 million pesos (about US$27.6 million) for 2002, with an additional 30% coming from the states. But in addition to the substantially expanded resources, the possible investment projects have been greatly expanded. Whereas PRODEFOR was mostly limited to financing management plans, projects can now be presented for a wide range of forest production and diversification activities. Now, training, silvicultural treatments, certification, technical studies for harvesting of NTFPs, ecosystem services projects, and ecotourism projects can all qualify for funds, with amounts in the range of US$50 to US$100,000 available for ecotourism and logging road projects.

At the same time, the Program for Forest Conservation and Management (Programa para la Conservación y Manejo Forestal; PROCYMAF), a World Bank/government of Mexico program to promote and strengthen community forest management, is being expanded to include 10 states over the next several years. PROCYMAF, in association with PRODEFOR, is the first Mexican government program since the 1970s that has made a concerted effort to promote community forest management and the formation of CFEs in Mexico, with Oaxaca being the primary focus of its work through 2002. In the 1998–2000 period, PROCYMAF in Oaxaca was able to incorporate 32 new communities into community logging activities, a notable achievement for such a short period (PROCYMAF 2000). The existence of the PRODEFOR and PROCYMAF programs since 1997, and their current rather dramatic expansion, is the most decided public policy support for CFEs in Mexico since the late 1970s and early 1980s. This opportunity needs to be seized by forest advisors, communities, and NGOs to use the new government and multilateral resources that ensure that community forest management (CFM) remains as a permanent part of forest policies in Mexico. Deeply entrenched suspicions of government action need to be overcome to recognize this historic opportunity.

But as new and more favorable public policies are consolidated, the question of how many more new CFEs can be promoted in Mexico becomes urgent. Very little is known about the periods of formation of CFEs in Mexico, that is, how many CFEs were formed in what years or historical periods. Survey information from Oaxaca confirms the general impression that most existing CFEs were probably legally formed by the end of the 1980s. For 15 sawmill communities in Oaxaca, the average founding date was 1984, and the average date for roundwood communities is 1988. Only the stumpage communities on average legally organized themselves more recently, with an average date of 1994 (Antinori 2000). But other CFEs continued to be established in the 1990s, for example, the CFE San José Zaragoza in the Mixteca region of Oaxaca, established in 1994. How many more new CFEs have been established in the 1990s? PROCYMAF staff suggests that nearly all communities with logging permits in Oaxaca now have their own logging team headed by a trained *jefe de monte*, which would mean that the period of neo-*rentismo* has ended in Oaxaca, an important historical achievement which has been insufficiently recognized (Juan Manuel Barrera, personal communication, 2002). In the numerous other forestry states, how many more new CFEs can be created? Was the promotion of forest communities themselves "high-graded" during the community forestry "boom" years of the 1970s and 1980s? Did government agencies and NGOs identify and create most of the CFEs that can be created? The experience of PROCYMAF in its first three years of operation in Oaxaca is illustrative. As mentioned above, it was able to start CFEs in 32 new communities for a collective forest estate of 75,593 hectares, with an average of 2,362 hectares each. This is relatively small forest estate. Although there are examples of successful CFEs mounted on even smaller forest estates, it still suggests the potential for new CFE creation is concentrated in the small communities, and that few, if any, large forest communities do not have CFEs. The new ones that are incorporating now are the ones with very marginal forests, and the marginal costs of incorporating new communities will be high.

PROCYMAF has identified three major problems associated with trying to extend the CFE model into additional Mexican forest communities. (1) Communities lack leadership or have severe internal conflicts that prevent them from responding. (2) In the Mixteca region of Oaxaca, in particular, there has been widespread parcelization of the forest resulting in a "covert privatization" of the forest (although this is not necessarily a barrier to mounting a CFE). (3) On the northern Pacific coast of Oaxaca, there are few providers of forest technical services (FTS), which are being dominated by a private plywood factory in Puerto Escondido. PROCYMAF has also discovered that communities do not necessarily want to autonomously manage their own forest. In relatively remote (but heavily impacted by migration) areas like the Mixteca region of Oaxaca, there are few examples of community-managed forests, and people show little interest in the concept. It takes considerable talking, visiting, and training before communities begin to understand the idea. Some communities with good commercial forests may never pursue logging, and the strategy here should be to make the leap directly into more benign ecosystem service sales.

For the 2001–2003 period PROCYMAF developed strategies that included a regional focus, a thematic focus (diversification), ecotourism, resin tapping, and water bottling, as well as an emphasis on financing management plans, helping communities demand more of FTS providers, and strengthening community technical teams (Gerardo-Segura, personal communication, 2003). As previously noted, they will also be expanding into a total of 10 states over the next several years.

Future Paths of Mexican CFEs

As a part of the development of a more diversified strategy for Mexican CFEs, it may be helpful to imagine what the future paths of CFEs might be, given their competitive positions at the present. Figure 14.1 maps out these paths. First, a substantial diversified, entrepreneurial sector is beginning to emerge, and there are probably more cases of this path than have been popularly recognized. These entrepreneurial CFEs are investing in modernized equipment, exploring new markets, investing in human capital, and diversifying their activities into the sale of ecosystem services and non-timber forest products of various kinds. The second path, the "small CFE path," is probably where the bulk of Mexican CFEs are. These CFEs are generally not modernizing their equipment, have continuing problems with administration and organization of the CFE, and may have varying degrees of internal debate over the purpose and direction of the CFE. Nonetheless, these CFEs should be regarded as small community businesses that have found their niche in the marketplace, that are profitable in spite of it all, and can probably continue to survive without expanding in the immediate future. Few of these small CFEs ever seem to go out of business entirely, which is to be contrasted with the very high rate of failure of most small businesses in the private sector.

These CFEs are under various internal and external pressures, however, and some percentage will probably be undergoing major transformation over the next decade. Some of these CFEs, following the third path, may abandon logging entirely and undertake either of two different paths. First, they might undertake the sale of ecosystem services, whether though ecotourism, sales of watershed services, or carbon sequestration projects. Others may abandon logging entirely because the opportunity costs be-

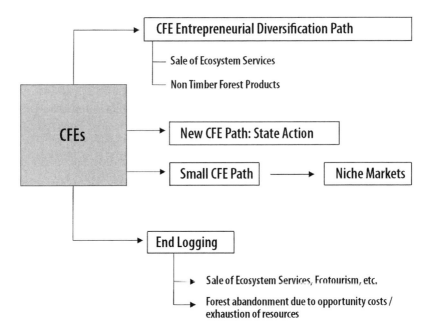

Figure 14.1 Four future paths for Mexican CFEs.

come too high, and most of the CFE staff would migrate. Others may end logging because they have simply exhausted the commercial supplies of timber due to decades of overexploitation by both outside interests and the CFE. Finally, in the fourth path, the combined actions of PROCYMAF and PRODEFOR are engaged in the first major effort at state promotion of CFEs since the 1970s. This would be likely to produce a new stratum of small, fragile CFEs with small forest resources. CFEs in this stratum would require continued state support to survive and find their own niches in the marketplace and, as noted, some communities might elect to skip the logging stage of community forest development entirely.

Twenty Lessons Learned from the CFE Experience in Mexico

In this section, 20 lessons that have been learned from over 25 years of concerted development of a CFE sector in Mexico will be presented. These lessons are derived from both the chapters in this book and data in reports and published works (Bray and Merino 2003; Bray and Merino-Pérez 2002). The lessons are divided into global lessons, which can apply to CFEs anywhere in the world, and national lessons, which may apply more specifically to Mexico, although it is hoped that many of these national lessons may also have some value for emerging experiences elsewhere.

Global Lessons

1. *The devolution of public and private forestlands to local communities with common pool resource regimes and clear tenure status* can *create economic equity, social peace, democratization of power, and improved forest ecosystem management.* Mexico is a unique historical case that may prove the hypothesis that delivering forests to local communities will bring a wide range of benefits. Mexico's major agrarian revolution early in the twentieth century eventually drove a massive transfer of forest assets to local communities, whereas less dramatic efforts are now under way globally.

2. *Mexican CFEs represent a unique global case, where hundreds of communities are managing common property forests for the commercial production of timber. As such, it is a model for many other forest communities in developing countries.* This model can be viewed as a form of co-management on privately held communal lands, in a common property form that is neither declining nor emergent, but is a decades-old persisting form of state rural administration. Mexico is a global model, and in this sense is the "face of the future" in community forest management. Emerging CFEs in Clayquot Sound in Vancouver and elsewhere are beginning to face many of the same problems with which Mexican CFEs have grappled for decades (Gill 2002). Mexico demonstrates that local communities can master complex industrial processes and produce for the market with the right support.

3. *The strength of CFEs in Mexico shows that assets can be accumulated at the community level (public goods), and not just at the household level.* There is substantial evidence that community-level assets, where each family may be regarded as shareholder, have substantially increased due to CFEs. There is no direct evidence that CFEs serve to help in the accumulation of assets at the household level. In the best cases, increased flows of income may be invested in the consumption of education.

4. *Government actions, at times supplemented by NGO action, can create new social capital in rural areas and thereby increase the economic competitiveness of community enterprises.* Mexican government efforts to promote CFEs,

with varying motives and at varying periods, as well as efforts to support second- and third-level organizations, were instrumental in creating the organizational and institutional forms of social capital which undergird the CFE sector.

5. *Visionary community leadership and demonstration effects can create social capital and relative social peace, even from a base of conflict-ridden, nonindigenous communities in the space of 10–20 years.* The case of El Balcón (see Torres-Rojo et al., this volume) demonstrates that even situations of great conflict can be pacified, and civil society built, by the concerted action of constructing a CFE and a second-level organization. Social learning through producer exchanges is also key. Just as integrated civic groups have been an important force in forestalling ethnic violence in India (Varshney 2000), they may be an important source in diminishing rural violence in forest communities in Mexico.

6. *Communities and CFEs should be aware that some of their great strengths in establishing CFEs, their traditional social capital, can also serve as a barrier to further development of CFEs which could better serve the community.* Communities that are not willing to make some adaptations in their traditional structures and practices may continue to confront administrative problems with their CFEs, community conflict around them, and a reduced flow of financial resources.

National Lessons

7. *Mexican CFEs should not be regarded as a backward, noncapitalist economic sector to be dismantled, as is the neoliberal impulse, but promoted as a uniquely Mexican contribution to the global economy, a Mexican grassroots version of communitarian capitalism in Asia.* Mexican CFEs have demonstrated that they have uniquely local ways of organizing themselves on the basis of a common property resource, and that these local traditions may be sources of strength in the national and international marketplace. This also stands as a global model for the local common property communities that are attempting to organize themselves for commercial production, demonstrating that they do not have to abandon traditional forms of organization, practices, and culture in order to be competitive in the marketplace.

8. *Two specific organizational innovations help to make the relationship between the community and CFEs more efficient: (1) the establishment of a new super-*

visory Community Forest Council and (2) the institutionalization of a professional manager, with preference given to providing the necessary training to young people in the community. Several communities, inspired by the traditional Council of Elders in Oaxaca, have created new organizational supervisory organs that have proven to be more effective than the General Assembly at overseeing CFE operations, and that serve to separate CFE administration from community politics. Communities must also pay greater attention to creating a role for professional managers.

9. *The most vertically integrated Mexican CFEs make increased investments in improving forest management and diversification of their enterprises.* The most vertically integrated CFEs are investing in better forest ecosystem management and are evolving toward corporate diversified structures that give them increased resilience in dealing with shifts in markets.

10. *The most dynamic, diversified, and vertically integrated CFEs will also be in communities that show high migration rates.* In these cases, the CFE provides an option for those young people who would rather stay in their communities than migrate, and it will probably reduce the total number of those who do migrate. But migration will continue to be very dynamic from these communities because of their overall economic development. CFEs only increase the number of options for those who may want to stay.

11. *Small ejidos can successfully manage their forests and successfully unite to undertake vertical integration steps that are not possible for any one community.* In a 25–community organization in the Sierra Norte of Puebla, 18 of the communities organized themselves to establish a sawmill. This demonstrates that if communities can overcome mistrust, they can gain more value-added from their timber production. The fact that the average forest size in these communities is 213 hectares also shows that even very small forests can be successfully managed for timber.

12. *In accordance with common property theory, large heterogeneous communities, particularly ones characterized by geographic and ethnic divisions, are more likely to have severe conflicts in attempting to administer a common property resource.* Experiences in Chihuahua, Oaxaca, and elsewhere suggest it will be extremely difficult to develop successful CFEs in these circumstances. Agrarian reform authorities may want to consider allowing the partition of communities with these characteristics that are continually wracked by

conflicts, or they may want to take more decided external interventions to help resolve conflicts.

13. *There is no one way to organize a successful community enterprise and its relation to the common pool resource.* The stocks and flows of a forest resource may be divided up in a multitude of ways, and even parcelization of the forest resource for some individual uses need not be a barrier to mounting a successful CFE on the same resource. Promoters of CFEs need to be flexible. There are multiple institutional pathways to CFE success.

14. *Work groups represent an authentic grassroots solution to the persisting problem of CFE corruption, and should be accepted as a viable alternative model to unified CFEs.* While work groups present new challenges in the administration of FTS, forest management, and marketing, these problems are not insurmountable (see Wilshusen, this volume).

15. *Investment in human capital, both through short-term training and longer term formal education of young community members, is a key element in the success of CFEs.* NGOs and government agencies have invested much time and energy in training for years, but new ways need to be found to institutionalize this process. Communities need to be given models of how to establish fellowship programs in areas needed by the community that tie the recipient to a period of community service. Prosperous communities can finance these themselves, while government or foundation funds will be needed in poorer communities. Community-to-community exchanges, as carried out by PROCYMAF, should continue to be a key element in training programs.

16. *Mexican CFEs are highly profitable undertakings, and this is true at all levels of integration.* This finding should change the development approach to CFEs. They should no longer be viewed as welfare basket cases, but as viable community enterprises that have been successful at generating jobs and income, but which need more investments to do what they do even better.

17. *Mexican CFEs vertically integrate in order to seek control over local economic development, that is, to generate jobs and better control over forest extraction.* Mexican forest communities should be encouraged to continue to seek local economic development through vertical integration, but they also need analyses to help them understand when vertical integration is

indicated (by size of resource) and when it may not be. There is a strong relationship between size of forest resource and vertical integration. Promoters should no longer stigmatize some communities as *rentistas* when classical *rentismo*, based on a stumpage fee, no longer exists. For many communities, selling timber on the stump, with little direct participation, may be the optimal economic decision.

18. *Most CFEs have survived in the post-NAFTA period, and some have been able to become internationally competitive. Despite some notable failures in foreign investment, there are successful models of partnership between U.S. timber companies and Mexican CFEs.* The case of El Balcón (see Torres-Rojo et al., this volume) and probably some cases in Durango as well, show that Mexican CFEs can successfully compete in U.S. markets and partner with U.S. businesses.

19. *While a relatively small number of CFEs may be internationally competitive, most others seem to have local market niches where they will probably be able to survive for a time yet, but they will need government and foundation support to establish a new market niche for certified wood produced by communities.* Most CFEs may be thought of as small community businesses, like small businesses everywhere, which may not be very dynamic or expansive, but which continue to survive because they have found a local market niche. Mexican timber is generally of very high quality, one competitive advantage that even small CFEs have.

20. *Mexican forest communities with CFEs, particularly those that are not major income generators, are increasingly divided between pro- and anti-logging groups within the community. Both traditional peasant conservationism, which identifies forests with water, and emergent forms associated with urban environmentalism, work to place pressure on some CFEs.* Some promoters of CFEs have seen these conservationist forces within communities as "the enemy," but communities should be allowed to work out these debates on their own. For some communities, it may be a natural social and economic evolution to abandon logging and move on to other forest management options.

Final Thoughts

For many years it appeared as if Mexico's success in the development of timber-producing CFEs was a unique historical event, attributable to

Mexico's agrarian reforms over the twentieth century. But it is now becoming clear that land tenure reforms and government programs in other countries are gradually beginning to create the conditions that will allow timber CFEs to emerge elsewhere. Some 20 CFEs have emerged in the Guatemalan Petén in the last decade, operating under 25-year concessions from the government (Gretzinger 1998), and CFEs are also emerging in Peru and Brazil (Loayza Villegas and Chota Valera 1996; d'Oliveira 1998; Samantha Stone, personal communication, 2002). The number of indigenous timber management projects in Bolivia has expanded from 9 to 32 in 1999–2002 (Cronkleton 2002). Eight villages and 59 hamlets are also undertaking community logging in Indonesia (Nolan 2001). Joint management for timber production has also emerged in Madhya Pradesh in India (Scherr et al. 2003), and Salafsky et al. (2001a, 2001b) identify several additional CFEs worldwide. The Nuu-chah-nulth Nation in British Columbia is engaged in a significant new CFE initiative in partnership with a multinational timber company (Gill 2002). This emergence makes Mexico far more significant as a global model, and makes it even more crucial to draw the appropriate lessons from its experience.

It is common in the literature to refer to "successful CFEs," but the term is seldom defined. Peter Taylor (see Chapter 7), a rural sociologist who has conducted research on both the Mondragon cooperative in Spain and Mexican CFEs in Durango and Quintana Roo, has provided a compelling discussion of successful CFEs:

> I've come to believe that the cooperative world could learn a lot from the Mexican case. Mexican *ejidos* and agrarian communities' collective enterprises . . . look a lot like those successful cooperatives ("success" meaning that they survive over several generations of participants, over the long run consistently benefit more than a handful of people, and include the possibility of renegotiating governance arrangements if necessary). I've attended numerous general assembly meetings in *ejidos* and agrarian communities and from the first, have been struck by how much they resemble general assemblies in Mondragón. They often drag on, the topic goes all over the place, certain people talk too much, there's not enough technical mastery of the issues, but at the end, they very often end up in a place that works. People who've participated in the debate then have some commitment to the decision made, because they've been part of the process. At a minimum, they are willing to lose if they have to, because they know they can come back at the next meeting and have another go. *Ejidos* and agrarian communities are more

stable than most ordinary cooperatives, even with all their problems, because their economic relationships are embedded in a network of political, social, cultural, and other economic ties. There is a lot of conflict, but as long as the people have good reason to stick around and work through it, the community can survive and with it, the collective economic enterprise. Lots of cooperatives fold when things get tough because people don't have other reasons to stick around and work through the conflict. If collective enterprise and community, more broadly defined, overlap, then people don't just walk away, even when they lose an argument. Another way to put this is, because of their unique history, the Mexican *ejidos* and agrarian communities have a lot of social capital to work with when it comes to implementing a collective economic enterprise like community-based forestry. (Peter Taylor, email, 7 June 2001)

By this standard, it may be the case that Mexico has hundreds of successful CFEs. Too often, the Mexican CFE sector has been seen as an undifferentiated mass, with nearly all of them being inefficient, conflict-ridden, on the brink of collapse, and in need of massive government and NGO help to survive, basically as a part of rural welfare programs. This book suggests a different picture. CFEs at all levels of integration can be highly profitable. The Mexican government, in some periods more than others, has played a key role in the creation of the CFE sector, and this needs to be more clearly recognized. Community forestry organizations and advocates, who frequently found themselves in intense struggles with government actors, may understandably have had difficulty accepting this notion. But the Mexican government has been a very complex actor, and should feel proud of what it has created, with major prodding from emerging, democratic civil society, and understand that it has helped to create what can be called "the Mexican model of Community Forest Management."

A new government-led marketing campaign for the entire CFE sector, in close collaboration with second- and third-level organizations and forest NGOs, is an important further step that government and international donors could be taking now. As has been argued, Mexico's CFEs represent a distinctive productive sector within the global forest products industry. A publication relations campaign could be mounted within the forest products industry and for the public that "sells" the Mexican CFE sector as one that uniquely combines high-quality wood products with "green seal" forest management, and social justice and equity. This should also involve a major push for certification and the development of schemes for the sale of ecosystem services. If it is true that Mexico is the face of the future in global community forestry, then for Mexico, the future is now. Thus, Mexican community forestry stands at the brink of even greater achievements. It is an optimal moment for all of its stakeholders to join together in a concerted effort to take it to the next level of equity, democracy, and sustainability.

References

Antinori, C. M. 2000. Vertical integration in Mexican common property forests. PhD diss., University of California, Berkeley.

Bray, D. B., and L. Merino. 2003. A case study of El Balcón Ejido, Guerrero. In *Confronting Globalization: Economic Integration and Popular Response in Mexico*, ed. T. A. Wise, H. Salazar, and L. Carlsen, 65–80. Bloomfield, CT: Kumarian Press.

Bray, D. B., and L. Merino Pérez. 2002. *The Rise of Community Forestry in Mexico: History, Concepts, and Lessons Learned from 25 Years of Community Forestry Timber Production*. Mexico City: Ford Foundation.

Cronkleton, P. 2002. Collaboration and adaptation in the marketing of timber by indigenous peoples in lowland Bolivia. Paper presented at Working Forests in the Tropics: Conservation through Sustainable Management, 25–26 February, University of Florida, Gainesville.

d'Oliveira, M. V. N., E. M. Braz, D. F. R. Burslen, and M. D. Swaine. 1998. Small-scale natural forest management. *Tropical Forest Update* 8:5–7.

Gill, I. 2002. The first nations reclaim a temperate rain forest. In *Sustainable Solutions: Building Assets for Empowerment and Sustainable Development*. Environment and Development Affinity Group, Ford Foundation. URL: http://www.fordfound.org/publications/recent_articles/docs/Solutions_81-85.pdf.

Gretzinger, S. P. 1998. Community forest concessions: An economic alternative for the Maya Biosphere Reserve in the Petén, Guatemala. In *Timber, Tourists, and Temples: Conservation and Development in the Maya Forest of Belize, Guatemala, and Mexico*, ed. R. B. Primack, D. B. Bray, H. A. Galleti, and I. Ponciano, 111–124. Washington, DC: Island Press.

Guerrero, M. T., C. Reed, and B. Vegter. 2000. *La industria forestal y los recursos naturales en la Sierra Madre de Chihuahua: Impactos sociales, económicos y ecológicos*. Mexico City: Comisión de Solidaridad y Defensa de los Derechos Humanos, A.C., and Texas Center for Policy Studies.

Loayza Villegas, M., and G. Chota Valera. 1996. An indigenous Amazonian community and its forest. *Tropical Forest Update* 6:10–11.

Merino-Pérez, L. 1997. Organización social de la producción forestal comunitaria: Siete estudios de caso. In *Semillas para el cambio en el campo: Medio ambiente, mercados y organización campesina*, ed. L. Paré, D. B. Bray, J. Burstein, and B. S. M. Vásquez, 141–154. Mexico City: UNAM; IIS; La Sociedad de

Solidaridad Social Sansekan Tinemi y Saldebas; Servicios de Apoyo Local al Desarrollo de Base en México.

Nolan, T. M. 2001. Community-based forest management: Commercial harvesting of the rainforest of Indonesia. *International Forestry Review* 3:231–235.

PROCYMAF. 2000. *Proyecto de conservación y manejo sustentable de recursos forestales en México: Balance de tres años de ejecución.* Mexico City: SEMARNAP.

Salafsky, N., H. Cauley, B. Balachander, et al. 2001a. A Systematic test of an enterprise strategy for community-based biodiversity conservation. *Conservation Biology* 15:1585–1595.

Salafsky, N., M. Henderson, and M. Leighton. 2001b. Community-based timber production: A viable strategy for promoting wildlife conservation? In *The Cutting Edge: Conserving Wildlife in Logged Tropical Forests*, ed. R. A. Fimbel, A. Grajal, and J. G. Robinson, 575–594. New York: Columbia University Press.

Scherr, S. J., A. White, and D. Kaimowitz. 2003. *A New Agenda for Conservation and Poverty Reduction: Making Forest Markets Work for Low-Income Producers.* Washington, DC: Forest Trends/Center for International Forestry Research.

Varshney, A. 2000. *Ethnic Conflict and Civic Life: Hindus and Muslims in India.* New Haven: Yale University Press.

Acronyms Used in the Book

AGN-PF	Archivo General de la Nación, Ramo Política Forestal (General National Archives, Forest Policy Branch)
AHPEM-B	Archivo Histórico del Poder Ejecutivo de Michoacán, Ramo Bosques (Historical Archive of the Executive Authority of Michoacán)
ANP	Áreas Naturales Protegidas (Protected Natural Areas)
ARIC	Asociación Rural de Interés Colectivo (Rural Collective Interest Association)
ASARCO	American Smelting and Refining Company
ASETECO	Asistencia Técnica para las Comunidades Oaxaqueñas (Technical Assistance to Oaxacan Communities, A.C.)
BOLFOR	Proyecto de Manejo Forestal Sostenible—Bolivia (Bolivian Sustainable Forestry Project)
BR	Biosphere Reserves
CATIE	Centro Agronómico Tropical de Investigación y Enseñanza (Tropical Agronomy Center for Research and Teaching)
CBC	Comisariado de Bienes Comunales (Mayor for Communal Property)
CCMSS	Consejo Civil Mexicano para la Silvicultura Sostenible (Mexican Civil Council for Sustainable Silviculture)
CDM	Clean Development Mechanism
CEMDA	Centro Mexicano de Derecho Ambiental (Mexican Center for Environmental Law)
CESPEDES	Centro de Estudios del Sector Privado para el Desarrollo Sustentable (Private Sector Center for the Study of Sustainable Development)
CFE	Community forest enterprise
CFM	Community forest management
CFO	Compañía Forestal de Oaxaca (Oaxaca Forest Company)
CICY	Centro de Investigación Científica de Yucatán (Yucatan Center for Scientific Research)

CIFOR	Center for International Forestry Research
CIOAC	Central Independiente de Obreros Agrícolas y Campesinos (Independent Organization of Agricultural Workers and Peasants)
CITES	Convention on International Trade in Endangered Species of Wild Fauna and Flora
CMO	Compañía Maderas de Oaxaca (Timber Company of Oaxaca)
CNC	Confederación Nacional Campesina (National Campesino Federation)
CODREMI	Coordinadora para el Desarrollo de la Región Mixe (Mixe Development Coordination)
COFYAL	Yánesha Forestry Cooperative
COINBIO	Proyecto de Conservación de la Biodiversidad por Comunidades Indígenas de los Estados de Oaxaca, Michoacán, y Guerrero, México (Campesino Biodiversity Conservation)
CONABIO	Comisión Nacional de la Biodiversidad (National Commission on Biodiversity)
CONAFOR	Comisión Nacional Forestal (National Forest Commission)
CONAPO	Consejo Nacional de Población (National Council on Population)
CONACYT	Comisión Nacional de Ciencia y Tecnología (National Commission for Science and Technology)
CPR	Common property regime; also common pool resources
CRIM	Centro Regional de Investigaciones Multidisciplinarias (Regional Center for Multidiscipline Research)
dbh	Diameter at breast height (the diameter of the stem of a tree measured at 1.30 m above the soil level)
DFID	Department for International Development (UK)
DGDF	Dirección General de Desarrollo Forestal (General Office of Forest Development)
ECOSUR	Colegio de la Frontera Sur (College of the Frontera Sur)
ERA	Estudios Rurales y Asesoría Campesina (Rural Studies and Advising)
FAO	Food and Agriculture Organization (United Nations)
FAPATUX	Fábricas de Papel Tuxtepec (Tuxtepec Paper Factory)
FIFONAFE	Fideicomiso del Fondo Nacional de Fomento Ejidal (National Trust Fund for *Ejido* Development)
FOVIGRO	Forestal Vincente Guerrero (Vicente Guerrero Forest Company)
FSC	Forest Stewardship Council
FTS	Forest technical services
GATT	General Agreement on Tariffs and Trade
GPS	Global positioning system
IASCP	International Association for the Study of Common Property
IBRD	International Bank for Reconstruction and Development
INE	National Ecology Institute

INEGI   Instituto Nacional de Estadística, Geografía e Informática (National Institute of Statistics and Geography)
ITTO   International Tropical Timber Organization
IXETO   Ixtlán-Etla-Oaxaca (Ixtlán-Etla Community Union)
JFM   Joint Forest Management
LIF   Low inundated forest
LKS   Lesser-known species
LUCAS   Land Use Change and Analysis System
LUCC   Land use/land cover change
MDS   Método de Desarrollo Silvicultura (Silvicultural Development Method)
MIQROO   Maderas Industrializados de Quintana Roo (Industrial Timber of Quintana Roo)
MMOM   Método Mexicano de Ordenación de Montes (Mexican Method of Forest Management)
NAFTA   North American Free Trade Agreement
NGO   Nongovernmental organization
NTFP   Non-timber forest product
ODRENASIJ Organización para la Defensa de los Recursos Naturales y el Desarrollo Social de la Sierra Juárez (Organization for the Defense of Natural Resources of the Sierra Juárez)
OEPFZM   Organización de Ejidos Productores Forestales de la Zona Maya (Forest *Ejido* Organization of the Mayan Zone)
PA   Protected area
PEF   Plan Estratégico Forestal (Strategic Forest Plan)
PEFC   Pan-European Forest Certification
PFA   Permanent forest area
PNF   Plan Nacional Forestal 2001–2006 (National Forest Program 2001–2006)
PNG   Papua New Guinea
PNUMA   Programa de las Naciones Unidas para el Medio Ambiente (United Nations Program for the Environment)
PPF   Plan Piloto Forestal (Forest Pilot Plan)
PPM   Parcelas Permanentes de Muestreo (Permanent Sampling Plots)
PRA   Participatory Rural Appraisal
PROCAMPO Programa de Apoyo Directo al Campo (Program of Direct Support to the Countryside)
PROCEDE   Programa de Certificación de Derechos Ejidales y Titulación de Solares (Certification Program for *Ejido* Parcels and for Titling of Urban Plots)
PROCYMAF Programa para la Conservación y Manejo Forestal (Program for Forest Conservation and Management)
PRODEFOR Programa de Desarrollo Forestal (Forest Development Program)
PRODEPLAN Programa para el Desarrollo de Plantaciones Forestales (Program for the Development of Forest Plantations)

PROFEPA	Procuraduría Federal de Protección Ambiental (Federal Attorney General for Environmental Protection)
PROGRESA	Programa de Educación, Salud, y Alimentación (Program for Education, Health, and Nutrition)
PRONARE	Procuraduría Federal de Protección al Ambiente (National Reforestation Program)
RAN	Registro Agrario Nacional (National Agrarian Registry)
RAN-M	Registro Agrario Nacional, Morelia (National Agrarian Registry, Morelia)
SAO	Servicios Ambientales de Oaxaca (Oaxaca Environmental Services)
SAP	Structural Adjustment Plan
SARH	Secretaría de Agricultura y Recursos Hidráulicos (Secretariat of Agriculture and Hydraulic Resources)
SC	*Sociedad civil* (civil society)
SCS	Scientific Certification Systems
SDF	Semideciduous dry forest
SEDESOL	Secretaría de Desarrollo Social (Secretariat of Social Development)
SEF	Semi-evergreen forest
SEMARNAP	Secretaría del Medio Ambiente, Recursos Naturales, y Pezca (Secretariat of the Environment, Natural Resources, and Fisheries)
SEMARNAT	Secretaría de Medio Ambiente y Recursos Naturales (Secretariat of the Environment and Natural Resources)
SFF	Subsecretaría Forestal (Forestry Undersecretariat)
SGS	Sociéte Générale de Surveillance
SICODESI	Sistema de Conservación y Desarrollo Silvícola (System of Conservation and Silvicultural Development)
SIMAP	Secretaría de Infraestructura, Medio Ambiente, y Pesca (Secretariat of Infrastructure, Environment, and Fisheries)
SLIMF	Small and Low Intensity Managed Forests
SPFEQR	Sociedad de Productores Forestales Ejidales de Quintana Roo (Sociedad Sur) (Society of Forest Production of *Ejidos* of Quintana Roo [Southern Society])
SPR	Sociedades de Producción Rural (Rural Production Societies)
SRA	Secretaría de Reforma Agraria (Secretariat of Agrarian Reform)
STF	Servicios técnicos forestales (technical forest service provider)
SWOT	Strengths, Weaknesses, Opportunities, and Threats
TRF	Tropical rainforest
UACH	Universidad Autónoma de Chapingo (Autonomous University of Chapingo)
UAF	Unidades de Administración Forestal (Forest Administration Units)

UAM   Universidad Autónoma Metropolitana (Autonomous Metropolitan University)

UBC   University of British Columbia

UCEFO   Unión de Comunidades y Ejidos Forestales de Oaxaca (Union of Forest Communities and *Ejidos* of Oaxaca)

UCIRI   Unión de Comunidades Indígenas del Istmo (Union of Indigenous Communities of the Isthmus)

UEFHG   Unión de Ejidos Forestales "Hermenegildo Galeana" (Hermenegildo Galeana *Ejido* Union)

UIEFs   Unidades Industriales de Explotación Forestal (Industrial Forest Exploitation Units)

UNAM   Universidad Nacional Autónoma de México (National Autonomous University of Mexico)

UNECOFAEZ   Unión de Ejidos y Comunidades de Producción Forestal y Agropecuaria del Noroeste del Estado de Durango General Emiliano Zapata (Emiliano Zapata Union of Forest and Livestock *Ejidos* and Communities of Northwestern Durango)

UNESCO   United Nations Educational, Scientific, and Cultural Organization

UNOFOC   Unión Nacional de Organizaciones Forestales Comunales (National Community of Communal Forest Organizations)

UPMPF   Unidades de Producción de Materia Prima Forestal (Forest Raw Material Production Units)

USAID   U.S. Agency for International Development

UZACHI   Unión de Comunidades Zapoteco-Chinanteca (Union of Zapotec-Chinantec Communities)

VFC   Village Forest Committees

WRI   World Resources Institute

WTO   World Trade Organization

About the Contributors

ENRIQUE ALATORRE-GUZMÁN has a degree in biology from UAM-Xochimilco. He has long experience in community technical assistance in forest management in Mexico. He was in charge of the certification office of CCMSS from 1997 to 2003 with the SmartWood Program. Currently he is an independent consultant and an organic producer of macadamia nuts and other products.

SHRINIDHI AMBINAKUDIGE is a doctoral candidate in the Department of Geography at Florida State University, Tallahassee. He worked for several years as a research assistant at the Institute for Social and Economic Change, Bangalore, India, in a research project on forest use in the Western Ghats of India. Currently he is working on his dissertation on differential impacts of environmental change on people's livelihood in the Western Ghats of India.

CAMILLE ANTINORI is a private consultant and senior research associate in climate change studies at the Lawrence Berkeley National Laboratory, Berkeley, California. Her research focuses on property rights, contracts, and governance in natural resource management. She is currently a principal investigator for a national survey project to identify and research the community forestry sector in Mexico.

DEBORAH BARRY has a degree in geography from the University of California, Berkeley. She is the founder of PRISMA, a Salvadoran NGO specializing in agrarian environmental research. Since 1998 she has been a program officer with the Ford Foundation.

CHRISTOPHER R. BOYER teaches history and Latin American and Latino Studies at the University of Illinois at Chicago. His first book, on the interactive construction of campesino political identity in Mexico, is titled *Becoming Campesinos: Politics, Identity, and Agrarian Struggle in Postrevolutionary Michoacán, 1920–1935*, and was released by Stanford University Press in 2003. He has also published a number of articles and book chapters dealing with agrarian history, labor history, and Catholic nationalism in postrevolutionary Mexico. He is currently at work on a book on the social history—and social conflict—regarding the use of the forest in the states of Michoacán and Chihuahua between 1880 and the present.

DAVID BARTON BRAY has a PhD in anthropology from Brown University. At the Inter-American Foundation, he was foundation representative for Paraguay and Argentina from 1986 to 1989 and for Mexico from 1989 to 1997. He was chair of the Department of Environmental Studies at Florida International University from 1997 to 2002 and is currently professor there.

FRANCISCO CHAPELA is an agronomist specializing in forest management and social organization. He has devoted most of his professional career to supporting indigenous organizations in Oaxaca and Veracruz. He collaborated with Estudios Rurales y Asesoría Campesina, A.C., a nonprofit technical assistance NGO, and was its president from 1997 to 2002. He was the contact person who promoted the Forest Stewardship Council in Mexico from 1999 to 2001. He currently coordinates a GEF-funded pilot project co-executed by Nacional Financiera and the Comisión Nacional Forestal to support indigenous communities' biodiversity and conservation initiatives in Oaxaca, Guerrero, and Michoacán, known as the Campesino Biodiversity Conservation project.

ELVIRA DURÁN graduated with a degree in biology from UAM, Mexico City. She received her PhD in 2004 from UNAM. She is currently based at the Academic Unit of Morelia, Institute of Geography, UNAM, leading the geobotany group.

PATRICIA GEREZ-FERNÁNDEZ studied biology at UNAM and received a master's degree in forest sciences from the Yale School of Forestry and Environmental Studies. She is coauthor of the first analysis published on the status of biodiversity and its conservation in Mexico (in 1984). In the last 10 years she has been focused on research in sustainable management of community-owned forests in Mexico. She was involved in field evaluations of community forestlands for certification and was the coordinator of all forest operations certified in Mexico, under the SmartWood Program, from 2001 to 2003. Her fieldwork and research have been supported by the MacArthur Foundation's Environment and Population Fellowship Program, National Council for Sciences and Technology (CONACYT), Center for Studies on Social Anthropology (CIESAS), Mexican Foundation for Nature Conservation (FMCN). Recently, she was awarded the Conservation Program Fellowship by the Overbrook Foundation/CERC–Columbia University. Currently, she is an independent consultant and researcher.

ALEJANDRO GUEVARA-SANGINÉS is an associate professor in the Economics Department, Universidad Iberoamericana, Mexico City. He has a PhD in economics from the University of Madrid, a master's degree in public policy from the University of California, Berkeley, and a master's degree in development economics from the University of East Anglia in Norwich, England. His main research interests focus on poverty and the environment. In 1999 he was awarded the National Prize of Public Administration for his work on this topic.

DAN KLOOSTER is an assistant professor of geography at Florida State University in Tallahassee, where he devotes most of his time to teaching courses in environmental studies, Latin American geography, and development studies. His community forestry research in Mexico has addressed common property theory, timber smuggling, deforestation dynamics, and adaptive management in forests used for fuelwood. Currently, he is investigating the role of international forest certification in Mexico.

RODOLFO LÓPEZ-ARZOLA has been working with indigenous communities with forestry resources mainly in Oaxaca but also in Chiapas and Chihuahua; over the past 25 years he has worked on the creation of community forest enterprises (CFEs) and educational programs in the same communities. The model of the CFEs promoted by the NGO ASETECO, A.C., in Oaxaca, is the one that currently dominates as part of a communal enterprise culture already established in the state of Oaxaca, with 70 of them operating for 15 years and having won national and international awards.

JEAN-FRANÇOIS MAS received his PhD from Paul Sabatier University, Toulouse, France, in 1998 as a specialist on remote sensing. He worked as an associate researcher at the University of Campeche (EPOMEX) until 2000. He has been involved in the coordination of the last two national forest inventories of Mexico. He is currently head of the laboratory of remote sensing and geographic information systems at the Academic Unit of Morelia, the Institute of Geography, UNAM.

LETICIA MERINO-PÉREZ has a master's degree in sociology, another in population and development, and a PhD in anthropology. She has advised forest unions in Mexico and has worked as a consultant for the World Bank, SEMARNAT, and the Ford Foundation. She is an instructor at the Institute of Ecology, the Latin American Faculty of Social Sciences, in Mexico and Guatemala. She is also a faculty member at the Institute of Social Research, UNAM.

MARÍA ANGÉLICA NAVARRO-MARTÍNEZ has a degree in biology from UNAM and a master's degree in forest science from the Universidad Autónoma Chapingo. She has been an associate researcher at El Colegio de la Frontera Sur since 1996. Her major interest areas include the population ecology of trees, forest ecology, and forest management.

GERARDO SEGURA-WARNHOLTZ has a PhD in forest ecology from the University of Washington. He served on the faculty of the Ecology Institute at UNAM, and since 1996 has been director of the Programa de Conservación y Manejo Forestal (PROCYMAF), a program jointly funded by the World Bank and Mexico to promote community forestry.

PETER LEIGH TAYLOR is an associate professor of sociology at Colorado State University. He does research in Mexico and Latin America on community-based forestry, and on forest and Fair Trade coffee certification as market-based social change mechanisms.

JUAN MANUEL TORRES-ROJO has a degree in forest engineering from the Universidad Autónoma Chapingo and his PhD in forest economics from Oregon State University. He served as the director of the Mexican government's National Reforestation Program (PRONARE), and in recent years has been a researcher in the Economy Division of the Centro de Investigación y Docencia Económicas (CIDE) in Mexico City. He is currently director of the Economics Division at CIDE.

ALEJANDRO VELÁZQUEZ obtained his PhD from the University of Amsterdam, the Netherlands, in landscape ecology. He served as head of the Laboratory of Biogeography of the Faculty of Sciences at UNAM. He is currently director of the Institute of Geography, UNAM, Academic Unit at Morelia, Michoacán.

HENRICUS F. M. VESTER received his undergraduate degree in forestry from the University of Wageningen, The Netherlands, in 1987, and his PhD in biology from the University of Amsterdam in 1997. He has been senior scientist at El Colegio de la Frontera Sur, Chetumal, Mexico, since 1997 and a member of the National System of Researchers in Mexico (SNI 1). His major interests are tree architecture, forest dynamics, biodiversity, and sustainable forest management.

PETER R. WILSHUSEN is an assistant professor of environmental studies at Bucknell University in Lewisburg, Pennsylvania. He completed his PhD in environmental sociology and policy at the University of Michigan in 2003. His scholarly interests focus on the politics of international conservation and development initiatives. He is currently examining how processes of globalization impact agrarian communities and the environment in Latin America.

Index

Abies religiosa (fir), 285, 292, 299
agrarian reform, 4, 14–15, 28, 31, 35, 40, 59, 92–93, 125–126, 134, 241, 243, 247–248, 341, 346; changes and additions of 1992, 126–130, 133, 137, 140, 151–154, 243
agricultural land demand, 229–230
agriculture, 32, 45, 52–54, 83, 100, 102, 108, 115, 121, 156, 184, 189–190, 192, 225, 227, 229–231, 233, 243, 258, 263, 296, 305, 319
agroforestry, 101, 104, 308
Alseis yucatensis, 198–199, 202
Altamirano (Quintana Roo), 218
Amazon, 197, 317
Andres Quintana Roo, 218
anthropogenic permanence, 223
Assembly, General Community, 81, 99–101, 116, 123, 129, 152, 157, 160–161, 169, 173–174, 248–249, 254, 290, 343, 346
Australia, 307–308
authorized (extraction) volumes, 51, 120, 157, 254, 291

Bajitos (Guerrero), 218
Bajos de Balsamar (Guerrero), 218
beekeeping, 159
Belize, 183, 319
Betania (Quintana Roo), 218
biodiversity, 5, 63, 73, 75, 92, 101, 105, 108, 185, 229, 293; logging and, 189, 191–196, 206, 215, 229
bioprospecting, 103, 241
Biosphere Reserves, 58, 62
Blomia cupanoides, 199
Bolivia, 308, 317–318, 321
Bonampak, 233
Bosencheve, 233
Bourreria pulcra, 196
Brazil, 197, 300, 308, 346
Brosimum alicastrum (ramón), 187, 195, 199, 202
Bursera simarouba (chacá), 195, 199, 202–205
butterflies, Monarch, 18, 27, 28, 41, 232
Byrsonoma bucidaefolia, 202

Cabo San Lucas, 233
caciquismo, 249
Caesalpinia gaumeri, 202
Caesalpinia mollis (chacte viga), 195
Cafetal-Limones (Quintana Roo), 218
Cajón del Diablo, 233
Calakmul, 232–233
Calles, Plutarco Elías, 29
Camacho, Manuel Ávila, 27
Cameroon, 314
Campeche, 5, 7
campesinos (peasants) as social agents, 126

Canada, 131, 252–253, 267, 299–300, 341, 346

Cancún (Quintana Roo), 156

Canelas (Durango), 133–138, 143

Cañón del Río Blanco, 233

Cañón del Sumidero, 233

Caoba (Quintana Roo), 20, 152–163, 169–178

Caobas (Quintana Roo), 158

carbon sequestration, 101, 103–105, 121, 339

Cárdenas, Alberto, 336

Cárdenas, Cuauhtémoc, 113, 336

Cárdenas, Lázaro, 29, 31, 34, 36, 51

cargo system, 116, 248–250

Cascada de Bassaseachic, 233

Cascadas de Agua Azul, 233

Castellanos, León Jorge, 95, 98

CBC (Comisariado de Bienes Comunales), 22, 101, 116, 135–136, 143, 152, 242, 249–251, 290

CCMSS (Mexican Civil Council for Sustainable Silviculture), 79–80, 138

Cedrela odorata (Spanish Cedar, Cedro), 156, 200; harvested volumes in Quintana Roo 1938–2000, 184; history of exploitation in Quintana Roo, 183–184; relative abundance of, 195

cellulose, 131–132

Central planning era, 34–40

Cerro de Garnica, 233

Cerro de la Estrella, 233

Cerro de la Silla, 233

certification, 19, 20, 52, 65, 71–87, 296, 318, 320, 347; in Durango, 126, 133, 138–142; expense of, 82, 140, 144–145; industry support of, 140–141; international schemes, 72; market demand for, 72, 145; rationale for pursuing, 139–142, 144; state support of, 141, 145; total certified area in Mexico, 79; total Mexican community operations certified, 79; volume of certified timber produced in Mexico, 79

CFE (Community Forest Enterprise): certification/FSC and, 75–76, 80–81, 82–85; concessionaires and, 113–114, 245–246, 255–258; definition of, 4; degree of participation in, 174–175, 290; DGDF and, 56–58, 114–118; distribution of benefits/profit from, 137–138, 152, 156–157, 159–160, 162, 166–169, 220, 232, 249, 288–289, 341, 344; economic integration of, 22, 241–269; economic rationale of, 106, 232, 241, 273; as entrepreneurial firm, 273–299; as forest conservation strategy, 216, 229–233, 293; future paths of, 339–340; global comparison of economic benefits, 321, 323–324, 346; global lessons of, 340–342; historical formation of, 22, 54–55, 153, 219 220, 245–246, 337–338; numbers nationally, 320; organizational structure of, 101, 105, 116, 119, 125–149, 151, 179, 249–250, 283, 289–290, 341, 343, 346; profitability of, 263–265, 273, 344; social capital and, 93–94, 99–102, 220, 342; typologies of, 9–13

CFO (Oaxaca Forest Company), 112–113, 244–245

CFM (Community Forest Management), 4, 24. *Also see* CFE

Chanca Derrepente (Quintana Roo), 218

Chan-Kin, 233

Chan Santa Cruz (Quintana Roo), 218

charcoal, 131–132, 261, 314

Chetumal, 186

Chiapas, 5, 52, 54

Chichan Há (SPR, Quintana Roo), 158–161, 173

chicle (*Manilkara zapota*), 51, 79, 153, 154, 187, 195, 199, 202, 319

Chihuahua, 5, 7, 17, 52, 54, 78, 79, 335–336, 343

Chile, 132, 140–141, 300

Chimalapas, 5

China, 307–308

Chiquitano Lomerio (Bolivia), 317–318
Chunhuaz (Quintana Roo), 218
CIOAC (Central Independiente de
   Obreros Agrícolas), 275, 283
CITES (Convention on International
   Trade in Endangered Species), 189
Coccoloba aculpensis, 202
Coccoloba cozumelensis, 202
Coccoloba spicata, 202
coffee, 258
Cofre de Perote, 233
COINBIO (Campesino Biodiversity
   Conservation), 64
Comisión Nacional de Desmontes, 53
common property resources and
   management, 241; in the market
   economy, 265; theory, 13–17, 125
Community Forestry: definition, 305;
   global typology, 324
Community Forestry Organizations,
   19, 347. *Also see* CIOAC, OEPFZM,
   UCEFO, UEFHG, UZACHI
Community Forest Technicians, 120,
   123, 164. *Also see* Technical Service
   Providers
community–private company forest
   partnerships, 22, 241, 253–254,
   265–267, 276, 345
CONAFOR (National Forest Commission), 64–66, 80, 140, 336
concessions and concessionaires, 10,
   18, 34–40, 50–57, 94–96, 106, 112–
   114, 143, 153, 183, 188, 219, 241, 244,
   263, 306, 309, 312–313, 317, 319–
   320, 322, 335; human capital and,
   255–258; social capital and, 255–258
Coniferous and Oak forests, 5, 115
conservation policy, 215, 303
Constitución de 1857, 233
contract theory, 242–243, 252–253,
   260
Cordia dodecandra (siricote), 195
Cordon Grande (Guerrero), 218
Corredor Biológico Chichinautzin,
   233
Costa Grande region (Guerrero),
   274–275

cost structure of production activities,
   El Balcón, 293–294
credit, 39–40, 159, 161, 175–176, 282,
   287
Cuatro Cruces (Guerrero), 218, 274
Cuauhtemóc (Quintana Roo), 218
Cumbres de Ajusco, 233
Cumbres de Majalca, 233
Cumbres de Monterrey, 233

Danaus plexippus. *See* butterflies
deforestation: causes, 6, 131, 215, 229–
   230, 305; LUCC definition, 224;
   rates, 5–7, 42, 53–54, 223–224
De la Madrid, Miguel, 41, 56
Demand conditions of firm competitive advantage, 277–279; in El
   Balcón, 284–286
Dendropanax arboreus (sac chaca), 195,
   202–205
De Quevedo, Miguel Angel, 30–31, 51
Desierto del Carmen o Nixongo, 233
Desierto de los Leones, 233
determinants of firm competitive
   advantage, 277–279
DGDF (General Office of Forest
   Development), 56–59
disturbance, mahogany and forest dynamics in Quintana Roo, 188–190,
   201–208
drought, 190
drying kilns, 282, 284, 287
Durango, 5, 7, 19, 20, 52, 54, 56, 64,
   78, 79–80, 95, 125–149, 345–346
Dzibilchaltún, 233
Dzoyola (Quintana Roo), 218

Echeverría, Luis, 53, 95
ecoforestry, 313, 323
ecological paternalism, 29–34
economic paternalism, 35
economics: community forestry's
   contribution to forest sector,
   126, 246; determinants of firm
   competitive advantage, 277–279;
   ecosystem management, 316, 343;
   firm strategy, structure and rivalry,

279, 288–293; forests in Durango's economy, 130–131; forests in Mexican economy, 7; forward integration of CFEs, 255–269; importance of timber to community economies, 171; international comparisons and competition, 131–132, 139–141, 273, 274, 284–285; intracommunity timber sales, 161–171; prior markets in noncommercial timber goods, 256, profitability of CFEs, 263–265, 273, 276; related supporting industries, 278; vertical integration of CFEs, 241–269, 296, 343–345

economics, environmental, 93

ecotourism, 337, 339–340. *Also see* tourism

eco-units, 192, 201–208

El Asoleadero (Michoacán), 29–48

El Balcón (Guerrero), 22, 80–81, 218, 273–300, 342, 345

El Chico, 233

El Citatorio, 233

El Jabalí, 233

El Moreno (Guerrero), 218

El Potosí, 233

El Rosario (Michoacán), 18, 27–48

El Tepozteco, 233

El Triunfo, 233

El Veladero, 233

El Vizcaíno, 234

endemic tree species, 196, 205

environmental/ecosystem services, 64, 66, 145, 232, 321, 339–340, 348

environmental impact assessments, 319

ERA (Rural Studies and Advising), 19, 97, 100–102

Eugenia capuli, 202

Europe, 268

Exothia paniculata, 205

factor conditions of firm competitive advantage, 277–278; in El Balcón, 279–284

Fair Trade Labeling Organization, 145

FAPATUX (Tuxtepec Paper Factory), 94–96, 106, 112–114, 244–245, 255

Felipe Carrillo Puerto (Quintana Roo), 154, 185–186, 217

Ficus, 205

FIFONAFE (National Trust Fund for *Ejido* Development), 275

Filomeno Mata (Quintana Roo), 218

finished product communities, 246–247, 251, 254–256, 262, 265

fire, 57, 63, 65, 136, 188, 190, 231, 292

firewood. *See* fuelwood

FOGIVRO (Vicente Guerrero Forest Company), 219, 275, 280

forest architecture, 191–192, 200–206

forest communities, numbers of, 8–9, 80

Forest Law: *of 1926*, 30–34, 51, 244; *of 1940*, 34–35, 52; *of 1960*, 54, 119, 242; *of 1986*, 58, 97–98, 123, 128, 246; *of 1992*, 59, 128; *of 1997*, 61, 128; *of 1999*, 128, 250

Forest Planning Unit (Unidad de Ordenación Forestal), 38

forest population structure, 191, 197–198

forest products: cellulose, 131–132; charcoal, 131–132, 261, 314; fuelwood, 131–132, 261, 279, 306, 310, 314; furniture, 131–132, 242; lumber, 131–132; palettes, 242; plywood, 131–132, 338; pulp, 30, 253, 255; railway ties, 131–132, 219; veneer, 131–132

forest types and extent: controlled by communities internationally, 308; in Durango, 130; in El Balcón Guerrero, 279; nationally, 4, 243, 308; in Oaxaca, 112, 343

forest vegetation classification schemes, 4–5, 187, 221

Fox, Vicente, 18, 83, 336

Fresnos de Puerto Rico, 218

FSC (Forest Stewardship Council), 19, 71, 138, 318, 320; certified area in Durango region, 140; (community) operations certified nationally by, 77, 139; FSC certified (community) operations in Durango,

139; international certified numbers and area of, 74; principles of good forest management of, 73, 138–139
fuelwood, 131–132, 261, 279, 306, 310, 314
furniture, 131–132, 242

GATT (General Agreement on Tariffs and Trade), 58, 96, 125
geology, 91–92, 220
Germany, 183, 219, 310
globalization, impacts on community forestry, 125–145
Gogorrón, 234
governance, community. *See* Assembly; General Community
GPS, 221
Grutas de Cacahuamilpa, 234
Guaiacum sanctum, 195
Guatemala, 319–321, 323–324, 346
Guattarda combsii, 202
Guerrero, 4, 5, 54, 56, 64, 79–81, 216–233, 273–300, 335–336
Guyana, 308
Gymnanthes lucida (yaiti), 195, 205

Hampea trilobata, 196
harvested volumes, 37; calculation of by MIQROO in Quintana Roo, 188; in El Balcón, Guerrero, 284, 292; of pine and Oak in Durango, 134; in Quintana Roo (1938–2000), 184; in two *ejidos* in Quintana Roo, 156–159
Hidalgo, 56, 78
hierarchy of forest organization theory, 191–192
high and medium evergreen forest (selva alta and mediana perennifolia), 221, 230
high-grading, 245, 338
history of forest policy, 18, 21, 28–48, 49–69; internationally, 305–326
history of traditional indigenous resource management, 92–93, 305–307, 317

human capital, 19, 106–107, 255–258, 275, 280–281, 298, 344
Humedades (Guerrero), 218
hunting, 293
hurricanes, 186–188, 190

illegal logging, 38, 42–43, 54, 55, 57, 60, 63, 72, 128–129, 132, 174–175, 305, 319, 336
India, 308, 310–312, 321, 323–324, 346
Indonesia, 308–310
industrial organization theory, 242–243
Insurg. José María Morelos, 234
Insurg. Miguel Hidalgo y Costilla, 234
International Paper Company, 336
inundated forest, 187
ITTO (International Tropical Timber Organization), 82
Ixtlán de Juárez (Oaxaca), 112
Iztaccíhuatl-Popocatépetl, 234

Jalisco, 54, 64, 336
jefe de monte (logging foreman), 12–13, 116, 164, 290, 338
JFM (joint forest management), 310–312, 321, 346

Kampokolche (Quintana Roo), 218

Lacandon (Chiapas), 5, 6
Lacan-Tun, 234
Laguna Kaná (Quintana Roo), 186, 189, 191–193, 198, 200, 218
Lagunas de Chacahua, 234
Lagunas de Montebello, 234
Lagunas de Zempoala, 234
La Laguna (Guerrero), 275
La Lajita (Guerrero), 274
La Michilía, 234
land disputes, 275
land use planning, 98–99
La Primavera, 234
La Trinidad (Guerrero), 218
La Trinidad (Oaxaca), 114, 120
liberalism. *See* neoliberalism

livestock. *See* agriculture
livestock land demand, 229–230
LKS (lesser-known [tree] species), 187–189
logging bans/forest bans, 54, 58, 63, 71, 98, 320
logging foreman. *See jefe de monte*
logging permits, 9, 61, 128, 217
logging roads, 101, 337; in El Balcón, 283–284; initial stock of in Oaxaca, 256, 263
Lol-Ché (SPR, Quintana Roo), 159
Lomas de Padierna, 234
Lonchocarpus xuul, 202
LUCC (land use/land cover change), 6, 21, 216–235; definitional categories of, 223; rates of in *ejidos* vs. protected areas, 221–233
Luhea speciosa, 202
Lysoma latisiliquum (tzalam), 195, 202, 205

Machiche (SPR, Quintana Roo), 161–162, 167
mahogany (*Swietenia macrophylla*), 153, 154, 156–157, 166; community buyers of, 167; genetic erosion of, 189; growth increment of, 198–200, 219–221; harvested volumes in Quintana Roo (from 1938–2000), 184; harvested volumes in two *ejidos* in Quintana Roo, 156–159, 161–162; history of exploitation in Quintana Roo, 183–184; impact of logging on, 188–189; population dynamics of, 196–200; population structure of, 191, 197–198; regeneration of, 21, 184–208; relative abundance of, 195; reproduction strategy of, 187–188; seedling ecology of, 187, 191, 196–198, 205; size and, 196, 201–208
Malawi, 314
Malinche or Matlalcuéyatl, 234
management plans, 157, 217, 250, 264, 310, 314, 319–320, 337; FSC and, 73, 78–79, 123; mahogany and, 198–

199, 207–208; MDS, 20, 99, 120, 291; MIQROO and, 183–184, 188; MMOM, 99, 106, 117, 217, 220, 291; PPF and, 189; SICODESI, 219–220, 245, 291, 296–297; work groups and, 136
management power, degrees of in international community forestry, 322–324
mangroves, 185, 187
Manilkara zapota. See chicle
Mapamí, 234
maps, 221–223
marginalization, degrees of, 280, 299
Mariposa Monarca, 234
Maya, 183
mechanical training index, 256, 258, 263
Mesa Verde (Guerrero), 274
Metopium brownei (chechem), 195, 202–205
Mexican Forestry Society, 30
Mexican model of community forestry, 305, 347
Mexican Revolution, 4, 14, 18, 32, 50, 125, 243
Mexico State, 56
Michoacán, 5, 7, 9, 17, 27–48, 64, 78, 79, 81, 112, 283, 289
migration, 24, 29, 40, 66, 133–135, 141, 143, 154, 177, 343
MIQROO (Industrial Timber of Quintana Roo), 153, 183, 188, 199, 219
MMOM (Mexican Method of Forest Management), 99, 106, 117, 217, 220, 291
Mixteca (Oaxaca), 244, 338
Montes Azules, 232, 234
mushrooms, 102–103, 261, 280

NAFTA (North American Free Trade Agreement), 60, 125, 131, 157, 284, 299–300, 345
Naranjal Poniente (Quintana Roo), 191, 198, 218
National Forest Inventory, 4, 221

National Land Use Inventory of 2001, 6
natural forest management, 306
natural permanence, 223
Nayarit, 54
Nectandra coreacea, 202
neoliberalism, impacts of on community forestry, 40, 56–57, 125–145, 151, 305
Nevado de Toluca, 234
NGO (nongovernmental organization), 17, 19, 76, 85, 100, 151, 309, 311, 313, 318–320, 323, 325, 327, 336, 338, 344, 347
Noh-Bec, 154, 156, 188, 196–197
Novartis, 101–103
NTFP, 62, 65, 79, 83, 85, 99, 108, 241, 242, 261, 267, 280, 309, 316, 319–320, 339–340
Nueva Loria (Quintana Roo), 218
Nuevo Zoquiapam (Oaxaca), 114

oak forests, 221
Oaxaca, 4, 5, 17, 19, 20, 21, 52, 54, 56, 62, 78, 79, 82–83, 91–110, 111–124, 242–270, 336–338, 343
Obregón, Alvaro, 29
ODRENASIJ (Organization for the Defense of Natural Resources of Sierra Juárez), 114
OEFHG (Organization of *Ejidos* Hermenegildo Galeana), 217–233, 283, 286–287
OEPFZM (Forest *Ejido* Organization of the Mayan Zone), 191, 217–233
Ottoschulzia pallida, 202

Palenque, 234
palettes, 242
Pantanos de Centra, 234
Papua New Guinea, 307, 312–313, 321, 323–324
participatory rural appraisals, 62
permanent forest areas, 101, 154, 183–184, 207
Peru, 317, 323, 346

Petcacab (Quintana Roo), 20, 152–158, 160–178, 191, 198
Petén, 319, 346
Pico de Orizaba, 234
Pico de Tancítaro, 234
pine forests, 221, 230, 279
pine oak forest, 4, 32, 99, 130, 221, 230, 279
pine resin, 34, 36, 51, 338
Pinos Caribe (SPR; Quintana Roo), 158–161
Pinus ayacahuite, 293, 299
Pinus chiapensis, 293
Pinus herrerae, 299
Pinus michoacana, 284, 299
Pinus oocarpa, 299
Pinus patula, 293
Pinus pseudostrobulus, 284, 293, 299
Pinus teocote, 299
Piscidia piscipula (jabin), 195, 198–199
Pitos, Pitales y Letrados (Guerrero), 218
Plan de Ayala (SPR, Quintana Roo), 160
Plan Nacional Forestal, 63
Plan Piloto Forestal, 17, 152, 183, 189, 219
plantations, 61–62, 64–65, 73, 132, 156, 159, 279, 292–295, 309
Platanillo (Guerrero), 218
Platymiscium yucatanum (granadillo), 195
Playa del Carmen (Quintana Roo), 156
plywood, 131–132, 338
Pocitos (Guerrero), 274, 280
policy. *See* Forest Law, Agrarian Reform
Polinkín (Quintana Roo), 154, 175
Porter's Diamond, 276–279
Pouteria campechiana, 202–205
Pouteria reticulata (zapotillo), 195, 198–199, 202
prices of pine and fir, 284–286
PROCAMPO (Program of Direct Support to the Countryside), 157, 160, 176, 287

PROCEDE (Certification Program for *Ejido* Parcels), 127, 135
PROCYMAF (Program for Forest Conservation and Management), 61, 64–65, 83, 325, 337–341, 344
PRODEFOR (Forest Development Program), 61, 64–65, 79, 83, 156–157, 287, 297, 336–337, 340
PRODEPLAN (Program for the Development of Forest Plantations), 61–62, 64–65, 287, 336
producers' organizations, 153, 158; producers' cooperatives, 31–34, 37, 38, 44, 310, 347
PROFEPA (Federal Attorney General for Environmental Protection), 61, 81, 336
PROGRESA (Program for Education; Health and Nutrition), 287
PRONARE (National Reforestation Program), 156–157, 297
ProSelva (SPR, Quintana Roo), 160
protected areas, 6, 21, 58, 62–63, 306; alternatives to, 216, 306; community-created, 293; effectiveness, 215–216; LUCC in, 221, 224–235
Protium copal, 202
Pseudobombax ellipticum (amapola), 195, 202
Puebla, 5, 56, 114, 343
Puebla Plan, 56
Pueblos Mancomunados (Oaxaca), 112, 113–114
pulp, 253, 255, 309; substitution program, 244

Quintana Roo, 5, 7, 17, 20, 21, 52, 54, 64, 76, 78, 79, 81, 151–179, 183–213, 216–233, 346

railway ties, 131–132, 219
RAN (National Agrarian Registry), 158
Randia longiloba, 196
reforestation, 100, 117, 160, 170, 189, 231, 280, 318. *Also see* PRONARE

Reforma Agraria (Quintana Roo), 218
related supporting industries, 278; in El Balcón, 286–287
remittances, 258
Rentismo logging, 51, 55, 275, 335, 345; neo-*rentismo*, 335, 345
revegetation, 223
Ría Celestún, 234
Ría Lagartos, 234
roundwood communities, 246–247, 251, 254, 275, 338
roundwood production volume, 8

Sahel, 313–314
Salinas de Gortari, Carlos, 40, 59–60
San Alonso (Chihuahua), 336
San Andrés el Alto (Oaxaca), 112, 115, 122
San Antonio el Alto (Oaxaca), 112, 115, 122
San José de la Montaña (Quintana Roo), 154, 158, 160
San Juan Atepec (Oaxaca), 112, 114
San Juan Nuevo Parangaricutiro (Michoacán), 63, 81, 283, 289
San Juan Tierra Negra (Oaxaca), 336
San Miguel Aloapan (Oaxaca), 115
San Miguel Cajonos (Oaxaca), 114
San Miguel Mixtepec (Oaxaca), 115, 122
San Pablo Macuiltianguis (Oaxaca), 95, 113
San Pedro el Alto (Oaxaca), 112–115, 120, 122
Santa Catarina Ixtepeji (Oaxaca), 112, 114–115, 117
Santa Lucía (Guerrero), 218
Santa María Poniente (Quintana Roo), 218
Santa María Zaniza (Oaxaca), 112, 115
Santa Marta (Durango), 133–138, 143
Santiago Textitlán (Oaxaca), 113–115
Santiago Xochiltepec (Oaxaca), 115
SARH (Secretariat of Agriculture and Hydraulic Resources), 56–57, 59–60, 112, 118–119, 120
satellite imagery, 221

sawmills, 131–132, 136, 255, 258, 275, 282, 298, 343

sawnwood communities, 246–247, 251, 255–256, 262, 265, 337

sawnwood production volume, 8

scientific forestry, 30–34

SDF (low semideciduous dry forest, or selva baja subcaducifolia), 187, 196, 221

Sebastiana adenophora, 196

SEDESOL (Secretariat of Social Development), 156, 159, 286

SEF (semi-evergreen forest), 187, 190, 221, 230; species richness in, 192–196, 206

Selva El Ocote, 234

selva mediana caducifolia, 221

SEMARNAP. *See* SEMARNAT

SEMARNAT, 16, 60, 64, 136, 156, 250, 254, 286, 336

Senegal, 314–315, 323–324

Señor (Quintana Roo), 186

Sian Ka'an, 234

Sierra de Ajos/Bavispe, 234

Sierra de Álvarez, 234

Sierra de Manantlán, 234

Sierra de Quila, 234

Sierra de San Pedro Mártir, 234

Sierra la Mojonera, 234

silviculture, 24, 65, 75, 120, 157, 184–185, 189, 191, 264, 290–291

Simaruba glauca (negrito), 195, 202

Simira salvadorensis (cactekok), 195, 201–205

Sinaloa, 53

SLIMF (Small and Low Intensity Managed Forests), 76

SmartWood, 72, 76, 138

social capital, 19, 62, 66, 93–94, 99–102, 106–107, 220, 282–283, 325, 342

social forestry, 306, 321

Sociedad Sur, 153, 155, 157–158, 164–168, 172, 176–177

socioproduction, 114

soils: in Quintana Roo, 186–187; and mahogany, 187, 189, 200, 207

Spain, 346

species abundance of trees in SEF, Quintana Roo, 195

species richness of trees in SEF, Quintana Roo, 191–194, 206; of epiphytes in SEF, Quintana Roo, 193–194

SPR (Rural Production Society), 158, 161; list of SPRs in Caoba, Quintana Roo, 159; in Petcacab, Quintana Roo, 162–163

SRA (Secretariat of Agrarian Reform), 54–55, 57, 59, 112, 118–119, 121

structural adjustment policies, 40, 56, 59–60, 96

stumpage communities, 242, 247, 251, 254–256, 260, 262–265, 338

stumpage fee, 10, 244, 275, 335, 345

Sudan, 308

Sufricaya (SPR, Quintana Roo), 161–162, 167, 173

Suharto, 309–310

sustainability: definition of, in community forestry, 126; international support for, 145–146; work groups and, 136–138, 142–143

sustainable landscapes; definition, 23

Swartzia cubensis, 202

Swietenia macrophylla. *See* Mahogany

SWOT analysis, 296

Tabi (Quintana Roo), 218

Tanzania, 308, 314

Technical Forest Service Providers, 55, 57, 60–65, 85, 94, 97–98, 105, 117–118, 121–122, 128, 132, 136, 164–168, 172, 217, 242, 250–251, 276, 281, 286, 290, 338

Técpan de Galeana (Guerrero), 217–233, 273–300

tequio, 248

Tlaxcala, 114

Tlaxiaco (Oaxaca), 244

tourism, 41, 127, 156, 177

trade theory, 278

transaction cost economics, 242–243, 251–252, 254, 263, 265–268

transect study, 191–193
Trapich (Quintana Roo), 218
tree nurseries, 160, 169–170, 292–293, 318
Tres Garantías, 158
Tres Reyes (Quintana Roo), 218
tropical deciduous forests (selvas bajas caducifolias), 221, 230
tropical dry forest, 187, 221
tropical montane forests, 5
tropical rainforest, 4–5, 309, 310, 312, 317; species richness in, 192
tropical seasonal forests, 5
Tulúm, 218, 234
Tuxtepec (Oaxaca), 255

UCEFO (Union of Forest Communities and *Ejidos* of Oaxaca), 19–20, 111–124
UIEF (Industrial Forest Exploitation Unit), 34–40, 244, 250, 255, 258–259
United Kingdom, 151
UPMPF (Forest Raw Material Production Unit), 114
Uruapan (Michoacán), 31–32, 34, 36
USA, 22, 131, 154, 177, 252, 267, 284, 287, 299–300, 316, 322
USAID (U.S. Agency for International Development), 317
usos y costumbres community governance, 248–249
UZACHI (Union of Zapotec-Chinantec Communities), 19, 91–110

Valle de los Cirios, 234
value-added timber processing: in Durango, 131–132, 137; in Quintana Roo, 161

vegetation composition study, 191–193
veneer, 131–132
Veracruz, 5, 56, 114, 255
vertical integration: costs and benefit of to CFEs, 242–269, 344; degrees of, 10, 131
Village Forest Committees, 311, 314
violence, 274–275, 282, 296, 306, 342
Vitex gaumeri, 202–205
Volcán Nevado de Colima, 234

Westwood Forest Products, 276, 282, 284, 286–287, 299
women's rights, 23, 24, 81
work groups, 20, 344; in Durango, 133–149; in Quintana Roo, 151–178
World Bank, 307, 314, 337

xate palm, 319
X-Hazil (Quintana Roo), 186, 191–193, 197, 200–202
Xicoténcatl, 234
X-Maben (Quintana Roo), 218
X-Pichil (Quintana Roo), 186, 218

Yaxley (Quintana Roo), 218
Yazchilán, 234
Yoactun (Quintana Roo), 218
Yucatán Peninsula: ecosystem resilience, 190; endemism in, 192; geography of, 185; tree diversity in, 193–195

Zapote Negro (SPR, Quintana Roo), 161–162
Zedillo, Ernesto, 18, 60, 64
Zimbabwe, 313
Zoquiapan y Anexas, 234
Zygia stevensonii, 205